PASTRIES, AND HOT FRUIT DESSERTS, PAST

TS · COOKIES · CAKES · SPECIAL DESSERTS

PASTRIES, AND HOT FRUIT DESSERTS, PAST

TS · COOKIES · CAKES · SPECIAL DESSERTS

PASTRIES, AND HOT FRUIT DESSERTS, PAST

TS · COOKIES · CAKES · SPECIAL DESSERTS

PASTRIES, AND HOT FRUIT DESSERTS, PAST

TS · COOKIES · CAKES · SPECIAL DESSERTS

PASTRIES, AND HOT FRUIT DESSERTS, PAST

TS · COOKIES · CAKES · SPECIAL DESSERTS

PASTRIES, AND HOT FRUIT DESSERTS, PAST

TS · COOKIES · CAKES · SPECIAL DESSERTS

PASTRIES, AND HOT FRUIT DESSERTS, PAST

TS · COOKIES · CAKES · SPECIAL DESSERTS

PASTRIES, AND HOT FRUIT DESSERTS, PAST

TS · COOKIES · CAKES · SPECIAL DESSERTS

PASTRIES, AND HOT FRUIT DESSERTS, PAST

THE

GOOD HOUSEKEEPING

ILLUSTRATED BOOK OF

DESSERTS

THE
GOOD HOUSEKEEPING
ILLUSTRATED BOOK OF
DESSERTS

HEARST BOOKS
A DIVISION OF STERLING PUBLISHING CO., INC.
NEW YORK

A DORLING KINDERSLEY BOOK

Created and produced by
Carroll & Brown Ltd.
London, England

Editorial Director: Jeni Wright
Art Director: Denise Brown
Designers: Sally Powell
            Wendy Rogers
            Joanna Pocock

Library of Congress Cataloging-in-Publication Data available upon request

10 9 8 7 6 5 4 3 2 1

Published by Hearst Books,
A Division of Sterling Publishing Company, Inc.
387 Park Avenue South, New York, N.Y. 10016

Good Housekeeping and Hearst Books are trademarks owned by
Hearst Magazines Property, Inc., in USA, and Hearst Communications, Inc., in Canada.

www.goodhousekeeping.com

Distributed in Canada by Sterling Publishing
ᶜ/ₒ Canadian Manda Group, One Atlantic Avenue, Suite 105
Toronto, Ontario, Canada M6K 3E7A
Distributed in Australia by Capricorn Link (Australia) Pty. Ltd.
P.O. Box 704, Windsor, NSW 2756 Australia

Printed in China

Sterling ISBN 1-58816-200-1

CONTENTS

FOREWORD

Come and join Good Housekeeping's celebration of desserts. In this, our first cookbook devoted entirely to a single subject, we present the sweet treats from our magazine that have become our favorites and yours. Each recipe has had the thorough testing and retesting in our Food Department Kitchens that will ensure successful results with the least expenditure of time and effort.

We all know that desserts can be good for you as well as just plain good. Desserts can add heartiness to the light menu and lighten a substantial one. They can supply nutritional foods, such as milk or fruit or grain products, that are missing from the rest of the meal or from the entire day's fare.

Even if you are watching your waistline, you can enjoy our desserts in thinner slices or smaller servings, and still conform to healthwise eating.

Among the recipes in this book you'll find wonderful new ways with beloved old favorites, like Walnut-Crunch Pumpkin Pie and Banana Brown Betty. You'll see how easy it is to make classics like Baklava, Apple Strudel, and Crème Brûlée. If simple recipes are your choice, try one of the Fruit Fools or Cherries en Gelée. If you like to hear "oohs" and "ahs" as you bring on dessert, opt for Curly Chocolate Cake or Irish-Cream Triangle Cake. Swan Cream Puffs or Meringue Mushrooms are sure to delight children of all ages from six to 96.

Full-color photographs of each recipe show you what to expect, and step-by-step instructions – many of them illustrated – guide you through every technique in preparation. And, to make great desserts more glorious, we have included dozens of garnishes, decorations, and serving tips to help you make every dish as pleasing to the eye as it is to the palate.

Thanks are due to the Food Department staff whose hard work and dedication to the art as well as the skills of cooking have resulted in these fabulous desserts. Special thanks, too, to Susan Deborah Goldsmith and Ellen Connelly, who helped with the planning, recipe selection and updating, writing, and proofreading of this book. A special word of thanks to Amy Carroll and Denise Brown of Carroll & Brown, and Jeni Wright, who devoted two years to the production of this volume.

We hope that our dessert collection gives you as much pleasure to prepare and enjoy, as it did for us to put it together.

The Editors of Good Housekeeping

SPECIAL DESSERTS

7-78

SPECIAL DESSERTS

In this chapter are desserts that call for a show-off setting – your prettiest glass bowls to reveal textures, and dainty china plates and dishes to enhance colors. Our mousses, soufflés, custards, creams, and puddings are generally soft and smooth, easy to serve and to eat, and stunningly varied in color and flavor. Many, like Tiramisù, take their shape from the dish in which they are served; others, like Zuccotto, from the mold in which they were placed to set or to firm up. Our jewel-toned fresh fruit desserts can put the taste of summer on your table any time, thanks to the year-round availability of many familiar fruits, and add exotic new varieties to the list of dessert possibilities. Rounding out this chapter are tender crepes and blintzes, and meringue desserts as appealing as Meringue Mushrooms and as elegant as Strawberry and Almond Dacquoise.

CONTENTS

Mousses and Soufflés

Light and fluffy mousses and soufflés – made from fruit, chocolate, and even bread pudding – are right for any occasion, from everyday meals for family and friends to special events when you want to impress. And because cold mousses can be made ahead, they're perfect for entertaining.

CHOCOLATE MOUSSE

🥄 12 servings
⏱ Begin early in day or day ahead

4 large egg yolks

2 cups milk

1/4 cup sugar

1/4 teaspoon salt

1 envelope unflavored gelatin

6 1-ounce squares semisweet chocolate, chopped

2 1-ounce squares unsweetened chocolate, chopped

1 teaspoon vanilla extract

2 cups heavy or whipping cream

Whipped cream and finely chopped pistachios (see right) for garnish

1 In 3-quart saucepan, with wire whisk, beat egg yolks, milk, sugar, and salt until blended. Evenly sprinkle gelatin over mixture; let stand 1 minute to soften gelatin slightly. Stir in chopped chocolate.

2 Cook over low heat, stirring frequently, about 15 minutes or until gelatin completely dissolves, chocolate melts, and mixture thickens and coats a spoon well (mixture should be about 170° to 175°F. but do not boil or it will curdle).

3 Stir vanilla extract into chocolate mixture. Beat with wire whisk or hand beater to blend chocolate completely.

4 Remove saucepan from heat; cover and refrigerate until mixture mounds slightly when dropped from a spoon, about 1½ hours, stirring occasionally.

5 In small bowl, with mixer at medium speed, beat heavy or whipping cream until stiff peaks form. With rubber spatula or wire whisk, fold whipped cream into chocolate mixture.

6 Pour mousse into twelve 6-ounce individual soufflé dishes or 1½-quart serving bowl; cover and refrigerate 4 hours or until set.

> **TO SERVE**
> Garnish mousse with whipped cream and finely chopped pistachios.

Piping whipped cream:
Using decorating bag with medium star tube, pipe whipped cream in shell shape at edge of each chocolate mousse.

Chopping pistachios:
With sharp knife, on cutting board, finely chop shelled pistachios. Use to sprinkle over whipped cream and chocolate mousse.

RASPBERRY AND VANILLA MOUSSE

16 servings
Begin about 5 hours before serving or early in day

2 10-ounce packages frozen raspberries in syrup, thawed

2 envelopes unflavored gelatin

2 large eggs

1 cup milk

²/₃ cup sugar

1 ¹/₂ teaspoons vanilla extract

3 cups heavy or whipping cream

14 gingersnap cookies, crushed (about ³/₄ cup)

Raspberries and mint leaves for garnish

1 Over 3-quart saucepan, with back of spoon, press and scrape thawed raspberries with their syrup firmly against medium-mesh sieve to separate seeds from pulp; discard seeds.

2 Evenly sprinkle 1 envelope gelatin over raspberry puree; let stand 1 minute to soften gelatin slightly.

3 Over medium heat, cook raspberry mixture until gelatin completely dissolves, stirring frequently.

4 Cover and refrigerate until mixture mounds slightly when dropped from a spoon, about 1¹/₂ hours, stirring occasionally.

5 Meanwhile, in 2-quart saucepan, with wire whisk, beat eggs, milk, and ¹/₃ cup sugar until blended. Evenly sprinkle remaining 1 envelope gelatin over mixture; let stand 1 minute to soften gelatin slightly.

6 Cook gelatin mixture over low heat, stirring frequently, about 10 minutes or until gelatin completely dissolves and mixture thickens and coats a spoon well (mixture should be 170° to 175°F. but do not boil or it will curdle). Stir in vanilla extract.

7 Cover and refrigerate until mixture mounds slightly when dropped from a spoon, stirring occasionally.

8 About 10 minutes before gelatin mixtures are ready, in large bowl, with mixer at medium speed, beat heavy or whipping cream and remaining ¹/₃ cup sugar until stiff peaks form.

9 With rubber spatula or wire whisk, gently fold half the whipped cream into each gelatin mixture.

10 In 2 ¹/₂-quart serving bowl, layer half the crushed gingersnaps, then vanilla cream, rest of gingersnaps, then raspberry cream. Cover and refrigerate until set, about 3 hours.

TO SERVE
Garnish mousse with raspberries and mint leaves.

The different layers of Raspberry and Vanilla Mousse can be seen if the dessert is made in a glass bowl

MARBLED MOUSSE

🥄 16 servings
🕐 Begin early in day

1 ³/₄ cups milk
¹/₄ teaspoon salt
3 large egg yolks
1 cup sugar
2 envelopes unflavored gelatin
2 1-ounce squares unsweetened chocolate, melted and cooled
3 teaspoons vanilla extract
3 cups heavy or whipping cream
5 teaspoons shortening
7 1-ounce squares semisweet chocolate

1 In 2-quart saucepan, blend milk, salt, egg yolks, and ³/₄ cup sugar. Evenly sprinkle gelatin over mixture; let stand 1 minute to soften gelatin slightly. Cook over low heat, stirring often, about 30 minutes or until gelatin completely dissolves and mixture coats a spoon well (mixture should be about 170° to 175°F. but do not boil or it will curdle).

2 Pour half the egg-yolk mixture into small bowl; add unsweetened chocolate and 1 teaspoon vanilla extract. With wire whisk, beat just until blended. Into remaining egg-yolk mixture, stir remaining 2 teaspoons vanilla extract.

3 Cover and refrigerate both mixtures until they mound slightly when dropped from a spoon, 20 to 25 minutes, stirring occasionally.

4 In large bowl, with mixer at medium speed, beat heavy or whipping cream and remaining ¹/₄ cup sugar until stiff peaks form.

5 With rubber spatula or wire whisk, gently fold half the whipped cream into each chilled egg-yolk mixture.

6 Alternately spoon chocolate and vanilla mousse mixtures into 9" by 3" springform pan. With knife or metal spatula, swirl mixtures together to create marbled design. Cover and refrigerate 4 hours or until set.

7 Meanwhile, cut waxed paper into 12" by 7 ¹/₂" rectangle; place on cookie sheet. In heavy 1-quart saucepan over low heat, melt shortening and 5 squares semisweet chocolate, stirring frequently.

8 Spread melted chocolate over waxed-paper rectangle (see Box, right); refrigerate until firm.

9 Cut chocolate rectangle into strips (see Box, right); peel off paper. Place chocolate strips on cookie sheet; refrigerate.

10 Make chocolate curls: With heat of hands, slightly soften remaining 2 squares semisweet chocolate. Draw blade of vegetable peeler along smooth surface of chocolate to make wide chocolate curls. Place curls on plate; refrigerate.

11 Remove chocolate strips from refrigerator; let stand 5 minutes to soften slightly. Remove side of springform pan; place mousse on cake stand or plate. Cover side of mousse with chocolate strips (see Box, below).

12 With toothpick, gently place chocolate curls in center of mousse.

MAKING CHOCOLATE FRAME

Spreading melted chocolate: With metal spatula, quickly spread warm melted chocolate over waxed-paper rectangle to evenly cover; refrigerate until firm, about 30 minutes.

Cutting chocolate into strips: With sharp knife, cut chocolate rectangle lengthwise into five 1 ¹/₂-inch-wide strips.

Covering side of mousse: Place chocolate strips one at a time around mousse. Press each strip gently with metal spatula to fit shape of mousse and overlap slightly.

*If you like, top each serving of
Marbled Mousse with colorful
juicy berries*

QUICK CHOCOLATE-ALMOND MOUSSE

6 servings
Begin about
30 minutes before
serving

*1 envelope unflavored
gelatin*

*1 cup heavy or whipping
cream*

*1 6-ounce package
semisweet-chocolate pieces
(1 cup)*

3 ice cubes

³/₄ cup milk

¹/₄ cup sugar

³/₄ teaspoon almond extract

*Whipped cream and toasted
sliced almonds (see Box,
right) for garnish*

**TOASTING SLICED
ALMONDS**
In skillet or saucepan
over medium heat, cook
small quantity sliced
almonds until golden,
stirring frequently with
wooden spatula.

Cool almonds before
using.

---

1 In 1-quart saucepan,
evenly sprinkle gelatin
over ¹/₂ cup heavy or
whipping cream; let stand
1 minute to soften.

2 Cook over medium
heat until tiny bubbles
form around edge of pan
and gelatin completely
dissolves, stirring
frequently.

3 Pour hot mixture into
blender or food
processor with knife blade
attached; add chocolate
pieces. Cover and blend
until chocolate melts.

4 To chocolate mixture,
add ice cubes.

5 Add milk, sugar,
almond extract, and
remaining ¹/₂ cup heavy or
whipping cream; blend
until smooth.

6 Pour mixture
into six 6-ounce
freezersafe glasses
or bowls; chill in
freezer 15 minutes
until dessert is set.
Remove mousse from
freezer and keep
refrigerated if not serving
right away.

7 Garnish each mousse
with whipped cream
and toasted sliced
almonds.

WARM BANANA SOUFFLÉS

4 servings
Begin 30 minutes before serving

Nonstick cooking spray

3 medium-sized bananas (about 1 pound)

2 teaspoons lemon juice

1 teaspoon vanilla extract

4 large egg whites

3 tablespoons confectioners' sugar plus extra for sprinkling

1 Preheat oven to 450°F Spray four 10-ounce soufflé dishes with nonstick cooking spray.

2 Mash bananas with lemon juice and vanilla extract.

3 In small bowl, with mixer at high speed, beat egg whites until soft peaks form; gradually sprinkle in 3 tablespoons confectioners' sugar, beating until sugar completely dissolves and whites stand in stiff peaks.

TO SERVE
When soufflés are done, remove from oven and sprinkle tops lightly with confectioners' sugar; serve immediately.

4 With rubber spatula or wire whisk, gently fold beaten egg whites into banana mixture, one-third at a time.

5 Spoon mixture into soufflé dishes; set dishes in jelly-roll pan for easier handling.

6 Bake 15 minutes or until soufflés are puffed and browned.

BREAD PUDDING SOUFFLÉ

🍴 8 servings
⏰ Begin about 2 ½ hours before serving or early in day

Bread Pudding (see Box, right)

6 large eggs, separated

1 cup sugar

½ cup confectioners' sugar

1 ½ teaspoons cornstarch

⅛ teaspoon ground cinnamon

½ cup heavy or whipping cream

½ cup milk

1 tablespoon bourbon whiskey (optional)

1 tablespoon margarine or butter

Confectioners' sugar and shredded orange peel for garnish

1 Prepare Bread Pudding.

2 About 1 hour before serving, preheat oven to 350°F. Grease 2 ½-quart soufflé dish.

3 In double boiler over hot, not boiling, water, with wire whisk, beat egg yolks and ½ cup sugar until mixture is frothy and shiny, about 5 minutes. (Or, mix in 1½-quart heatsafe bowl set over hot water in 3-quart saucepan, making sure bowl does not touch water.)

4 Spoon Bread Pudding into large bowl; stir in egg-yolk mixture. Set aside.

5 In another large bowl, with mixer at high speed, beat egg whites until soft peaks form; gradually sprinkle in confectioners' sugar, beating until sugar completely dissolves and whites stand in stiff peaks.

6 With rubber spatula or wire whisk, gently fold egg-white mixture into bread-pudding mixture. Spoon into soufflé dish. Bake 35 to 40 minutes until knife inserted in center comes out clean.

7 Meanwhile, prepare sauce: In 2-quart saucepan, with wire whisk or spoon, mix cornstarch, cinnamon, and remaining ½ cup sugar; slowly stir in heavy or whipping cream and milk until smooth. Cook over medium heat, stirring constantly, until mixture thickens and boils; boil 1 minute. Remove from heat; stir in bourbon and margarine or butter.

BREAD PUDDING

Preheat oven to 350°F. In oven, in 8" by 8" baking dish, melt 4 tablespoons margarine or butter (½ stick); remove dish from oven. In bowl, with wire whisk, mix 2 large eggs, 1 cup heavy or whipping cream, ½ cup sugar, ¼ cup golden or dark seedless raisins, 1 tablespoon vanilla extract, and ⅛ teaspoon ground cinnamon. Arrange six 1-inch-thick slices French bread in baking dish, turning bread to coat both sides with melted margarine or butter. Pour egg mixture over bread; let stand 5 minutes. Turn bread slices; let stand 10 minutes. Cover dish with foil. Set dish in large roasting pan; place on oven rack. Fill pan with boiling water to come halfway up side of dish. Bake 40 minutes, uncovering pudding during last 10 minutes to slightly brown top. (Custard should still be soft, not firm.) Remove dish from water in roasting pan; cover pudding and refrigerate if not using right away to complete soufflé.

TO SERVE

When soufflé is done, remove from oven and sprinkle top lightly with confectioners' sugar and shredded orange peel; serve immediately. Pass sauce in bowl.

INDIVIDUAL CHOCOLATE SOUFFLÉS
WITH COFFEE CREAM

TO SERVE
When soufflés are done, remove from oven and sprinkle tops lightly with confectioners' sugar; serve immediately. Let each person, with spoon, break up top of soufflé, then spoon on some coffee cream.

6 servings
Begin 1 hour before serving

1 tablespoon all-purpose flour

About ¼ cup sugar

½ cup milk

2 1-ounce squares unsweetened chocolate, chopped

4 large eggs, separated

½ teaspoon vanilla extract

⅛ teaspoon salt

1 cup heavy or whipping cream

2 tablespoons coffee-flavor liqueur

Confectioners' sugar for sprinkling

1 In 2-quart saucepan, with wire whisk or spoon, mix flour and 2 tablespoons sugar; slowly stir in milk until smooth. Cook over medium heat, stirring constantly, until mixture boils and thickens; cook 1 minute.

2 Remove saucepan from heat. Stir in chocolate until melted.

3 Rapidly beat egg yolks all at once into chocolate mixture until well blended. Refrigerate mixture to cool to lukewarm, about 10 minutes, stirring occasionally. Stir in vanilla extract.

4 Preheat oven to 375°F. Grease six 6-ounce soufflé dishes; lightly sprinkle with sugar.

5 In small bowl, with mixer at high speed, beat egg whites and salt until soft peaks form; gradually sprinkle in 2 tablespoons sugar, beating until sugar completely dissolves and whites stand in stiff peaks.

6 With rubber spatula or wire whisk, gently fold chocolate mixture into beaten egg whites until blended.

7 Spoon chocolate soufflé mixture into prepared soufflé dishes.

8 Place filled dishes in jelly-roll pan for easier handling.

9 Bake soufflés 15 to 20 minutes until puffy and brown and knife inserted in side comes out clean.

10 Meanwhile, prepare coffee cream: In small bowl, with mixer at medium speed, beat heavy or whipping cream until soft peaks form. Add coffee-flavor liqueur; beat until evenly mixed. Spoon into small serving bowl.

SWEETENED WHIPPED CREAMS

Sweetened whipped cream is the perfect garnish for desserts, and the ideal accompaniment for fresh fruit salads, as well as fruit and nut pies and tarts, hot puddings, and ice-cream sundaes.

To make Sweetened Whipped Cream:
In bowl, with hand beater or with mixer at medium speed, beat *1 cup heavy or whipping cream*, well chilled, *1 to 2 tablespoons sugar*, and *½ teaspoon vanilla or almond extract* just until soft or stiff peaks form, depending on use. Yield: About 2 cups.

Chocolate Whipped Cream
Place *2 tablespoons instant-cocoa mix* (or *2 tablespoons sugar* and *2 tablespoons unsweetened cocoa*) in small bowl; add *1 cup heavy or whipping cream*. Beat just until soft or stiff peaks form. Yield: About 2 cups.

Orange Whipped Cream
Beat cream as above, with *1 teaspoon shredded orange peel* and *⅛ teaspoon orange extract*. Yield: About 2 cups.

Berry Whipped Cream
Beat cream as above, until soft peaks form. Fold in *½ cup drained, crushed, slightly sweetened strawberries, raspberries, or blackberries.* Yield: About 2 ½ cups.

ORANGE-LIQUEUR SOUFFLÉ

8 servings
Begin 2 hours before serving

4 tablespoons margarine or butter (¹/₂ stick)

¹/₃ cup all-purpose flour

¹/₈ teaspoon salt

1 ¹/₂ cups milk

About 3 tablespoons sugar

4 large egg yolks

¹/₃ cup orange-flavor liqueur

1 tablespoon grated or finely shredded orange peel

6 large egg whites

1 cup heavy or whipping cream (optional)

Confectioners' sugar for sprinkling

1 In 2-quart saucepan over low heat, melt margarine or butter; stir in flour and salt until blended. Gradually stir in milk; cook, stirring constantly, until mixture boils and thickens; cook 1 minute.

2 Remove saucepan from heat. With wire whisk, beat 3 tablespoons sugar into milk mixture. Rapidly beat in egg yolks all at once until well mixed. Refrigerate egg-yolk mixture to cool to lukewarm, stirring occasionally. Stir in orange-flavor liqueur and grated orange peel.

3 Preheat oven to 375°F. Grease 2-quart soufflé dish; lightly sprinkle with sugar; shake off excess.

4 In large bowl, with mixer at high speed, beat egg whites until stiff peaks form. With rubber spatula or wire whisk, gently fold egg-yolk mixture, one-third at a time, into beaten egg whites.

5 Spoon mixture into prepared dish. With back of metal spoon, about 1 inch from edge of dish, make 1¹/₂-inch-deep indentation all around in soufflé mixture (center will rise slightly higher than edge, making top-hat effect when soufflé is done).

Making indentation in soufflé mixture for top-hat effect

6 Bake soufflé 30 to 35 minutes until knife inserted under top hat comes out clean.

7 Meanwhile, if serving with cream, in small bowl, with mixer at medium speed, beat cream until soft peaks form. Cover; refrigerate.

> *TO SERVE*
> *When soufflé is done, remove from oven and sprinkle top lightly with confectioners' sugar; serve immediately. Pass whipped cream in bowl to spoon onto each serving, if you like.*

SUCCESSFUL SWEET SOUFFLÉS

Hot sweet soufflés consist of a thick sauce of flour, margarine or butter, milk, sugar, egg yolks, and flavorings folded into stiffly beaten egg whites. For success every time, follow these simple guidelines:

• Always cook flour and margarine or butter first to get rid of raw taste of uncooked flour.

• Boil milk mixture for 1 minute so that smooth sauce is formed.

• Fold sauce gently into egg whites, taking care not to stir whites or they will lose their volume.

• Bake soufflé on rack slightly below center of oven so that mixture itself is centered and has sufficient room to rise.

• Do not open oven door before end of baking time; cold air could cause soufflé to fall.

FRESH-APPLE SOUFFLÉ

🍴 4 servings
⏱ Begin about 1 hour before serving

3 medium-sized cooking apples (about 1 pound)

3 tablespoons sugar

1/2 teaspoon almond extract

5 large egg whites

Confectioners' sugar

1 Peel apples; cut into quarters; with sharp knife, remove cores.

2 Cut apples into bite-sized chunks. In 2-quart saucepan over high heat, heat apples and 1/4 cup water to boiling. Reduce heat to low; cover and simmer 8 to 10 minutes, stirring occasionally, until apples are tender. Stir in sugar and almond extract. Remove saucepan from heat; refrigerate apple mixture in saucepan to cool.

3 Preheat oven to 450°F. In large bowl, with mixer at high speed, beat egg whites until stiff peaks form.

4 With rubber spatula or wire whisk, gently fold egg whites into cooled apple mixture until evenly incorporated.

5 Spoon mixture into 1½-quart soufflé dish.

6 Bake 15 minutes or until soufflé is puffy and lightly browned.

> *TO SERVE*
> *When soufflé is done, remove from oven and sprinkle top lightly with confectioners' sugar; serve immediately.*

Custards and Creams

Velvety smooth, soft and pleasing, custards and creams are easy and quick to make. Most can be prepared ahead, making them excellent to round out menus in which other foods require last-minute attention. Fruit Fools are the exception; they must be made just before serving, but preparation takes only 20 minutes. In these pages you'll find desserts ranging from simple family-pleasing "comfort food" like Skillet Custards to sophisticated, party desserts like Zuccotto.

SKILLET CUSTARDS

 6 servings

Begin about 3 hours before serving or early in day

4 large eggs

3 cups milk

⅓ cup sugar

1 teaspoon vanilla extract

¼ teaspoon salt

6 tablespoons maple syrup or maple-flavor syrup

1 11-ounce can mandarin-orange sections, drained, for garnish

1 In 8-cup measuring cup, with wire whisk, beat eggs, milk, sugar, vanilla extract, and salt until well blended.

2 Carefully pour milk mixture into six 6-ounce custard cups.

3 Set custard cups in 12-inch skillet; slowly fill skillet with water to come halfway up sides of custard cups.

4 Over medium heat, heat water in skillet to boiling.

5 Cover skillet and remove from heat; let custards stand in covered skillet 15 minutes.

6 Remove custard cups from skillet; refrigerate until well chilled, about 2 hours. If not serving right away, cover chilled desserts with plastic wrap.

7 Just before serving, on top of each custard, pour 1 tablespoon maple syrup.

> *TO SERVE*
> *Garnish each custard with some mandarin-orange sections.*

CHOCOLATE CUPS

 8 servings

Begin about 2 hours before serving or early in day

1 6-ounce package semisweet-chocolate pieces (1 cup)

1 tablespoon shortening

1 package vanilla-flavor instant pudding and pie filling for 4 servings

1 1/4 cups milk

3/4 cup heavy or whipping cream

2 tablespoons orange-flavor liqueur

Unsweetened cocoa

Lemon leaves for garnish

1 Place fluted paper or foil baking cup in each of eight 2 1/2 inch-muffin-pan cups.

2 In heavy 1-quart saucepan over low heat, heat semisweet-chocolate pieces and shortening, stirring frequently, until melted and smooth.

3 Starting from top rim of each baking cup, drizzle chocolate, 1 heaping measuring teaspoon at a time, down inside of cup.

4 About 3 of these teaspoons will line each cup. If necessary, spread chocolate over cup bottom.

5 Refrigerate until firm, about 30 minutes. With cool hands, remove 1 chocolate-lined baking cup at a time from refrigerator; gently but quickly peel baking cup from each one, leaving chocolate cup.

6 Set chocolate cups on chilled dessert platter and refrigerate.

7 In medium bowl, with wire whisk, prepare instant pudding as label directs, but use only 1 1/4 cups milk.

8 In small bowl, with mixer at medium speed, beat heavy or whipping cream until stiff peaks form.

9 With rubber spatula or wire whisk, fold whipped cream and orange-flavor liqueur into pudding until blended.

10 Spoon filling into cups. Refrigerate at least 30 minutes or until filling is well chilled.

TO SERVE
Sprinkle cocoa through small sieve lightly over cream filling in chocolate cups. Garnish with lemon leaves.

CRÈME CARAMEL

6 servings

Begin about
3 ½ hours before
serving or early
in day

½ cup sugar

4 large eggs

2 cups milk

1 teaspoon vanilla extract

¼ teaspoon salt

Cracked Caramel (page 300), physalis, or lime julienne and citrus-fruit sections for garnish

1 Preheat oven to 325°F. Grease six 6-ounce custard cups, or oval-, or heart-shaped molds.

2 In small saucepan over medium heat, heat ¼ cup sugar until melted and a light caramel color, stirring constantly. Immediately pour into prepared cups or molds.

3 In large bowl, with wire whisk or fork, beat eggs and remaining ¼ cup sugar until well blended; beat in milk, vanilla extract, and salt until well mixed. Pour mixture into cups or molds.

4 Set cups or molds in 13" by 9" baking pan; place on oven rack. Fill pan with boiling water to come halfway up sides of cups or molds. Bake 50 to 55 minutes until knife inserted in center of custard comes out clean.

5 Remove cups or molds from water in baking pan. Refrigerate until well chilled, about 2 hours. If not serving right away, cover chilled desserts with plastic wrap.

6 Meanwhile, prepare Cracked Caramel.

TO SERVE
With small spatula, loosen custards from cups or molds. Invert each custard onto a chilled dessert plate; allow syrup to drip onto custard..Add garnish of your choice just before serving.

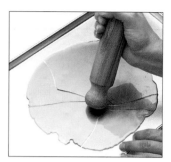

Cracked Caramel Garnish: *With 1 end of rolling pin, sharply tap hardened caramel until it cracks into small pieces.*

Physalis Garnish: *Also called husk tomato, ground cherry, and Chinese lantern. Carefully peel back inedible husk to resemble flower petals.*

Lime Julienne Garnish: *With vegetable peeler, remove peel from lime, leaving bitter white pith behind. Cut peel into fine strips.*

CRÈME BRÛLÉE WITH TROPICAL FRUITS

- 6 servings
- Begin early in day or day ahead

2 cups heavy or whipping cream

4 large egg yolks

1/4 cup sugar

1/2 teaspoon vanilla extract

3 tablespoons brown sugar

Fruits: Prepared papayas, mangoes, kiwifruit, and tamarillos, or other favorite fruits such as pineapple, lychees, carambolas (star fruits), and bananas

1 In 1-quart saucepan over medium heat, heat heavy or whipping cream until tiny bubbles form around edge of pan.

2 Meanwhile, in heavy 2-quart saucepan, with wire whisk or fork, beat egg yolks with sugar until well blended. Slowly stir in hot cream. Cook over medium-low heat, stirring constantly, until mixture thickens and coats a spoon well, about 15 minutes (mixture should be about 170° to 175°F. but do not boil or it will curdle). Stir in vanilla extract.

3 Pour cream mixture into six 3- to 4-ounce heatsafe ramekins. Cover and refrigerate until well chilled, about 6 hours.

4 About 1 hour before serving, preheat broiler if manufacturer directs. Place brown sugar in small sieve; with spoon, press sugar through sieve over top of chilled cream mixture.

5 Broil 2 to 3 minutes until sugar just melts. Chill. The melted sugar will form a crisp crust over the custard. If the crust is done too early, the sugar will become soft and lose its crisp texture.

Accompany ramekins of Crème Brûlée with choice of fruits, for guests to help themselves

TROPICAL FRUITS

There are many new and exciting tropical fruits available in supermarkets today, and it's a matter of personal taste which ones you serve with Crème Brûlée.

Papayas
Available all year, they should be greenish-yellow to almost yellow, and yield to thumb pressure when ripe. Refrigerate until ready to serve.

Mangoes
Available all year, with best supplies May through August, they should be plump with yellowish or orange skin. To test a mango for ripeness, press on the skin gently - it should yield slightly. Keep mangoes refrigerated until ready to serve as they taste best when cold.

Kiwifruit
Also known as "Chinese gooseberries", these are available all year, but are best June through December. When ripe, kiwifruit should yield to gentle pressure. Refrigerate until ready to serve.

Tamarillos
Sometimes called "tree tomatoes", these fruits have blood-red or bright-yellow skin, and long, tapering stems. When ripe, the skin should feel soft if pressed, and the seeds inside will be black.

HAWAIIAN TAPIOCA WITH CUSTARD CREAM

6 servings
Begin about
2 ½ hours before
serving or early
in day

*2 cups fruit juicy red
Hawaiian punch or
grape juice*

½ cup sugar

*⅓ cup quick-cooking
tapioca*

½ teaspoon salt

1 cup Burgundy wine

*Custard Cream (see Box,
right)*

1 In 3-quart saucepan,
mix first 4 ingredients;
let stand 5 minutes to
soften tapioca. Cook over
medium heat, stirring
constantly, until it thickens
and begins to boil, about
5 minutes.

2 Add wine and con-
tinue cooking 5 more
minutes, stirring con-
stantly.

3 Spoon pudding into
six 12-ounce wine
glasses or dessert bowls;
cover and refrigerate until
well chilled, about 2 hours.

4 Meanwhile, prepare
Custard Cream;
refrigerate.

TO SERVE
*Top each serving of
tapioca with some
Custard Cream.*

CUSTARD CREAM
In 2-quart saucepan,
combine *1 ¾ cups half-
and-half* or light cream,
*3 tablespoons sugar,
1 tablespoon cornstarch,
dash salt,* and *1 large egg
yolk.* Cook over medium-
low heat, stirring
constantly, until mixture
coats a spoon well, about
15 minutes (mixture
should be about 170° to
175°F. but do not boil or
it will curdle).

Remove custard from
heat. Stir in *½ teaspoon
vanilla extract*; pour into
bowl. To keep skin from
forming as custard cools,
press plastic wrap
directly onto
surface of
Custard
Cream.

BUTTERSCOTCH SQUARES

🍴 15 servings
⏰ Begin 5 ½ hours before serving or day ahead

1 4-ounce can slivered blanched almonds (1 cup)

1 cup all-purpose flour

½ cup margarine or butter (1 stick)

¾ cup plus 2 tablespoons confectioners' sugar

1 8-ounce package cream cheese, softened

2 cups heavy or whipping cream

1 teaspoon vanilla extract

2 packages butterscotch-flavor sugar-free instant pudding and pie filling for 4 servings

3 cups milk

1 With sharp knife, finely chop ⅔ cup slivered almonds and coarsely chop remaining ⅓ cup almonds.

2 Preheat oven to 350°F.

3 In medium bowl, with fingers, mix flour, margarine or butter, finely chopped almonds, and ¼ cup confectioners' sugar until crumbly.

4 With fingers, press mixture firmly into ungreased 13" by 9" baking dish.

5 Bake crust 15 to 20 minutes until golden brown. Cool crust in dish on wire rack.

6 While crust is cooling, in same bowl with spoon, beat cream cheese and ½ cup confectioners' sugar until light and fluffy.

7 In small bowl, with mixer at medium speed, beat heavy or whipping cream and vanilla extract until stiff peaks form.

8 With rubber spatula or wire whisk, fold 1 cup whipped cream into cream-cheese mixture; spread over crust. Reserve remaining whipped cream.

9 In large bowl, with wire whisk, prepare pudding mixes as labels direct, but prepare both packages together and use only 3 cups milk. Spread pudding over cream-cheese layer.

10 Fold remaining 2 tablespoons confectioners' sugar into reserved whipped cream; spread over pudding. Refrigerate until firm, about 4 hours.

11 Meanwhile, in small saucepan over medium heat, cook remaining ⅓ cup coarsely chopped almonds until golden, stirring frequently; cool.

TO SERVE
Cut dessert lengthwise into 3 strips, then cut each strip crosswise into 5 pieces. Sprinkle toasted chopped almonds on squares.

SAUCY GARNISHES

There's more to serving a sauce than just spooning it over a dessert. It can be made into an eye-catching garnish that's quick and surprisingly easy to do; all that's needed is a bit of imagination coupled with a steady hand.

Fruit purees, syrups, soft custard, cream, and sauces can all be used effectively. The garnish on White-Chocolate and Cranberry Trifle (pages 34 to 35), for example, is a delicate "feathering" of ruby-red cranberry-raspberry sauce on snowy whipped cream. Simple chocolate syrup piped onto plain custard is all that's needed to decorate Cherries en Gelée (page 52) so attractively.

The designs on these two pages should help get you started. Each combines two different ingredients of contrasting color yet compatible flavor. Choose from a wide variety of ingredients – colorful fruit sauces and purees, glistening jellies and preserves, rich dark chocolate, golden custard.

Cream Wisps
Spoon raspberry sauce onto plate. With small writing tube, pipe dots of heavy cream in a circle 1 inch from edge of sauce. Draw tip of knife or toothpick through 1 edge of each dot to form the shape of a wisp. Use as a garnish for ice creams, sorbets, and sherbets.

Chocolate Spider Web
Spoon slightly whipped cream onto plate. With small writing tube, pipe 2 concentric circles of chocolate syrup on cream. Beginning in center, draw tip of knife or toothpick to edge of cream at regular intervals, alternating first in one direction and then in the other. Use as a garnish for molded desserts and individual slices of cakes and pies.

Cream Hearts

Heat jellied cranberry sauce or currant jelly until melted, stirring until smooth; cool. Spoon sauce onto plate. With small writing tube, pipe dots of heavy cream in a circle 1 inch from edge of sauce, and in heart shape in center. Draw tip of knife or toothpick through dots to make heart shapes. Use as a garnish for poached fruit.

Fudge Chevrons

Spoon custard sauce onto plate. With small writing tube, pipe parallel lines of fudge sauce on custard. Draw tip of knife or toothpick across lines at regular intervals, alternating first in one direction and then in the other. Use as a garnish for ice cream.

Cream Sunburst

Spoon chocolate custard sauce onto plate. With small writing tube, pipe semi-circular lines of heavy cream at regular intervals. Starting at smallest circle, draw tip of knife or toothpick across lines, toward edge of plate. Use as a garnish for individual slices of pies and tarts.

On Raspberry Pond

With small writing tube, pipe free-form decorative shape of strained raspberry jelly or preserves on plate. Carefully spoon in heavy or whipping cream to fill shape. If you like, add extra garnish of fruit and mint leaves. Use as a garnish for fresh fruit and fruit salads.

ZUCCOTTO (FLORENTINE CREAM CAKE)

This delicious dessert comes from Italy, where it is traditionally made in a special pumpkin-shaped mold (zuccotto means "little pumpkin" in Italian). Here we've used a simple 2 1/2 - quart mixing bowl, which works just as well as a special zuccotto mold, and gives an equally good shape.

🥄 12 servings

🕐 Begin early in day or day ahead

1 16- to 17-ounce package pound-cake mix

1/4 cup almond-flavor liqueur

6 1-ounce squares semisweet chocolate

2 cups heavy or whipping cream

4 teaspoons instant espresso-coffee powder

1 package vanilla-flavor instant pudding and pie filling for 6 servings

2 1/4 cups milk

1 teaspoon almond extract

2 tablespoons slivered blanched almonds, chopped

2 tablespoons sugar

1 Prepare cake mix as label directs for 9" by 5" loaf pan; cool completely.

2 Line 2 1/2-quart bowl with plastic wrap. Cut cake into 1/2-inch-thick slices; cut each cake slice diagonally in half to make 2 triangles.

3 Sprinkle almond-flavor liqueur over cake triangles. Line bowl with triangles; reserve remaining triangles.

4 In heavy 1-quart saucepan over low heat, heat 4 squares semisweet chocolate, stirring often, until melted and smooth; cool slightly. Coarsely grate remaining 2 squares chocolate.

5 In small bowl, with mixer at medium speed, beat 1 1/4 cups heavy or whipping cream and 2 teaspoons instant espresso-coffee powder until stiff peaks form.

6 In large bowl, with wire whisk, prepare instant pudding as label directs, but use only 2 1/4 cups milk. Fold whipped-cream mixture, almond extract, and grated chocolate into pudding.

Covering cake in bowl with pudding mixture

7 Cover cake in bowl with two-thirds of pudding mixture.

8 Fold melted chocolate into remaining pudding mixture; use to fill center of dessert.

9 Cover top of dessert with remaining cake triangles.

10 Cover bowl and refrigerate at least 4 hours.

11 Meanwhile, in small saucepan over medium heat, cook chopped almonds until golden, stirring frequently; cool.

12 In small bowl, with mixer at medium speed, beat remaining ³/₄ cup heavy or whipping cream with sugar and remaining 2 teaspoons instant espresso-coffee powder until soft peaks form.

13 Unmold dessert onto chilled platter; discard plastic wrap. Frost dessert with whipped-cream mixture; sprinkle toasted chopped almonds on top.

DECORATIVE FINISHES FOR ZUCCOTTO

You can garnish the Zuccotto very simply with toasted chopped almonds as in our main photograph (page 28), or sift cocoa powder or confectioners' sugar over the top for an equally attractive finish. Another more decorative idea, which echoes the almond and coffee flavors of the Zuccotto, is our Daisy Design, and it only takes a few extra minutes to do.

Daisy Design
A simple daisy made from blanched or toasted almonds and coffee-bean candies, is quick and effective to do. Gently press coffee-bean candy into whipped-cream frosting for center of daisy, then press slivered almonds around candy for petals. If you like, make 1 large daisy on top of Zuccotto, or several small daisies around sides.

TO SERVE
Cut Zuccotto into slices and arrange on dessert plates to reveal different layers inside.

STRAWBERRY-ORANGE CHARLOTTE

14 servings
Begin early in day or day ahead

2 envelopes unflavored gelatin

³/₄ cup orange juice

4 large egg yolks

1 ¹/₂ cups milk

1 14-ounce can sweetened condensed milk

1 10-ounce package frozen strawberries in heavy syrup, thawed

¹/₃ cup strawberry preserves

¹/₄ cup orange-flavor liqueur

3 tablespoons cornstarch

2 3- to 4¹/₂-ounce packages ladyfingers

2 cups heavy or whipping cream

1 tablespoon confectioners' sugar

Strawberries for garnish

1 In 3-quart saucepan, evenly sprinkle gelatin over orange juice; let stand 1 minute. Cook over medium heat until gelatin dissolves, stirring frequently.

2 In small bowl, with wire whisk, beat egg yolks, milk, and sweetened condensed milk until blended. Gradually beat egg-yolk mixture into gelatin mixture. Cook over medium-low heat, stirring constantly, until mixture thickens and coats a spoon well, about 15 minutes (mixture should be about 170° to 175°F. but do not boil or it will curdle).

3 Pour custard mixture into large bowl; cover and refrigerate until mixture mounds slightly when dropped from a spoon, about 1 ¹/₂ hours, stirring occasionally.

4 Meanwhile, in food processor with knife blade attached or in blender, blend strawberries with their syrup and strawberry preserves until smooth.

5 Pour mixture into 2-quart saucepan; stir in liqueur, cornstarch, and *¹/₄ cup water.* Cook over medium-high heat, stirring constantly, until mixture boils and thickens; boil 1 minute. Remove from heat.

6 Separate ladyfingers into halves. Line 9" by 3" springform pan with ladyfinger halves.

7 Brush bottom layer of ladyfingers with ¹/₄ cup strawberry mixture (see Box, below). Reserve any remaining ladyfingers to serve with ice cream another day. Cover pan with plastic wrap; set aside. Pour remaining strawberry mixture into bowl; refrigerate until cool, stirring occasionally.

8 In small bowl, with mixer at medium speed, beat 1 ¹/₂ cups heavy or whipping cream until stiff peaks form. With rubber spatula or wire whisk, fold whipped cream into custard mixture.

9 Spoon half the custard mixture over ladyfingers in bottom of springform pan. Spoon ²/₃ cup strawberry mixture over custard layer. Add remaining custard mixture (see Box, below.) Drop heaping spoonfuls of remaining strawberry mixture on top of custard. Using metal spatula or knife, swirl mixtures together to create marbled design (see Box, below). Refrigerate until firm, at least 4 hours or overnight.

10 When ready to serve, carefully remove side of springform pan from charlotte; place charlotte on cake plate or stand. In small bowl, with mixer at medium speed, beat confectioners' sugar and remaining ¹/₂ cup heavy or whipping cream until stiff peaks form. Spoon into decorating bag with medium star tube; pipe in pretty design around top edge of charlotte. Cut strawberries into halves; use to garnish charlotte.

MAKING MARBLED DESIGN

Brushing bottom layer of ladyfingers: Evenly spread ¹/₄ cup strawberry mixture over ladyfingers.

Adding remaining layer of custard mixture: Over second layer of strawberry mixture, spoon rest of custard mixture.

Swirling mixtures: *With metal spatula, swirl strawberry and custard mixtures to create marbled design.*

Strawberry-Orange Charlotte looks extra pretty with a satin ribbon tied around its center

TIRAMISÙ

16 servings

Begin 3 hours before serving or early in day

1 16-ounce container mascarpone cheese (see Box, below right)

$1/2$ teaspoon salt

$1/2$ cup plus 2 tablespoons confectioners' sugar

3 tablespoons plus $1/3$ cup coffee-flavor liqueur

$1 1/2$ teaspoons vanilla extract

3 1-ounce squares semi-sweet chocolate, grated

$1 1/2$ cups heavy or whipping cream

2 teaspoons instant espresso-coffee powder

2 3- to 4 $1/2$-ounce packages ladyfingers

1 In large bowl, with wire whisk or fork, beat mascarpone, salt, $1/2$ cup confectioners' sugar, 3 tablespoons coffee-flavor liqueur, 1 teaspoon vanilla extract, and two-thirds of grated chocolate. (Set aside remaining chocolate for top of dessert.)

2 In small bowl, with mixer at medium speed, beat 1 cup heavy or whipping cream until stiff peaks form. With rubber spatula or wire whisk, fold whipped cream into cheese mixture.

3 In small bowl, stir instant espresso-powder, remaining $1/3$ cup coffee-flavor liqueur, remaining $1/2$ teaspoon vanilla extract, and 2 tablespoons water.

4 Separate ladyfingers into halves. Line 2 $1/2$-quart glass or crystal bowl with one-fourth of ladyfingers; brush with 2 tablespoons of espresso mixture. Spoon one-third of cheese mixture over ladyfingers. Repeat with ladyfingers, espresso mixture, and cheese mixture to make 2 more layers. Top with remaining ladyfingers, gently pressing ladyfingers into cheese mixture. Brush ladyfingers with remaining espresso mixture. Sprinkle remaining grated chocolate over top of dessert, reserving 1 tablespoon for garnish.

5 In small bowl, with mixer at medium speed, beat remaining $1/2$ cup cream and remaining 2 tablespoons confectioners' sugar until stiff peaks form.

6 Spoon whipped-cream mixture into decorating bag with large star tube. Pipe large rosettes on top of dessert.

Now you don't have to dine at an Italian restaurant to enjoy this great dessert! See how easy it is to make at home

7 Sprinkle reserved grated chocolate on whipped-cream rosettes. Refrigerate until chilled and to blend flavors, at least 2 hours.

MASCARPONE CHEESE

Mascarpone, a fresh, double-cream cheese, is one of the great Italian cheeses available in cheese shops, specialty stores, and deli departments of many supermarkets. It is buttery-smooth in texture, slightly nutty or tangy in flavor, and superb with fruit as well as in recipes.

Mascarpone Cheese Substitute

If mascarpone cheese is not available when making Tiramisù, substitute *two 8-ounce packages cream cheese*, softened, and delete salt; in step 1, in large bowl, with mixer at medium speed, beat cream cheese and *3 tablespoons milk* until smooth and fluffy. Increase confectioners' sugar for cheese mixture to $2/3$ cup, and beat in with coffee-flavor liqueur and vanilla extract. Stir in grated chocolate.

RASPBERRY-ORANGE TRIFLE

🍴 16 servings

🕐 Begin about 1 hour before serving or early in day

⅓ cup orange-flavor liqueur

¼ cup orange juice

1 10¾- to 12-ounce frozen ready-to-serve pound cake, thawed

2 12-ounce jars seedless raspberry jam

3 cups heavy or whipping cream

2 packages vanilla-flavor instant pudding and pie filling for 4 servings

2 cups milk

½ teaspoon orange-flavor extract

1 large orange

4 1-ounce squares semisweet chocolate

Cranberries and lemon leaves for garnish

1 In 1-cup measure, combine orange-flavor liqueur and orange juice. With serrated knife, cut pound cake horizontally into 3 layers.

2 Brush cut sides and top of pound cake generously with orange-liqueur mixture.

3 In medium bowl, with fork or wire whisk, stir raspberry jam until smooth. Spread bottom layer of pound cake with ¼ cup raspberry jam; top with middle layer. Spread ¼ cup raspberry jam over middle layer.

4 Replace top of pound cake. Slice layered pound cake crosswise into ½-inch-thick slices.

5 In large bowl, with mixer at medium speed, beat heavy or whipping cream until stiff peaks form.

6 In another large bowl, prepare vanilla-flavor pudding and pie filling as label directs, but use only 2 cups milk and add orange extract. Grate peel from orange; add to pudding mixture. With wire whisk or rubber spatula, fold whipped cream into pudding mixture.

7 In heavy 1-quart saucepan over low heat, heat chocolate, stirring frequently, until melted and smooth; remove saucepan from heat.

8 In 4-quart glass bowl, place 2 cups pudding mixture. Spread with half the remaining raspberry jam, then 1 cup pudding mixture. Drizzle with half the melted chocolate.

9 Arrange some layered pound-cake slices around side of bowl.

10 Cut remaining pound-cake slices into chunks and layer in bowl; drizzle with remaining chocolate.

11 Spread enough pudding mixture to cover cake (2 to 3 cups). Spoon remaining raspberry jam around edge of bowl.

12 Spoon remaining pudding mixture into decorating bag with large star tube. Pipe pudding, inside ring of raspberry jam, to make a pretty design. Cover bowl and refrigerate.

> **TO SERVE**
> With knife, remove any remaining peel and white membrane from orange and cut out sections. Garnish trifle with orange sections, cranberries, and lemon leaves.

WHITE-CHOCOLATE AND CRANBERRY TRIFLE

Give your holiday table a festive look when you serve this stunning trifle for dessert. No-one will be able to resist its luscious layers of fruit, cream, and pound cake. Made ahead of time and kept in the refrigerator, its flavor improves, so it's the perfect dessert for easy entertaining.

 12 servings

Begin early in day or day ahead

White-Chocolate Custard (see Box, page 35)

1 10 ³/4- to 12-ounce frozen ready-to-serve pound cake, thawed

1 16-ounce can jellied cranberry sauce

¹/3 cup raspberry-flavor liqueur

1 ¹/2 cups heavy or whipping cream

¹/4 cup confectioners' sugar

1 teaspoon vanilla extract

Chopped pistachio nuts for garnish

1 Prepare White-Chocolate Custard; refrigerate until cool, about 1 hour.

2 Cut pound cake into ³/4-inch chunks. In small bowl, with fork, stir jellied cranberry sauce and raspberry-flavor liqueur until smooth.

3 In 3-quart glass serving bowl, place half the cake chunks.

4 Reserve 2 tablespoons cranberry-raspberry sauce mixture; spoon half the remaining sauce mixture over cake.

5 Top sauce mixture with half the White-Chocolate Custard. Repeat layering with cake, sauce mixture, and custard. Cover and refrigerate at least 4 hours.

6 In small bowl, with mixer at medium speed, beat heavy or whipping cream, confectioners' sugar, and vanilla extract until stiff peaks form. Reserve 1 cup whipped-cream mixture; spread remaining cream over trifle.

7 Spoon reserved cranberry-raspberry sauce mixture into small decorating bag with small writing tube (or, use paper cone with tip cut to make ¹/8 -inch-diameter hole) and use to decorate top of trifle (see Box, below).

8 Spoon reserved whipped-cream mixture into decorating bag with large star tube. Pipe around edge of trifle (see Box, below). Garnish with pistachios.

DECORATING TOP OF TRIFLE

Filling decorating bag: *Into small decorating bag with small writing tube, spoon reserved cranberry-raspberry sauce mixture.*

Making feather design: *Draw tip of knife across lines at ¹/2-inch intervals, alternating first in one direction and then in the other.*

Piping parallel lines: *On whipped-cream mixture on trifle, pipe cranberry-raspberry sauce mixture in parallel lines, ¹/2 inch apart.*

Piping cream: *Using decorating bag with large star tube, pipe reserved whipped-cream mixture around edge of trifle.*

WHITE-CHOCOLATE CUSTARD

In 3-quart saucepan, with wire whisk, mix *1/2 cup sugar, 1/4 cup cornstarch, and 1/4 teaspoon salt;* slowly stir in *4 cups milk* until smooth. Cook over medium heat, stirring constantly, until mixture boils and thickens; boil 1 minute. Remove saucepan from heat. In cup, with fork, beat *4 large egg yolks;* stir in about 1/2 cup hot milk mixture. Slowly pour egg mixture back into milk mixture, stirring rapidly to prevent lumping; cook over medium-low heat, stirring constantly, until mixture thickens and coats a spoon well (mixture should be about 170° to 175°F.). Remove saucepan from heat. Stir in *6 ounces white chocolate,* chopped, and *2 teaspoons vanilla extract,* until chocolate melts and mixture is smooth. To keep skin from forming as custard cools, press plastic wrap directly onto surface of hot custard.

This simple garnish of feathering plus piped cream makes your dessert look like the work of a master chef!

BUTTERMILK MOLD WITH PEACH SAUCE

10 servings

Begin about 3 ½ hours before serving or early in day

3 cups buttermilk

⅓ cup sugar

2 envelopes unflavored gelatin

3 tablespoons lemon juice

1 teaspoon grated lemon peel

1 envelope whipped-topping mix (½ 2.6-ounce package)

½ cup milk

½ teaspoon vanilla extract

2 10-ounce packages frozen peaches in syrup, thawed

2 teaspoons cornstarch

Shredded lemon peel for garnish

1 In 2-quart saucepan, stir 1 ½ cups buttermilk with sugar until blended. Evenly sprinkle gelatin over buttermilk mixture; let stand 1 minute to soften gelatin slightly.

2 Cook over medium heat, stirring frequently, until gelatin completely dissolves. Remove saucepan from heat. Into buttermilk mixture, stir lemon juice, lemon peel, and remaining 1 ½ cups buttermilk.

3 Cover and chill until mixture mounds slightly when dropped from spoon, about 45 minutes, stirring occasionally.

4 In small bowl, prepare whipped-topping mix as label directs with milk and vanilla extract; set aside.

5 In large bowl, with mixer at high speed, beat buttermilk mixture until foamy, about 30 seconds.

6 To buttermilk mixture, add whipped topping; beat at high speed until mixture is smooth and creamy, about 30 seconds.

7 Pour mixture into 1 ½-quart mold; cover and refrigerate until dessert is firm, about 2 hours.

8 Meanwhile, prepare peach sauce: Into 1-quart saucepan, drain syrup from peaches; set peaches aside. Into peach syrup, stir cornstarch; cook over medium heat until mixture thickens and boils, stirring constantly; boil 1 minute. Gently stir in peaches. Cover sauce and refrigerate.

TO SERVE
Unmold dessert onto chilled platter. Arrange peaches on top of dessert and around bottom. Spoon sauce over; garnish with shredded lemon peel.

FRUIT FOOLS

4 servings
Begin about 20 minutes before serving

PEACH

3 medium-sized ripe peaches

2 tablespoons sugar

1 cup heavy or whipping cream

1/8 teaspoon almond extract

Mint leaves for garnish

1 Peel, halve, and pit peaches. Reserve 1 peach half for garnish. Cut remaining peaches into chunks.

2 In blender at medium speed, blend peach chunks and sugar until smooth.

3 In small bowl, with mixer at medium speed, beat heavy or whipping cream and almond extract until stiff peaks form.

4 With rubber spatula or wire whisk, fold peach puree into whipped-cream mixture.

TO SERVE
Spoon mixture into parfait glasses or dessert dishes; garnish with reserved fruits and mint leaves.

RASPBERRY

1 10-ounce package frozen quick-thaw raspberries in light syrup, thawed

1 cup heavy or whipping cream

1/8 teaspoon almond extract

Raspberries and mint leaves for garnish

1 Over large bowl, with back of spoon, press and scrape thawed raspberries with their syrup firmly against medium-mesh sieve to separate seeds from pulp; discard seeds.

2 In small bowl, with mixer at medium speed, beat heavy or whipping cream and almond extract until stiff peaks form.

3 With rubber spatula or wire whisk, fold whipped-cream mixture into raspberry puree.

Peach Fool

Raspberry Fool

KIWIFRUIT

3 large kiwifruit

2 tablespoons sugar

1 cup heavy or whipping cream

1/8 teaspoon vanilla extract

Mint leaves for garnish

1 Peel kiwifruit. Cut 1 kiwifruit crosswise in half. Reserve 1 half for garnish. Cut remaining kiwifruit into chunks.

2 In blender at medium speed, blend kiwifruit chunks and sugar until smooth.

3 In small bowl, with mixer at medium speed, beat heavy or whipping cream and vanilla extract until stiff peaks form.

4 With rubber spatula or wire whisk, fold kiwifruit puree into whipped-cream mixture.

Kiwifruit Fool

CHOCOLATE BOX WITH BERRIES AND CREAM

This spectacular dessert is simple to make when you follow our step-by-step directions below, yet your guests cannot fail to be impressed with your skills. And the combination of rich dark chocolate with fresh strawberries and cream is the perfect choice for any special occasion or celebration.

9 servings

Begin about 3 hours before serving or early in day

6 1-ounce squares semisweet chocolate

1 tablespoon shortening

2 3-ounce packages cream cheese, softened

4 tablespoons butter (1/2 stick), softened

1 1/2 cups confectioners' sugar

1/3 cup unsweetened cocoa

2 tablespoons milk

1 teaspoon vanilla extract

2 cups heavy or whipping cream

2 pints strawberries

Mint leaves for garnish

1 Line 9" by 9" baking pan with foil; press out wrinkles so chocolate box will come off foil smoothly (see Box, below).

2 In heavy 1-quart saucepan over low heat, heat semisweet chocolate and shortening, stirring frequently, until melted and smooth.

3 Pour melted-chocolate mixture into foil-lined pan and swirl around sides and bottom, keeping edges as even as possible (see Box, below). Refrigerate 1 minute, then swirl chocolate mixture around inside of pan a second time, to reinforce sides of chocolate box. Refrigerate until chocolate is firm, about 30 minutes.

4 Meanwhile, prepare filling: In large bowl, with mixer at medium speed, beat cream cheese and butter until smooth (do not use margarine or filling will be too soft to cut). Add confectioners' sugar, cocoa, milk, and vanilla extract; beat until light and fluffy.

5 In small bowl, with mixer at medium speed, beat 1 1/2 cups heavy or whipping cream until stiff peaks form. With rubber spatula or wire whisk, fold whipped cream into cream-cheese mixture.

6 Remove foil-lined chocolate box from pan, then gently peel foil from sides and bottom (see Box, below). Place chocolate box on platter. Spread cream-cheese filling evenly in chocolate box. Refrigerate until filling is well chilled and firm, about 2 hours.

7 In small bowl, with mixer at medium speed, beat remaining 1/2 cup heavy or whipping cream until stiff peaks form. Spoon whipped cream into decorating bag with large rosette tube.

8 Pipe whipped cream in 1-inch-wide border on filling around chocolate box. Cut larger strawberries in half and arrange over entire top of cream-cheese filling. Garnish top of dessert with mint leaves. Serve remaining strawberries with dessert.

> *TO SERVE*
> *If you can find strawberries with long stems, they will make this dessert even prettier.*

MAKING CHOCOLATE BOX

Pouring chocolate: Slowly pour warm melted-chocolate mixture into foil-lined baking pan.

Swirling chocolate: *Gently tilt pan from side to side so chocolate swirls around sides and bottom.*

Removing chocolate box: *Carefully lift foil to remove chocolate box from pan.*

Meringues

Light and delicate, crisp and sweet, meringue serves as the crust for pie-like Pavlova; makes the layers for cake-like dacquoise; becomes petite tart shells to hold fillings of cream, fruit, and frozen mixtures; and, shaped as mushrooms, makes a stunning addition to the cookie tray. Small, meringues, spooned or piped into dollops like whipped cream, can top soft puddings, or garnish cakes and tortes; bake as for Miniature Meringue Shells (page 42).

PAVLOVA

12 servings
Begin 3 1/2 hours before serving or early in day

3 large egg whites

1/4 teaspoon cream of tartar

1/4 teaspoon salt

3/4 cup sugar

5 kiwifruit

1 1/2 cups heavy or whipping cream

3/4 teaspoon almond extract

1 Line cookie sheet with foil. Using 9-inch round plate or cake pan as guide, with tooth-pick, outline a circle on foil on cookie sheet.

2 Preheat oven to 275°F. In small bowl, with mixer at high speed, beat egg whites, cream of tartar, and salt until soft peaks form. Beating at high speed, gradually sprinkle in sugar, 2 table-spoons at a time, beating well after each addition until sugar completely dissolves and whites stand in stiff, glossy peaks.

3 Inside circle on cookie sheet, spoon meringue mixture, shap-ing meringue into a "nest" about 1 1/2 inches high around edge. Bake 1 1/4 hours or until meringue is lightly browned and crisp.

4 Cool meringue on cookie sheet on wire rack 10 minutes. With metal spatula, carefully loosen and remove me-ringue from foil to wire rack to cool completely. When meringue is cool, place on serving plate.

5 With sharp knife, peel off skin and thinly slice kiwifruit.

6 In small bowl, with mixer at medium speed, beat heavy or whipping cream and almond extract until stiff peaks form.

OTHER FRUIT TOPPINGS

Though kiwifruit remains the classic topping for Pavlova, other fruits can be used instead. Combine any or all of the following fruits with kiwifruit, or use them on their own.

- Halved strawberries.

- Peeled and sliced peaches.

- Peeled and cut-up papaya.

- Pineapple chunks.

TO SERVE
Spoon two-thirds of cream into meringue; reserve a few kiwifruit slices; arrange remainder on cream. Top with remain-ing cream and reserved kiwifruit.

DATE AND WALNUT DACQUOISE

16 servings

Begin about 2 ½ hours before serving or early in day

1 4-ounce can walnuts (1 cup)

½ 10-ounce container pitted dates (1 cup)

5 large egg whites

⅛ teaspoon cream of tartar

⅛ teaspoon salt

1 cup sugar

3 tablespoons unsweetened cocoa

Mocha Butter-Cream Filling (see Box, above right)

Confectioners' sugar for sprinkling

1 Set aside few pieces of walnuts and few dates to use for garnish later. Coarsely chop remaining walnuts and cut remaining dates into ½-inch pieces.

2 In 10-inch skillet over medium heat, toast chopped walnuts until golden brown, stirring occasionally; remove skillet from heat.

3 Line 2 cookie sheets with foil. Using 9-inch round plate or cake pan as guide, with toothpick, outline 1 circle on foil on each cookie sheet; set aside.

4 In large bowl, with mixer at high speed, beat egg whites, cream of tartar, and salt until soft peaks form. Beating at high speed, gradually sprinkle in sugar, 2 tablespoons at a time, beating well after each addition until sugar completely dissolves and whites stand in stiff, glossy peaks.

5 Preheat oven to 350°F. In small bowl, with spoon, mix cut-up dates with ¼ cup egg-white mixture to separate pieces. With rubber spatula, gently fold cocoa, date mixture, and chopped walnuts into remaining egg-white mixture.

6 Inside each circle on cookie sheets, spoon half the egg-white mixture; with metal spatula, evenly spread meringue to cover entire circle. Place cookie sheets with meringue on 2 oven racks; bake 15 minutes. Switch cookie sheets between upper and lower racks so meringue browns evenly; bake 15 minutes longer or until meringue layers are crisp on the outside, but still soft and chewy on the inside.

7 Cool meringues on cookie sheets on wire racks 10 minutes. With metal spatula, carefully loosen and remove meringues from foil to wire racks to cool completely. (If not assembling dessert right away, meringue layers can be stored, covered, up to 1 day ahead.)

8 When meringues are cool, prepare Mocha Butter-Cream Filling.

MOCHA BUTTER-CREAM FILLING
In large bowl, with mixer at low speed, beat *one 16-ounce package confectioners' sugar, 6 tablespoons margarine* or butter (¾ *stick*), *softened, ½ cup unsweetened cocoa, ⅓ cup hot coffee,* and *½ teaspoon vanilla extract* until blended. Increase speed to medium; beat until butter cream has an easy spreading consistency, adding more coffee if necessary.

9 To assemble cake: Place 1 meringue layer, flat-side up, on cake plate. Cover evenly with Mocha Butter-Cream Filling; spread to ½ inch from edge. Top with second meringue layer, flat-side down; press down gently. Cover; refrigerate until filling is firm.

TO SERVE
Sprinkle with confectioners' sugar; garnish with reserved walnuts and dates. While firm, cut into wedges; allow to soften 5 minutes at room temperature.

MERINGUE SHAPES

MERINGUE SHELLS

🥄 6 shells
🕐 Begin about 3 hours before serving or day ahead

3 large egg whites

1/8 teaspoon cream of tartar

3/4 cup sugar

1/2 teaspoon vanilla extract

1 Preheat oven to 275°F. Line large cookie sheet with foil.

2 In small bowl, with mixer at high speed, beat egg whites and cream of tartar until soft peaks form. Sprinkle in sugar, 2 tablespoons at a time, beating well after each addition until sugar completely dissolves and whites stand in stiff, glossy peaks. Beat in vanilla.

3 Spoon meringue into large decorating bag with medium star tube. Pipe meringue into six 4-inch rounds, about 1 inch apart, on foil-lined cookie sheet.

4 Pipe remaining meringue in decorative star border around edge of each meringue round.

5 Bake meringues 45 minutes. Turn oven control off; leave meringues in oven 45 minutes longer to dry completely.

6 Cool meringues on cookie sheet on wire rack 10 minutes. With metal spatula, carefully loosen and remove meringues from foil to wire rack to cool completely.

7 If not using meringues right away, store in tightly covered container.

MINIATURE MERINGUE SHELLS
Prepare meringue as for Meringue Shells (above), through step 2. With medium writing tube, pipe into thirty 1 1/2-inch rounds on foil-lined cookie sheet. With teaspoon, shape into nests. Bake 30 minutes. Turn oven control off; leave in oven 30 minutes longer. Cool as above in step 6. Yield: 30 miniature shells.

MERINGUE MUSHROOMS

1 Preheat oven to 200°F. Line large cookie sheet with foil. Prepare meringue as in step 2 of Meringue Shells (left).

2 With large writing tube, pipe meringue onto foil-lined cookie sheet in 24 mounds, each about 1 1/2 inches in diameter, to resemble mushroom caps.

3 Pipe remaining meringue upright onto cookie sheet in twenty-four 1 1/4-inch lengths, to resemble stems.

4 Bake 1 3/4 hours. Turn oven control off; leave meringues in oven 30 minutes longer. Cool completely on cookie sheet on wire rack.

5 In heatproof glass measuring cup, in pan of simmering water, melt *two 1-ounce squares semisweet chocolate*; cool slightly.

6 With tip of small knife, cut small hole in center of underside of mushroom cap. Place a little melted chocolate in hole; spread underside of cap with chocolate.

7 Carefully insert pointed end of stem into hole in center of underside of mushroom cap.

8 Repeat with remaining caps and stems. Let chocolate dry and set, about 1 hour. Store in tightly covered container. Before serving, sprinkle lightly with *unsweetened cocoa*. Yield: 24 mushrooms.

Meringue Shells filled with ice cream or whipped cream, topped with a variety of different-colored fresh fruits, make glorious table centerpieces

Miniature Meringue Shells and Meringue Mushrooms make mouthwatering bite-sized desserts

STRAWBERRY AND ALMOND DACQUOISE

🍴 16 servings
🕐 Begin early in day

½ 4-ounce can slivered blanched almonds (½ cup)

6 large egg whites

¼ teaspoon cream of tartar

1 cup sugar

2 pints strawberries

Chocolate Butter-Cream Filling (see Box, below)

2 cups heavy or whipping cream

1 In skillet over medium heat, cook almonds until golden, stirring frequently; cool. In blender or food processor, blend almonds until finely ground; set aside.

2 Line 2 large cookie sheets with foil. Using 8-inch round plate or cake pan as guide, with toothpick, outline 2 circles on foil on each cookie sheet.

3 Preheat oven to 275°F. In large bowl, with mixer at high speed, beat egg whites and cream of tartar until soft peaks form. Beating at high speed, gradually sprinkle in sugar, 2 tablespoons at a time, beating well after each addition until sugar completely dissolves and whites stand in stiff, glossy peaks.

4 Into egg-white mixture, with wire whisk or rubber spatula, carefully fold ground toasted almonds.

5 Spoon one-fourth of mixture inside each circle on cookie sheets; with metal spatula, evenly spread meringue to cover entire circle.

6 Place cookie sheets with meringue on 2 oven racks; bake 30 minutes. Switch cookie sheets between racks so meringue browns evenly; bake 30 minutes longer or until golden.

7 Cool meringues on cookie sheets on wire racks 10 minutes. With metal spatula, loosen and remove meringues from foil to wire racks; cool completely.

8 Hull and thinly slice enough strawberries to make 1½ cups. Prepare Chocolate Butter-Cream Filling.

9 On serving plate, place 1 meringue layer; spread with one-third of butter cream; top with one-third of sliced strawberries. Make 2 more layers and top with last meringue layer (see Box, right).

10 In small bowl, with mixer at medium speed, beat heavy or whipping cream until stiff peaks form. Spoon 1⅓ cups whipped cream into decorating bag with large star tube; set aside. Spread remaining whipped cream on top and side of cake. With cream in decorating bag, garnish top edge of cake.

11 Refrigerate cake 4 hours to soften meringue layers slightly for easier cutting.

12 Cut 16 slices from remaining strawberries; press into cream on side of cake. Hull remaining strawberries and cut into halves. Pile strawberry halves on center of cake.

CHOCOLATE BUTTER-CREAM FILLING

In large bowl, with mixer at low speed, beat *one 16-ounce package confectioners' sugar, 6 tablespoons margarine* or butter (*¾ stick), softened, 3 tablespoons milk* or half-and-half, *½ cup unsweetened cocoa,* and *1½ teaspoons vanilla extract* until smooth. Add more milk, if necessary, until an easy spreading consistency.

ASSEMBLING THE DACQUOISE

Spreading top layer of butter-cream filling: *With metal spatula, evenly spread third layer of butter cream over third meringue layer.*

Topping with strawberries: *Arrange remaining sliced strawberries over butter cream.*

Topping with meringue: *Place fourth meringue layer on top to complete dacquoise.*

TO SERVE
After the dacquoise has
been spread with whipped
cream, use a 4-tined fork to
make attractive vertical
lines all around side;
then garnish with sliced
strawberries.

Crepes and Blintzes

Crepes can be folded, rolled, or stacked, with or without a filling, to make a different-looking dessert every time you serve them. One side is always browner than the other; so have the pale side up when you fold or roll the crepes, so that the browner, more attractive side is visible.

FREEZING CREPES

Crepes can be prepared and frozen up to 2 months ahead. After stacking crepes with waxed paper between them, allow them to cool, then wrap stack tightly in foil; label and freeze; use within 2 months. To thaw, let stand, wrapped, at room temperature about 2 hours. Use as directed in recipes.

CREPES

12 crepes

Margarine or butter, melted

1 ¹/₂ *cups milk*

²/₃ *cup all-purpose flour*

¹/₂ *teaspoon salt*

3 large eggs

5 Using metal spatula, work around crepe to loosen it from pan.

2 With pastry brush, brush bottoms of 7-inch crepe pan and 10-inch skillet with melted margarine or butter.

3 Over medium heat, heat both pans.

6 Invert crepe into hot skillet. Cook other side about 30 seconds. Meanwhile, start cooking another crepe in crepe pan.

7 Slip cooked crepe onto waxed paper. Repeat until all batter is used, stacking crepes, with waxed paper between them. Use immediately or wrap in foil and refrigerate.

1 In medium bowl, with wire whisk, beat 2 tablespoons melted margarine or butter (¹/₄ stick) and remaining ingredients until smooth. Cover and refrigerate batter at least 2 hours (to give flour time to absorb liquid, so that batter is thicker and easier to handle).

4 Pour scant ¹/₄ cup batter into crepe pan; tip pan to evenly coat bottom. Cook crepe 2 minutes or until top is set and underside slightly browned.

CREPES SUZETTE

6 servings
Begin about 3 ½ hours before serving or early in day

12 crepes (page 46)

1 large orange

4 tablespoons margarine or butter (½ stick)

2 tablespoons sugar

¼ cup orange-flavor liqueur

Orange slices and shredded orange peel for garnish

1 Prepare crepes. (If using frozen crepes, let stand, wrapped, at room temperature about 2 hours until thawed.)

2 About 30 minutes before serving, grate ½ teaspoon peel from orange. Cut orange crosswise in half; squeeze enough juice from orange halves to measure ⅓ cup.

3 Prepare sauce: In 10-inch skillet or chafing dish, over low heat, heat orange peel, orange juice, margarine or butter, and sugar until margarine or butter melts.

4 Fold each crepe in half, then fold each one again into quarters.

5 Arrange crepes in sauce in skillet or chafing dish and heat through.

6 In very small saucepan over low heat, gently heat liqueur until warm; remove saucepan from heat. Ignite liqueur with match; pour flaming liqueur over crepes.

FLAMBÉ

Flambé is the French word for flamed, and generally refers to foods that are bathed in flaming spirits, usually brandy, cognac, or high-proof liqueur. Flaming burns off some of the alcohol, and when the flames die down, the food, now deliciously flavored, is ready to enjoy. Crepes Suzette is one of the best-known desserts that uses this classic French cooking technique, and so too does Cherries Jubilee (see recipe below). Here are some tips for success.

• Use a skillet or chafing dish, preferably shallow to let more oxygen reach the flames and keep them alive longer so they burn off more alcohol.

• Serving dishes should be heatproof; don't use your fine crystal.

• Use wooden matches or long fireplace matches, not book matches, for igniting the spirit.

• Gently warm the spirit before igniting it. Heat it in a very small metal saucepan or measuring cup over a low heat - such as a candle - until it's warm but not hot.

• Hold lighted match over warm spirit to ignite vapors, then slowly pour flaming spirit over food. Or, if there isn't much liquid in skillet, pour warm spirit into the skillet (don't stir) and then light it.

• Rock or shake skillet gently to keep the flames alive as long as possible.

• When flames die, serve the food immediately.

CHERRIES JUBILEE

Just before serving: Scoop *1 ½ pints vanilla ice cream* into 6 dessert bowls. At table, in 10-inch skillet or chafing dish, melt *one 10-ounce jar red currant jelly*; stir until smooth. Add *two 17-ounce cans pitted dark sweet cherries*, drained; heat until simmering. Pour in *½ cup brandy*; heat, without stirring, 1 minute. Light brandy with match. Spoon flaming cherries over ice cream. Makes 6 servings.

TO SERVE
When flame dies down, place crepes on warm plates; garnish with orange slices and peel.

CHEESE BLINTZES WITH CHERRY SAUCE

6 servings
Begin about
3 ½ hours before
serving or early
in day

12 crepes (page 46)

*1 12-ounce container
cottage cheese
(1 ½ cups)*

*2 3-ounce packages cream
cheese, softened*

¼ cup sugar

*½ teaspoon vanilla
extract*

*1 pound sweet cherries,
pitted*

¼ cup sugar

1 Prepare crepes. (If using frozen crepes, let stand, wrapped, at room temperature about 2 hours until thawed.)

2 About 30 minutes before serving, in small bowl, with mixer at medium speed, beat cottage cheese, cream cheese, sugar, and vanilla extract until smooth.

3 Spread about 1 tablespoon of cheese mixture on each crepe.

4 Fold one side and then its opposite side slightly toward center.

5 Roll up crepe, jelly-roll fashion, in opposite direction.

6 Prepare cherry sauce: In cook-and-serve skillet over medium heat, in ⅔ cup boiling water, heat cherries to boiling. Reduce heat to low; cover and simmer 5 minutes or until tender. During last minute of cooking, add sugar.

7 To cherry sauce in skillet, add filled crepes. Over low heat, simmer 10 minutes to heat through.

> **TO SERVE**
> *Place 2 blintzes on each plate and spoon over sauce.*

PINEAPPLE CREPES

6 servings
Begin about 3 1/2 hours before serving or early in day

12 crepes (page 46)

Vanilla Custard Cream (see Box, right)

1 large pineapple

2 1/2-pints raspberries

6 tablespoons confectioners' sugar

1/3 cup brandy (optional)

Fresh raspberries for garnish

1 Prepare crepes. Prepare Vanilla Custard Cream and refrigerate.

2 About 45 minutes before serving, with sharp knife, cut crown and stem ends from pineapple; cut off rind. Slice pineapple lengthwise in half; remove core from each half. Cut pineapple halves crosswise into 1/4-inch-thick slices; set aside.

3 Over medium bowl, with back of spoon, press and scrape raspberries firmly against medium-mesh sieve to separate seeds from pulp; discard seeds. Set pulp aside.

4 Preheat broiler if manufacturer directs. Place 3 crepes on large cookie sheet. On each crepe, spread about 2 tablespoons Vanilla Custard Cream; arrange several slices pineapple over custard cream.

5 Spread about 2 more tablespoons custard cream over pineapple; top with another crepe and slice of pineapple. Sprinkle about 1 tablespoon confectioners' sugar over each filled crepe.

6 Place cookie sheet in broiler at closest position to source of heat; broil filled crepes 6 to 8 minutes until sugar caramelizes. Remove cookie sheet from oven; with pancake turner, slide filled crepes onto large dessert or dinner plates; keep warm. Repeat to make 3 more filled crepes.

TO SERVE
Spoon raspberry puree around warm crepes. Sprinkle each serving with about 1 tablespoon brandy, and if you like, sprinkle with more confectioners' sugar. Garnish with fresh raspberries.

VANILLA CUSTARD CREAM

In 1-quart saucepan over medium heat, heat *1 cup milk* to boiling; remove from heat. In medium bowl, with wire whisk, beat *3 large egg yolks, 1/2 teaspoon vanilla extract,* and *1/3 cup sugar* until thick and lemon-colored; beat in *1/4 cup all-purpose flour.* Add *1/2 cup hot milk,* mixing well with wire whisk; pour egg mixture back into remaining milk in saucepan, stirring constantly. Cook over medium-low heat, stirring constantly, until mixture thickens and boils. Reduce heat to low; cook 1 minute. Remove to small bowl. To keep skin from forming as custard cream cools, press plastic wrap directly onto surface.

APPLE DESSERT PANCAKE

 8 servings

🕐 Begin about 40 minutes before serving

1 large Golden Delicious apple

4 tablespoons butter ($\frac{1}{2}$ stick)

1 teaspoon ground cinnamon

$\frac{1}{4}$ cup plus $\frac{1}{3}$ cup sugar

$\frac{1}{3}$ cup all-purpose flour

$\frac{1}{3}$ cup milk

$\frac{1}{2}$ teaspoon baking powder

$\frac{1}{8}$ teaspoon salt

4 large eggs, separated

1 Peel and core apple; cut into $\frac{1}{8}$-inch-thick slices. Set aside.

2 In 10-inch skillet with all-metal handle (or handle covered with heavy-duty foil), over medium-low heat, melt butter (do not use margarine because it separates from sugar during cooking). Stir in cinnamon and $\frac{1}{4}$ cup sugar; remove skillet from heat.

3 In butter mixture in skillet, arrange apple slices, overlapping them slightly (see Box, below). Repeat with smaller circle of apple slices in center.

4 Return skillet to low heat; cook 10 minutes or until apples are tender-crisp (see Box, below).

5 Meanwhile, preheat oven to 400°F. In medium bowl, with fork, beat flour, milk, baking powder, salt, and egg yolks until blended; set aside.

6 In small bowl, with mixer at high speed, beat egg whites and remaining $\frac{1}{3}$ cup sugar until soft peaks form. With rubber spatula, gently fold egg-white mixture into egg-yolk mixture.

7 Cover apple slices in skillet with egg mixture (see Box, below); with rubber spatula, spread batter evenly.

8 Bake pancake 10 minutes or until golden brown. Remove skillet from oven. Carefully invert dessert onto large platter to serve.

PLACING APPLES AND PANCAKE MIXTURE IN SKILLET

Arranging apple slices: Around edge of skillet, place apple slices in a circle. Do not crowd apple slices – overlap them slightly so they cook evenly.

Testing apple slices for doneness: With tines of fork, gently pierce apple slices. They are "tender-crisp" when easy to pierce.

Covering apple slices: With large metal spoon, carefully pour egg mixture over apple slices, taking care not to shift them.

Fruit Desserts

When eaten by itself at the peak of its freshness, fruit is truly a "natural" dessert. But it can also be transformed into myriad excitingly different desserts, ranging from simple mixtures such as Gingered Fruit (below) and Sacramento Fruit Bowl (page 62) to more elaborate preparations such as Grape Clusters in Shimmering Lemon-Cheese Gel (pages 60 to 61). Importing has extended the availability of many familiar fruits, and given us new and exotic kinds, like figs, carambola (star fruit), and papaya, to add flavor, color, and texture to desserts.

GINGERED FRUIT

12 servings

Begin about 1 ½ hours before serving or early in day

2 17-ounce cans apricot halves in heavy syrup

1 17-ounce jar figs in heavy syrup

3 large Red Delicious apples

3 large pears

¾ pound seedless red grapes

¾ pound seedless green grapes

⅓ cup finely chopped preserved ginger in syrup

2 tablespoons lemon juice

1 Into large bowl, pour apricot halves with their syrup and figs with their syrup.

2 With sharp knife, cut unpeeled apples and pears into bite-sized chunks; discard cores.

3 Add apples and pears to fruit mixture in bowl with grapes, ginger, and lemon juice; toss to mix well.

4 Cover and refrigerate at least 1 hour to blend flavors.

This combination of fresh and canned fruits can be enjoyed the year round!

CHERRIES EN GELÉE

🥄 8 servings
🕐 Begin early in day
or day ahead

*2 16 ½- to 17-ounce cans
pitted dark sweet cherries
in heavy syrup*

*1 envelope unflavored
gelatin*

*1 package cherry-flavor
gelatin for 4 servings*

½ cup cream sherry

*Snow-White Custard (see
Box, right)*

*1 tablespoon chocolate
syrup*

*Citrus Curls (page 66) for
garnish*

1 Into 2-cup glass measuring cup, drain syrup from both cans of cherries; set cherries aside.

2 Add enough *water* to cherry syrup to measure 2 cups liquid.

3 In 2-quart saucepan, evenly sprinkle unflavored gelatin over cherry-syrup mixture; let stand 1 minute to soften. Cook over medium heat until gelatin completely dissolves, stirring frequently.

4 Remove saucepan from heat; stir in cherry-flavor gelatin until dissolved. Stir in sherry.

5 Pour gelatin mixture into large bowl; cover and refrigerate until gelatin mixture mounds slightly when dropped from a spoon, about 1 hour, stirring occasionally.

6 When gelatin mixture is ready, gently stir in cherries. Spoon gelatin mixture into eight 4-ounce molds. Cover and refrigerate until gelatin is firm, about 3 hours or overnight.

7 Meanwhile, prepare Snow-White Custard; refrigerate.

SNOW-WHITE CUSTARD

In 1-quart saucepan, with wire whisk, beat *4 large egg yolks* and *⅓ cup sugar* until blended. Stir in *2 cups half-and-half* or light cream and cook over medium-low heat, stirring constantly, until mixture thickens and coats a spoon well, about 25 minutes (mixture should be about 170° to 175°F. but do not boil or it will curdle).

Remove saucepan from heat; stir in *½ teaspoon vanilla extract.* To keep skin from forming as custard cools, press plastic wrap directly onto surface of hot custard.

8 To serve, unmold each gelatin into a large goblet or dessert bowl; spoon custard around gelatin.

9 With chocolate syrup in small decorating bag with very small writing tube (or paper cone with tip cut to make ⅛-inch-diameter hole), make wisps (see Cream Wisps, page 26). Garnish each serving with a Citrus Curl.

Cherries and sherry account for the superb taste of this so-simple dessert

CELEBRATION POACHED PEARS

🍴 12 servings

🕐 Begin about 4 ½ hours before serving or early in day

1 32-ounce jar cranberry-juice cocktail

½ cup sugar

1 medium-sized lemon, cut in half

12 medium-sized firm pears (about 7 pounds)

¼ cup red currant jelly

Mint for garnish

1 In 8-quart Dutch oven or saucepot, combine cranberry-juice cocktail, sugar, lemon halves, and 2 cups water.

2 With vegetable peeler, peel 6 pears, being careful to leave stems on.

3 With sharp knife, cut peeled pears lengthwise into halves. With teaspoon, scoop out cores and stringy portions from pear halves.

4 As each pear half is peeled and cored, place it in cranberry-juice mixture, turning to coat completely to help prevent pears from darkening.

5 Over high heat, heat pear mixture to boiling. Reduce heat to low; cover and simmer 10 to 15 minutes until pears are tender. With slotted spoon, remove pear halves to large bowl.

6 Repeat steps 2 through 5 with remaining 6 pears.

7 After all pears are poached, over high heat, heat cranberry-juice mixture in Dutch oven to boiling; cook about 20 minutes, uncovered, or until liquid is reduced to about 1 ½ cups.

> **PEARS**
> Bartlett, Anjou, and Bosc are the best varieties of pear for cooking.
> If you have a melon baller, you can use it to remove cores from pears easily and without waste, instead of a teaspoon. After scooping out core, run melon baller from core to stem and blossom end of pear to remove stringy portion.
> To prevent peeled or cut-up pears browning if left to stand, sprinkle them with lemon juice.

8 Stir red currant jelly into hot liquid until dissolved. Pour hot syrup over pear halves in bowl; cool. Cover and refrigerate until pears are chilled, about 3 hours, turning them occasionally.

> **TO SERVE**
> Arrange pear halves in deep platter; pour syrup over pears. Garnish with mint leaves.

DESSERT PIZZA

12 servings

Begin about 1 hour before serving or early in day

Nonstick cooking spray

1 20-ounce package refrigerated sugar or chocolate-chip cookie dough

1 package vanilla-flavor instant pudding and pie filling for 4 servings

1 ¼ cups milk

¼ teaspoon almond extract

1 medium-sized banana, sliced

1 ½-pint blackberries

4 kiwifruit, peeled and sliced

5 large plums, thinly sliced

1 Preheat oven to 350°F.

2 Spray 14-inch pizza pan with nonstick cooking spray.

3 With floured hands, press cookie dough in pizza pan to evenly cover bottom.

4 Bake dough 12 to 15 minutes until golden brown.

5 Cool cookie crust in pizza pan on wire rack.

6 In medium bowl, with wire whisk, prepare instant pudding as label directs, but use only 1 ¼ cups milk and add almond extract.

If you like, go ahead and use a pizza wheel to cut the dessert!

7 Remove cooled cookie crust to serving platter. Evenly spread pudding on top of cookie crust.

8 Arrange fruits in attractive pattern on top of pudding. Cover and refrigerate dessert if not serving right away.

Letting dessert stand in refrigerator before serving will soften crust slightly for easier cutting

ELEGANT ORANGES IN LIQUEUR

🍴 8 servings

⏱ Begin about 1 ½ hours before serving or early in day

8 large seedless oranges

3 tablespoons light corn syrup

½ 12-ounce jar orange marmalade (½ cup)

¼ cup orange-flavor liqueur

½ teaspoon ground ginger

½ teaspoon grenadine syrup

1 With sharp knife, carefully cut off peel and white portion from oranges, being sure to remove thin membrane that covers pulp; reserve peel.

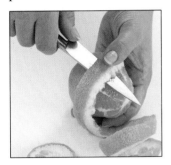

2 Place oranges on dessert plates or in deep serving platter; set oranges aside.

3 Trim off white membrane from several pieces of reserved orange peel. Cut orange peel into matchstick-thin strips to measure about ½ cup, loosely packed. Discard remaining pieces of orange peel.

4 In heavy small saucepan over medium-high heat, cook orange-peel strips and corn syrup until liquid becomes thick and coats strips.

5 Remove coated peel to waxed paper; then, with fork, separate into individual strips.

6 Leave coated orange peel to cool on waxed paper.

7 In same saucepan over medium-high heat, heat orange marmalade, orange-flavor liqueur, ground ginger, grenadine syrup, and _½ cup water_ to boiling. Cook 1 minute.

8 Remove saucepan from heat; cool sauce slightly. Pour cooled sauce over oranges. Serve at room temperature, or cover and refrigerate to serve chilled later.

TO SERVE
Garnish oranges with candied-orange-peel strips. Accompany each plate with knife, fork, and spoon.

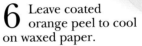

PEARS WITH ZABAGLIONE CREAM

4 servings
Begin about
10 minutes before
serving

2 large pears

1/2 cup heavy or whipping cream

1 tablespoon Marsala wine

1 teaspoon confectioners' sugar

Mint for garnish

1 Cut each pear lengthwise into halves; with teaspoon or melon baller, scoop out core, then run melon baller from core to stem and blossom ends of pear halves to remove stringy portion.

2 Cut each pear half lengthwise into thin slices, almost but not all the way through the stem end.

3 Place each pear half, cut-side down, on dessert plate; spread pear slices open to form fans.

ZABAGLIONE

There are a number of classic dessert recipes using wine and eggs, and Italian Zabaglione is probably the most well known. Its key ingredient, Marsala, is a fortified wine, which means that it contains both wine and brandy, and has a dark, rich flavor similar to sweet, aged sherry.

Traditionally, Zabaglione is made with egg yolks, cooked over a double boiler until thickened, but this method of cooking eggs is no longer recommended. Using heavy or whipping cream, as in our recipe here, gives a similar delicious taste.

4 In small bowl, with mixer at medium speed, beat heavy or whipping cream, Marsala, and confectioners' sugar until soft peaks form.

5 Spoon some zabaglione cream on each plate with pear. Garnish with mint.

POACHED PEACHES WITH BAY LEAVES

12 servings

Begin early in day or day ahead

1 24-ounce bottle white grape juice

1 1/2 cups cranberry-juice cocktail

1 cup white wine

8 bay leaves

About 1/2 cup sugar

12 large peaches (about 5 pounds)

Bay leaves for garnish

PEELING PEACHES

1 In saucepan of rapidly boiling water, with slotted spoon, dip peaches about 15 seconds.

2 With slotted spoon, immediately transfer peaches to saucepan of cold water.

3 Lift peaches out of water; carefully peel off skins with sharp knife.

1 In 8-quart saucepot or Dutch oven, mix white grape juice, cranberry-juice cocktail, white wine, bay leaves, 1/2 cup sugar (or to taste, depending on sweetness of peaches), and 2 cups water.

2 Peel peaches (see Box, above right). Add peaches to fruit-juice mixture in saucepot as soon as they are peeled to prevent darkening.

3 Over high heat, heat peaches and juice mixture to boiling. Reduce heat to low; cover and simmer 5 to 10 minutes, occasionally basting peaches with juice mixture in saucepot.

4 Spoon peaches and juice mixture into large bowl. Cover, then refrigerate at least 6 hours or overnight. Discard bay leaves before serving.

Here peaches are served garnished with additional bay leaves

FRUIT CONTAINERS

Many fruits come "pre-packaged" in pretty casings which, once freed of their fillings, can be carved and cut, for more spectacular servings.

The peel of melons and oranges can be given a scalloped edge, or formed into baskets, with or without a strip over the top for the handle; pineapples can be scooped out, part of their crowns intact, to make eye-catching fruit bowls. These shells can be filled simply with their own cut-up fruit to make easier eating.

Especially eye-catching effects are achieved by using contrasting fruits and shells: Red fruit, such as watermelon and raspberries stand out in green-fleshed melons, while rich green kiwifruit contrasts well with the amber flesh of papaya in its shell; or for a more delicate effect, fill with mixed pastel-shaded balls of cantaloupe, honeydew, and watermelon.

Cantaloupe Cup
Cut cantaloupe crosswise in half. Hollow out halves, then fill with balls of cantaloupe, honeydew or Gallia, and watermelon. For added color, sprinkle with a few blueberries, then garnish with a small sprig of mint.

Gallia Bowl
Cut slice off top of Gallia melon; scoop out seeds from center. Heap center with watermelon balls and raspberries, allowing them to spill out over the top of the melon flesh.

Watermelon Basket
Into small round watermelon, make horizontal cut from each end 2 inches from top (do not cut through); leave 1-inch strip in center. Then make two vertical cuts from top of melon down to horizontal cuts, to create handle. Scoop out melon. If you like, cut scalloped edge around rim of basket. Fill with watermelon, cantaloupe, honeydew or Gallia melon balls, and garnish with sprigs of mint.

Papaya Boat

Slice papaya lengthwise in half. Remove seeds; scoop out flesh and cut into bite-sized chunks. Fill papaya halves with chunks of papaya and honeydew melon. Top with kiwifruit triangles and garnish with sprig of mint.

Grapefruit Half

Cut grapefruit crosswise through center in sawtooth pattern. Scoop out sections. Fill with peeled whole clementines and raspberries. Garnish with sprig of mint.

Pineapple Boat

Cut pineapple lengthwise in half. Cut out core and chunks of flesh. Cut thin slice from underside. Fill shell with kiwifruit and pineapple; crown with strawberry half.

Filled Fruits

Cut deep "X" in top of figs, kiwifruit, and strawberries (peel kiwifruit first). Gently spread fruit apart to make "petals"; pipe whipped cream into center of each fruit.

GRAPE CLUSTERS
IN SHIMMERING LEMON-CHEESE GEL

🍴 10 servings
⏱ Begin early in day

Mint leaves

2 packages lemon-flavor gelatin for 4 servings

1 16-ounce container cottage cheese (2 cups)

1 tablespoon sugar

1 teaspoon grated lemon peel

$^1\!/_2$ teaspoon vanilla extract

$^1\!/_4$ pound seedless green grapes

$^3\!/_4$ pound seedless red grapes

1 Chop enough mint leaves to make 2 teaspoons; set aside.

2 In small bowl, stir 1 package lemon-flavor gelatin with *$^1\!/_2$ cup boiling water* until gelatin is completely dissolved. In blender at high speed, blend gelatin mixture, cottage cheese, sugar, lemon peel, vanilla extract, and chopped mint until smooth. Pour into 8" by 3" springform pan; cover and chill until almost set, about 20 minutes.

3 In medium bowl, stir remaining package lemon-flavor gelatin with *2 cups boiling water* until gelatin is dissolved. Chill until cool but not set, about 1 hour.

4 While mixture is chilling, with sharp knife, cut each green grape and each grape from $^1\!/_4$ pound red grapes lengthwise into halves.

5 With kitchen shears, cut remaining red grapes into small bunches; wrap in plastic wrap and refrigerate for garnish.

6 Make grape clusters on cheese layer in springform pan (see Box, right). Carefully pour enough lemon gelatin over grape design just to cover grapes so grapes do not float.

7 Cover pan and refrigerate until gelatin is almost set, about 20 minutes. Leave remaining lemon gelatin at room temperature so it does not set.

8 Pour remaining lemon gelatin over grapes (see Box, right). Cover and refrigerate until set, about 3 hours.

9 Unmold dessert from pan (see Box, right).

Layers of cheese and lemon gelatin look beautiful topped with clusters of grapes

MOLDING DESSERT

Making grape clusters: *Arrange green-grape halves and red-grape halves in 2 clusters on cheese layer in springform pan.*

Pouring lemon gelatin over grapes: *Carefully pour remaining lemon-gelatin mixture over grape design; some grapes may extend out of gelatin.*

Unmolding dessert: *With metal spatula dipped in hot water, gently loosen edge of dessert from pan; remove side of pan.*

SACRAMENTO FRUIT BOWL

12 servings
Begin early in day

1 1/2 cups sugar

2 tablespoons anise seeds

3 tablespoons lemon juice

1/2 teaspoon salt

1 small pineapple

1 small honeydew melon

1 small cantaloupe

2 oranges

2 large nectarines or
4 apricots

2 large red plums

1/2 pound seedless green
grapes

2 kiwifruit

1 In 2-quart saucepan over medium heat, heat *2 cups water* with sugar, anise seeds, lemon juice, and salt to boiling; cook 15 minutes or until mixture becomes a light syrup. Remove saucepan from heat; refrigerate to chill well.

2 Meanwhile, prepare pineapple (see Box, above right).

3 Cut honeydew melon and cantaloupe into wedges; discard seeds. Cut peel from melon and cantaloupe, then cut pulp into bite-sized chunks.

4 With sharp knife, carefully cut off peel and white portion from oranges; cut along both sides of each dividing membrane and lift out orange sections from center.

5 Cut nectarines or apricots and plums into halves and remove pits; slice. Cut grapes into halves.

6 In large serving bowl, combine cut-up fruit. Pour chilled syrup through strainer over fruit. Cover and refrigerate until well chilled, stirring frequently.

PREPARING A PINEAPPLE

1 With large sharp knife, cut crown and stem ends from pineapple.

2 Stand pineapple on one cut end; cut off rind in large strips.

3 Cut pineapple from core in large strips; discard core.

4 Then cut pineapple strips into bite-sized chunks.

TO SERVE
Peel and slice kiwifruit.
Gently stir kiwifruit slices
into fruit mixture.

SUMMER FRUITS
WITH ALMOND-YOGURT CHANTILLY

🥄 8 servings

🕐 Begin about 30 minutes before serving or early in day

Almond-Yogurt Chantilly (see Box, right)

4 large kiwifruit

4 medium-sized plums

2 large peaches

2 medium-sized bananas

1 small cantaloupe

1/2 cup raspberries

1/2 cup blueberries

1/2 cup blackberries

Lemon leaves and sliced almonds for garnish

---

1 Prepare Almond-Yogurt Chantilly; spoon into small serving bowl; cover and refrigerate until ready to serve.

2 About 20 minutes before serving, with sharp knife, peel kiwifruit; cut each lengthwise in half.

3 Cut each plum and peach into halves; discard pits. Peel bananas; cut each crosswise into halves, then cut each half lengthwise into 2 pieces.

4 With sharp knife, cut cantaloupe into thin wedges; remove seeds and cut peel from each wedge.

5 Arrange cut-up fruit on large platter. Top with raspberries, blueberries, and blackberries.

ALMOND-YOGURT CHANTILLY

In large bowl, with mixer at medium speed, beat *1 cup heavy or whipping cream, 1/3 cup confectioners' sugar,* and *1 teaspoon almond extract* until stiff peaks form. With rubber spatula or wire whisk, fold in *one 8-ounce container plain yogurt.*

TO SERVE
Garnish with lemon leaves; garnish Almond-Yogurt Chantilly with sliced almonds and pass to spoon over fruit.

PARTY FRESH FRUITCAKE

This spectacular showpiece is an artfully arranged selection of juicy, ripe melons, berries, kiwifruit, and pineapple – a more summery version of a fruitcake. It makes a wonderful centerpiece for the buffet table, and is ideal for barbecues and other informal events when guests can serve themselves. It can be prepared ahead of time too, as long as it is kept well wrapped in the refrigerator until you are ready to serve. The calorie-conscious will find the combination of fruit flavors absolutely delicious when eaten plain, but for those who don't mind throwing caution to the wind, a dollop of Crème Cointreau will make it sweeter.

20 servings
Begin about 3 hours before serving or early in day

4 large cantaloupes (about 3 pounds each)

2 medium-sized honeydews (about 4 pounds each)

2 large pineapples (about 4 pounds each)

4 large kiwifruit

1 pint strawberries

1 pint blueberries

1 pint raspberries

Crème Cointreau (see Box, page 65)

Mint sprig for garnish

1 Cut each cantaloupe and honeydew lengthwise into 4 wedges. With spoon, scoop out seeds. Cut wedges crosswise into 1-inch-thick slices; cut rind off each slice. Set aside.

2 Cut crown and rind off each pineapple. Cut pineapple lengthwise into halves; cut crosswise into ½-inch-thick slices. Cut out tough core of each slice. Cut enough pineapple slices into bite-sized pieces to measure 2 cups; set aside.

3 On 14-inch plate with rim (to catch any fruit juices), arrange half the nice large honeydew slices around rim. Reserve small honeydew slices.

Arranging honeydew slices around edge of plate

ALTERNATIVE FRUIT ARRANGEMENT

Using only four different kinds of fresh fruits, you can create just as eye-catching an arrangement as in our main recipe. Here, neat wedges of cantaloupe and honeydew melon are combined with slices of fresh pineapple and strawberry halves to create a more symmetrical version, and the pineapple crown provides a dramatic touch.

Four-Fruit Fresh Fruitcake

1 Cut each of *2 large cantaloupes* lengthwise into 3 wedges, and cut each of *2 medium-sized honeydews* lengthwise into 4 wedges. With spoon, scoop out seeds. Cut wedges crosswise into 1-inch-thick slices; cut rind off each slice.

2 Cut crown and rind off *2 large pineapples*; reserve one crown with pretty leaves for garnish. Cut each pineapple lengthwise in half; then cut crosswise into 1-inch slices. Cut out tough core of each slice.

3 On large round platter with rim (to catch any fruit juices), arrange enough center honeydew slices to make 14-inch ring; fill center of ring with end pieces; cut pieces to fit, if necessary. Repeat layering with cantaloupe, pineapple, and more honeydew slices, filling center of ring with end fruit pieces as you assemble each layer.

4 Place reserved pineapple crown on top of fruitcake. Cut *2 pints strawberries* in half; pile strawberries on top of cake around pineapple crown. Cover with plastic wrap; refrigerate 1 hour or until ready to serve.

4 Arrange layers of pineapple slices in center of plate.

5 Arrange half the nice large cantaloupe slices over honeydew slices on rim of plate. Reserve small cantaloupe slices.

6 Repeat with another layer of honeydew and cantaloupe slices. With remaining pineapple and reserved small melon slices, fill in gaps or holes in center to form level top.

7 Peel kiwifruit; cut into wedges. Arrange kiwifruit carefully on top of fruitcake.

8 Make neat piles of strawberries, blueberries, raspberries, and reserved bite-sized pieces of pineapple to cover rest of top of fruitcake.

9 Cover fruitcake with plastic wrap and refrigerate to chill, at least 1 hour or until ready to serve.

10 Meanwhile, prepare Crème Cointreau.

CRÈME COINTREAU
In small bowl, with mixer at medium speed, beat *2 cups heavy or whipping cream* and *¹/₄ cup confectioners' sugar* just until soft peaks form. Gradually beat in *¹/₄ cup orange-flavor liqueur.*

Spoon cream into serving bowl; cover and refrigerate until ready to serve.

TO SERVE
Garnish center of chilled fruitcake with mint sprig. Pass Crème Cointreau separately.

FRUIT GARNISHES

Fruit used for garnish adds little in the way of calories, but much in terms of color, brightness, and a fresh look to a wide range of desserts.

Like all carefully chosen garnishes, the fruit should be appropriate in size, shape, taste, and color to the food it is served on.

Choose fruit that is as near perfect as possible, and leave it until the last moment to prepare, to prevent discoloration.

Small items such as strawberries and cherries are attractive whole with their stems and hulls left on, but cut into fans and blossoms or dipped into sugar, they take on a new dimension; the peel of citrus fruit such as lemons, limes, and oranges, is readily shaped into curls, julienne, and twists; while slices, rounds, and chunks of brightly colored kiwifruit, warmer-shaded nectarine, and coolly neutral pineapple can be used to good effect on contrasting bases or combined with berries.

Strawberry Fans
Starting just below hull, thinly slice strawberry lengthwise several times, leaving strawberry connected at hull end. Press down gently to fan out slices slightly.

Citrus Curls
Using stripper or canelle knife, remove long thin strips of peel from citrus fruit. Coil peel around to create curls. Use curls individually or mix colors together.

Lemon Twists
With sharp knife, cut lemon crosswise into thin slices. Make 1 cut from center to edge of each slice, then twist cut edges in opposite directions.

Lemon Cartwheels
With stripper or canelle knife, make vertical grooves at regular intervals in peel of whole lemon. With sharp knife, cut fruit crosswise into thin slices.

Cherry Blossoms
Starting just below stem end, make 8 cuts lengthwise in cherry, leaving cherry connected at stem end. Press down gently to fan out "petals" slightly and expose pit. Place cherry on mint leaf.

Frosted Cherries
Wash cherries but do not remove stems or pits. While still wet, dip bottoms in sugar until evenly coated; allow to dry before using.

Nectarine Slices

Cut nectarine (or peach) in half and twist apart; remove pit. Cut each half lengthwise into thin slices; sprinkle with lemon juice if not using immediately. Arrange in fan shape and add mint sprig.

Strawberry Halves

Select firm berries with fresh green hulls and stems. Cut strawberries lengthwise through centers, being careful to leave some stalk on each half. Arrange cut-side-up or cut-side-down, or alternate for a more striking effect.

Citrus Julienne

With vegetable peeler, remove peel from citrus fruit in lengthwise strips. Lay strips on top of each other; cut into julienne.

FRUIT COMBINATIONS

Eye-catching arrangements of fruit can be used to good effect as garnishes on plates and platters when the dessert you are serving is simple. Experiment with different fruits, grouping them together to create dramatic designs and stunning shapes.

Honeydew Slices

Cut melon lengthwise into wedges. Remove seeds and cut flesh from rind. Cut wedges into thin slices and arrange in fan shape, adding a few red currants for contrast.

Pineapple and Raspberry Clusters

Cut crown and stem ends from pineapple. Stand pineapple on one cut end; cut off rind in large strips. Cut pineapple crosswise into thin slices and remove core. Cut slice into 4 wedges; arrange as slice. Fill center with raspberries and mint sprig.

Kiwifruit Slices

With sharp knife, remove fuzzy skin from kiwifruit, then, cut fruit crosswise into thin slices. Combine with blueberries for extra effect.

MORE-THAN-BERRIES SHORTCAKE

Whipped cream and strawberries are the usual filling and topping for a traditional summer shortcake; this deluxe version goes one step further, combining a variety of different-colored fresh fruits with sweetened whipped cream for a more dramatic effect. Of course you don't have to use the fruits that we have suggested here, so long as you are careful to choose ripe, juicy fruits in season and aim for a good contrast of bright colors, and interesting shapes and flavors. This is the perfect dessert to serve at casual neighborly get-togethers, such as a summer brunch on the patio or a picnic on the lawn.

16 servings
Begin about 1 hour before serving or early in day

3 medium-sized nectarines (1 pound)

6 tablespoons sugar

¹/₄ cup packed light brown sugar

2 ¹/₂ cups all-purpose flour

³/₄ cup margarine or butter (1 ¹/₂ sticks)

1 tablespoon baking powder

¹/₂ teaspoon salt

1 large egg

³/₄ cup milk

¹/₂ pound sweet cherries

1 large kiwifruit

1 ¹/₂-pint blackberries or blueberries

1 cup heavy or whipping cream

1 Cut nectarines into halves and remove pits; slice. In medium bowl, toss nectarines with 2 tablespoons sugar. Cover and refrigerate.

2 Preheat oven to 450°F. Grease 9-inch round cake pan.

3 In small bowl, with fork, mix brown sugar and ¹/₂ cup flour. With pastry blender or 2 knives used scissor-fashion, cut 4 tablespoons margarine or butter (¹/₂ stick) into flour mixture until mixture resembles size of peas. Set topping aside.

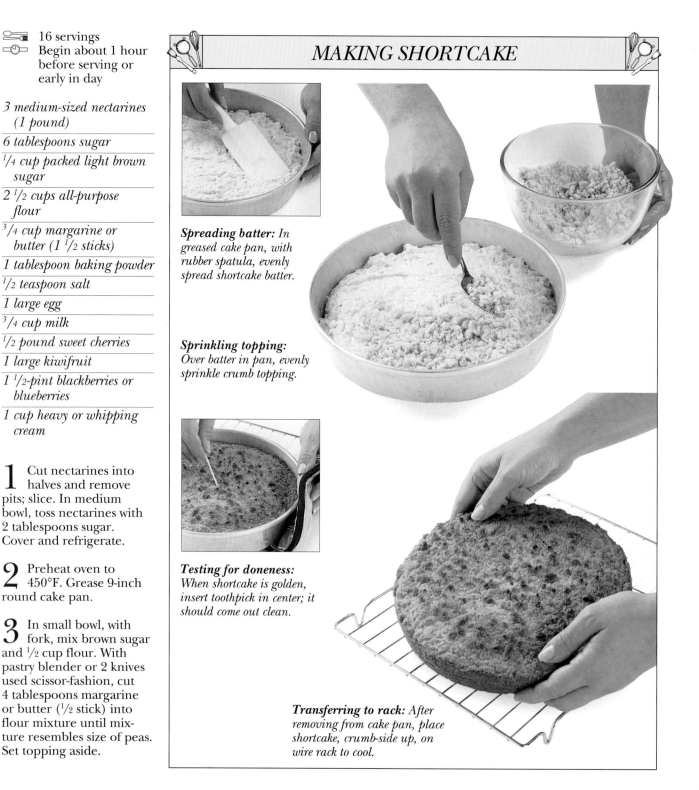

MAKING SHORTCAKE

Spreading batter: In greased cake pan, with rubber spatula, evenly spread shortcake batter.

Sprinkling topping: Over batter in pan, evenly sprinkle crumb topping.

Testing for doneness: When shortcake is golden, insert toothpick in center; it should come out clean.

Transferring to rack: After removing from cake pan, place shortcake, crumb-side up, on wire rack to cool.

4 In large bowl, with fork, mix baking powder, salt, remaining 2 cups flour, and 2 tablespoons sugar.

5 With pastry blender or 2 knives used scissor-fashion, cut remaining 1/2 cup margarine or butter (1 stick) into flour mixture until mixture resembles coarse crumbs.

6 In another small bowl, with fork, beat egg slightly; stir in milk. Add egg mixture all at once to flour mixture; stir just until flour mixture is moistened.

7 Spread shortcake batter in pan and sprinkle with topping, then bake 20 minutes or until golden (see Box, page 68). Cover with foil during last 5 minutes of cooking if topping is browning too quickly.

8 Carefully remove shortcake from pan; transfer to wire rack (see Box, page 68); cool slightly, about 10 minutes. (Or, cool completely to serve later.)

9 Reserve several cherries with stems for garnish; stem and pit remaining cherries. With sharp knife, peel kiwifruit; cut into bite-sized pieces. Gently stir pitted cherries, kiwifruit, and blackberries or blueberries into nectarine mixture.

10 In small bowl, with mixer at medium speed, beat heavy or whipping cream and remaining 2 tablespoons sugar until stiff peaks form.

11 With long serrated knife, carefully split shortcake horizontally in half.

12 Place bottom half of shortcake, cut-side up, on dessert plate; top with all but 3/4 cup fruit. Spoon 1 1/2 cups whipped-cream mixture over fruit.

Spooning whipped-cream mixture over fruit

13 Place top half of shortcake, crumb-side up, on cream.

14 Pile reserved fruit in center of shortcake; top with remaining whipped cream and reserved cherries.

WARM FRUIT COMPOTE

4 servings
Begin about
20 minutes
before serving

*4 ounces pitted prunes
(about ¹/₂ cup)*

*4 ounces dried apricot
halves (about ¹/₂ cup)*

¹/₂ cup apple juice

*2 teaspoons light brown
sugar*

*¹/₄ teaspoon ground
cinnamon*

1 large banana

*Whipped Topping
(see Box, right)*

1 In 2-quart saucepan over high heat, heat prunes, apricots, apple juice, brown sugar, and ground cinnamon to boiling.

2 Reduce heat to low; cover and simmer 10 minutes, stirring often.

*Stirring banana into
dried-fruit mixture*

3 Meanwhile, with sharp knife, cut banana into 1-inch chunks. Prepare Whipped Topping.

4 Remove saucepan from heat. With rubber spatula, gently stir banana into dried-fruit mixture.

WHIPPED TOPPING

In small bowl, with mixer at medium speed, beat *¹/₄ cup well-chilled evaporated skimmed milk* and *1 tablespoon confectioners' sugar* until stiff peaks form.

Evaporated skimmed milk whips better if partially frozen.

---

*TO SERVE
Spoon warm fruit and
Whipped Topping onto
4 dessert plates.*

SUMMER FRUIT MÉLANGE

🍴 12 servings
🕐 Begin about
30 minutes
before serving

1 small lemon

1 6-ounce can frozen pineapple-juice concentrate, thawed

³/₄ teaspoon minced peeled gingerroot or ¹/₄ teaspoon ground ginger

¹/₄ teaspoon salt

1 8-pound piece watermelon

5 large nectarines or peaches (about 2 ¹/₂ pounds)

3 medium-sized plums (about 1 pound)

1 pint strawberries

Fresh mint leaves for garnish

1 From lemon, grate 1 tea-spoon peel and squeeze 1 tea-spoon juice.

2 In large bowl, with spoon or wire whisk, mix lemon peel, lemon juice, pineapple-juice concentrate, ginger, and salt.

3 Cut watermelon into bite-sized pieces; discard rind.

4 Cut nectarines or peaches and plums into wedges; discard pits from fruit.

5 Hull strawberries and cut each berry length-wise in half if berries are large.

6 Add fruit to pine-apple-juice mixture in bowl. With rubber spatula, gently toss to mix well.

TO SERVE
Transfer fruit mélange to large serving bowl; garnish with mint leaves.

CHERRIES GLACÉS

🍴 10 servings
⏰ Begin early in day or day ahead

2 pounds sweet cherries

1 12-ounce package semisweet-chocolate pieces (2 cups)

1 cup half-and-half or light cream

1 ½ teaspoons vanilla extract

1 Wash cherries but do not remove stems or pits; pat cherries dry with paper towels.

2 Place cherries in single layer in jelly-roll pan; place in freezer until 15 minutes before serving.

3 About 15 minutes before serving, remove cherries from freezer; let stand at room temperature to soften slightly. Do not allow cherries to thaw completely.

4 Meanwhile, in heavy 2-quart saucepan over low heat, heat chocolate pieces and half-and-half or light cream, stirring frequently, until chocolate is melted and smooth. Remove saucepan from heat; stir in vanilla extract.

TO SERVE
Arrange cherries in large bowl. Pour chocolate sauce into small bowl. Let each person dip partially frozen cherries into chocolate sauce.

CREAM-FILLED STRAWBERRIES

🥄 6 servings

🕐 Begin about 30 minutes before serving or early in day

18 jumbo strawberries

1 cup heavy or whipping cream

1 package vanilla-flavor instant pudding and pie filling for 4 servings

1 cup milk

1 teaspoon almond extract

1 Cut stem ends off strawberries. With sharp knife, cut deep "X" in top of each fruit.

2 With fingertips, gently spread each strawberry apart to make "petals"; set aside.

3 In small bowl, with mixer at medium speed, beat heavy or whipping cream until stiff peaks form.

4 In large bowl, with wire whisk, prepare instant pudding as label directs but use only 1 cup milk. With wire whisk or rubber spatula, gently fold whipped cream and almond extract into prepared instant pudding.

5 Spoon almond-cream mixture into decorating bag with large writing tube. Pipe cream mixture into strawberries.

Piping almond-cream mixture into strawberries

6 Cover and refrigerate strawberries if not serving right away.

ALTERNATIVE FRUIT

When figs are in season, you can fill them with almond-flavored cream, in the same way as we have done with strawberries.

Almond-Cream Figs

1 With sharp knife, cut stem ends off *12 medium-sized figs*, then cut deep "X" in top of each fruit.

2 With fingertips, gently spread each fig apart to make "petals".

3 Fill figs with almond-cream mixture as for Cream-Filled Strawberries.

Puddings

Of all the different kinds of desserts, puddings are the ones to call "comfort food." Look for variety in texture as well as flavor: smooth and custardy, like Baked Lemon-Cake Puddings; or substantial, like Creamy Rice Pudding; or moist and rich, like Hot Fudge Cake Pudding.

ORANGE PUDDING CUPS

🥄 6 servings
🕐 Begin 1 ½ hours before serving

3 large oranges

1 package vanilla-flavor instant pudding and pie filling for 4 servings

1 cup milk

1 cup heavy or whipping cream

½ teaspoon almond extract

Orange peel for garnish

Zigzag Cups: *With sharp pointed knife, cut crosswise through center of each orange in sawtooth pattern, so that each orange half has zigzag edge.*

Personalized Cups: *With stripper or canelle knife, carve initials of each guest in orange peel. Carve 2 sets of initials in each orange, then, with sharp knife, cut orange crosswise in half.*

Striped Cups: *With stripper, cut thin strips from orange peel, working from top to bottom of orange. With sharp knife, cut orange crosswise in half.*

1 Prepare orange cups of your choice (see above right). With sharp knife, cut thin slice off bottom of each half so orange halves stand level. Carefully remove fruit from orange halves; cut fruit into small bite-sized pieces. Set fruit and orange cups aside.

2 In medium bowl, with wire whisk, prepare instant pudding as label directs, but use only 1 cup milk.

3 In small bowl, with mixer at medium speed, beat heavy or whipping cream and almond extract until stiff peaks form. Reserve a few pieces of cut-up fruit for garnish. With rubber spatula, fold whipped-cream mixture and remaining cut-up fruit into pudding.

4 Spoon pudding mixture into orange cups. Cover and refrigerate, about 1 hour. To serve, garnish with reserved fruit and orange peel.

CREAMY RICE PUDDING

16 servings
Begin about 2 hours before serving or early in day

2 quarts milk

½ teaspoon salt

1 cup regular long-grain rice

½ cup dark seedless raisins

¾ cup sugar

1 tablespoon vanilla extract

2 12-ounce cans evaporated milk

4 large eggs

Ground cinnamon

Fresh or Maraschino cherries for garnish

1 In 4-quart saucepan over medium heat, heat milk and salt to simmering; stir in rice. Reduce heat to low; cover and simmer 45 to 50 minutes until rice is very tender and mixture is thick, stirring occasionally. Stir in raisins.

2 Preheat oven to 350°F. Grease 13" by 9" baking dish; set in large roasting pan.

3 In large bowl, with wire whisk or fork, beat sugar, vanilla extract, evaporated milk, and eggs until blended; gradually stir in hot rice mixture.

4 Place baking dish in pan on oven rack; carefully pour rice mixture into baking dish (mixture will almost fill dish). Fill roasting pan with boiling water to come halfway up sides of baking dish. Bake 40 to 45 minutes until knife inserted in center of pudding comes out clean.

5 Make Cinnamon Lattice on top of pudding (see Box, right).

TO SERVE
Garnish pudding with cherries. Serve warm or refrigerate to serve cold later.

CINNAMON LATTICE

Hold ruler diagonally across 1 corner of baking dish, about 1 inch in from edge of pudding. Holding cinnamon jar in other hand, evenly shake spice through sprinkler hole along ruler edge. Shake excess spice off ruler. Repeat at 1-inch intervals.

Repeat in opposite direction to form lattice pattern.

BAKED LEMON-CAKE PUDDINGS

6 servings

Begin about 1 ³/₄ hours before serving or early in day

2 medium-sized lemons

2 large eggs, separated

¹/₄ teaspoon salt

³/₄ cup sugar

1 cup milk

3 tablespoons all-purpose flour

2 tablespoons margarine or butter (¹/₄ stick), melted

1 Preheat oven to 350°F. Grease six 6-ounce custard cups.

2 Finely grate lemon peel to measure 1 tablespoon.

3 Squeeze juice from lemons to measure ¹/₃ cup; set aside.

4 In small bowl, with mixer at high speed, beat egg whites and salt until soft peaks form; gradually sprinkle in ¹/₂ cup sugar, beating until sugar completely dissolves and whites stand in stiff peaks.

5 In large bowl, using same beaters and with mixer at medium speed, beat egg yolks with remaining ¹/₄ cup sugar until blended; add lemon peel and juice, milk, flour, and margarine or butter, and beat until well mixed, occasionally scraping bowl with rubber spatula.

6 With wire whisk or rubber spatula, gently fold beaten egg whites into egg-yolk mixture just until mixed.

7 Into prepared custard cups, carefully pour batter.

8 Set custard cups in 13" by 9" baking pan; place on oven rack. Fill baking pan with boiling water to come halfway up sides of custard cups. Bake 40 to 45 minutes until pudding tops are golden and firm. (Puddings separate into cake layer on top, sauce layer underneath.)

9 Cool puddings in custard cups on wire rack.

LEMON-CAKE PUDDING

If you like, you can make 1 large pudding instead of 6 individual ones. Grease 1-quart casserole. Prepare batter as for individual puddings; pour into casserole; bake 55 to 65 minutes.

HOT FUDGE CAKE PUDDING

🍴 12 servings

⏱ Begin about 45 minutes before serving

2 1-ounce envelopes unsweetened baking chocolate flavor

1 ½ cups buttermilk baking mix

1 cup milk

2 teaspoons vanilla extract

1 cup sugar

2 tablespoons unsweetened cocoa

Whipped Cream (see Box, right) or ice cream (optional)

1 Preheat oven to 350°F. Into large bowl, measure chocolate flavor, buttermilk baking mix, milk, vanilla extract, and ⅔ cup sugar. With wire whisk, beat ingredients together until smooth. Pour batter into 12" by 8" baking dish.

WHIPPED CREAM

Indispensable as an ingredient in many dessert dishes, whipped cream can be made from two different creams of varying fat content. Heavy cream contains at least 36 percent fat while whipping cream is slightly lighter, containing at least 30 percent fat. When whipped, cream doubles in volume, and it should stay whipped for a few hours before it begins to "weep." The following should help ensure a perfect outcome every time:

- Before starting to beat, be sure that cream, bowl, and beaters are well chilled.

- Start with slow speed on mixer. This will stabilize cream by incorporating small air bubbles into it.

- Finish beating at medium speed, until stiff enough. Longer beating may break cream down into butter and whey.

- If not using whipped cream immediately, cover and refrigerate.

2 In small bowl, mix cocoa and remaining ⅓ cup sugar; sprinkle over batter in baking dish.

4 Bake 25 minutes. (Batter separates into cake layer on top, sauce layer underneath.)

5 Serve immediately or sauce will be absorbed by cake.

TO SERVE
Serve with whipped cream or softened ice cream, if you like.

Pouring batter into baking dish

3 Over mixture in baking dish, carefully pour 1 ½ cups boiling water; do not stir.

FRENCH-BREAD PUDDING

🥄 10 servings
🕐 Begin about 1 hour before serving or early in day

1 24-inch-long loaf French or Italian bread (about 8 ounces)

4 tablespoons margarine or butter (1/2 stick), softened

3 cups half-and-half or light cream

1/3 cup sugar

1 1/2 teaspoons imitation maple flavor

1/8 teaspoon salt

4 large eggs

3 tablespoons maple or maple-flavor syrup

Heavy or whipping cream (optional)

1 Preheat oven to 350°F. Cut bread diagonally into 1/2-inch-thick slices, each about 5 inches long.

2 Spread one side of each bread slice with margarine or butter.

3 In 10-inch quiche dish or round baking dish with side at least 1 1/2 inches high, arrange bread slices, buttered-side up, to fill dish, overlapping slices if necessary.

4 Place one end slice of bread in center. (Save remaining end to use for bread crumbs another day.)

5 In medium bowl, with wire whisk or fork, beat half-and-half or light cream, sugar, imitation maple flavor, salt, and eggs until well mixed. Slowly pour egg mixture over bread slices in quiche dish.

6 With fork, gently press bread slices into egg mixture.

7 Bake 45 to 50 minutes until knife inserted in center of pudding comes out clean. Remove pudding to wire rack; brush with maple or maple-flavor syrup.

TO SERVE
Serve pudding warm or refrigerate to serve cold later. Serve pudding with heavy or whipping cream, if you like.

CAKES
79-146

CAKES

Here we have a dazzling assortment of cakes and tortes for all occasions, from elegant dinner parties and special holidays to a cozy cup of tea with a friend – try our indulgently rich White-Chocolate Cheesecake, or West Indian Fruitcake, so colorful and tasty! Cappuccino Cake with its creamy espresso frosting and Chocolate Buttermilk Torte – moist chocolate cake laced with orange-flavor liqueur – are as eye-catching as they are delicious. Our recipes range from temptingly sumptuous Chocolate Truffle Cake to old-fashioned Carrot Bundt Cake – there is even an ultra-light, cholesterol-free recipe for the health-conscious dessert lover! In this chapter you'll find every kind of cake: easy but spectacular Irish-Cream Triangle Cake, made with a cake mix, or the more fancifully decorated Raspberry Laced Vanilla Cake, with helpful directions on piping whipped cream. Be sure to use the tips for spreading frosting and using chocolate and flower garnishes to make your luscious cakes even lovelier to look at!

CONTENTS

Cakes and Tortes

There's a cake for every occasion, every holiday, every season. There are lavish cakes to glorify grand celebrations such as weddings, and simple cakes to accompany afternoon tea or bring a family repast to a happy ending. Tortes are cakes that are richer and/or more elaborate. Most of the recipes in this section start "from scratch"; but our Mother's Day Cake and Flag Cake turn packaged mix into spectacularly delicious (and deliciously spectacular) treats.

CINNAMON-CREAM TORTE

16 servings
Begin up to 3 days ahead

³/₄ cup margarine or butter (1 ¹/₂ sticks), softened
¹/₂ cup sugar
1 tablespoon ground cinnamon
1 large egg
1 ¹/₂ cups all-purpose flour
2 cups heavy or whipping cream
Unsweetened cocoa

1 Preheat oven to 375°F. Tear 9 sheets of waxed paper, each about 8 ¹/₂ inches long. On 1 sheet of waxed paper, trace bottom of 8-inch round cake pan. Evenly stack all the waxed paper with the marked sheet on top. With kitchen shears, cut out rounds (see Box, above right).

2 Into large bowl, measure margarine or butter, sugar, cinnamon, egg, and 1 cup flour. With mixer at low speed, beat ingredients until well mixed, constantly scraping bowl with rubber spatula. Increase speed to medium; beat until light and fluffy, about 3 minutes, occasionally scraping bowl. With spoon, stir in remaining ¹/₂ cup flour to make a soft dough.

3 With damp cloth, moisten 1 large or 2 small cookie sheets. Place 2 waxed-paper rounds on large cookie sheet, or 1 on each small cookie sheet, then, with metal spatula, spread ¹/₄ cup dough in very thin layer on each round (see Box, right).

4 Bake 6 to 8 minutes until lightly browned around the edges. Cool on cookie sheet on wire rack 5 minutes; with pancake turner, carefully remove cookies, still on waxed paper, to wire rack to cool completely (see Box, right).

MAKING COOKIE LAYERS

Cutting waxed-paper rounds: *Holding stack of waxed paper, with kitchen shears, carefully cut out nine 8-inch rounds, using top marked sheet as guide.*

Placing rounds on cookie sheet: *On moistened large cookie sheet, place 2 waxed-paper rounds, side by side. (Or place 1 round on 1 small cookie sheet.)*

Spreading dough on waxed paper: *With metal spatula, spread very thin, even layer of dough on each waxed-paper round.*

Removing cookies to wire rack: *With pancake turner, transfer each cookie, still on waxed paper, to wire rack.*

Peeling off paper: *With fingers, carefully peel waxed paper off cookie.*

5 Allow cookie sheet to cool before spreading waxed-paper rounds with more dough. (The more cookie sheets you have the faster you can bake the cookies.) Repeat until all dough is baked, to make 9 cookies in all. If not assembling cake right away, stack cooled cookies carefully on flat plate; cover with plastic wrap and store in cool, dry place.

6 Early on day of serving, in small bowl, with mixer at medium speed, beat heavy or whipping cream until stiff peaks form.

7 Carefully peel off paper from 1 cookie (see Box, page 82); place on cake plate. Spread with about ½ cup whipped cream. Repeat layering until all cookies are used, ending with whipped cream.

8 Sprinkle cocoa through sieve lightly over whipped cream. If you like, with dull edge of knife, mark 16 wedges on top of cake. Refrigerate at least 4 hours to let cookies soften slightly for easier cutting.

GINGER-CREAM TORTE

If you like, you can change the flavor of this spectacular-looking torte from cinnamon to ginger.

Substitute *1 tablespoon ground ginger* for the ground cinnamon in the cookie dough, then, for garnish, omit sprinkling whipped-cream top of torte with cocoa and instead make decorative pattern of finely chopped *crystalized ginger* on each marked wedge of torte.

Cinnamon-Cream Torte marked into wedges ready to serve

DOUBLE-CHOCOLATE MOUSSE CAKE

This luscious, rich mousse cake is the best chocolate dessert ever – dark, moist, fully flavored, and soul satisfying! There is no flour in it; but the torte holds together beautifully when cut into slices for serving. Candied violets add an elegant finishing touch on top of the cake.

🍴 16 servings
🕐 Begin early in day or day ahead

2 8-ounce packages semisweet chocolate (16 1-ounce squares)

2 cups margarine or butter (4 sticks)

1 cup sugar

1 cup half-and-half or light cream

1 tablespoon vanilla extract

1/2 teaspoon salt

8 large eggs

Chocolate Glaze (see Box, page 85)

1 cup heavy or whipping cream

Candied violets for garnish

1 Preheat oven to 350°F. Grease 10" by 3" springform pan.

2 In heavy 3-quart saucepan over low heat, heat semisweet chocolate, margarine or butter, sugar, half-and-half or light cream, vanilla extract, and salt, stirring frequently, until chocolate melts and mixture is smooth.

3 In large bowl, with wire whisk or fork, beat eggs slightly; slowly beat warm chocolate mixture into eggs until well blended.

4 Pour batter into springform pan so that it spreads evenly.

5 Bake 45 minutes or until toothpick inserted in cake 2 inches from edge comes out clean. Cool cake completely in pan on wire rack.

Pouring batter into pan

> **TO SERVE**
> *Garnish cream around top edge of cake with candied violets.*

6 When cake is cool, carefully remove side of pan; wrap cake, still on pan bottom, in plastic wrap and refrigerate until well chilled, at least 6 hours.

7 Prepare Chocolate Glaze.

8 Unwrap cake; remove from pan bottom. Line cake plate with waxed-paper strips. Place cake on plate and spread with warm glaze (see Box, right). Discard waxed paper.

9 In small bowl, with mixer at medium speed, beat heavy or whipping cream until stiff peaks form. Spoon whipped cream into decorating bag with medium star tube (see Box, right) and pipe cream around top edge of cake. Refrigerate cake if not serving right away.

CHOCOLATE GLAZE

In heavy 2-quart saucepan over low heat, heat *one 6-ounce package semisweet-chocolate pieces* (1 cup) and *2 tablespoons margarine* or butter, stirring frequently, until melted and smooth. (If pan is too thin, it will transfer heat too fast and burn chocolate.)

Remove pan from heat; beat in *3 tablespoons milk* and *2 tablespoons light corn syrup.*

GLAZING AND GARNISHING CAKE

Placing cake on plate: *On cake plate lined with waxed-paper strips (to catch glaze as it drips), carefully place well-chilled cake.*

Spreading glaze over cake: *With metal spatula, evenly spread warm glaze over top and down side of cake.*

Filling decorating bag with cream: *Into decorating bag with medium star tube, spoon whipped cream. Twist end of bag to enclose cream.*

Piping cream: *Around top edge of cake, pipe scrolls of whipped cream to make continuous circle.*

PUMPKIN-CRUNCH TORTE

🍴 16 servings

⏰ Begin about 3 hours before serving or early in day

Crunch Topping (see Box, right)

1 ¼ cups sugar

¾ cup margarine or butter (1 ½ sticks), softened

½ 16-ounce can solid pack pumpkin (1 cup), not pumpkin pie mix, or 1 cup Mashed Cooked Pumpkin (see Box, page 87)

2 ½ cups all-purpose flour

½ cup plain yogurt

1 tablespoon pumpkin pie spice

2 ¼ teaspoons baking powder

¾ teaspoon baking soda

½ teaspoon salt

3 large eggs

2 cups heavy or whipping cream

Vanilla-wafer crumbs for garnish

1 Prepare Crunch Topping; set aside topping in pans. Preheat oven to 350°F.

2 In large bowl, with mixer at low speed, beat sugar and margarine or butter just until blended. Increase speed to high; beat 10 minutes or until light and fluffy, scraping bowl often with rubber spatula. Reduce speed to low; add pumpkin and next 7 ingredients; beat until well mixed, constantly scraping bowl. Increase speed to high; beat 2 minutes, occasionally scraping bowl (batter will be thick).

3 Spoon batter over Crunch Topping in pans; spread evenly with rubber spatula.

4 Stagger 4 cake pans on 2 oven racks, so layers are not directly on top of one another. Bake 20 minutes or until toothpick inserted in center of each cake layer comes out clean, rotating pans between upper and lower racks after 10 minutes.

5 Cool cake layers in pans on wire racks 10 minutes. With spatula, loosen each cake layer from edge of pan.

6 Invert cake layers onto wire racks to cool completely.

7 In small bowl, with mixer at medium speed, beat heavy or whipping cream until stiff peaks form.

CRUNCH TOPPING

1 ½ cups walnuts, finely chopped

1 ½ cups vanilla-wafer crumbs (about 36 cookies)

1 ½ cups packed light brown sugar

¾ cup margarine or butter (1 ½ sticks), melted

1 In large bowl, with spoon, mix walnuts, vanilla-wafer crumbs, light brown sugar, and margarine or butter until well blended.

2 Into each of four 9-inch round cake pans, measure one-fourth of topping.

3 With fingers, evenly pat topping to cover bottoms of pans.

8 On cake plate, place 1 cake layer, crunch-topping-side up; top with one-fourth of whipped cream.

9 Repeat layering, ending with a cake layer, topping-side up. Spoon remaining cream around top edge of cake; sprinkle lightly with vanilla-wafer crumbs. Refrigerate if not serving right away.

USING FRESH OR FROZEN PUMPKIN

Fresh pumpkin is in season in October. Look for firm, bright pumpkins, free from blemishes. Store in a cool, dry place and cook within 1 month. Mashed cooked pumpkin can be frozen until you are ready to use.

Mashed Cooked Pumpkin

Halve pumpkin and scoop out seeds and stringy portions. Cut pumpkin into chunks. In saucepan over medium heat, in *1 inch boiling water*, heat pumpkin to boiling. Reduce heat to low, cover and simmer 25 to 30 minutes or until tender. Drain, cool slightly, and remove peel. Return pumpkin to saucepan and mash with potato masher. Drain well.

CHOCOLATE BUTTERMILK TORTE

🍴 16 servings
🕐 Begin about 3 hours before serving or early in day

1 1/2 cups sugar

10 tablespoons margarine or butter (1 1/4 sticks)

1 2/3 cups all-purpose flour

1 1/2 cups buttermilk

2/3 cup unsweetened cocoa

1 1/2 teaspoons baking soda

1 teaspoon vanilla extract

1/2 teaspoon salt

1/2 teaspoon instant espresso-coffee powder

2 large eggs

4 1-ounce squares semisweet chocolate

Butter-Cream Frosting (see Box, above right)

3 tablespoons orange-flavor liqueur (optional)

1 Preheat oven to 350°F. Grease 10" by 2 1/2" springform pan; line bottom of pan with waxed paper; grease waxed paper.

2 In large bowl, with mixer at low speed, beat sugar and margarine or butter just until blended. Increase speed to high; beat 10 minutes or until light and fluffy, scraping bowl often with rubber spatula. Reduce speed to low; add flour, buttermilk, cocoa, baking soda, vanilla extract, salt, espresso-coffee powder, and eggs; beat until well mixed, constantly scraping bowl. Increase speed to high; beat 2 minutes, occasionally scraping bowl.

3 Spoon batter into springform pan, spreading evenly.

4 Bake 45 minutes or until toothpick inserted in center of cake comes out clean.

5 Cool cake in pan on wire rack 10 minutes. With spatula, loosen cake from edge of pan; invert onto wire rack. Peel off paper. Cool completely.

6 While cake is cooling, with semisweet-chocolate squares, make Semisweet Chocolate Curls (page 158).

7 Prepare Butter-Cream Frosting.

8 Place cake on large platter. If you like, with skewer or fork, make holes in top of cake all over; sprinkle orange-flavor liqueur evenly over cake.

BUTTER-CREAM FROSTING

In large bowl, with mixer at medium speed, beat *one 16-ounce package confectioners' sugar, 6 tablespoons margarine or butter (3/4 stick), softened, 3 tablespoons milk or half-and-half, and 1 1/2 teaspoons vanilla extract* until smooth. Add more milk if necessary until frosting is smooth, with an easy spreading consistency.

9 Spoon 3/4 cup Butter-Cream Frosting into decorating bag with large writing tube; set aside. Cover top and side of cake with remaining frosting. With frosting in decorating bag, pipe circle of small dollops around edge on top of cake, then pipe another circle of smaller dollops 3 inches from edge of cake. Press some chocolate curls onto side of cake; sprinkle remaining curls in between 2 circles of dollops on top of cake. Refrigerate cake if not serving right away.

BITTERSWEET CHOCOLATE TORTE

12 servings

Begin about 2 ½ hours before serving or early in day

3 3-ounce bars bittersweet chocolate, coarsely chopped

¾ cup unsalted butter (1 ½ sticks)

6 large eggs, separated

1 cup sugar

¼ cup all-purpose flour

¼ teaspoon salt

2 1-ounce squares semisweet chocolate

1 tablespoon confectioners' sugar

Whipped Cream (see Box, page 77)

1 Preheat oven to 325°F. Grease and flour 9" by 2 ½" springform pan.

2 In heavy 2-quart saucepan over low heat, heat bittersweet chocolate and butter, stirring frequently, until melted and smooth. Remove pan from heat.

3 In small bowl, with mixer at high speed, beat egg whites until soft peaks form; gradually sprinkle in ¼ cup sugar, beating until sugar completely dissolves and whites stand in stiff peaks.

4 In large bowl, using same beaters and with mixer at high speed, beat egg yolks and remaining ¾ cup sugar until very thick and lemon-colored, about 5 minutes. Reduce speed to low; add melted chocolate mixture, beating until well mixed.

5 To mixture, add flour and salt; continue beating at low speed until blended, occasionally scraping bowl with rubber spatula.

6 With rubber spatula or wire whisk, gently fold beaten egg whites into chocolate mixture, one-third at a time.

7 Spoon batter into pan, spreading evenly. Bake 30 to 35 minutes (torte will rise and crack on top while baking).

8 Torte is done when batter appears set but when toothpick inserted in center comes out moist (but center should not be runny).

9 Cool torte completely in pan on wire rack (torte will fall as it cools).

10 Meanwhile, using semisweet-chocolate squares, make Semisweet Chocolate Curls (page 158).

11 With spatula, loosen torte from side of pan; remove pan side.

> ### TO SERVE
> Sprinkle top of torte with confectioners' sugar; garnish with chocolate curls. Serve with whipped cream.

CAPPUCCINO CAKE

🥄 14 servings
🕐 Begin about 2 ½ hours before serving or early in day

5 large eggs, separated

1 ⅓ cups confectioners' sugar

½ teaspoon almond extract

3 tablespoons unsweetened cocoa plus extra for sprinkling

½ cup heavy or whipping cream

1 8-ounce package cream cheese, softened

1 tablespoon milk

½ teaspoon vanilla extract

1 1-ounce square semisweet chocolate, coarsely grated

Espresso Butter-Cream Frosting (see Box, above right)

Coffee-bean candies for garnish

1 Preheat oven to 400°F. Grease 15 ½" by 10 ½" jelly-roll pan; line bottom with waxed paper; grease and flour paper.

2 In small bowl, with mixer at high speed, beat egg whites until soft peaks form.

3 Gradually sprinkle in ½ cup confectioners' sugar, beating until sugar completely dissolves and whites stand in stiff peaks.

4 In large bowl, with mixer at high speed, beat egg yolks until very thick and lemon-colored. Reduce speed to low; add almond extract, ½ cup confectioners' sugar, and 3 tablespoons cocoa; beat until well mixed, occasionally scraping bowl.

ESPRESSO BUTTER-CREAM FROSTING

In cup, mix *2 tablespoons hot tap water* and *2 teaspoons instant espresso-coffee powder* until coffee dissolves. In large bowl, with mixer at low speed, beat *2 cups confectioners' sugar* and *1 cup margarine* or butter (2 sticks), softened, until just mixed. Increase speed to high; beat 10 minutes or until fluffy, scraping bowl often. Reduce speed to medium; gradually beat in espresso mixture until smooth, occasionally scraping bowl. If frosting is made in advance, store until needed in tightly covered container to prevent crust forming on top.

5 With rubber spatula or wire whisk, gently fold beaten egg whites into egg-yolk mixture, one-third at a time.

6 Spoon batter into pan, spreading evenly. Bake 15 minutes or until top of cake springs back when lightly touched with finger.

7 Sprinkle clean cloth towel with cocoa. When cake is done, immediately invert cake onto towel. Carefully peel waxed paper from cake. If you like, cut off crisp edges. Cool cake completely.

8 While cake is cooling, prepare cream-cheese filling: In small bowl, with mixer at medium speed, beat heavy or whipping cream until stiff peaks form.

ASSEMBLING CAKE LAYERS

Placing bottom layer on plate: On center of cake plate, place 1 cake piece, bottom side up.

Spreading with filling: With metal spatula, spread half the cream-cheese filling over bottom cake layer on plate.

Finishing cake layers: On top of second layer of cream-cheese filling, place third cake layer.

9 In large bowl, with mixer at medium speed, beat cream cheese, milk, and vanilla extract until fluffy. Reduce speed to low; beat in remaining ⅓ cup confectioners' sugar. Stir in grated chocolate. With rubber spatula, fold in whipped cream. Chill until ready to use.

10 Prepare Espresso Butter-Cream Frosting. Spoon ¾ cup frosting into decorating bag with small star tube.

11 With serrated knife, cut cake crosswise into 3 equal pieces.

12 Place 1 cake piece on cake plate and spread with half the cream-cheese filling (see Box, page 90).

13 Repeat layering, finishing with cake layer (see Box, page 90).

14 Spread frosting on sides and top of cake. Use frosting in decorating bag to pipe lattice top and pretty border. Place a candy in each lattice diamond. Refrigerate cake if not serving right away.

TRIPLE CHOCOLATE TORTE

 10 servings

Begin about 4 hours before serving or early in day

1 cup all-purpose flour

³/₄ cup sugar

³/₄ cup sour cream

¹/₂ cup margarine or butter (1 stick), softened

¹/₄ cup unsweetened cocoa

1 ¹/₂ teaspoons vanilla extract

¹/₂ teaspoon baking powder

¹/₂ teaspoon baking soda

¹/₄ teaspoon salt

1 large egg

6 1-ounce squares semisweet chocolate

Chocolate Glaze (see Box, above right)

Confectioners' sugar for sprinkling

1 Preheat oven to 350°F. Grease 9-inch round cake pan; line bottom of pan with waxed paper; grease waxed paper.

2 In large bowl, with mixer at low speed, beat first 10 ingredients until blended, occasionally scraping bowl with rubber spatula.

3 Spoon batter into pan, spreading evenly. Bake 30 to 35 minutes until toothpick inserted in center comes out clean. Cool cake in pan on wire rack 10 minutes. With spatula, loosen cake from edge of pan; invert onto wire rack; peel off waxed paper. Cool completely.

4 Meanwhile, in heavy 1-quart saucepan over low heat, heat semisweet chocolate squares, stirring frequently, until melted and smooth. Pour onto 2 large cookie sheets, spread evenly, and make Pencil-Thin Chocolate Curls (see Box, below).

CHOCOLATE GLAZE

In heavy 1-quart saucepan over low heat, heat *three 1-ounce squares semisweet chocolate, 3 tablespoons margarine or butter, and 2 teaspoons light corn syrup,* stirring frequently, until melted and smooth. Remove saucepan from heat; stir frequently until glaze cools and thickens slightly.

5 Repeat with chocolate on second cookie sheet to make as many curls as possible. (Consistency of chocolate is very important. If it is too soft, it will not curl; if too hard, it will crumble. If chocolate is too firm, let stand at room temperature a few minutes until soft enough to work with; if too soft, return to refrigerator.) Refrigerate curls until firm.

6 Make Chocolate Glaze.

7 Brush away crumbs from cake. Place cake on wire rack set over waxed paper.

8 Spoon glaze over top and side of cake (some glaze will drip onto waxed paper).

9 Let cake stand at room temperature until glaze is firm, about 45 minutes.

10 Place cake on plate. Arrange chocolate curls on top; sprinkle with confectioners' sugar.

PENCIL-THIN CHOCOLATE CURLS

Spreading chocolate: With metal spatula, spread melted chocolate over cookie sheets to cover evenly. Refrigerate until firm but not brittle, about 10 minutes.

Making curls: *Place 1 chocolate-covered cookie sheet on damp cloth on work surface (damp cloth keeps cookie sheet from moving while working). Using straight-edged knife or long metal spatula, push blade across chocolate to form long, thin curls.*

Transferring curls: With toothpick, transfer curls to another cookie sheet.

CHOCOLATE TRUFFLE CAKE

16 servings
Begin 3 hours before serving or day ahead

2 8-ounce packages unsweetened-chocolate squares (16 1-ounce squares)

1 cup plus 6 tablespoons margarine or butter (2 3/4 sticks), at room temperature

3 large eggs

2 teaspoons vanilla extract

2 2/3 cups all-purpose flour

2 cups sugar

1 1/4 teaspoons baking soda

1/2 teaspoon salt

2 1/2 cups confectioners' sugar

3/4 cup heavy or whipping cream

10 1-ounce squares semi-sweet chocolate

Rose for garnish

1 Grease three 9-inch round cake pans. Preheat oven to 325°F.

2 In heavy 4-quart saucepan over low heat, heat 12 squares unsweetened chocolate, 1 cup margarine or butter (2 sticks), and 2 1/2 cups water, stirring frequently, until melted and smooth. Remove from heat; cool slightly.

3 In large bowl, with wire whisk or fork, beat eggs and vanilla extract. Gradually beat in warm chocolate mixture.

4 To chocolate mixture, add flour, sugar, baking soda, and salt; continue beating with wire whisk or fork until batter is smooth and well blended.

5 Pour batter into cake pans. Bake 25 to 30 minutes until toothpick inserted in center of cake comes out clean. Cool cakes in pans on wire racks 10 minutes. Remove from pans; cool cakes completely on wire racks.

6 Meanwhile, prepare truffle mixture: In heavy 2-quart saucepan over low heat, heat remaining 4 squares unsweetened chocolate, stirring frequently, until melted; cool slightly. With spoon, stir in confectioners' sugar, remaining 6 tablespoons margarine or butter (3/4 stick), and 1/4 cup heavy or whipping cream until mixture is smooth and blended.

7 Prepare glaze: In heavy 2-quart saucepan over low heat, heat 8 squares semisweet chocolate and remaining 1/2 cup heavy or whipping cream, stirring frequently, until melted, smooth, and slightly thickened; keep warm.

8 Assemble and glaze cake (see Box, below). Refrigerate cake until glaze is set, about 30 minutes.

9 Remove cake to plate. Pipe border with remaining truffle mixture (see Box, below). Grate remaining 2 squares semisweet chocolate; sprinkle around top edge of cake.

> *TO SERVE*
> *Just before serving, garnish cake with fresh rose.*

ASSEMBLING, GLAZING, AND GARNISHING CAKE

Assembling cake: *With metal spatula, spread 1 cake layer with 1/2 cup truffle mixture. Top with second cake layer, pressing down gently but firmly. Spread with another 1/2 cup truffle mixture; top with third cake layer.*

Glazing cake: *Over assembled cake, pour prepared glaze. With metal spatula, spread glaze to completely cover top and side of cake.*

Piping border: *With rosette tube, pipe border of remaining truffle mixture around bottom of cake.*

FLAG CAKE

🍴 30 servings
⏰ Begin about
3 ½ hours before
serving or early
in day

2 16- to 17-ounce packages
pound-cake mix

1 ½ cups milk

4 large eggs

3 cups heavy or whipping
cream

⅓ cup confectioners' sugar

1 ½ teaspoons vanilla
extract

½ pint blueberries

2 ½-pints raspberries

1 Preheat oven to
350°F. Grease and
flour 13" by 9" baking pan.

2 In large bowl, with
mixer at low speed,
beat both packages of
pound-cake mix with milk
and eggs just until
blended. Increase speed
to medium; beat 4 min-
utes, occasionally scraping
bowl with rubber spatula.

3 Spoon batter into
baking pan, spreading
evenly. Bake 45 to 50
minutes until toothpick
inserted in center of cake
comes out clean. Cool
cake in pan on wire rack
15 minutes. With spatula,
loosen cake from edge of
pan; invert onto wire rack
to cool completely.

4 In small bowl, with
mixer at medium
speed, beat heavy or
whipping cream, confec-
tioners' sugar, and vanilla
extract until stiff peaks
form.

5 Place cake on large
platter. Spread 3 cups
whipped-cream mixture
on sides and on top of
cake. Arrange blueberries
and raspberries on top of
cake to resemble the
American flag, with
blueberries representing
the background for the
stars and raspberries
representing the 7 red
stripes, leaving space
between each row of
raspberries.

6 Spoon remaining
whipped-cream
mixture into decorating
bag with medium star
tube; pipe 6 lines between
raspberries to represent
the white stripes on the
flag.

7 Pipe decorative
border around
bottom edge of cake.
Refrigerate cake if not
serving right away.

*This Old Glory will surely
bring a happy ending to any
July 4th celebration!*

SIX-LAYER TOFFEE TORTE

20 servings

Begin about 3 1/2 hours before serving or early in day

2 2/3 cups all-purpose flour

2 cups sugar

1 cup margarine or butter (2 sticks), softened

1 cup buttermilk

3/4 cup unsweetened cocoa

2 teaspoons baking soda

1 1/2 teaspoons vanilla extract

1/4 teaspoon salt

2 large eggs

2 1/2 teaspoons instant-coffee powder or granules

10 1.4-ounce chocolate-covered toffee candy bars

2 cups heavy or whipping cream

3 tablespoons light brown sugar

Semisweet Chocolate Curls (page 158) for garnish

1 Preheat oven to 350°F. Grease and flour three 8-inch round cake pans.

2 Into large bowl, measure first 9 ingredients. With mixer at low speed, beat ingredients until just blended, constantly scraping bowl with rubber spatula.

3 Dissolve 2 teaspoons instant coffee in *1 cup boiling water*; add to bowl. Increase speed to medium; beat 2 minutes, occasionally scraping bowl.

4 Spoon batter into pans, spreading evenly. Bake 25 to 30 minutes until toothpick inserted in center of cake comes out clean. Cool cakes in pans on wire racks 10 minutes. With spatula, loosen layers from edges of pans; invert onto wire racks to cool completely.

5 Meanwhile, finely chop toffee bars. In cup, dissolve remaining 1/2 teaspoon instant coffee in *1 teaspoon hot water*; cool.

6 With serrated knife, cut each cake layer horizontally into halves to make 6 thin layers.

7 In small bowl, with mixer at medium speed, beat heavy or whipping cream, brown sugar, and dissolved instant coffee until stiff peaks form.

8 Place 1 cake layer on cake plate; spread with about 1/2 cup whipped-cream mixture. Reserve about two-thirds of finely chopped toffee bars; sprinkle layer with about one-fifth of remaining finely chopped toffee bars.

9 Repeat layering, ending with a cake layer. Thinly spread remaining whipped-cream mixture over side and top of cake. Gently press reserved chopped toffee bars onto side and top of cake. Garnish with chocolate curls before serving.

CHOCOLATE-COCONUT CAKE

This spectacular four-layer treat boasts flakes of coconut in the cake batter; a generous measure of chopped walnuts in the candy-sweet filling; airy unsweetened whipped cream to accent the chocolate flavor; and paper-thin, dainty "ruffles" of slivered fresh coconut to crown the whole.

14 servings
Begin 3 hours before serving or early in day

Unsweetened cocoa

3 1-ounce squares unsweetened chocolate

2 cups cake flour

1 1/2 cups sugar

1 1/4 cups buttermilk

1/2 cup shortening

1 1/2 teaspoons baking soda

1 teaspoon salt

1 teaspoon vanilla extract

1/2 teaspoon baking powder

3 large eggs

1 3 1/2-ounce can flaked coconut (1 1/3 cups)

Chocolate-Walnut Filling (see Box, above right)

1 cup heavy or whipping cream

Coconut Ruffles (page 99) for garnish

CHOCOLATE-WALNUT FILLING
In 3-quart saucepan over medium heat, heat *1 cup evaporated milk*, *1/2 cup packed brown sugar*, *1/2 cup margarine* or *butter* (1 stick), *two 1-ounce squares unsweetened chocolate*, and *3 large egg yolks*, slightly beaten, until chocolate melts and mixture will coat a spoon well, about 10 minutes, stirring often (mixture should be about 170° to 175°F. but do not boil or it will curdle). Remove from heat; stir in *one 8-ounce can walnuts* (2 cups), chopped, and *1 teaspoon vanilla extract*. Cool slightly until thick enough to spread, stirring occasionally.

---

1 Preheat oven to 350°F. Grease two 9-inch round cake pans; dust bottoms and sides of pans with cocoa.

2 In heavy 1-quart saucepan over low heat, melt chocolate, stirring often, until smooth; remove from heat.

3 Into large bowl, measure next 9 ingredients; add melted chocolate. With mixer at low speed, beat until mixed, scraping bowl often with rubber spatula. Increase speed to high; beat 2 minutes, occasionally scraping bowl. Stir in coconut.

4 Spread batter evenly in pans. Bake 25 to 30 minutes until toothpick inserted in center of cake comes out clean.

5 Cool cakes in pans on wire racks 10 minutes. With spatula, loosen cakes from edges of pans; invert onto wire racks to cool completely.

6 When cakes are cool, prepare Chocolate-Walnut Filling. In small bowl, with mixer at medium speed, beat heavy or whipping cream until stiff peaks form.

7 Cut each cake horizontally into 2 layers; place 1 layer on cake plate and spread with half the Chocolate-Walnut Filling (see Box, page 99).

8 Top with a second cake layer; spread with half the cream. Top with another cake layer (see Box, page 99); spread with remaining filling. Top with last cake layer; spread with remaining cream (see Box, page 99).

TO SERVE
Garnish top of cake with Coconut Ruffles. Sprinkle some cocoa through sieve over center. Refrigerate if not serving right away.

ASSEMBLING CAKE LAYERS

Cutting cake into layers: *With serrated knife, cut each cake horizontally into halves to make 4 thin layers.*

Starting to assemble cake: *On cake plate, place 1 cake layer, cut side up.*

Spreading with first layer of filling: *On first cake layer, with metal spatula, spread half the Chocolate-Walnut Filling.*

Topping with third cake layer: *Over cream layer, place cake layer, cut side up.*

Spreading with cream: *On last cake layer, with metal spatula, spread remaining whipped cream.*

COCONUT RUFFLES

With skewer and hammer, puncture eyes of fresh coconut. Drain coconut juice into bowl. Add to orange juice or other fruit drinks. Open shell by hitting very hard with hammer. Hit firmly all around middle.

With small sharp knife, pry out coconut meat in pieces.

With vegetable peeler, draw blade along curved edge of coconut piece to make wafer-thin, wide ruffles with brown edging.

Remaining coconut meat can be peeled and shredded for later use; refrigerate and use within 1 to 2 days.

BRIDAL SHOWER CAKE

75 servings

Begin early in day or day ahead

Cake

3 cups sugar

1 1/2 cups margarine or butter (3 sticks), softened

4 1/2 cups cake flour

1 1/2 cups milk

2 tablespoons baking powder

2 1/4 teaspoons vanilla extract

3/4 teaspoon salt

6 large eggs

Orange Curd

2 large oranges

1 cup margarine or butter (2 sticks)

1 1/2 cups sugar

4 large eggs

Vanilla Butter-Cream Frosting (see Box, above right)

Red food coloring

Flowers for garnish (pages 134 to 135)

1 Preheat oven to 350°F. Grease one 10-inch round cake pan, one 8-inch round cake pan, and one 6-inch round cake pan. Line bottoms with waxed paper; grease paper.

2 In large bowl, with mixer at low speed, beat sugar and margarine or butter just until blended. Increase speed to high; beat 10 minutes or until light and fluffy, scraping bowl often with rubber spatula. Reduce speed to low; add next 6 ingredients; beat until well mixed, constantly scraping bowl. Increase speed to high; beat 2 minutes, occasionally scraping bowl.

3 Evenly spread about 5 2/3 cups batter in 10-inch pan, 3 cups batter in 8-inch pan, and remaining batter in 6-inch pan. Place 10-inch layer on lower oven rack and other 2 layers on upper rack.

4 Bake 50 minutes or until toothpick inserted in center of 6-inch and 8-inch layers comes out clean. Cool 2 small layers in pans on wire racks 30 minutes. Bake 10-inch layer 30 minutes longer or until toothpick inserted in center comes out clean. Cool large layer in pan on wire rack 30 minutes.

5 Loosen cake layers from edges of pans; invert onto wire racks. Peel off paper. Cool completely.

6 While cakes are baking, prepare Orange Curd: From oranges, grate 4 teaspoons peel and squeeze 2/3 cup juice. In 3-quart saucepan over low heat, stir orange peel, juice, margarine or butter, and sugar until margarine melts. With wire whisk, beat in eggs. Cook, stirring constantly, until mixture is very thick and coats a spoon well, about 35 minutes (mixture should be about 170° to 175°F. but do not boil or it will curdle). Cover and refrigerate until firm, about 2 hours.

7 When cakes are cool, prepare Vanilla Butter-Cream Frosting. Spoon 1 cup frosting into decorating bag with medium star tube; set aside. Spoon about 1/4 cup frosting into small bowl; tint a pale pink color with red food coloring.

8 With serrated knife, cut each cake horizontally in half to make 6 thin layers.

9 For bottom tier, place bottom half of 10-inch cake layer, cut-side up, on large cake plate; spread with about 1 1/4 cups Orange Curd to within 1/2 inch of edge. Top with top half of 10-inch cake layer; spread with about 3/4 cup frosting.

VANILLA BUTTER-CREAM FROSTING

In large bowl, with mixer at low speed, beat *one and one half 16-ounce packages confectioners' sugar (5 2/3 cups)* and *2 3/4 cups margarine or butter (5 1/2 sticks)*, softened, just until mixed. Increase speed to high; beat 10 minutes. Reduce speed to medium; beat in *1/4 cup heavy or whipping cream* and *1 tablespoon vanilla extract*, scraping bowl often.

10 Place bottom half of 8-inch cake layer, cut-side up, on center of 10-inch tier; spread with about 1 cup Orange Curd to within 1/2 inch of edge. Top with top half of 8-inch cake layer; spread with about 2/3 cup frosting.

11 Place bottom half of 6-inch cake layer, cut-side up, on center of 8-inch tier; spread with remaining Orange Curd. Top with top half of 6-inch cake layer.

12 Spread remaining frosting on sides and top of cake. Use frosting in decorating bag to pipe border around bottom of cake, and around top edge of each tier.

13 Spoon pink frosting into small decorating bag with small writing tube (or, paper cone with tip cut to 1/8-inch-diameter hole); pipe bead border around bottom edge of top and middle tiers. Refrigerate cake if not serving right away. Garnish with flowers just before serving.

RASPBERRY ICEBOX CAKE

10 servings
Begin about 6 hours before serving or early in day

2 cups heavy or whipping cream

2 tablespoons sugar

1 teaspoon vanilla extract

2 tablespoons seedless raspberry preserves

2 ½-pints raspberries

1 8 ½-ounce package chocolate wafers

1 In large bowl, with mixer at medium speed, beat heavy or whipping cream, sugar, and vanilla extract until stiff peaks form. Reserve half the whipped-cream mixture in another bowl; cover and refrigerate.

2 In small bowl, with fork, mash raspberry preserves and ½ pint raspberries until pureed. With wire whisk or rubber spatula, gently fold raspberry mixture into remaining whipped-cream mixture just until blended.

3 On one side of each of 6 chocolate wafers, spread about 2 teaspoons raspberry whipped cream.

4 Stack wafers on top of each other. Top stack with a plain wafer.

Stacking wafers together

5 Repeat stacking wafers on top of each other until all wafers are used, making 5 stacks of 7 wafers each.

6 Turn each stack on its side; place stacks, side by side, in a long roll on platter.

7 Frost roll with reserved whipped cream. Cover and refrigerate 5 hours or until wafers have softened.

8 Top cake with remaining raspberries just before serving.

TO SERVE
Slice Raspberry Icebox Cake on an angle, to reveal its luscious layers.

MOTHER'S DAY CAKE

16 servings

Begin about 3 hours before serving or early in day

1 package lemon-cake mix for 2-layer cake

2 medium-sized lemons

4 cups confectioners' sugar

1/2 cup margarine or butter (1 stick), softened

Red food coloring

Pink satin bow, freesias, and/or other flowers for garnish (pages 134 to 135)

1 Preheat oven to 350°F. Generously grease and flour 12-inch round pizza pan with at least a 3/4-inch-high rim to be used for hat brim and 1 1/4-quart heatsafe bowl to be used for hat's crown.

2 Prepare cake mix as label directs. Pour 3 1/2 cups cake batter into greased bowl; pour remaining batter into pizza pan, spreading evenly.

3 Bake batter in pizza pan about 15 minutes or until toothpick inserted in center of cake comes out clean. Cool cake in pan on wire rack 10 minutes; with spatula, loosen cake and invert onto wire rack to cool completely.

4 Bake batter in bowl about 50 minutes or until toothpick inserted in center of cake comes out clean. Cool cake in bowl on wire rack 10 minutes; with spatula, loosen cake and invert onto wire rack to cool completely.

5 Meanwhile, prepare icing: Grate 1 1/2 teaspoons peel from lemons and squeeze 5 tablespoons juice. Place peel and juice in large bowl; add confectioners' sugar, and margarine or butter. With mixer at low speed, beat until smooth, scraping bowl often.

6 Spoon about 1/4 cup icing into small bowl; stir in enough red food coloring to tint icing a pretty pink color. Cover bowls with plastic wrap.

7 Place cake brim on flat cake plate or tray; spread with 1 cup white icing (see Box, below). Place cake crown on center of cake brim and spread with 1 1/4 cups white icing (see Box, below).

8 Spoon remaining white icing into small decorating bag with petal tube; pipe ruffle around edge of cake brim.

9 Spoon pink icing into small decorating bag with small writing tube (or, paper cone with tip cut to 1/8-inch-diameter hole).

10 Pipe dots with pink icing over cake crown to make pretty design.

MAKING HAT SHAPE

Spreading icing on cake brim: With metal spatula, evenly spread 1 cup white icing on cake brim, occasionally dipping spatula into bowl of water to smooth out icing.

Spreading icing on cake crown: With metal spatula, evenly spread 1 1/4 cups white icing on cake crown.

Placing crown on brim: On center of cake brim, carefully place cake crown (if bottom of cake crown is very rounded, cut off thin slice to make flat).

TO SERVE
Attach satin bow to base of crown; garnish cake with flowers.

GRANDMA'S 1-2-3-4 CAKE

12 servings
Begin about 3 hours before serving or early in day

2 cups sugar

1 cup margarine or butter (2 sticks), softened

3 cups cake flour

1 cup milk

1 tablespoon baking powder

1 1/2 teaspoons vanilla extract

1/2 teaspoon salt

4 large eggs

Confectioners' sugar

Fresh cherries for garnish

1 Preheat oven to 350°F. Grease and flour 9-inch fluted tube pan (about 3 quarts).

2 In large bowl, with mixer at low speed, beat sugar and margarine or butter just until blended. Increase speed to high; beat 10 minutes or until light and fluffy, scraping bowl often with rubber spatula.

3 Reduce speed to low; add flour, milk, baking powder, vanilla extract, salt, and eggs; beat until well mixed, constantly scraping bowl. Increase speed to high; beat 2 minutes, occasionally scraping bowl.

4 Spoon batter into pan, spreading evenly.

5 Bake 50 to 55 minutes until toothpick inserted in center of cake comes out clean. Cool cake in pan on wire rack 10 minutes; with spatula, loosen cake and invert onto wire rack to cool completely.

6 Sift confectioners' sugar over cake.

TO SERVE
Garnish around side of cake with fresh cherries.

TOASTED ALMOND CAKES

Makes 8
Begin about 2 hours before serving or early in day

1 cup blanched almonds
1 1/2 cups all-purpose flour
1 cup sugar
2 teaspoons baking powder
1/2 teaspoon salt
2 large eggs
2/3 cup milk
2 tablespoons salad oil
1 teaspoon almond extract
Strawberries for garnish

1 In small skillet over medium heat, cook blanched almonds until golden, stirring often; cool. In blender at medium speed or in food processor with knife blade attached, finely grind toasted almonds. (If using blender, grind nuts in 2 batches.)

2 Preheat oven to 350°F. Generously grease eight 5-inch baking shells.

3 In large bowl, mix ground almonds, flour, sugar, baking powder, and salt.

4 In small bowl, with fork, beat eggs slightly; stir in milk, salad oil, and almond extract. Stir liquid mixture into flour mixture just until flour is moistened.

5 Spoon batter evenly in shells, leaving 1/2-inch border all around shell.

Spooning batter in baking shell

6 To keep shells level while baking, arrange batter-filled shells on top of 2 large muffin pans, or arrange filled shells on crumpled pieces of foil in jelly-roll pan.

7 Bake 20 to 25 minutes until toothpick inserted in center of cakes comes out clean.

8 Cool cakes in shells on wire racks 5 minutes. Run tip of knife around edge of shells to loosen cakes; invert cakes onto wire racks to cool completely. Garnish with strawberries.

These pretty little tea cakes are delicious made with walnuts or pecans too!

CURLY CHOCOLATE CAKE

Covered with plump chocolate curls, this yummy chocolate cake looks a perfect picture, making it an unforgettably delicious treat for family and friends. And don't worry about making the chocolate curls – if you follow our simple directions in the step-by-step box on this page, you will find they're really easy to make.

DELUXE CHOCOLATE CURLS

Pouring melted chocolate: *Into 15 ¹/₂" by 10 ¹/₂" jelly-roll pan, pour melted chocolate; use rubber spatula to scrape all chocolate from saucepan.*

Spreading melted chocolate: *With same rubber spatula, spread chocolate to evenly cover entire bottom of pan. Refrigerate until firm but not brittle, about 10 minutes.*

16 servings

Begin about 4 hours before serving or early in day

1 ¹/₃ cups sugar

¹/₂ cup margarine or butter (1 stick), softened

1 ²/₃ cups all-purpose flour

1 ¹/₂ cups buttermilk (see Box, page 107)

²/₃ cup unsweetened cocoa

1 ¹/₄ teaspoons baking soda

¹/₂ teaspoon salt

1 ¹/₂ teaspoons vanilla extract

3 large eggs

2 ¹/₂ 8-ounce packages semisweet chocolate (20 1-ounce squares)

Cocoa Frosting (see Box, page 107)

Confectioners' sugar for sprinkling

1 Preheat oven to 350°F. Grease 10" by 2 ¹/₂" springform pan; line bottom of pan with waxed paper; grease waxed paper.

2 In large bowl, with mixer at low speed, beat sugar and margarine or butter just until blended. Increase speed to high; beat 10 minutes or until light and fluffy, scraping bowl often with rubber spatula. Reduce speed to low; add flour, buttermilk, cocoa, baking soda, salt, vanilla extract, and eggs; beat until well mixed, constantly scraping bowl. Increase speed to medium; beat 2 minutes, occasionally scraping bowl.

3 Spoon batter into pan, spreading evenly. Bake 55 to 60 minutes until toothpick inserted in center of cake comes out clean. Cool cake in pan on wire rack 10 minutes.

Forming curls: *Place jelly-roll pan on damp cloth on work surface (damp cloth keeps pan from moving while working). Holding teaspoon at 30° angle, scrape chocolate into curls (if chocolate softens and sticks to spoon, place pan in refrigerator several minutes). With toothpick, transfer curls to another jelly-roll pan; refrigerate.*

4 With spatula, loosen cake from edge of pan; invert onto wire rack; peel off waxed paper. Cool completely.

5 Meanwhile, in heavy 1-quart saucepan over low heat, heat 5 squares chocolate, stirring frequently, until melted and smooth; use to make Chocolate Curls (see Box, page 106). Repeat 3 more times to make 4 batches of curls in all.

6 Prepare Cocoa Frosting.

7 Place cake on large platter; spread frosting evenly over side and top of cake. With toothpick, carefully press chocolate curls onto frosting, completely covering cake.

8 Refrigerate cake if not serving right away.

COCOA FROSTING

In large bowl, with mixer at low speed, beat *2 2/3 cups confectioners' sugar, 3/4 cup unsweetened cocoa, 6 tablespoons margarine or butter (3/4 stick), softened, 1/3 cup milk, 2 tablespoons light corn syrup, 1 teaspoon vanilla extract, and 1/4 teaspoon salt,* until blended. Increase speed to high; beat until frosting is smooth and glossy. Add more milk if necessary until frosting is an easy spreading consistency.

TO SERVE
Sprinkle top of cake lightly with confectioners' sugar.

BUTTERMILK

Buttermilk once was the liquid left behind after milk had been churned and the fat removed. Today it is cultured by the addition of a lactic acid bacteria, which gives it its tangy flavor and smooth, rich body. Traditionally, it is used to make biscuits, quick breads, and cakes.

Substitute for Buttermilk

If you cannot obtain buttermilk, use this: In 1-cup measure, mix *1 tablespoon white vinegar* or lemon juice and enough *milk* to make 1 cup; let stand 5 minutes to thicken.

CHOCOLATE GARNISHES

A chocolate butterfly perched atop a simple dessert will delight the sophisticated dinner party guest as much as it will enchant the children at a birthday party. More, the ease with which it can be made will delight the cook as well (pages 110 and 130). Like most chocolate garnishes, butterflies require no special skill, but they do need time for the chocolate to firm up.

To melt chocolate for making garnishes: Place *one 6-ounce package semisweet-chocolate pieces* (1 cup) and *2 teaspoons shortening* in heavy, small saucepan over low heat. Heat about 5 minutes until melted and smooth, stirring often with rubber spatula. If using for piping garnishes, let cool.

Chocolate-Dipped Fruits
Small fruits like grapes, cherries, and strawberries dipped in melted chocolate look very pretty arranged around edge of a cake or dessert, or grouped together in clusters in center.

NONTOXIC LEAVES
These nontoxic leaves are safe for making chocolate leaves: Gardenia, grape, lemon, magnolia, nasturtium, rose, violet.

Do not use the following leaves in contact with chocolate or other foods: Amaryllis, azalea, caladium, daffodil, delphinium, dieffenbachia, English ivy, hydrangea, jonquil, larkspur, laurel, lily of the valley, mistletoe, narcissus, oleander, poinsettia, rhododendron.

Wash nontoxic leaves in warm, soapy water; rinse and dry well before use.

Chocolate Leaves
A variety of leaves is brushed with different kinds of melted chocolate to make interesting shapes and colors. Grouping chocolate leaves together to make a flower shape is especially effective in center of dessert or cake.

Chocolate Cups
Miniature paper or foil baking cups are used as molds for melted chocolate, then peeled off when chocolate is firm. Filled with piped whipped cream, frosting, or tiny pieces of fruit, they look pretty on the edge of platters and plates.

Lacy Lattice
Melted chocolate piped free-hand in lattice design on waxed paper is refrigerated until firm, then carefully lifted off.

Chocolate Heart
Heart shape is cut out of melted and chilled semisweet chocolate with cookie cutter, then piped with melted white chocolate. Hole is punched with fine skewer for ribbon to be threaded through.

Pencil-Thin Chocolate Curls
Elegant scrolls are made by pushing knife or spatula across surface of melted and cooled chocolate.

Chocolate Ruffles
These are made in the same way as Pencil-Thin Chocolate Curls (left), but knife or spatula is pushed only halfway across surface of chocolate.

Dainty Daisy
Melted semisweet chocolate is piped over daisy design on waxed paper, then left to set before being flooded with melted white chocolate. Daisy is refrigerated until firm, then lifted off paper.

Simple Curls
Simple chocolate curls can be made quickly and easily using a vegetable peeler; draw it along chocolate square to produce short, plump shapes.

Fleur-de-Lis
Shape of fleur-de-lis is drawn on waxed paper, then melted chocolate piped over. Garnish is refrigerated until firm before being carefully lifted off and placed on dessert or cake.

Marbled Triangles
Melted semisweet and white chocolate are swirled together to make marbled design, then refrigerated until firm. Triangles are then cut out with small cutter.

CHOCOLATE-DIPPED FRUIT

WHITE-CHOCOLATE CURLS

CHOCOLATE BUTTERFLIES

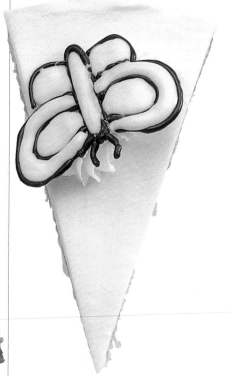

Cherries dipped in melted semisweet and white chocolates

Pencil-Thin Chocolate Curls (see Box, page 92), together with White-Chocolate Curls (below)

Two-Tone Butterfly made with piped melted semisweet and white chocolates

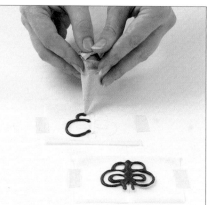

1 *Rinse fruit under running cold water but do not remove stems; pat completely dry with paper towels; set fruit aside. (For dipping, fruit should be at room temperature.)*

2 *Melt chocolate in heavy, small saucepan (page 108); let cool slightly.*

3 *With fingers, hold stem of 1 fruit at a time and dip it into chocolate, leaving part of fruit uncovered.*

4 *Shake off excess chocolate; place fruit on waxed paper. Let stand until chocolate is set, about 10 minutes; remove fruit from waxed paper.*

1 *Hold bar of white chocolate between palms of hands; let heat of hands soften chocolate slightly, about 5 minutes.*

2 *Slowly and firmly draw blade of vegetable peeler across wide side of chocolate for wide curls, thin side for thin curls.*

3 *Use toothpick to transfer curls, to avoid breaking them.*

Note: *For Semisweet Chocolate Curls, see page 158.*

1 *With pencil, draw butterflies on rectangles of waxed paper. Place rectangles on clean flat surface, pencil-side down; tape to work surface.*

2 *Spoon melted semisweet chocolate (page 108) into paper cone with ⅛-inch-diameter hole (or use small decorating bag with small writing tube).*

3 *Pipe melted semisweet chocolate onto waxed-paper rectangle in thin continuous lines over butterfly outline. Refrigerate until set.*

4 *Spoon melted white chocolate into clean paper cone; pipe inside outline. Refrigerate until firm, about 1 hour.*

CHOCOLATE TRIANGLES

Semisweet- and white-chocolate triangles

1 Tape sheet of waxed paper onto clean work surface.

2 With metal spatula, spread melted chocolate (page 108) onto waxed paper. Refrigerate until chocolate is set.

3 With small decorative cutter, cut out chocolate shapes. Refrigerate shapes until firm.

CHOCOLATE SQUIGGLES

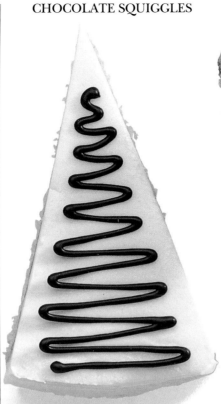

Semisweet-chocolate squiggles

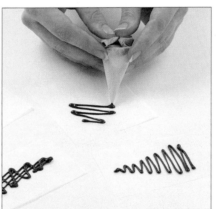

1 Spoon melted chocolate (page 108) into paper cone with tip cut to ⅛-inch-diameter hole.

2 Onto waxed-paper rectangles, pipe melted chocolate in free-hand squiggle designs.

3 Refrigerate chocolate squiggles until firm.

4 With metal spatula, carefully lift chocolate squiggles off paper.

CHOCOLATE LEAVES

Chocolate leaves in different colors and shapes

1 Rinse leaves of your choice (see Box, page 108); pat dry with paper towels.

2 With pastry brush, small painting brush, or small metal spatula, spread layer of melted chocolate (page 108) on underside of leaves (using underside will give a more distinctive leaf design).

3 Refrigerate chocolate-coated leaves until chocolate is firm, about 30 minutes.

4 With cool hands, carefully peel each leaf from chocolate.

MAPLE-WALNUT TORTE

16 servings

Begin about 4 hours before serving or early in day

1 16-ounce can walnuts (4 cups)

1/3 cup all-purpose flour

1 teaspoon baking powder

1/4 teaspoon salt

5 large eggs, separated

3/4 cup sugar

2 tablespoons salad oil

2 1/4 teaspoons imitation maple flavor

3 cups heavy or whipping cream

1/4 cup confectioners' sugar

1 In blender at medium speed or in food processor with knife blade attached, finely grind 3 cups walnuts with flour, baking powder, and salt. (If using blender, blend ingredients in batches.)

2 Preheat oven to 350°F. Grease two 9-inch round cake pans; line bottoms of pans with waxed paper; grease waxed paper.

3 In small bowl, with mixer at high speed, beat egg whites until soft peaks form; gradually sprinkle in 1/4 cup sugar, beating until sugar completely dissolves and whites stand in stiff peaks.

4 In large bowl, using same beaters and with mixer at high speed, beat egg yolks, salad oil, and remaining 1/2 cup sugar until very thick and lemon-colored, about 5 minutes. Add 1 teaspoon imitation maple flavor; beat until blended. With rubber spatula or wire whisk, gently fold nut mixture and beaten egg whites into yolk mixture just until blended.

5 Spoon batter into pans, spreading evenly. Bake 20 to 25 minutes until top of cake springs back when lightly touched with finger. Immediately loosen edges of cakes from sides of pans; invert cakes onto wire racks and peel off waxed paper. Cool completely.

6 In small bowl, with mixer at medium speed, beat heavy or whipping cream, confectioners' sugar, and remaining 1 1/4 teaspoons imitation maple flavor until stiff peaks form. Spoon 2 1/2 cups whipped-cream mixture into decorating bag with large rosette tube; reserve for garnish. Chop remaining 1 cup walnuts for garnish.

7 With serrated knife, cut each cake layer horizontally into halves to make 4 thin layers.

8 Place 1 cake layer on cake plate; spread with one-fourth of whipped-cream mixture.

9 Repeat layering, ending with a cake layer. Spread remaining one-fourth whipped-cream mixture on side of cake.

10 Reserve 1/4 cup chopped walnuts; press remaining chopped walnuts into cream on side of cake. Pipe whipped cream in decorating bag on top of cake in parallel lines.

11 Sprinkle reserved chopped walnuts in between lines of cream on top of cake.

12 Refrigerate cake if not serving right away.

OUR FAVORITE MISSISSIPPI MUD CAKE

16 servings

Begin about 3 hours before serving or early in day

1 ¹/₂ cups margarine or butter (3 sticks), softened

³/₄ cup walnuts, finely chopped

³/₄ cup vanilla-wafer crumbs (about 18 cookies)

³/₄ cup packed light brown sugar

1 ¹/₂ cups all-purpose flour

1 cup sugar

¹/₃ cup unsweetened cocoa

¹/₂ teaspoon salt

1 teaspoon vanilla extract

4 large eggs

1 3 ¹/₂-ounce can flaked coconut (1 ¹/₃ cups)

1 ¹/₂ cups miniature marshmallows

Chocolate Glaze (see Box, below)

Grated Chocolate Curls (page 116) for garnish

CHOCOLATE GLAZE
In heavy 1-quart saucepan over low heat, heat *one 8-ounce package semisweet-chocolate squares* (eight 1-ounce squares), *3 tablespoons margarine* or butter, and *3 tablespoons water*, stirring frequently, until melted and smooth. Remove from heat; stir in *1 ¹/₂ teaspoons vanilla extract*. Let chocolate mixture cool to room temperature; then add *3 tablespoons confectioners' sugar*, beating with spoon until well blended and a thick spreading consistency.

1 Preheat oven to 350°F. Grease two 9-inch round cake pans; line bottoms with waxed paper.

2 In 2-quart saucepan over low heat, heat ¹/₂ cup margarine or butter (1 stick) until melted. Remove from heat; stir in walnuts, vanilla-wafer crumbs, and brown sugar. Divide mixture equally between cake pans and pat to cover bottoms of pans evenly.

3 In large bowl, with mixer at low speed, beat flour, sugar, cocoa, salt, vanilla extract, eggs, coconut, and remaining 1 cup margarine or butter (2 sticks) until blended, constantly scraping bowl with rubber spatula. Increase speed to medium; beat 1 minute.

4 Spoon batter into pans, spreading evenly. Bake 30 minutes or until toothpick inserted in center comes out clean. Immediately, with spatula, loosen cake layers from edges of pans; invert onto wire racks and carefully peel off waxed paper.

5 While still hot, carefully place 1 cake layer, crumb-mixture-side up, on cake plate; top with marshmallows.

6 Immediately place second cake layer, crumb-mixture-side up, on top of marshmallows so marshmallows will melt.

7 Insert long metal or wooden skewer in center of cake to keep top layer from sliding.

8 Refrigerate cake until completely cool and marshmallows are set.

9 When cake is cool, prepare Chocolate Glaze.

10 Remove skewer from cake. Spread glaze over top and side of cake. Garnish with Grated Chocolate Curls. Allow glaze to set before serving.

VALENTINE CAKE

20 servings

Begin about 3 hours before serving or early in day

1 cup sugar

3/4 cup margarine or butter (1 1/2 sticks), softened

2 1/3 cups cake flour

3/4 cup milk

2 1/2 teaspoons baking powder

1 teaspoon vanilla extract

1/2 teaspoon salt

3 large eggs

Vanilla Butter-Cream Frosting (see Box, page 115)

Red and green food colorings

3/4 cup raspberry preserves

2 tablespoons orange-flavor liqueur

1 Preheat oven to 350°F. Grease and flour three 8-inch heart-shaped cake pans.

2 In large bowl, with mixer at low speed, beat sugar and margarine or butter just until blended. Increase speed to high; beat 10 minutes or until light and fluffy, scraping bowl often with rubber spatula. Reduce speed to low; add cake flour, milk, baking powder, vanilla extract, salt, and eggs; beat until well mixed, constantly scraping bowl. Increase speed to medium; beat 1 minute, occasionally scraping bowl.

3 Spoon batter into pans, spreading evenly. Bake 20 minutes or until toothpick inserted in center comes out clean. Cool cake layers in pans on wire racks 10 minutes. With spatula, loosen cake layers from edges of pans; invert onto wire racks to cool completely.

4 Meanwhile, prepare Vanilla Butter-Cream Frosting. In medium bowl, mix about 2 3/4 cups frosting with enough red food coloring to tint a pretty pink. In cup, mix about 1/3 cup frosting with enough green food coloring to tint a leaf green. Leave remaining white frosting in large bowl.

5 In small bowl, stir raspberry preserves with orange-flavor liqueur.

6 Place 1 cake layer on cake plate; spread with half the raspberry mixture. Repeat layering, ending with cake layer.

7 Spread top and side of cake with pink frosting, reserving about 1/3 cup. Spoon white frosting into decorating bag with coupler and rosette tube; use to pipe decorative border around bottom edge of cake (see Box, right).

8 Using white frosting in same decorating bag with medium ruffle tube, pipe double ruffle border around top edge of cake (see Box, right). If cake and/or frosting become very soft, refrigerate until firm enough to work with.

DECORATING CAKE

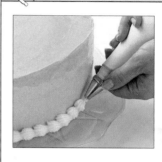

Piping bottom border: Using decorating bag with coupler and rosette tube, pipe decorative border of white frosting around bottom edge of cake.

Piping top border: Using white frosting in same decorating bag with medium ruffle tube, pipe double ruffle border around top edge of cake.

Piping rosebuds: Using decorating bag with small writing tube, pipe 1 deep-pink rosebud on end of each stalk.

9 With decorating bag and small writing tube and medium leaf tube, pipe green frosting to resemble stems and leaves on top of cake.

10 Into reserved ⅓ cup pink frosting, stir enough additional red food coloring to tint a deep pink; spoon into decorating bag with small writing tube (or, use paper cone with tip cut to make ⅛-inch-diameter hole).

11 Pipe pink dots inside ruffle border on top of cake and pipe rosebuds on ends of stalks (see Box, page 114). Refrigerate cake if not serving right away.

Pretty as a picture, Valentine Cake is a delicious way to say "I love you"

VANILLA BUTTER-CREAM FROSTING
In large bowl, with mixer at medium speed, beat *4 cups confectioners' sugar, 1 cup margarine* or butter (2 sticks), softened, and *1 cup shortening* until just mixed. Increase speed to high; beat 10 minutes or until light and fluffy, scraping bowl often with rubber spatula. Reduce speed to medium; gradually beat in *¼ cup heavy or whipping cream* and *2 teaspoons vanilla extract* until smooth, occasionally scraping bowl.

DREAMY CHOCOLATE CAKE

16 servings

Begin about 5 hours before serving or early in day

4 1-ounce squares semisweet chocolate

2 large eggs, separated

1 ¹/₃ cups plus 2 tablespoons sugar

¹/₂ cup margarine or butter (1 stick), softened

2 ¹/₄ cups all-purpose flour

¹/₂ cup sour cream

1 teaspoon baking powder

1 teaspoon baking soda

¹/₂ teaspoon orange extract

¹/₄ teaspoon salt

1 6-ounce package semisweet-chocolate pieces (1 cup)

2 tablespoons shortening

Chocolate Cream (see Box, page 117)

1 cup heavy or whipping cream

Candied violets for garnish

1 Grease and flour 10" by 3" springform pan.

2 In heavy 1-quart saucepan over low heat, heat semisweet-chocolate squares, stirring frequently, until melted and smooth. Remove saucepan from heat.

3 In small bowl, with mixer at high speed, beat egg whites until stiff peaks form.

4 Preheat oven to 350°F. In large bowl, using same beaters and with mixer at medium speed, beat egg yolks, 1 ¹/₃ cups sugar, and margarine or butter until light and fluffy, about 5 minutes, occasionally scraping bowl with rubber spatula.

5 Reduce speed to low; add melted chocolate, flour, sour cream, baking powder, baking soda, orange extract, salt, and 1 cup water; beat until well mixed, constantly scraping bowl. Increase speed to medium; beat 2 minutes, occasionally scraping bowl.

6 With rubber spatula or wire whisk, gently fold beaten egg whites into chocolate mixture.

7 Spoon batter into pan, spreading evenly. Bake 45 minutes or until cake springs back when lightly touched with finger. Cool cake in pan on wire rack 10 minutes. With spatula, loosen cake from edge of pan; carefully remove side of pan, leaving cake on pan bottom. Cool completely on wire rack.

8 While cake is cooling, in heavy 1-quart saucepan over low heat, heat semisweet-chocolate pieces and shortening, stirring frequently, until melted and smooth; use to make Grated Chocolate Curls (see Box, below).

9 Prepare Chocolate Cream.

10 Remove cake from pan bottom. With serrated knife, cut cake horizontally into 2 layers. Place 1 cake layer on cake plate; spread with one-third Chocolate Cream. Top with second cake layer.

GRATED CHOCOLATE CURLS

Making chocolate block: Into foil-lined or disposable 5 ³/₄" by 3 ¹/₄" loaf pan, pour melted chocolate mixture. Refrigerate until chocolate is set, about 2 hours.

Unmolding chocolate block: Remove chocolate block from pan; carefully peel off foil.

Grating chocolate curls: Using coarse side of grater, grate along 1 long side of chocolate block to make long, thin curls (if chocolate appears too brittle to curl, let stand at room temperature 30 minutes to soften slightly).

11 Spread remaining Chocolate Cream over top and side of cake. Carefully press chocolate curls onto side of cake.

12 In small bowl, with mixer at medium speed, beat heavy or whipping cream and remaining 2 tablespoons sugar until stiff peaks form. Spoon whipped-cream mixture into decorating bag with large star tube; use to pipe border and lattice design on top of cake. Garnish with candied violets.

CHOCOLATE CREAM

In 2-quart saucepan over medium heat, heat *1 1/2 cups heavy or whipping cream, eight 1-ounce squares semisweet chocolate,* and *4 tablespoons margarine* or butter (1/2 stick) to boiling, stirring constantly until mixture is smooth. Pour mixture into large bowl; let cool completely at room temperature. With mixer at high speed, beat chocolate mixture until light and fluffy.

MOCHA ROULADE

🍴 16 servings

⏰ Begin about 3 hours before serving or early in day

6 large eggs, separated

$1/3$ cup plus $3/4$ cup sugar

$3/4$ cup all-purpose flour

1 teaspoon baking powder

$1/4$ teaspoon salt

$1/2$ cup unsweetened cocoa plus extra for sprinkling

White-Chocolate Butter-Cream Frosting (see Box, right)

White-Chocolate Curls (page 110) and Semisweet Chocolate Curls (page 158) for garnish

1 Grease two 15 $1/2$" by 10 $1/2$" jelly-roll pans; line pans with waxed paper; grease waxed paper.

2 In small bowl, with mixer at high speed, beat egg whites until soft peaks form; gradually sprinkle in $1/3$ cup sugar, beating until sugar completely dissolves and whites stand in stiff peaks.

3 Preheat oven to 375°F. In large bowl, using same beaters and with mixer at high speed, beat egg yolks and remaining $3/4$ cup sugar until very thick and lemon-colored. Reduce speed to low; add flour, baking powder, salt, and $1/2$ cup cocoa; beat until well mixed, occasionally scraping bowl with rubber spatula. With rubber spatula or wire whisk, gently fold beaten egg whites into egg-yolk mixture, one-third at a time.

WHITE-CHOCOLATE BUTTER-CREAM FROSTING

In heavy 1-quart saucepan over medium heat, heat *3 tablespoons milk* until tiny bubbles form around edge of pan; remove saucepan from heat. With wire whisk, beat in *2 ounces white chocolate*, chopped; mix until chocolate melts. Stir in $1/4$ *cup coffee-flavor liqueur*. Refrigerate until cool, about 30 minutes, stirring occasionally.
In large bowl, with mixer at low speed, beat *1 cup confectioners' sugar* and $3/4$ *cup butter* (1 $1/2$ sticks), softened (do not use margarine; frosting will separate), just until mixed. Increase speed to high; beat 10 minutes or until light and fluffy, scraping bowl often with rubber spatula. Reduce speed to medium; gradually beat in white-chocolate mixture until smooth, occasionally scraping bowl.

4 Spoon batter into pans, spreading evenly. Bake 8 to 10 minutes until tops of cakes spring back when lightly touched with finger.

5 Sprinkle 2 clean cloth towels with cocoa. When cakes are done, immediately invert cakes onto towels.

6 Carefully peel waxed paper from cakes. If you like, cut off crisp edges. Starting at narrow end of each cake roll, roll cakes with towels, jelly-roll fashion. Place cake rolls, seam-side down, on wire racks; cool completely, about 1 hour.

MAKING ROULADE

Spreading first cake with frosting: With metal spatula, spread top of 1 cake evenly with about $3/4$ cup frosting.

Joining cakes: Along narrow end of second cake, place a narrow end of filled cake roll.

Rolling cakes together: Roll second cake around first cake roll.

7 Meanwhile, prepare White-Chocolate Butter-Cream Frosting.

8 Unroll 1 cooled cake; spread with about ³/₄ cup frosting (see Box, page 118). Starting at same narrow end, roll cake without towel. Unroll second cake; spread with about ³/₄ cup frosting. Join cakes and roll together (see Box, page 118).

9 Place cake roll on serving plate; spread remaining frosting over cake roll. Garnish with chocolate curls. Refrigerate cake if not serving right away.

CUTTING ROULADE

It is important to slice roulade cleanly, so that filling is seen at its best. For perfect results, dip long serrated knife in tall glass of hot water before slicing. Wipe blade with paper towel after each slice and dip again in hot water.

Baking batter in 2 jelly-roll pans creates thin layers that make this cake roll extra pretty and different

FILBERT AND MAPLE-CREAM ROLL

16 servings

Begin about 2 hours before serving or early in day

5 large eggs, separated

1 cup confectioners' sugar plus extra for sprinkling

²/₃ cup all-purpose flour

³/₄ teaspoon baking powder

1 teaspoon vanilla extract

¹/₄ teaspoon salt

Maple-Cream Filling (see Box, below right)

1 cup filberts (also called hazelnuts)

1 cup heavy or whipping cream

Lemon leaves for garnish

MAKING JELLY ROLL

1 Sprinkle clean cloth towel with confectioners' sugar. When cake is done, immediately invert onto towel.

2 With fingers, carefully peel waxed paper from cake. If you like, cut off crisp edges.

3 Starting at 1 narrow end, roll cake with towel. Place cake roll, seam-side down, on wire rack; cool completely, about 30 minutes.

1 Grease 15 ¹/₂" by 10 ¹/₂" jelly-roll pan; line pan with waxed paper; grease waxed paper.

2 In small bowl, with mixer at high speed, beat egg whites until soft peaks form; gradually sprinkle in ¹/₂ cup confectioners' sugar, beating until sugar completely dissolves and whites stand in stiff peaks.

3 Preheat oven to 375°F. In large bowl, using same beaters and with mixer at high speed, beat egg yolks and ¹/₂ cup confectioners' sugar until very thick and lemon-colored. Reduce speed to low; add flour, baking powder, vanilla extract, and salt; beat until well mixed, constantly scraping bowl with rubber spatula.

4 With rubber spatula or wire whisk, gently fold beaten egg whites into egg-yolk mixture, one-third at a time.

5 Spoon batter into pan, spreading evenly. Bake 12 to 15 minutes until cake springs back when lightly touched with finger.

6 Make jelly roll (see Box, above).

7 While jelly roll is cooling, prepare Maple-Cream Filling; cool.

8 In small skillet over medium heat, cook filberts until golden, stirring frequently; cool. Coarsely chop 12 toasted filberts and reserve some whole ones for garnish; finely chop remaining toasted filberts.

9 In small bowl, with mixer at medium speed, beat heavy or whipping cream until stiff peaks form.

MAPLE-CREAM FILLING
In 2-quart saucepan, with wire whisk or spoon, mix *2 tablespoons all-purpose flour* and *¹/₄ teaspoon salt*; slowly stir in *²/₃ cup milk* and *¹/₃ cup maple syrup* or maple-flavor syrup until smooth. Cook over medium heat, stirring constantly, until mixture boils and thickens; cook 1 minute. Remove saucepan from heat. In cup, with fork, beat *2 large egg yolks* slightly; stir in small amount of hot maple mixture. Slowly pour egg mixture back into remaining maple mixture in pan, stirring rapidly to prevent lumping; cook over low heat, stirring constantly, until mixture thickens and coats a spoon well, about 5 minutes (mixture should be about 170° to 175°F. but do not boil or it may curdle). Remove saucepan from heat; stir in *³/₄ teaspoon imitation maple flavor*. Pour filling into bowl. To keep skin from forming as filling cools, press plastic wrap directly onto surface of hot filling.

10 Unroll cooled jelly roll; spread top of cake evenly with Maple-Cream Filling. Spread half the whipped cream on filling; sprinkle with finely chopped filberts. Starting at same narrow end, roll cake without towel; place on platter.

11 Spoon remaining whipped cream into decorating bag with large rosette tube; pipe whipped cream on jelly roll to make attractive design.

12 Sprinkle reserved coarsely chopped filberts on whipped cream. Refrigerate roll if not serving right away.

TO SERVE
Garnish platter with lemon leaves and reserved whole filberts, if you like.

RASPBERRY-LACED VANILLA CAKE

24 servings

Begin about 3 hours before serving or early in day

1 1/2 cups margarine or butter (3 sticks), softened

1 1/4 cups sugar

3 cups all-purpose flour

2/3 cup milk

1 tablespoon baking powder

1/2 teaspoon salt

1 1/2 teaspoons vanilla extract

1/4 teaspoon baking soda

4 large eggs

Raspberry Butter-Cream Frosting (see Box, right)

1 12-ounce jar red raspberry preserves

1 Grease and flour three 9-inch round cake pans.

2 Preheat oven to 350°F. In large bowl, with mixer at low speed, beat margarine or butter and sugar just until blended. Increase speed to high; beat 10 minutes or until light and fluffy, scraping bowl often with rubber spatula. Reduce speed to low; add flour and next 6 ingredients; beat until well mixed, constantly scraping bowl. Increase speed to high; beat 2 minutes, occasionally scraping bowl.

3 Spoon batter into pans, spreading evenly. Bake 25 minutes or until toothpick inserted in center of cakes comes out clean. Cool in pans on wire racks 10 minutes. With spatula, loosen cake layers from edges of pans; invert onto wire racks to cool completely.

4 Meanwhile, prepare Raspberry Butter-Cream Frosting. Spoon 2 cups frosting into decorating bag with small star tube; set aside.

5 With serrated knife, cut each cake layer horizontally into halves to make 6 thin layers.

6 Assemble cake layers with raspberry preserves and frosting (see Box, below).

7 With metal spatula, spread remaining frosting on side and top of cake.

8 Use frosting in decorating bag to pipe lattice top and pretty border around top and bottom edges of cake. Refrigerate cake if not serving right away.

RASPBERRY BUTTER-CREAM FROSTING

In large bowl, with mixer at low speed, beat *3 cups confectioners' sugar* and *2 cups margarine* or butter (4 sticks), softened, until just mixed. Increase speed to high. Beat 10 minutes or until light and fluffy, scraping bowl often with rubber spatula. Reduce speed to medium; gradually beat in *1/4 cup raspberry-flavor liqueur* and *1 teaspoon vanilla extract* until smooth, occasionally scraping bowl.

ASSEMBLING CAKE LAYERS

Placing cake on plate: Place bottom half of 1 cake layer, cut-side up, on cake plate.

Spreading with raspberry preserves: With metal spatula, spread cake layer with 1/3 cup raspberry preserves. Top with top half of cake layer.

Spreading frosting: Spread second cake layer with about 1/2 cup frosting. Repeat layering, ending with cake layer.

RASPBERRY-STRAWBERRY CREAM CAKE

16 servings

Begin about 3 hours before serving or early in day

1 3/4 cups cake flour

3/4 cup milk

3/4 cup margarine or butter (1 1/2 sticks), softened

1 tablespoon baking powder

3/4 teaspoon salt

1/2 teaspoon baking soda

4 large eggs

1 1/2 cups plus 2 teaspoons sugar

1 tablespoon plus 1 teaspoon vanilla extract

Raspberry-Custard Filling (see Box, page 125)

2 pints strawberries

3 1/2 cups heavy or whipping cream

1 Grease and flour two 9-inch round cake pans.

2 Preheat oven to 375°F. Into large bowl, measure flour, milk, margarine or butter, baking powder, salt, baking soda, eggs, 1 1/2 cups sugar, and 1 tablespoon vanilla extract. With mixer at low speed, beat ingredients just until blended, constantly scraping bowl with rubber spatula. Increase speed to high; beat 3 minutes, occasionally scraping bowl.

3 Spoon batter into pans, spreading evenly. Bake 25 minutes or until toothpick inserted in center of cake comes out clean. Cool cake layers in pans on wire racks 10 minutes. With spatula, loosen cake layers from edges of pans; invert onto wire racks to cool completely.

4 Meanwhile, prepare Raspberry-Custard Filling.

5 Hull 1 pint strawberries and cut each in half; set aside.

6 With serrated knife, cut each cake layer horizontally into halves to make 4 thin layers in all.

7 In small bowl, with mixer at medium speed, beat heavy or whipping cream, remaining 2 teaspoons sugar, and remaining 1 teaspoon vanilla extract until stiff peaks form.

8 Place 1 cake layer on plate; spread with about 1 cup whipped-cream mixture. Arrange half the strawberry halves on top of cream.

PIPING WHIPPED CREAM

Coupler and tube

Heavy or whipping cream can be whipped to double its volume and will stay stiff for several hours. For perfect results, chill bowl, beater, and cream before beating. Whisk until stiff peaks form, but be careful not to overbeat as this causes cream to become granular and it will then turn to butter. Refrigerate whipped cream if not using immediately. After piping design onto cake, refrigerate until ready to serve. Here we show you how, with decorating bag and star tube, you can make a wide range of different shapes and designs.

Decorating bag fitted with coupler and tube

9 Top strawberries with second cake layer, pressing down gently but firmly; spread Raspberry-Custard Filling over layer.

10 Top Raspberry-Custard Filling with third cake layer; repeat with whipped cream and strawberry halves. Top with remaining cake layer.

11 Frost top and side of cake with one-third of remaining whipped cream. Spoon remaining whipped cream into decorating bag with large star tube; use to decorate top and side of cake.

12 From remaining 1 pint strawberries, arrange 3 whole strawberries on top of cake. Cut each of remaining berries in half; use to garnish side of cake. Refrigerate cake if not serving right away.

RASPBERRY-CUSTARD FILLING

Thaw *one 10-ounce package frozen quick-thaw raspberries in syrup*; drain, reserving *1/2 cup syrup*; set aside. In 2-quart saucepan, combine *1 envelope unflavored gelatin, 4 teaspoons sugar, 4 teaspoons all-purpose flour,* and *1/4 teaspoon salt*. In medium bowl, with wire whisk or fork, beat *2 large egg yolks* with *1 cup milk* and reserved raspberry syrup until well mixed; stir into gelatin mixture. Let stand 1 minute to soften gelatin slightly. Cook over low heat, stirring constantly, until mixture thickens and coats a spoon well, about 15 minutes (mixture should be about 170° to 175°F. but do not boil or it may curdle). Remove saucepan from heat; stir in raspberries. Cover and refrigerate custard until mixture mounds slightly when dropped from a spoon, about 30 minutes to 1 hour, stirring occasionally. In small bowl, with mixer at medium speed, beat *1/2 cup heavy or whipping cream* until stiff peaks form; with rubber spatula or wire whisk, fold into custard. Refrigerate filling until firm enough to spread, about 20 minutes.

IRISH-CREAM TRIANGLE CAKE

🍴 16 servings

⏱ Begin about 4 hours before serving or early in day

---

2 8-ounce packages semisweet-chocolate squares (16 1-ounce squares)

1 1/2 cups heavy or whipping cream

1/2 cup cream liqueur

1 package white-cake mix for 2-layer cake

4 tablespoons unsweetened cocoa

Strawberries for garnish

1 Coarsely chop semi-sweet chocolate. Place in large bowl. In 2-quart saucepan over medium heat, heat heavy or whipping cream and cream liqueur until tiny bubbles form around edge of pan; pour hot cream mixture into bowl with chocolate. With mixer at medium speed, beat until chocolate melts and mixture is smooth. Cover and refrigerate chocolate ganache until thickened, about 1 1/2 hours.

2 Meanwhile, preheat oven to 350°F. Grease and flour two 15 1/2" by 10 1/2" jelly-roll pans.

3 Prepare cake mix as label directs. Spoon half the batter into 1 jelly-roll pan, spreading evenly. Stir 3 tablespoons cocoa into remaining batter; spoon into second pan, spreading evenly.

4 Bake cakes 10 minutes or until toothpick inserted in center comes out clean. Cool cakes in pans on wire racks 10 minutes. With spatula, loosen cakes; invert onto wire racks to cool completely.

5 With serrated knife, using cardboard strip as guide, cut each cake lengthwise into halves, to make 4 equal strips in all.

6 With mixer at medium-high speed, beat chilled chocolate ganache until thick with an easy spreading consistency.

7 Place 1 white-cake layer on large cookie sheet; spread with 1/3 cup chocolate ganache. Top with 1 chocolate-cake layer; spread with 1/3 cup chocolate ganache.

8 Repeat layering, ending with chocolate-cake layer. Set aside remaining ganache.

9 Cover cake and place in freezer until chocolate-ganache filling is firm, about 1 hour.

10 Assemble and frost cake (see Box, right). Sprinkle remaining 1 tablespoon cocoa through sieve over cake.

11 Remove cake to serving plate; refrigerate if not serving right away.

12 To serve, garnish cake with straw–berries.

ASSEMBLING CAKE

Cutting cake diagonally: *Place frozen cake on work surface with long side parallel to edge. With long serrated knife, slice cake diagonally in half from upper rear corner to lower front corner, to make 2 long triangles. With pancake turners, place 1 cake half on foil-covered cardboard strip, cut-side facing outward.*

Spreading first cake half with chocolate ganache: *On uncut side of cake half on foil-covered cardboard strip, with metal spatula, evenly spread 1/3 cup chocolate ganache.*

Joining cake halves: *Place second cake half, cut-side facing outward, along-side first cake half. Gently press 2 halves together to form 1 large triangle.*

Frosting cake: *Spread sloping sides of triangle cake with remaining chocolate ganache.*

*Everyone is going to wonder
how you make this beautiful
cake. Don't tell them that it
really is easy!*

CARROT BUNDT CAKE

16 servings
Begin about 4 hours before serving or early in day

3 cups all-purpose flour

2 1/2 cups sugar

1 tablespoon baking soda

1 tablespoon ground cinnamon

1 teaspoon salt

4 large eggs

1 1/2 cups salad oil

1 teaspoon vanilla extract

2 cups packed shredded carrots (about 3 medium-sized carrots)

1 8-ounce can walnuts (2 cups), chopped

1 cup apple sauce

1 1/4 cups confectioners' sugar

1 Preheat oven to 325°F. Grease and flour 10-inch Bundt pan.

2 In large bowl, with spoon, mix flour, sugar, baking soda, cinnamon, and salt.

3 In small bowl, with fork, beat eggs slightly; stir in oil and vanilla extract. Stir egg mixture, shredded carrots, walnuts, and apple sauce into flour mixture just until flour is moistened.

4 Spoon batter into pan, spreading evenly. Bake 1 hour 20 minutes or until toothpick inserted in center of cake comes out clean. Cool cake in pan on wire rack 10 minutes.

5 With spatula, loosen cake from edge of pan; invert onto wire rack to cool completely.

CREAMY CHEESE FROSTING

In large bowl, with mixer at medium speed, beat *one and one-half 8-ounce packages cream cheese*, softened, *1/2 cup margarine* or butter (1 stick), softened, *1 tablespoon lemon juice*, and *1 1/2 teapoons vanilla extract* until smooth. Gradually beat in *5 1/2 cups confectioners' sugar* until smooth.

6 Prepare confectioners' sugar icing: In small bowl, with spoon, mix confectioners' sugar and *5 teaspoons water* until smooth and an easy spreading consistency.

7 Place cake on platter. With spatula, spread confectioners' sugar icing on cake.

ALTERNATIVE SHAPE

For a different look, you can bake two layers of carrot cake mixture, then sandwich layers together with frosting.

Carrot Layer Cake
In step 4, spoon batter into two greased and floured 9-inch round cake pans; bake for 40 to 45 minutes until toothpick inserted in center of cakes comes out clean. Cool cake layers in pans on wire racks 10 minutes; invert onto wire racks to cool completely. Make Creamy Cheese Frosting (see Box, above left).

Place 1 cake layer, rounded side down, on platter. With spatula, spread cake evenly with 1 cup frosting. Place second cake layer, rounded side up, on top of first cake layer. Spread top and side of cake with remaining frosting, swirling to make attractive design.

CHOCOLATE-CREAM CAKE

16 servings

Begin about 3 hours before serving or early in day

1 8-ounce package semisweet-chocolate squares (8 1-ounce squares)

6 large eggs, separated

1/3 cup sugar

1/3 cup all-purpose flour

1 4-ounce can sliced blanched almonds (1 cup)

Chocolate-Cream Filling (see Box, above right)

3 tablespoons unsweetened cocoa

1 Preheat oven to 350°F. Grease 10" by 3" springform pan.

2 Grate 4 squares semisweet chocolate; set aside.

3 In small bowl, with mixer at high speed, beat egg whites until stiff peaks form.

4 In large bowl, using same beaters and with mixer at high speed, beat egg yolks and sugar until very thick and lemon-colored. Reduce speed to low; add flour; beat until well mixed, occasionally scraping bowl with rubber spatula. With rubber spatula, stir in grated chocolate. With rubber spatula or wire whisk, gently fold beaten egg whites into egg-yolk mixture, one-third at a time.

5 Spoon batter into pan, spreading evenly. Bake 25 minutes or until toothpick inserted in center of cake comes out clean. Cool cake in pan on wire rack 5 minutes. With spatula, loosen cake from edge of pan; remove pan side. Loosen cake from pan bottom; slide onto wire rack to cool completely.

6 In skillet over medium heat, cook almonds until golden, stirring frequently; cool. Set aside.

7 Prepare Chocolate-Cream Filling. Spoon 2/3 cup filling into decorating bag with small star tube; set aside. Spoon another 2/3 cup filling into small bowl; reserve to cover side of cake.

8 In heavy small saucepan over low heat, heat remaining 4 squares chocolate and 2 tablespoons water, stirring frequently, until melted and smooth. Remove saucepan from heat.

9 With serrated knife, cut cake horizontally into 2 layers. Spread top cake layer with melted chocolate; let stand until chocolate sets slightly, about 10 minutes.

> ### CHOCOLATE-CREAM FILLING
> In large bowl, with mixer at medium speed, beat 3 cups heavy or whipping cream, 3/4 cup unsweetened cocoa, and 3/4 cup sugar until stiff peaks form.

10 Meanwhile, place bottom cake layer, cut-side up, on cake plate; spread with chocolate filling remaining in large bowl.

11 Cut top cake layer into 16 wedges. Place wedges on top of chocolate-cream-covered cake layer. Use chocolate filling in small bowl to cover side of cake. Pat toasted almonds onto side of cake. Sprinkle cocoa through sieve over top of cake. With knife, mark servings to show wedges. Use filling in decorating bag to pipe rosette on top of each wedge. Refrigerate cake if not serving right away.

MOCHA-CREAM BUTTERFLY CAKE

16 servings

Begin about 3 hours before serving or early in day

1 8-ounce package semisweet-chocolate squares (8 1-ounce squares)

8 large eggs, separated

1 cup sugar

1/2 cup all-purpose flour

Chocolate Butterflies (see Box, right)

1 teaspoon shortening

2 cups heavy or whipping cream

1/2 cup unsweetened cocoa

2 teaspoons instant-coffee granules or powder

1 Grate 6 squares chocolate (or, in food processor with knife blade attached, finely grind chocolate). Set aside.

2 In large bowl, with mixer at high speed, beat egg whites until stiff peaks form.

3 Preheat oven to 350°F. In another large bowl, using same beaters and with mixer at high speed, beat egg yolks and 1/2 cup sugar until very thick and lemon-colored, about 5 minutes. Reduce speed to low; add flour; beat until just mixed, occasionally scraping bowl with rubber spatula. With rubber spatula, stir in grated chocolate. Gently fold beaten egg whites into egg-yolk mixture, one-third at a time.

4 Evenly spread batter in ungreased 10" by 3" springform pan. Bake 40 to 45 minutes until top of cake springs back when touched with finger. Invert cake in pan on wire rack; cool completely in pan.

CHOCOLATE BUTTERFLIES

Making and folding waxed-paper rectangles: Cut waxed paper into five 4" by 2 1/2" rectangles. Fold each rectangle crosswise into halves to form 2" by 2 1/2" rectangle.

Making tracing of butterfly: With pencil, draw outline of half a butterfly on each folded rectangle using center fold for butterfly body (pressure of pencil point will mark bottom half of paper as well). Unfold rectangles and place on clean flat surface, tracing-side down. Tape rectangles to work surface about 2 inches apart with small pieces of cellophane or masking tape.

Piping chocolate butterfly: Pipe some chocolate mixture onto a waxed-paper rectangle in thin continuous lines over tracing and long centerfold to make a butterfly. Repeat with remaining chocolate to make several butterflies. Remove and discard tapes.

Molding butterflies: With pancake turner, carefully lift each piece of waxed paper and place, chocolate-side up, in 2 1/2-inch muffin-pan cup or in section of empty egg carton so that waxed paper is slightly bent on center fold. Refrigerate Chocolate Butterflies at least 1 hour or until chocolate is set.

Removing waxed paper: With cool hands, carefully peel off waxed paper. Keep butterflies refrigerated until ready to use.

5 Meanwhile, prepare Chocolate Butterflies: Cut waxed-paper rectangles and use to make tracings of butterflies (see Box, page 130). In heavy 1-quart saucepan over low heat, heat shortening and remaining 2 semisweet-chocolate squares, stirring frequently, until melted and smooth; cool 10 minutes for easier piping. Spoon chocolate mixture into paper cone with tip cut to make 1/8-inch-diameter hole (or use small decorating bag with small writing tube). Pipe butterflies and allow to cool (see Box, page 130).

6 When cake is cooled, prepare mocha cream: In large bowl, with mixer at medium speed, beat heavy or whipping cream, cocoa, instant coffee, and remaining 1/2 cup sugar until stiff peaks form. Spoon 1 1/4 cups mocha cream into decorating bag with medium star tube; set aside.

7 With metal spatula, loosen cake from side of pan; remove pan side. Loosen cake from pan bottom; remove pan bottom. With serrated knife, cut cake horizontally into 3 layers.

8 Place bottom cake layer, cut-side up, on cake plate; spread with 3/4 cup mocha cream in bowl. Repeat layering, ending with third cake layer, cut-side down.

9 Spread top of cake with thin layer of mocha cream; use remaining mocha cream to frost side of cake. Use mocha cream in decorating bag to pipe pretty design on top of cake. Refrigerate cake if not serving right away.

10 To serve, garnish cake with Chocolate Butterflies.

CANNOLI CAKE

16 servings
Begin early in day or day ahead

6 large eggs, separated

1 cup sugar

³/₄ cup all-purpose flour

1 tablespoon baking powder

¹/₂ teaspoon salt

2 teaspoons vanilla extract

2 large oranges

2 tablespoons orange-flavor liqueur (optional)

1 32-ounce container ricotta cheese

1 8-ounce package cream cheese, softened

1 cup confectioners' sugar

¹/₄ cup plus ¹/₃ cup semi-sweet-chocolate mini pieces

Vanilla-Cream Frosting (see Box, page 133)

1 Preheat oven to 375°F. In small bowl, with mixer at high speed, beat egg whites until soft peaks form; gradually sprinkle in ¹/₂ cup sugar, beating until sugar completely dissolves and whites stand in stiff peaks.

2 In large bowl, using same beaters and with mixer at low speed, beat egg yolks, flour, baking powder, salt, remaining ¹/₂ cup sugar, 1 teaspoon vanilla, and 2 tablespoons water until blended. With rubber spatula, gently fold beaten egg whites into egg-yolk mixture, one-third at a time.

3 Spoon batter into ungreased 10" by 3" springform pan. Bake 30 to 35 minutes until cake is golden and top springs back when lightly touched.

4 Invert cake in pan on wire rack; cool completely in pan.

MAKING FEATHER DESIGN

Piping circles on cake: Using paper cone with tip cut to make ¹/₈-inch-diameter hole, pipe melted chocolate on top of cake in concentric circles, starting in center and moving to edge of cake.

Drawing spokes toward center: Before chocolate hardens, quickly with tip of toothpick or small knife, draw lines in spoke fashion, about 1 ¹/₂ inches apart around edge of cake; alternate direction of each spoke, first from edge to center of cake, then from center to edge.

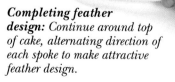

Completing feather design: Continue around top of cake, alternating direction of each spoke to make attractive feather design.

5 From oranges, grate 2 teaspoons peel and squeeze ¹/₃ cup juice (if not using liqueur, increase juice to ¹/₂ cup). Stir liqueur into juice; set aside.

6 In large bowl, with mixer at low speed, beat ricotta, cream cheese, grated orange peel, confectioners' sugar, and remaining 1 teaspoon vanilla extract until smooth. Stir in ¹/₄ cup semisweet-chocolate mini pieces.

WAXED-PAPER CONE

Cut square of waxed paper; fold in half into triangle. Lay triangle on flat surface so wide side is at top. Fold left-hand corner down to center point. Take right-hand corner; wrap it completely around folded left-hand corner, forming cone. Both corners meet at center point of original triangle.

Fold in these ends twice to hold together.

Fill cone two thirds full; fold top over.

7 With metal spatula, loosen cake from edge of pan; remove pan side. Loosen cake from pan bottom; remove pan bottom. With serrated knife, cut cake horizontally into 2 layers. Brush orange-juice mixture evenly over cut side of both layers.

8 Place bottom cake layer, cut-side up, on cake plate. Spoon ricotta-cheese filling on center of cake layer. Spread some filling out to edge, leaving center rounded to achieve a dome effect.

9 Cut a wedge out of remaining cake layer; arrange wedge and rest of cake layer over filling. (Cutting wedge will allow cake layer to bend, without cracking, to fit over dome shape.)

10 Prepare Vanilla-Cream Frosting; spread over top and down side of cake.

11 In heavy small saucepan over low heat, heat remaining ⅓ cup semisweet-chocolate mini pieces, stirring frequently, until melted and smooth.

12 Into waxed-paper cone (see Box, page 132), spoon melted chocolate. (Or, use small decorating bag with small writing tube.) With chocolate, make feather design on top of cake (see Box, page 132).

13 Refrigerate cake until filling is firm for easier cutting, about 3 hours.

VANILLA-CREAM FROSTING

In small bowl, with mixer at medium speed, beat *3 tablespoons margarine* or butter, softened, *3 tablespoons milk, 1 ³/₄ cups confectioners' sugar,* and *³/₄ teaspoon vanilla extract* until smooth, adding more milk if necessary until mixture has an easy spreading consistency. In large bowl, using same beaters and with mixer at medium speed, beat *2 cups heavy or whipping cream* until stiff peaks form; fold confectioners'-sugar mixture into whipped cream.

Cannoli Cake is layered with orange-flavored ricotta cheese and chocolate filling

FLOWERS FOR GARNISH

Many of the flowers that add color and freshness to the table as the centerpiece can be used to garnish desserts.

When choosing flowers to use with or on foods, keep two important points in mind. First, be sure the ones you want to use are nontoxic. If in doubt, check with your local horticultural society or Poison Control center. All of the flowers shown in this picture are nontoxic and safe to use with foods.

Next, use flowers that have been grown without the help of pesticides and other chemical sprays. Flowers from the florist have usually been sprayed. Flowers from a home garden, grown without insecticides, are best.

Flowers from a garden should be picked early in the day. Rinse blossoms, leaves, and stems briefly in cool water and shake dry. Keep flowers in water in the refrigerator and use as soon as you can, as they tend to wilt quickly.

Use flowers in many ways – as buds, or open flower heads, with or without the stem and/or leaves; or pull off individual petals and sprinkle them over the dessert.

Carnation

Pansy

Viola

Borage

Chrysanthemum

Variegated Geranium

Cornflower

Gypsophila
(Baby's Breath)

Lavender

Pink
Geranium

Marigold

Nasturtium

Day Lily

Honeysuckle

Gladiolus

Wild Rose

Freesia

Sweet Pea

Rose

COFFEE ANGEL RING

16 servings

Begin about 3 hours before serving or early in day

1 ¼ cups confectioners' sugar

1 cup cake flour

1 ⅔ cups egg whites (12 to 14 large egg whites)

3 tablespoons instant coffee granules or powder

1 ½ teaspoons cream of tartar

½ teaspoon salt

1 teaspoon vanilla extract

1 ¼ cups sugar

Coffee Icing (see Box, above right)

½ cup canned roasted, salted almonds, coarsely chopped

1 Preheat oven to 375°F. In small bowl, with fork, stir confectioners' sugar and cake flour; set aside.

2 In large bowl, with mixer at high speed, beat egg whites, instant coffee, cream of tartar, and salt until soft peaks form; beat in vanilla extract. Beating at high speed, gradually sprinkle in sugar, 2 tablespoons at a time, beating until sugar completely dissolves and whites stand in stiff peaks. With rubber spatula or wire whisk, fold in flour mixture just until flour disappears.

3 Pour batter into ungreased 10-inch tube pan. Bake cake 35 to 40 minutes, until top springs back when lightly touched with finger. Invert cake in pan on funnel or bottle; cool completely in pan.

4 With metal spatula, carefully loosen cake from pan; place on cake plate.

5 Prepare Coffee Icing; spread icing on top of cake. Sprinkle nuts on icing.

COFFEE ICING

In small bowl, stir *1 tablespoon instant coffee granules* or powder with *2 tablespoons very hot tap water* until coffee dissolves. Stir in *1 ½ cups confectioners' sugar* until smooth.

NOTE FOR DIETERS!
Omit the Coffee Icing and nuts for a delicious low-calorie, no-fat cake!

Cheesecakes

Our cheesecakes are the ideal party dessert! They'll catch the eye on the dessert table because they are handsome to look at and sizeable enough to please a large group. They are smooth and creamy in texture, deliciously satisfying to eat; and the different flavors make it possible to fit cheesecake into any elegant menu, whatever the occasion. All of these recipes are do-ahead; but they can also be made up to a month ahead and frozen. Make as directed and cool completely; freezer-wrap closely and freeze. Thaw them, wrapped, several hours or overnight in the refrigerator; *then* add any fruit or garnish just before serving.

MAPLE-PECAN CHEESECAKE

20 servings
Begin early in day or day ahead

Pastry

³/₄ cup all-purpose flour

¹/₂ cup margarine or butter (1 stick), softened

3 tablespoons sugar

1 large egg yolk

Filling

1 ¹/₄ cups pecan halves

3 8-ounce packages cream cheese, softened

¹/₂ cup sugar

4 large eggs

¹/₄ cup light corn syrup

2 tablespoons all-purpose flour

¹/₂ teaspoon salt

¹/₂ teaspoon imitation maple flavor

Extra pecans for garnish (optional)

1 First prepare pastry dough: In small bowl, with mixer at low speed, beat flour, margarine or butter, sugar, and egg yolk just until mixed. Shape dough into 2 balls; wrap with plastic wrap and refrigerate 1 hour.

2 Preheat oven to 400°F. Press one ball of dough onto bottom of 10" by 3" springform pan; keep remaining dough refrigerated.

3 Bake crust 8 minutes or until golden; cool in pan on wire rack. Turn oven control to 350°F.

4 While crust is cooling, prepare filling: Reserve ¹/₄ cup pecan halves for garnish; chop remaining pecans. In large bowl, with mixer at medium speed, beat cream cheese just until smooth; slowly beat in sugar, scraping bowl often with rubber spatula. Add eggs, corn syrup, flour, salt, and maple flavor; beat 2 minutes, occasionally scraping bowl. Stir in chopped pecans.

5 Press remaining dough around side of pan to within 1¹/₂ inches of top. Pour cream-cheese mixture into crust.

6 Bake cheesecake 45 minutes. Turn off oven; let cheesecake remain in oven 30 minutes. Remove cheesecake from oven; cool completely in pan on wire rack. Cover and refrigerate at least 3 hours or until well chilled.

7 When cheesecake is firm, with spatula, loosen pan side from cheesecake and remove; loosen cake from pan bottom; slide onto plate.

8 Just before serving, arrange reserved pecan halves on top of cheesecake, using a little extra corn syrup to help them stick. If you like, arrange extra pecans around edge of plate.

Stirring chopped pecans into cream-cheese mixture

LATTICE-TOP CHOCOLATE CHEESECAKE

16 servings
Begin early in day
or day ahead

Pastry

2 cups all-purpose flour

⅓ cup sugar

½ teaspoon baking powder

¼ teaspoon salt

10 tablespoons margarine
  or butter (1 ¼ sticks)

2 large egg yolks

2 tablespoons milk

Filling

1 8-ounce package
  semisweet-chocolate
  squares (8 1-ounce
  squares)

3 8-ounce packages cream
  cheese, softened

1 ½ cups sugar

1 16-ounce container sour
  cream (2 cups)

3 large eggs

1 teaspoon vanilla extract

½ teaspoon salt

Confectioners' sugar

1 First prepare pastry dough: In medium bowl, with fork, stir flour, sugar, baking powder, and salt. With pastry blender or two knives used scissor-fashion, cut margarine or butter into flour mixture until mixture resembles coarse crumbs.

2 With fork, stir in egg yolks and milk. With hand, mix just until dough holds together. On lightly floured surface, knead dough until smooth, about 2 minutes. Shape dough into 2 balls; wrap with plastic wrap and refrigerate 1 hour.

3 Preheat oven to 375°F. Grease bottom of 9" by 3" springform pan.

4 Press one ball of dough onto bottom of pan; keep remaining dough refrigerated. Bake crust 15 to 20 minutes until golden; cool in pan on wire rack.

5 While crust is cooling, prepare filling: In heavy 2-quart saucepan over low heat, heat chocolate, stirring frequently, until melted and smooth. Remove saucepan from heat; let chocolate cool to room temperature.

6 In large bowl, with mixer at medium speed, beat cream cheese just until smooth; slowly beat in sugar, scraping bowl often with rubber spatula. Add sour cream, eggs, vanilla extract, and salt; beat 1 minute, occasionally scraping bowl. Stir melted chocolate into cream-cheese mixture. Pour chocolate cream-cheese mixture into crust.

7 Divide remaining dough into 10 pieces. On lightly floured surface, with hand, roll each piece into 9-inch log.

8 Place 5 pastry logs, about 1 ½ inches apart, across top of cheesecake filling.

TO SERVE
Sprinkle lattice with
confectioners' sugar.

9 Lay remaining pastry logs across first pastry logs to form lattice top. Trim ends of logs even with side of pan.

10 Bake cheesecake 50 minutes, covering pan loosely with foil after 30 minutes if pastry begins to brown too quickly. Turn off oven; let cheesecake remain in oven 50 minutes. Remove cheesecake from oven; cool completely in pan on wire rack. Cover and refrigerate at least 4 hours or until well chilled.

11 When cheesecake is firm, with spatula, loosen pan side from cheesecake and remove; loosen cake from pan bottom; slide onto plate.

DELUXE CHEESECAKE

🍴 20 servings
🕐 Begin early in day
or day ahead

Pastry

1 1/4 cups all-purpose flour

*3/4 cup margarine or butter
(1 1/2 sticks), softened*

1/4 cup sugar

1 large egg yolk

*Grated peel of 1 small
lemon*

Filling

*5 8-ounce packages cream
cheese, softened*

1 3/4 cups sugar

5 large eggs

1/4 cup milk

*3 tablespoons all-purpose
flour*

2 large egg yolks

*Grated peel of 1 small
lemon*

*Fresh fruit brushed with
melted jelly (optional)*

1 First prepare pastry dough: In small bowl, with mixer at low speed, beat flour, margarine or butter, sugar, egg yolk, and grated lemon peel until well mixed. Shape dough into ball; wrap with plastic wrap and refrigerate 1 hour.

2 Preheat oven to 400°F. Press one-third of dough onto bottom of 10" by 2 1/2" springform pan; keep remaining dough refrigerated.

3 Bake crust 8 minutes or until golden; cool in pan on wire rack. Turn oven control to 475°F.

4 While crust is cooling, prepare filling: In large bowl, with mixer at medium speed, beat cream cheese just until smooth; slowly beat in sugar, scraping bowl often with rubber spatula. Add eggs, milk, flour, egg yolks, and lemon peel; beat 5 minutes, occasionally scraping bowl.

5 Press remaining dough around side of pan to within 1 inch of top. Pour cream-cheese mixture into crust.

6 Bake cheesecake 12 minutes. Turn oven control to 300°F.; bake 35 minutes longer. Turn off oven; let cheesecake remain in oven 30 minutes.

7 Remove cheesecake from oven; cool completely in pan on wire rack. Cover and refrigerate at least 4 hours or until well chilled.

8 When cheesecake is firm, with spatula, loosen pan side from cheesecake and remove; loosen cake from pan bottom; slide onto serving plate.

9 If you like, arrange fresh fruit on top of cheesecake and brush with melted jelly.

Deluxe Cheesecake is served plain here, but it can be topped with fresh fruit and melted jelly if you like

PUMPKIN-PRALINE CHEESECAKE

🍴 16 servings
🕐 Begin early in day
    or day ahead

45 gingersnap cookies

*6 tablespoons margarine or
butter (³/₄ stick), softened*

*4 8-ounce packages cream
cheese, softened*

*1 cup packed light brown
sugar*

*3 tablespoons all-purpose
flour*

*2 teaspoons ground
cinnamon*

*1 ¹/₂ teaspoons ground
ginger*

1 teaspoon ground allspice

1 teaspoon vanilla extract

³/₄ teaspoon salt

4 large eggs

*1 16-ounce can solid pack
pumpkin (not pumpkin
pie mix) (2 cups)*

¹/₃ cup sugar

*1 3-ounce can pecans
(1 cup), chopped*

*1 tablespoon light corn
syrup*

1 Place gingersnap
cookies, in batches, in
heavy-duty, closed plastic
bag and with rolling pin,
roll cookies into fine
crumbs. Or, in food
processor with knife blade
attached or in blender at
medium speed, blend
gingersnap cookies, in
batches, until fine crumbs
form. (You should have
about 2 ¹/₂ cups crumbs.)

2 In 9" by 2 ¹/₂" springform pan, with hand,
mix cookie crumbs and
margarine or butter; press
mixture onto bottom and
up side of pan to within
1 inch of top of pan.
Set aside.

3 Preheat oven to
350°F. In large bowl,
with mixer at medium
speed, beat cream cheese
just until smooth; slowly
beat in brown sugar,
scraping bowl often with
rubber spatula. Add flour,
cinnamon, ginger, allspice,
vanilla extract, salt, eggs,
and pumpkin; beat
3 minutes, occasionally
scraping bowl.

4 Pour cream-cheese
mixture into crust.
Bake cheesecake 1 hour.
Turn off oven; let cheesecake remain in oven
1 hour. Remove cheese-
cake from oven; cool
completely in pan on wire
rack. Cover and refriger-
ate at least 6 hours or until
well chilled.

5 Meanwhile, make
praline: In 1-quart
saucepan over low heat,
heat sugar and *3 tablespoons
water* until sugar dissolves,
stirring gently. Increase
heat to medium and boil
rapidly without stirring
until syrup turns a light
golden brown, about
6 minutes.

6 Working quickly,
stir in chopped pecans
and spread praline in a
thin layer on cookie sheet.

7 Cool praline, then
chop into small
pieces.

8 Store praline in tightly
covered container
until ready to use.

9 When cheesecake is
firm, with spatula,
loosen pan side from
cheesecake and remove;
loosen cake from pan
bottom; slide onto plate.
Gently spread corn syrup
on top of cake and
sprinkle with praline.

WHITE-CHOCOLATE CHEESECAKE

🍴 20 servings
🕐 Begin early in day or day ahead

1 8 ½-ounce package chocolate wafers

¾ cup margarine or butter (1 ½ sticks), softened

1 pound white chocolate or 5 3-ounce Swiss confectionery bars or 3 6-ounce packages white baking bars

4 8-ounce packages cream cheese, softened

¼ cup sugar

4 large eggs

2 tablespoons vanilla extract

White-Chocolate Curls (page 110) and unsweetened cocoa for garnish

3 Preheat oven to 350°F. In heavy 3-quart saucepan over very low heat, heat white chocolate, stirring frequently, until melted and smooth. If necessary, with wire whisk, beat chocolate until smooth. Remove saucepan from heat; let chocolate cool to room temperature.

4 In large bowl, with mixer at medium speed, beat cream cheese and remaining ½ cup margarine or butter (1 stick) just until smooth; slowly beat in sugar, scraping bowl often with rubber spatula. Add melted white chocolate, eggs, and vanilla extract; beat just until smooth.

5 Pour cream-cheese mixture into crust. Bake cheesecake 1 hour; cool in pan on wire rack. Cover and refrigerate at least 4 hours or until well chilled.

6 When cheesecake is firm, with spatula, loosen pan side from cheesecake and remove; loosen cake from pan bottom; slide onto plate.

7 Pile White-Chocolate Curls on top of cheesecake; sprinkle cocoa through sieve over chocolate curls.

1 Place chocolate wafers, in batches, in heavy-duty, closed plastic bag and with rolling pin, roll wafers into fine crumbs. Or, in food processor with knife blade attached or in blender at medium speed, blend wafers, in batches, until fine crumbs form.

2 In greased 10" by 2 ½" springform pan, with hand, mix wafer crumbs and 4 tablespoons margarine or butter (½ stick); press mixture onto bottom and up side of pan to within ½ inch of top of pan. Set aside.

TO SERVE
Serve White-Chocolate Cheesecake on dark plates to create a dramatic color contrast.

ESPRESSO CHEESECAKE

16 servings
Begin early in day
or day ahead

About 20 pair amaretti
cookies

6 tablespoons margarine or
butter ($^3/_4$ stick), softened

6 1-ounce squares
semisweet chocolate

4 8-ounce packages cream
cheese, softened

$^2/_3$ cup sugar

3 large eggs

$^1/_3$ cup milk

2 teaspoons instant
espresso-coffee powder

Chocolate Leaves (page
111), and small red
gumdrop candies for
garnish

1 Place amaretti cookies, in batches, in heavy-duty, closed plastic bag and with rolling pin, roll cookies into fine crumbs. Or, in food processor with knife blade attached or in blender at medium speed, blend cookies, in batches, until fine crumbs form. (You should have about 1 $^1/_2$ cups crumbs.)

2 In 9" by 3" springform pan, with hand, mix cookie crumbs and margarine or butter; press mixture onto bottom and up side of pan to within 1 inch of top of pan. Set aside.

3 Preheat oven to 350°F. In heavy 1-quart saucepan over low heat, heat semisweet chocolate, stirring frequently, until melted and smooth. Remove saucepan from heat.

4 In large bowl, with mixer at medium speed, beat cream cheese just until smooth; slowly beat in sugar, scraping bowl often with rubber spatula. Add melted chocolate, eggs, milk, and espresso-coffee powder; beat 3 minutes, occasionally scraping bowl.

5 Pour chocolate cream-cheese mixture into crust.

6 Bake cheesecake 45 minutes. Cool in pan on wire rack. Cover and refrigerate at least 4 hours or until well chilled.

7 When cheesecake is firm, with spatula, loosen pan side from cheesecake and remove; loosen cake from pan bottom; slide onto plate.

TO SERVE
Arrange Chocolate Leaves and candies in center of cheesecake.

MELTING CHOCOLATE

Great care must be taken when melting chocolate, to prevent it from burning. Overheated chocolate scorches easily and becomes bitter; so melt all forms slowly, using gentle heat. You can use any of these ways:

- Place chocolate in top of double boiler and melt over hot, *not boiling*, water.

- Or place in heavy 1-quart saucepan; melt over low heat – if pan is too thin, it will transfer heat too fast and burn chocolate.

- Or place chocolate in custard cup and set in pan of hot water.

- Or, for small amounts, leave chocolate blocks in original wrapper; place on piece of foil and set in warm spot on range.

- To speed melting, break up chocolate into smaller pieces; stir frequently.

- If melting chocolate in double boiler or custard cup, do not boil water to speed melting. Any moisture getting into chocolate will thicken or curdle chocolate.

- If chocolate thickens or curdles, add vegetable shortening (not margarine or butter) a little at a time and stir until of desired consistency.

TORTA DI RICOTTA

16 servings
Begin early in day
or day ahead

Pastry

2 cups all-purpose flour

*³/₄ cup margarine or butter
(1 ¹/₂ sticks), softened*

¹/₄ cup sugar

*2 tablespoons dry Marsala
wine*

¹/₂ teaspoon salt

2 large egg yolks

Filling

*1 32-ounce container
ricotta cheese (about
4 cups)*

1 cup sugar

*1 cup heavy or whipping
cream*

¹/₄ cup all-purpose flour

1 teaspoon vanilla extract

¹/₄ teaspoon salt

6 large eggs

*Grated peel of 2 medium-
sized oranges*

*Grated peel of 2 medium-
sized lemons*

Confectioners' sugar

Orange twists for garnish

1 First prepare pastry
dough: In large bowl,
with mixer at low speed,
beat flour, margarine or
butter, sugar, Marsala, salt,
and egg yolks just until
mixed. Shape dough into
a ball. Wrap with plastic
wrap and refrigerate
1 hour.

2 Preheat oven to
350°F. Into 10" by
2¹/₂" springform pan, press
three-fourths of dough
onto bottom and up side
of pan to within ³/₄ inch of
top; keep remaining
dough refrigerated. Bake
crust 15 minutes or until
golden; cool in pan on
wire rack.

3 While crust is cooling,
prepare filling: Into
large bowl, press ricotta
through fine sieve. With
mixer at medium speed,
beat ricotta just until
smooth; slowly beat in
sugar, scraping bowl often
with rubber spatula. Add
heavy or whipping cream,
flour, vanilla extract, salt,
eggs, orange and lemon
peel; beat until well
blended, occasionally
scraping bowl. Pour
cheese mixture into crust.

4 On lightly floured
surface, with floured
rolling pin, roll out
remaining dough into
10" by 5" rectangle. Cut
dough lengthwise into ten
¹/₂-inch-wide strips. Place
5 dough strips about
1 inch apart across filling.
Arrange remaining strips
at right angles to make a
lattice. Trim ends of strips
even with crust.

5 Bake cheesecake
1¹/₄ hours. Turn off
oven; let cheesecake
remain in oven 1 hour.
Remove cheesecake from
oven; cool completely in
pan on wire rack. Cover
and refrigerate at least
4 hours or until well
chilled.

6 When cheesecake is
firm, with spatula,
loosen pan side from
cheesecake and remove;
loosen cake from pan
bottom; slide onto plate.

7 Sprinkle cheesecake
with confectioners'
sugar. Arrange orange
twists around cake.

RICOTTA CHEESE

Ricotta cheese is a pure white, creamy, satiny-smooth
cheese with a fine, slightly moist texture and very
bland, sweetish flavor. Its nearest "relative" is cottage
cheese, but ricotta is smoother and creamier.

• Ricotta is made from
the whey left from the
making of other cheeses.
It is uncured, and so
should be used within a
few days after purchase.

• Cheesecake made of
ricotta – Torta di Ricotta –
is one of the great classic
dishes of Italy. For
another Italian-inspired
dessert using ricotta, see
Cannoli Cake (pages
132 to 133).

Fruitcakes

A beautifully decorated fruitcake makes a perfect centerpiece for holiday festivities and a delicious dessert to crown a feast or to accompany eggnog, mulled cider, coffee, or tea. Follow our easy storage tips if you want to enjoy your fruitcake even after the holidays are over.

MIXED-NUT FRUITCAKE

24 servings

Begin day ahead or up to 1 month ahead

2 8-ounce containers red candied cherries (2 cups)

1 12-ounce package pitted prunes (2 cups)

1 10-ounce container pitted dates (2 cups)

1 4-ounce container green candied cherries ($^1/_2$ cup)

$^1/_2$ cup cream sherry

2 12-ounce cans salted mixed nuts (5 cups)

1 6-ounce can pecans (2 cups)

1 $^1/_2$ cups all-purpose flour

1 cup sugar

1 teaspoon baking powder

6 large eggs, slightly beaten

1 In very large bowl or 6-quart saucepot, mix first 5 ingredients; let stand 15 minutes or until almost all liquid is absorbed, stirring often.

2 Meanwhile, generously grease 10-inch tube pan and line with foil, smoothing out foil as much as possible so cake does not have wrinkles on side and bottom; grease foil.

3 Preheat oven to 300°F. Stir mixed nuts and pecans into fruit mixture in bowl. Remove 1 $^1/_2$ cups fruit-and-nut mixture; set aside. Stir flour, sugar, and baking powder into remaining fruit-and-nut mixture in large bowl until well coated. Stir in eggs until well mixed.

4 Spoon batter into pan, spreading evenly. Sprinkle reserved fruit-and-nut mixture on top. Cover pan loosely with foil. Bake 2 hours.

5 Remove foil and bake 30 minutes longer or until knife inserted in cake comes out clean.

6 Cool cake in pan on wire rack 30 minutes; remove from pan and carefully peel off foil. Cool cake completely on rack.

7 Wrap fruitcake tightly in plastic wrap; refrigerate overnight so cake will be firm and easy to slice.

TO STORE FRUITCAKE

Keep cake, wrapped tightly in plastic wrap; store in cool place or refrigerator. If desired, sprinkle cake first with wine or brandy.

Alternatively, wrap cake in wine- or brandy-dampened cloth; over-wrap with plastic wrap. Redampen cloth weekly.

WEST INDIAN FRUITCAKE

24 servings

Begin early in day or day ahead

1 1/2 cups dry red wine or cranberry-juice cocktail

3/4 cup pitted prunes

3/4 cup dark seedless raisins

1 3.5-ounce container diced candied citron (scant 1/2 cup)

1 1/2 cups sugar

1 cup margarine or butter (2 sticks), softened

3 cups all-purpose flour

1 1/2 teaspoons baking powder

1 1/2 teaspoons baking soda

1 teaspoon vanilla extract

3/4 teaspoon salt

1/2 teaspoon ground cinnamon

3 large eggs

1 teaspoon grated lime peel

Lime Glaze (see Box, above right)

1 3.5-ounce container mixed candied fruit, chopped (scant 1/2 cup)

1 tablespoon light corn syrup

1 In 2-quart saucepan over high heat, heat first 4 ingredients to boiling.

2 Remove saucepan from heat; let stand 30 minutes to soften fruit.

3 In blender at low speed, blend fruit mixture, half at a time, until smooth; set aside.

4 Preheat oven to 325°F. Grease 10-inch Bundt pan or tube pan.

5 In large bowl, with mixer at low speed, beat sugar and margarine or butter just until blended. Increase speed to high; beat 10 minutes or until light and fluffy, scraping bowl often with rubber spatula. Reduce speed to low; add flour, baking powder, baking soda, vanilla extract, salt, cinnamon, eggs, and fruit mixture; beat until well mixed, constantly scraping bowl. Increase speed to high; beat 1 minute, occasionally scraping bowl. Stir in grated lime peel.

LIME GLAZE

In medium bowl, with spoon, stir *1 1/2 cups confectioners' sugar, 4 teaspoons hot tap water, 2 teaspoons lime juice, 1/2 teaspoon grated lime peel,* and *1/4 teaspoon salt* until smooth.

6 Spoon batter into pan, spreading evenly. Bake 1 hour or until toothpick inserted in cake comes out clean. Cool cake in pan on wire rack 10 minutes; remove cake from pan. Cool completely on rack.

7 To serve, prepare Lime Glaze. Spoon glaze over cake.

8 In small bowl, stir mixed candied fruit with corn syrup. Garnish top of cake with candied fruit.

West Indian Fruitcake with its festive garnish

MINCEMEAT CAKE

24 servings

Begin day ahead
or up to 1 month
ahead

1 10-ounce container pitted
dates (2 cups)

1 8-ounce package dried
figs, sliced (1 cup)

1 6-ounce can pecans
(2 cups)

1 4-ounce container green
candied cherries (¹/₂ cup)

1 4-ounce container red
candied cherries (¹/₂ cup)

4 cups all-purpose flour

6 large eggs, separated

1 ¹/₂ cups packed brown
sugar

1 cup sugar

1 cup margarine or butter
(2 sticks), softened

4 teaspoons baking powder

¹/₂ teaspoon ground
cinnamon

¹/₂ teaspoon ground
nutmeg

¹/₂ teaspoon ground allspice

1 27-ounce jar mincemeat

2 tablespoons light corn
syrup

1 Reserve ¹/₂ cup
each dates, figs, and
pecans, ¹/₄ cup each green
and red cherries. Dice
remaining dates and
cherries. In bowl, combine
diced dates, cherries, and
remaining figs and pecans;
coat with 1 cup flour.

2 Preheat oven to
300°F. Grease 10-inch
tube pan with removable
bottom.

3 In small bowl,
with mixer at
high speed, beat
egg whites
until stiff
peaks
form;
set aside.

4 In large bowl, using
same beaters and with
mixer at low speed, beat
brown sugar, sugar, and
margarine or butter just
until blended. Increase
speed to high; beat
10 minutes or until light
and fluffy, scraping bowl
often with rubber spatula.
Reduce speed to low; add
egg yolks, baking powder,
cinnamon, nutmeg, and
allspice; beat until well
mixed, constantly scraping
bowl. With spoon, stir in
mincemeat, fruit mixture,
and remaining flour. With
rubber spatula, gently fold
in beaten egg whites.

5 Spoon batter into
pan, spreading
evenly.

6 Bake 2 hours or until
toothpick inserted in
cake comes out clean and
cake pulls away slightly
from side of pan.

7 Cool cake in pan on
wire rack 30 minutes;
remove cake from pan and
cool completely on wire
rack.

8 When cake is cool,
prepare topping: In
2-quart saucepan over
medium heat, heat
reserved fruit and nuts
with corn syrup 5 minutes,
stirring; arrange on cake.

9 Let fruit-and-nut
topping cool and set.

10 Wrap fruitcake
tightly in foil or
plastic wrap; refrigerate
overnight so cake will be
firm and easy to slice.

PIES, TARTS, PASTRIES, AND HOT FRUIT DESSERTS

147-218

PIES, TARTS, PASTRIES, AND HOT FRUIT DESSERTS

Pie dough and pastry – timeless and simple – can be used in so many different and exciting ways! Just start with our basic recipes and a variety of fillings – you'll end up with old-fashioned favorites like Sugar-Frosted Apple Pie, Strawberry-Rhubarb Deep-Dish Pie, and Down-Home Peach Pie that your family will love. Make the most of summer and autumn harvests by trying Berries and Custard in Coconut Shell, or Individual Peach Cobblers – fruit desserts with a special touch. There are classic, old-world pastries like Baklava and Apple Strudel, comforting hot fruit desserts like Banana Brown Betty and Apple Pandowdy that are so quick to make, and magnificent recipes like Swan Cream Puffs and Fancy Phyllo Cups to add the crowning touch to an elegant meal.

CONTENTS

Pies

Pie for dessert can be as simple and homey or as elaborate and elegant as you wish. Much of its success depends on the crust, which should enhance, not compete with, the flavor of the filling and be crisp and tender, never soggy. For variety, on 2-crust pies, try a plain top crust one time, a lattice top the next. For crumb-crust pie, try different fillings and toppings. Be creative!

PASTRY FOR 2-CRUST PIE

2 cups all-purpose flour

1 teaspoon salt

³/4 cup shortening or butter-flavor shortening

5 to 6 tablespoons cold water

1 Make dough as for Pastry for 1-Crust Pie (see Box, right), steps 1 through 3.

2 Shape mixture into 2 balls, one slightly larger.

3 On lightly floured surface, with floured rolling pin, roll out larger ball of dough into round about ¹/8 inch thick and 1¹/2 inches larger all around than upside-down 8- to 9-inch pie plate.

4 Roll dough round gently onto rolling pin; transfer to pie plate and unroll. Gently ease dough into bottom and up side of pie plate to line evenly; trim dough edge, and fill as recipe directs.

5 For top crust, roll smaller ball of dough as for bottom crust; with sharp knife, cut few slashes or design in center of round; center top crust over filling in bottom crust.

6 Make Decorative Pie Edge (pages 152, 153, and 308); bake pie as directed in recipe.

MAKING PASTRY IN FOOD PROCESSOR

To save time, pastry can be made in the food processor, with excellent results. This is especially helpful if you are catering for a crowd and have a large number of pies to make.

1 Into food processor with knife blade attached, measure flour, shortening, and salt. Process 1 to 2 seconds until mixture forms fine crumbs.

2 Add cold water; process 1 to 2 seconds until dough forms on blades.

3 Remove dough from bowl; with hands, shape dough into ball.

PASTRY FOR 1-CRUST PIE

1 ¹/3 cups all-purpose flour

¹/2 teaspoon salt

¹/2 cup shortening or butter-flavor shortening

3 to 4 tablespoons cold water

1 In medium bowl, with fork, stir flour and salt.

2 With pastry blender or two knives used scissor-fashion, cut shortening or butter-flavor shortening into flour mixture until mixture resembles coarse crumbs.

3 Sprinkle cold water, a tablespoon at a time, into mixture. Mix lightly with fork after each addition, until dough is just moist enough to hold together.

8 Roll dough round gently onto rolling pin; transfer to pie plate and unroll.

4 In same bowl, with lightly floured hands, shape dough into smooth ball.

5 On lightly floured surface, with floured rolling pin, roll out dough into round about ⅛ inch thick.

9 Gently ease dough into bottom and up side of pie plate to line evenly.

10 Make Decorative Pie Edge (pages 152, 153, and 308); fill and bake pie as directed in recipe.

6 Roll from center to edge of dough to keep dough circular. Add more flour if dough begins to stick to work surface. Push sides in by hand if necessary and lift rolling pin slightly near edges to avoid making them too thin.

7 With sharp knife, cut dough round 1½ inches larger all around than upside-down 8- to 9-inch pie plate.

BAKED PIECRUST

Many 1-crust pies are made with uncooked fillings, so you will need to bake the piecrust beforehand. A crisp baked pastry crust that is to be filled with a chilled mixture should be thoroughly cooled before the filling is added.

1 Preheat oven to 425°F. Prepare Pastry for 1-Crust Pie.

2 With fork, prick bottom and side of crust in many places to prevent puffing during baking.

3 Bake 15 minutes or until golden.

4 Cool on wire rack; fill as directed in recipe.

DECORATIVE PIE EDGES

These eye-catching edges that finish off a pie so beautifully are not at all hard to make. Choose from Fluted, Sharp Fluted, and Ruffled Edges for either 2- or 1-crust pies; Leaf, Braided, and Heart Edges are suitable for 1-crust pies only.

1-Crust Pies

1 Line pie plate with dough (page 151); trim dough edge with kitchen shears, leaving about 1-inch overhang all around pie-plate rim.

2 Fold overhang under, then bring up over pie-plate rim.

3 Make decorative edge of your choice, then bake pie as directed in recipe.

2-Crust Pies

1 Trim edge of top crust with kitchen shears, leaving about 1-inch overhang all around pie-plate rim. Fold overhang under, then bring up over pie-plate rim.

2 Make decorative edge of your choice, then bake pie as directed in recipe.

FLUTED EDGE

Down-Home Peach Pie (page 174) with Fluted Edge

1 Pinch to form stand-up edge. Place 1 index finger on inside edge of dough and, with index finger and thumb of other hand, pinch dough to make flute.

2 Repeat around edge, leaving ¼-inch space between each flute.

SHARP FLUTED EDGE

Sugar-Frosted Apple Pie (page 161) with Sharp Fluted Edge

1 Pinch to form stand-up edge. Place pointed edge of small star- or diamond-shaped cookie cutter on inside edge of dough and, with index finger and thumb of other hand, pinch dough to make sharp flute.

2 Repeat around edge, leaving ¼-inch space between each flute.

LEAF OR HEART EDGE

*Honey-Crunch Pecan Pie
(page 164) with Leaf Edge*

1 *Prepare Pastry for 2-Crust Pie (page 150); use half to line pie plate.*

2 *Roll out remaining dough ¹/₈ inch thick. With sharp knife or small cookie cutter, cut out shapes (leaves or hearts).*

3 *Press each shape onto lightly moistened piecrust edge, overlapping shapes slightly or varying angles, to create desired effect.*

RUFFLED EDGE

*Sour-Cherry Pie
(page 172) with Ruffled Edge*

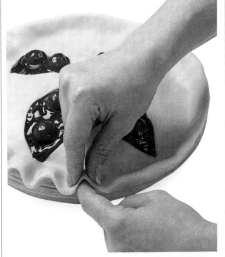

1 *Pinch to form stand-up edge. Place 1 index finger under outside edge of dough and, with index finger and thumb of other hand, pinch dough to form ruffle.*

2 *Repeat around edge, leaving ¹/₄-inch space between ruffles.*

BRAIDED EDGE

*Walnut-Crunch Pumpkin Pie
(page 165) with Braided Edge*

1 *Prepare Pastry for 2-Crust Pie (page 150); use half to line pie plate.*

2 *Roll out remaining dough ¹/₈ inch thick and cut into ¹/₄-inch-wide strips.*

3 *Gently braid strips together and press onto lightly moistened piecrust edge.*

4 *Join ends of braid together to cover edge completely.*

PEAR AND PINEAPPLE DEEP-DISH PIE

8 servings

Begin about 2 hours before serving or early in day

2 29-ounce cans pear halves

1 20-ounce can pineapple chunks in juice

3 tablespoons cornstarch

1/2 teaspoon ground nutmeg

1/2 teaspoon ground cinnamon

3 tablespoons margarine or butter

1 1/3 cups all-purpose flour

1/2 teaspoon salt

1/2 cup shortening or butter-flavor shortening

1 large egg yolk, slightly beaten

1 Drain pears, reserving 1 3/4 cups juice; thinly slice pear halves. Drain pineapple (save juice for use another day). Set pears and pineapple aside.

2 In 3-quart saucepan, mix cornstarch, nutmeg, cinnamon, and reserved pear juice. Cook over medium heat, stirring constantly, until mixture thickens and boils. Remove saucepan from heat; stir in pear slices and pineapple chunks.

3 Into 9" by 9" baking dish, pour pear and pineapple filling.

Pouring fruit mixture into baking dish

4 Cut margarine or butter into small pieces; sprinkle over fruit. Let cool to room temperature, about 30 minutes.

5 Meanwhile, prepare pastry dough: In medium bowl, with fork, stir flour with salt. With pastry blender or two knives used scissor-fashion, cut shortening into flour mixture until mixture resembles coarse crumbs. Sprinkle *3 tablespoons cold water*, a tablespoon at a time, into mixture, mixing lightly with fork after each addition until dough is just moist enough to hold together. Shape dough into ball.

6 Preheat oven to 425°F. On lightly floured surface, with floured rolling pin, roll out dough 1/8 inch thick to fit top of baking dish with 1-inch overhang; place over filling.

7 Turn overhang under to make stand-up edge. Make Rope Edge (see Box, right).

8 Cut a few slashes in crust to allow steam to escape during baking. Brush crust lightly with egg yolk.

9 Bake pie 25 to 30 minutes until filling is bubbly and crust is golden brown. Cool pie on wire rack 15 minutes before serving. Or, cool completely to serve cold later.

ROPE EDGE
Press right thumb into edge of crust at an angle, then pinch dough between thumb and knuckle of index finger. Place thumb in groove left by index finger.

Repeat all around edge of crust to create twisted rope effect.

CHOCOLATE CHEESE PIE

🍴 12 servings

🕐 Begin about 4 hours before serving or early in day

About 50 vanilla wafers

¹/₂ cup margarine or butter (1 stick), softened

2 1-ounce squares unsweetened chocolate

2 8-ounce packages cream cheese, softened

1 14-ounce can sweetened condensed milk

1 teaspoon vanilla extract

Candied Orange Peel (see Box, right)

1 Preheat oven to 375°F. Place vanilla wafers, in batches, in heavy-duty, closed plastic bag and with rolling pin, roll wafers into fine crumbs. Or, in food processor with knife blade attached or in blender at medium speed, blend wafers, in batches, until fine crumbs form. (You should have 2 cups crumbs.)

2 In 9-inch pie plate, with hand, mix vanilla-wafer crumbs with margarine or butter; press mixture onto bottom and up side of pie plate.

3 Bake crust 8 minutes or until golden; cool on wire rack.

4 In heavy small saucepan over low heat, heat chocolate, stirring frequently, until melted and smooth; remove saucepan from heat.

5 In large bowl, with mixer at medium speed, beat cream cheese, condensed milk, and vanilla extract until blended; beat in melted chocolate until smooth.

6 Pour chocolate mixture into crust. Cover and refrigerate until set.

7 Meanwhile, prepare Candied Orange Peel.

CANDIED ORANGE PEEL

Remove orange part of peel from 2 medium-sized oranges in long pieces (use fruit in salad another day); cut orange peel into ¹/₈-inch-thick matchstick-thin strips. In 2-quart saucepan over high heat, heat orange peel, ¹/₂ cup water, and ¹/₄ cup sugar to boiling. Reduce heat to medium and cook 10 to 15 minutes until orange peel is limp and translucent. Place 2 tablespoons sugar in small bowl. Drain orange peel and toss in bowl with sugar.

Spread orange peel on cookie sheet to dry.

TO SERVE
Arrange garland of Candied Orange Peel on top of Chocolate Cheese Pie, to give pie a colorful finishing touch.

STRAWBERRY-RHUBARB DEEP-DISH PIE

10 servings
Begin about 3 hours before serving or early in day

2 pints strawberries

1 pound rhubarb (without tops), or 1 16-ounce package frozen rhubarb

1 1/4 cups sugar

1/3 cup all-purpose flour

2 tablespoons quick-cooking tapioca

1/2 teaspoon vanilla extract

1/4 teaspoon salt

Pastry for 2-Crust Pie (page 150), or 1 10- to 11- ounce package piecrust mix

1 tablespoon margarine or butter

1 tablespoon milk

1 Hull strawberries and cut each in half. Cut rhubarb into 1/2-inch pieces. (If using frozen rhubarb, thaw and drain it.)

2 In large bowl, with rubber spatula, gently toss halved strawberries, rhubarb pieces, sugar, flour, tapioca, vanilla extract, and salt.

3 Let strawberry and rhubarb mixture stand 30 minutes to soften tapioca, stirring occasionally.

4 While strawberry and rhubarb mixture is standing, prepare pastry dough, or prepare piecrust mix as label directs.

5 On lightly floured surface, with floured rolling pin, roll out two-thirds of dough into 16-inch round.

6 Gently ease dough into bottom and up side of 9 1/2" by 1 1/2" deep-dish pie plate to line evenly; trim dough edge, leaving 1 1/2-inch overhang.

7 Into crust, spoon strawberry and rhubarb mixture.

8 Cut margarine or butter into small pieces; sprinkle on top of fruit mixture.

9 Preheat oven to 425°F.

10 Roll out remaining dough into 11-inch round. With fluted pastry wheel or knife, cut dough round into ten 3/4-inch-wide strips.

11 Over filling, place 5 strips, 1 inch apart; do not seal ends.

12 With remaining 5 strips, complete Diamond Lattice (see Box, page 157).

13 Trim ends of strips; moisten edge of bottom crust with water; press ends of strips gently to bottom crust to seal. Bring overhang up over strips; pinch edges to seal; make Ruffled or other Decorative Pie Edge (pages 152, 153, and 308). Brush lattice (not edge) with milk.

14 Bake pie 50 minutes or until fruit mixture begins to bubble and crust is golden brown.

15 Let pie stand 1 hour to allow juices to set slightly; serve warm. Or, cool pie completely to serve later.

Tossing strawberry and rhubarb mixture

ALTERNATIVE TO LATTICE

A quick-and-easy alternative pastry topping to the Diamond Lattice in our main picture (page 157) is this Cartwheel, in which the pastry strips are placed over the filling like the spokes of a wheel.

Cartwheel

1 With fluted pastry wheel or knife, cut dough into twelve 1/2-inch strips.

2 Arrange 6 strips over filling in "V" shapes.

3 Use more strips to make smaller "V" shapes inside larger ones.

4 If you like, cut out small shapes from dough trimmings and place in center of pie.

DIAMOND LATTICE

Taking pastry strips back:
Fold back every other strip three-fourths of its length.

Placing second cross-strip:
Arrange another cross-strip on filling, parallel to central strip and about 1 inch away.

Placing central cross-strip: *Arrange 1 strip diagonally across center of filling to start forming diamond shape, then take folded part of strips over central strip.*

Folding back alternate strips: *Fold back strips that were not folded back before.*

Replacing folded part of strips: *Take folded part of strips over second diagonal cross-strip. Continue folding back alternate strips and placing cross strips diagonally across filling to weave diamond pattern.*

BRANDY ALEXANDER PIE

10 servings
Begin about 2 hours before serving or early in day

1 8 1/2-ounce package chocolate wafers

4 tablespoons margarine or butter (1/2 stick), softened

1/3 cup brandy

1 package chocolate-flavor instant pudding and pie filling for 4 servings

1 package vanilla-flavor instant pudding and pie filling for 4 servings

1 1/2 cups milk

1/4 cup chocolate-flavor liqueur

1 cup heavy or whipping cream

Semisweet Chocolate Curls (see Box, right) for garnish

1 Place chocolate wafers, in batches, in heavy-duty, closed plastic bag; with rolling pin, roll chocolate wafers into fine crumbs. Or, in food processor with knife blade attached or in blender at medium speed, blend in batches.

2 In 9-inch pie plate, with hand, mix chocolate-wafer crumbs, margarine or butter, and 3 tablespoons brandy; press onto bottom and up side of pie plate.

Pressing chocolate-wafer mixture onto bottom and up side of pie plate

3 In large bowl, prepare instant puddings as labels direct, but mix both packages together and use only 1 1/2 cups milk in total; stir in chocolate-flavor liqueur and remaining brandy.

4 In small bowl, with mixer at medium speed, beat heavy or whipping cream until soft peaks form. With wire whisk or rubber spatula, gently fold cream into pudding mixture. Spoon mixture into crust.

5 Garnish pie with chocolate curls. Refrigerate at least 1 hour before serving.

SEMISWEET CHOCOLATE CURLS

With heat of your hand, slightly warm *two 1-ounce squares semisweet chocolate* to soften.

With vegetable peeler, slowly and firmly draw blade along smooth surface of chocolate to make chocolate curls.

Use wide side of chocolate for wide curls, thin side for thin curls. Transfer curls with toothpick.

If you like, you can use white chocolate instead of semisweet chocolate; see White-Chocolate Curls (page 110).

TO SERVE
Rich, dark, and chocolatey, Brandy Alexander Pie should be served chilled to be enjoyed at its best.

BLUEBERRY PIE

10 servings

Begin about 3 hours before serving or early in day

2 1/3 cups all-purpose flour

3/4 teaspoon salt

3/4 cup shortening or butter-flavor shortening

1 large egg

1 tablespoon white vinegar

2 pints fresh or frozen (thawed) blueberries (5 cups)

1 teaspoon grated lemon peel

1/2 teaspoon ground cinnamon

1/2 cup plus 2 teaspoons sugar

1 tablespoon margarine or butter

1 In large bowl, with fork, stir 2 cups flour with salt. With pastry blender or two knives used scissor-fashion, cut shortening into flour mixture until mixture resembles coarse crumbs. In cup, beat egg slightly; stir in vinegar and *3 tablespoons cold water*. Add egg mixture to flour mixture, mixing lightly with fork until dough will hold together. With hands, shape dough into 2 balls, one slightly larger.

2 On lightly floured surface with floured rolling pin, roll out larger ball of dough into round about 1 1/2 inches larger all around than upside-down 9-inch pie plate. Ease dough into pie plate to line evenly.

3 If using frozen blueberries, they should be drained. In large bowl, with rubber spatula, gently toss blueberries, lemon peel, cinnamon, 1/2 cup sugar, and remaining 1/3 cup flour.

4 Spoon blueberry mixture into crust. Cut margarine or butter into small pieces; sprinkle on top of blueberry mixture.

5 Preheat oven to 425°F. Roll out remaining dough as for bottom crust. Moisten edge of bottom crust with water; place top crust over filling.

6 Trim dough edge, leaving 1 1/2-inch overhang. Fold overhang under; make Sharp Fluted or other Decorative Pie Edge (pages 152, 153, and 308).

7 With sharp knife, cut 4-inch "X" in center of top crust.

8 Fold back points of "X" to make square opening in center of pie.

9 Sprinkle top of pie with remaining 2 teaspoons sugar.

10 Bake pie 40 minutes or until blueberry filling begins to bubble and crust is golden. If crust browns too quickly, cover edge loosely with foil. Cool pie on wire rack before serving.

Folding back points to make square

COCONUT-BANANA CREAM PIE

🍴 10 servings

🕐 Begin about 4 hours before serving or early in day

1 3 1/2-ounce can flaked coconut (1 1/3 cups)

2/3 cup old-fashioned or quick-cooking oats, uncooked

5 tablespoons margarine or butter

3 cups milk

1/3 cup cornstarch

1/4 teaspoon salt

3 large egg yolks

1/2 cup plus 2 teaspoons sugar

1 1/2 teaspoons vanilla extract

3 large bananas

1/2 cup heavy or whipping cream

Toasted sliced almonds for garnish

1 Preheat oven to 300°F. In 9-inch pie plate, with hand, mix coconut, oats, and 3 tablespoons softened margarine or butter.

2 Pat coconut mixture onto bottom and up side of pie plate.

3 Bake crust 15 minutes or until golden; cool on wire rack.

4 In 2-quart saucepan, combine milk, cornstarch, salt, egg yolks, 1/2 cup sugar, and remaining 2 tablespoons margarine or butter. Cook over medium-low heat, stirring constantly, until mixture boils and thickens; boil 1 minute. Remove saucepan from heat; stir in vanilla extract.

5 Cut 2 bananas into 1/4-inch-thick slices. Line cooled pie crust with sliced bananas; pour custard filling over banana.

6 Cover custard filling with plastic wrap; refrigerate until cold.

7 In small bowl, with mixer at medium speed, beat heavy or whipping cream with remaining 2 teaspoons sugar until stiff peaks form. With metal spatula, spread whipped-cream mixture over pie.

8 Cover and refrigerate pie until ready to serve.

> **TO SERVE**
> Slice remaining banana. Garnish pie with banana slices and toasted almonds.

SUGAR-FROSTED APPLE PIE

🍴 10 servings

🕐 Begin 2 hours before serving or early in day

8 medium-sized Golden Delicious apples

2 tablespoons all-purpose flour

2 teaspoons lemon juice

1/4 teaspoon salt

1/2 cup plus 1 tablespoon sugar

3/4 teaspoon plus 1/8 teaspoon ground cinnamon

Pastry for 2-Crust Pie (page 150)

1 tablespoon margarine or butter

Milk

7 slices American cheese

1 Peel and core apples; cut into thin slices (there should be about 8 cups). In large bowl, with rubber spatula, lightly toss apple slices, flour, lemon juice, salt, 1/2 cup sugar, and 3/4 teaspoon cinnamon; set aside.

2 Prepare pastry dough. On lightly floured surface, with floured rolling pin, roll out larger ball of dough into round about 1 1/2 inches larger all around than upside-down 9-inch pie plate. Ease dough into pie plate to line evenly; trim dough edge, leaving 1-inch overhang. Reserve dough trimmings.

3 Spoon apple mixture into crust. Cut margarine or butter into small pieces; sprinkle over apple filling.

4 Preheat oven to 425°F. Roll out remaining dough as for bottom crust; place over filling. Trim dough edge, leaving 1-inch overhang. Fold overhang under; make Sharp Fluted or other Decorative Pie Edge (pages 152, 153, and 308).

5 Reroll dough trimmings. With floured leaf-shaped cookie cutter or knife, cut 7 leaves, rerolling dough if necessary. Arrange leaves on top of pie. Lightly brush top of pie with milk.

6 With tip of knife, cut hole in top crust to allow steam to escape during baking.

7 In small bowl, mix remaining 1 tablespoon sugar with remaining 1/8 teaspoon cinnamon. Evenly sprinkle sugar mixture over pie. Set pie on cookie sheet and bake 45 minutes or until crust is golden and apples are tender.

8 Remove pie to wire rack; cool slightly. Cut each cheese slice into leaf shape. Gently tuck cheese leaves under pastry leaves on pie.

CUSTARD PEACH PIE

🍴 10 servings

🕐 Begin about 3 hours before serving or early in day

Pastry for 1-Crust Pie (see Box, page 150), or ¹/₂ 10- to 11-ounce package piecrust mix

5 medium-sized peaches (about 1 ¹/₂ pounds)

1 8-ounce container sour cream

3 large egg yolks

1 cup sugar

¹/₄ cup all-purpose flour

1 teaspoon vanilla extract

Streusel Topping

4 tablespoons margarine or butter (¹/₂ stick)

¹/₂ cup all-purpose flour

¹/₄ cup sugar

1 Prepare pastry dough, or prepare piecrust mix as label directs.

2 Preheat oven to 425°F. On lightly floured surface, with floured rolling pin, roll out dough into round about 1¹/₂ inches larger all around than upside-down 9-inch pie plate; ease dough into pie plate to line evenly.

3 Trim dough edge, leaving 1-inch overhang. Fold overhang under; make Fluted or other Decorative Pie Edge (pages 152, 153, and 308).

4 Peel 4 peaches and cut into ¹/₄-inch-thick slices with sharp knife.

5 In piecrust, arrange peach slices in concentric circles, overlapping them slightly.

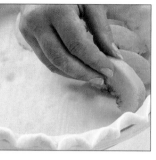

6 In medium bowl, with wire whisk or fork, beat sour cream, egg yolks, sugar, flour, and vanilla extract just until blended; pour over peaches in pie plate.

7 Bake pie 30 minutes, or just until custard mixture is beginning to set.

8 Meanwhile, prepare Streusel Topping: In small bowl, with hand, combine margarine or butter, flour, and sugar until mixture resembles coarse crumbs.

STREUSEL TOPPING
Streusel is a crust topping of flour, butter, and sugar, sprinkled and baked on breads, cakes, and muffins. The topping, to which spices are sometimes added, is of German origin, and was probably a favorite recipe brought over by 19th century immigrants.

9 After pie has baked 30 minutes, evenly sprinkle Streusel Topping over peaches and custard.

Sprinkling Streusel Topping over peaches and custard

10 Bake 15 minutes longer or until streusel is golden and knife inserted in center of pie comes out clean.

11 If crust browns too rapidly, cover loosely with foil.

12 Cool pie on wire rack 1 hour; serve warm. Or, cool completely to serve later.

Testing pie for doneness

TO SERVE
Cut remaining peach
into ¹/₄-inch-thick
slices; use to garnish
center of pie.

HONEY-CRUNCH PECAN PIE

10 servings

Begin about 4 hours before serving or early in day

Pastry for 2-Crust Pie (page 150), or
1 10- to 11-ounce package piecrust mix

4 large eggs

1 cup light corn syrup

1/4 cup packed brown sugar

1/4 cup sugar

2 tablespoons margarine or butter (1/4 stick), melted

1 tablespoon bourbon whiskey (optional)

1 teaspoon vanilla extract

1/2 teaspoon salt

1 3-ounce can pecans (1 cup), chopped

Honey-Crunch Topping (see Box, above right)

1 Prepare pastry dough or prepare piecrust mix as label directs. Divide dough into 2 pieces, 1 slightly larger.

2 Preheat oven to 350°F. On lightly floured surface, with floured rolling pin, roll out larger piece of dough into round about 1 1/2 inches larger all around than upside-down 9-inch pie plate.

3 Ease dough into pie plate to line evenly; trim dough edge, leaving 1/2-inch overhang. Fold overhang under. Make Leaf or other Decorative Pie Edge (pages 152, 153, and 308) with remaining dough.

4 In medium bowl, beat eggs slightly; stir in corn syrup, brown sugar, sugar, margarine or butter, bourbon, vanilla extract, and salt; stir in chopped pecans. Spoon into crust; bake pie 40 minutes.

5 Meanwhile, prepare Honey-Crunch Topping.

6 When pie has baked 40 minutes, remove from oven; spread topping over filling.

Spreading Honey-Crunch Topping over pecan filling

HONEY-CRUNCH TOPPING

In medium saucepan over medium heat, combine *1/3 cup packed brown sugar, 3 tablespoons honey,* and *3 tablespoons margarine* or butter; cook 2 to 3 minutes, stirring constantly, until sugar dissolves. Stir in *1 1/2 cups pecan halves.* Remove saucepan from heat.

7 Return pie to oven and bake 10 to 15 minutes longer until topping is bubbly and golden brown. Cover edge of piecrust with foil if necessary, to prevent overbrowning.

8 Cool pie on wire rack before serving.

Honey-Crunch Pecan Pie, perfect for Thanksgiving

WALNUT-CRUNCH PUMPKIN PIE

🍴 10 servings
🕐 Begin about 3 hours before serving or early in day

Pastry for 2-Crust Pie (page 150), or 1 10- to 11-ounce package piecrust mix

1 16-ounce can solid pack pumpkin (not pumpkin pie mix) (2 cups), or 2 cups Mashed Cooked Pumpkin (see Box, page 87)

1 12-ounce can evaporated milk

2 large eggs

³/₄ cup packed brown sugar or granulated brown sugar

1 ¹/₂ teaspoons ground cinnamon

¹/₂ teaspoon ground ginger

¹/₂ teaspoon ground nutmeg

¹/₂ teaspoon salt

Walnut-Crunch Topping (see Box, below)

¹/₂ cup heavy or whipping cream for garnish

1 Prepare pastry dough, or prepare piecrust mix as label directs. Divide dough into 2 pieces, 1 slightly larger.

2 Preheat oven to 400°F. On lightly floured surface, with floured rolling pin, roll out larger piece of dough to round about 1 ¹/₂ inches larger all around than upside-down 9-inch pie plate.

3 Ease dough into pie plate to line evenly; trim dough edge, leaving ¹/₂-inch overhang. Fold overhang under. With remaining dough, make Braided or other Decorative Pie Edge (pages 152, 153, and 308).

4 In large bowl, with mixer at medium speed, beat pumpkin and next 7 ingredients until well mixed.

5 Place pie plate on oven rack; pour pumpkin filling into crust. Bake pie 40 minutes or until knife inserted 1 inch from edge comes out clean.

6 Cool pie on wire rack about 1¹/₂ hours.

7 When pie is cool, preheat broiler if manufacturer directs. Prepare Walnut-Crunch Topping; spoon evenly over pie. About 5 to 7 inches from source of heat, broil pie 3 minutes or until topping is golden and sugar dissolves. Cool pie again on wire rack.

8 In small bowl, with mixer at medium speed, beat heavy or whipping cream until stiff peaks form. Garnish pie with cream.

WALNUT-CRUNCH TOPPING

In small saucepan over low heat, melt *4 tablespoons margarine* or *butter* (¹/₂ stick). Stir in *one 4-ounce can walnuts* (1 cup), chopped, and *³/₄ cup packed brown sugar* until well mixed.

PEANUT-BUTTER CUSTARD PIE

🍴 10 servings

🕐 Begin about 5 hours before serving or early in day

Pastry

1 ¼ cups all-purpose flour
¼ teaspoon salt
6 tablespoons margarine or butter (¾ stick)
1 large egg

Filling

3 large egg yolks
3 cups milk
½ cup sugar
⅓ cup cornstarch
¼ teaspoon salt
2 tablespoons margarine or butter (¼ stick)
¾ cup creamy peanut butter
1 ¼ teaspoons vanilla extract
¼ cup unsalted peanuts
½ cup heavy or whipping cream
2 tablespoons confectioners' sugar

1 First prepare pastry dough: In large bowl, with fork, stir flour and salt. With pastry blender or two knives used scissor-fashion, cut margarine or butter into flour mixture until mixture resembles coarse crumbs. In small bowl, with fork, lightly beat egg. Add egg to flour mixture, mixing lightly with fork until dough is just moist enough to hold together. With hands, shape dough into ball.

2 Preheat oven to 425°F. On lightly floured surface, with floured rolling pin, roll out dough into round about 1 ½ inches larger all around than upside-down 9-inch pie plate; ease dough into pie plate to line evenly.

3 Trim dough edge, leaving 1-inch overhang; reserve dough trimmings. Fold overhang under; make Fork-Scalloped Edge (see Box, right).

4 With remaining pastry scraps, cut several leaf-shaped pieces. Place on small cookie sheet.

5 With fork, prick bottom and side of piecrust in many places to prevent puffing and shrinkage during baking. Line piecrust with foil and evenly spread pie weights, dry beans, or uncooked rice over bottom.

6 Bake piecrust 10 minutes; remove weights, beans, or rice and foil and again prick piecrust.

7 Bake 5 minutes longer or until pastry is golden brown (if pastry puffs up, gently press it to pie plate with spoon). Bake leaves on cookie sheet on another rack during last 8 minutes of piecrust baking time or until golden brown. Cool on wire rack.

8 While piecrust is cooling, in 2-quart saucepan, with fork or wire whisk, beat egg yolks, milk, sugar, cornstarch, and salt until blended; add margarine or butter. Cook over medium-low heat, stirring constantly, until mixture boils and thickens and coats a spoon well, about 15 minutes; boil 1 minute.

9 Remove saucepan from heat; with whisk, stir in peanut butter and vanilla extract. Pour peanut-butter filling into cooled piecrust.

10 Reserve several whole peanuts for garnish; chop remaining peanuts. Sprinkle chopped peanuts around edge of filling. Cover and refrigerate pie until set, at least 4 hours.

TO SERVE
Top center of pie with whipped cream; garnish with pastry leaves and reserved whole peanuts.

---

11 In small bowl, with mixer at medium speed, beat heavy or whipping cream and confectioners' sugar until stiff peaks form.

FORK-SCALLOPED EDGE
Bring dough up over pie-plate rim; pinch to form stand-up edge. Place thumb against outside edge and press toward center while pressing down next to it with 4-tined fork. Repeat around edge, leaving alternate fork marks and ruffle effect.

For a wider ruffle, press down twice with fork, side-by-side, to make 8 marks between each ruffle, or overlap them to make 6 marks.

WALNUT FUDGE PIE

10 servings

Begin about 4 hours before serving or early in day

1 8-ounce can walnuts (2 cups), chopped

Pastry for 2-Crust Pie (page 150), or 1 10- to 11-ounce package piecrust mix

4 tablespoons margarine or butter (1/2 stick)

2 1-ounce squares unsweetened chocolate

1 cup sugar

1/3 cup milk

1/4 cup chocolate syrup

1 teaspoon vanilla extract

4 large eggs

Vanilla ice cream (optional)

TO SERVE
Accent the chocolate goodness of each serving of Walnut Fudge Pie with a scoop of vanilla ice cream.

---

1 Preheat oven to 350°F. Place walnuts in jelly-roll pan; toast in oven about 10 minutes or until golden brown, shaking pan occasionally. Set aside to cool. Do not turn oven off.

2 Meanwhile, prepare pastry dough or prepare piecrust mix as label directs. Divide dough into 2 pieces, 1 slightly larger.

3 On lightly floured surface, with floured rolling pin, roll out larger ball of dough into round about 1 1/2 inches larger all around than upside-down 9-inch pie plate. Ease dough into pie plate to line evenly; trim dough edge, leaving 1/2-inch overhang. Fold overhang under.

4 In 2-quart saucepan over low heat, heat margarine or butter and chocolate, stirring frequently, until melted and smooth. Remove saucepan from heat. With wire whisk, beat in sugar, milk, chocolate syrup, vanilla extract, and 3 eggs until blended. Stir in chopped walnuts. Pour walnut mixture into crust.

5 Roll out remaining dough 1/8 inch thick. With different-sized heart-shaped cookie cutters, cut out hearts for decorating edge of crust and top of pie.

Placing heart shapes over walnut filling

6 In cup, with fork, slightly beat remaining egg. Brush egg lightly over piecrust edge. Place hearts on edge of crust and walnut filling to make pretty design.

7 Brush hearts in center and on edge with beaten egg.

8 Bake pie 1 hour or until knife inserted in center of pie comes out clean. Cool pie on wire rack.

BLUEBERRY CELEBRATION PIE

10 servings

Begin 4 hours
before serving or
early in day

Pastry

1 1/2 cups all-purpose flour
1 tablespoon sugar
1/2 teaspoon salt
1/2 cup shortening or butter-flavor shortening
2 tablespoons finely chopped blanched almonds

Blueberry Filling

2 cups fresh or frozen (thawed) blueberries
2 tablespoons sugar
1 tablespoon cornstarch
1 tablespoon lemon juice
1 tablespoon grated lemon peel
2 tablespoons margarine or butter (1/4 stick)
2 teaspoons crème de cassis (optional)

White-Chocolate Filling

6 1 1/4-ounce white-chocolate candy bars with almonds
1 tablespoon shortening
1/4 teaspoon vanilla extract
1/8 teaspoon almond extract
1 cup heavy or whipping cream
2 tablespoons confectioners' sugar

Cream Layer

1 cup heavy or whipping cream
1/4 cup confectioners' sugar
1/4 teaspoon vanilla extract

1 Prepare pastry dough: In large bowl, with fork, stir flour, sugar, and salt. With pastry blender or two knives used scissor-fashion, cut shortening into flour mixture until mixture resembles coarse crumbs. Stir in almonds. Sprinkle 3 tablespoons cold water, a tablespoon at a time, into mixture, mixing lightly with fork after each addition until dough is just moist enough to hold together. With hands, shape dough into ball.

2 Preheat oven to 425°F.

3 On lightly floured surface, with floured rolling pin, roll out dough into round about 1 1/2 inches larger all around than upside-down 9-inch pie plate.

4 Ease dough into pie plate to line evenly. Trim dough edge, leaving 1/2-inch overhang; reserve dough trimmings. Fold overhang under.

5 With sharp knife, at regular intervals around edge of dough, cut out narrow sections, about 1/2-inch long.

Cutting out sections
from edge of dough

6 Place 1 thumb on inside edge of each section of dough, and, with index finger and thumb of other hand, pinch dough and press upward to make rounded "petal" shape.

7 Prick bottom and side of piecrust with fork in many places to prevent puffing and shrinkage during baking.

8 Bake piecrust 15 minutes or until golden; cool on wire rack.

9 Roll out dough trimmings. With small cookie cutters or knife, cut out few flowers and leaves for garnish.

10 Bake cutouts on ungreased cookie sheet about 10 minutes or until golden; cool.

11 Prepare blueberry filling: If using frozen blueberries, they should be drained. In 2-quart saucepan, mix sugar, cornstarch, lemon juice, and lemon peel; add 1 cup blueberries. Over low heat, cook, mashing berries with spoon and stirring, until mixture boils and thickens. Remove from heat; stir in margarine or butter, crème de cassis, and remaining blueberries, reserving a few blueberries for garnish. Cool.

12 For white-chocolate filling: Into heavy 2-quart saucepan, break candy bars into pieces. Over low heat, heat candy bars, shortening, and 2 tablespoons water, stirring frequently, until melted and smooth. Remove saucepan from heat; cool completely. Stir in vanilla and almond extracts. In small bowl, with mixer at medium speed, beat heavy or whipping cream and confectioners' sugar until stiff peaks form. Stir a few spoonfuls whipped-cream mixture into candy mixture to lighten, then with wire whisk or rubber spatula, gently fold in remaining cream.

13 For cream layer: In same bowl, using same beaters at medium speed, beat heavy or whipping cream, confectioners' sugar, and vanilla extract until stiff peaks form.

14 In cooled piecrust, with spoon, evenly spread blueberry filling.

15 Top blueberry filling with white-chocolate filling. Spread with whipped-cream mixture, reserving 1 tablespoon for garnish.

BLUEBERRIES

Big, sweet, succulent blueberries are purplish-blue in color with a powdery bloom – the "aristocrats" of soft fruit. They come in many varieties, cultivated and wild, and can be found as large as 1 inch in diameter!

• Blueberries are traditionally a summer fruit, at their best June through August.

• Just before using, remove any stems and discard any bruised, soft, or damaged berries; rinse gently in cold water, drain well, and dry on paper towels.

• To freeze blueberries, overwrap berries in store pint containers; freeze. Or, place them in single layer in jelly-roll pan; freeze until firm. Then transfer to freezer container to use up within 1 year.

• When using frozen blueberries, thaw only if recipe tells you to do so.

16 Decorate pie with pastry flowers, reserved whipped-cream mixture and blueberries, and pastry leaves.

Decorating top of pie

INDIVIDUAL APPLE PIES

6 servings

Begin about 2 hours before serving or early in day

Pastry

2 ¹/₂ cups all-purpose flour

1 cup unsalted butter (2 sticks), softened

¹/₃ cup sugar

2 large egg yolks, slightly beaten

1 tablespoon milk

Filling

8 medium-sized Golden Delicious apples (about 3 ¹/₂ pounds)

¹/₂ cup sugar

4 tablespoons unsalted butter (¹/₂ stick)

¹/₄ cup Calvados (optional)

Sugar for garnish

TO SERVE
Lightly dust Individual Apple Pies with sugar just before serving, to give pastry leaves a "frosted" look.

---

1 Prepare pastry dough: In large bowl, with fingertips, quickly mix flour, butter, and sugar until mixture resembles coarse crumbs. Add egg yolks and milk; mix until dough will hold together.

2 Shape two-thirds of dough into ball; wrap with plastic wrap and set aside. On waxed paper, with rolling pin, roll out remaining one-third of dough ¹/₈ inch thick. With 2 ¹/₂" by 1 ¹/₂" leaf-shape cookie cutter, cut out 36 leaves. With toothpick, press "vein" into each leaf; place on cookie sheet and refrigerate.

3 Divide larger ball of dough into 6 equal pieces. Press one piece of dough onto bottom and up side of each of six 4- or 4 ¹/₂-inch tart pans with removable bottoms; refrigerate.

4 Prepare filling: Peel and core apples; cut into ¹/₄-inch-thick slices. In 12-inch skillet over medium-high heat, heat sugar and butter until butter melts, stirring occasionally (do not use margarine because it separates from sugar during cooking). Sugar will not be completely dissolved.

5 Arrange apple slices on top of sugar mixture; heat to boiling (do not stir). Cook about 20 minutes, depending on juiciness of apples, until sugar mixture becomes caramel-colored; stir to combine apples with caramelized sugar. (Apples should still be slightly crunchy.) If using Calvados, pour it over apples; heat without stirring 1 minute. Remove skillet from heat; light Calvados with match, then let flame die out.

6 Preheat oven to 400°F. Spoon apple mixture into pie shells. Arrange 6 dough leaves on top of each pie, leaving some of filling uncovered. Arrange apple pies in jelly-roll pan for easier handling. Bake pies 25 to 30 minutes until pastry is golden (cover leaves with foil after 15 minutes if necessary to prevent overbrowning).

7 Cool pies on wire rack 10 minutes; serve warm. Or, cool completely to serve later. Remove sides and bottoms of pans before serving.

FLORIDA LIME PIE

🍴 8 servings

⏰ Begin 4 ½ hours before serving or early in day

1 ½ cups graham-cracker crumbs

¼ cup sugar

⅓ cup margarine or butter, softened

1 14-ounce can sweetened condensed milk

½ cup lime juice, preferably extracted from Key limes

2 teaspoons grated lime peel

2 large eggs, separated

Green food coloring (optional)

1 cup heavy or whipping cream

Lime garnish of your choice (see Box, above right)

4 Into piecrust, pour lime filling; smooth top. Bake pie 15 to 20 minutes until lime filling is just firm.

5 Cool pie on wire rack, then refrigerate until well chilled, about 3 hours.

6 In small bowl, with mixer at medium speed, beat heavy or whipping cream until stiff peaks form. Pipe or spread whipped cream around edge of filling.

TO SERVE
Top cream with Lime Kites or other Lime garnish of your choice.

LIME GARNISHES

The contrasting greens of lime peel and flesh make this a good choice for garnishing desserts, and a welcome change from the more usual orange and lemon garnishes.

Lime Cones
With sharp knife, cut lime crosswise into thin slices. Make 1 cut from center to edge of each slice, then curl slice around from center to form cone shape.

Lime Kites and Bow-Ties
With sharp knife, cut lime crosswise into thin slices, then cut each slice into quarters. Use singly, or place 2 kites together as shown above to make bow-tie shape.

1 Preheat oven to 325°F. In 9-inch pie plate, with hand, mix graham-cracker crumbs, sugar, and margarine or butter; press mixture onto bottom and up side of pie plate, making small rim.

2 In medium bowl, with wire whisk or fork, stir sweetened condensed milk with lime juice, grated lime peel, and egg yolks until mixture thickens. If liked, add sufficient green food coloring to tint mixture pale green.

3 In small bowl, with mixer at high speed, beat egg whites until stiff peaks form. With rubber spatula or wire whisk, gently fold egg whites into lime mixture.

SOUR-CHERRY PIE

🍴 10 servings

🕐 Begin about 4 hours before serving or early in day

2 16-ounce cans pitted tart cherries in water

1/3 cup packed brown sugar

1/4 cup cornstarch

1/2 teaspoon ground cinnamon

1/3 cup plus 2 teaspoons sugar

1 tablespoon margarine or butter

1 tablespoon vanilla extract

1 teaspoon almond extract

Pastry for 2-Crust Pie (page 150), or 1 10- to 11-ounce package piecrust mix

1 1/2 teaspoons milk

1 Drain liquid from canned cherries; reserve 1 cup liquid.

2 In 2-quart saucepan, combine brown sugar, cornstarch, cinnamon, reserved cherry liquid, and 1/3 cup sugar. Cook over low heat, stirring constantly, until mixture boils and thickens; boil 1 minute. Remove pan from heat; stir in margarine or butter, vanilla extract, and almond extract. Fold in cherries.

3 Prepare pastry dough or prepare piecrust mix as label directs. Divide dough into 2 pieces, 1 slightly larger.

4 Preheat oven to 425°F. On lightly floured surface, with floured rolling pin, roll out larger ball of dough into round about 1 1/2 inches larger all around than upside-down 9-inch pie plate; ease dough into pie plate to line evenly. Trim dough edge even with rim of pie plate; reserve dough trimmings.

5 Spoon filling into crust. Roll out remaining dough as for bottom crust. With leaf-shape cookie cutter, cut out leaves in top crust; reserve cutouts. Place top crust over filling. Trim edge of top crust, leaving 1/2-inch overhang; reserve dough trimmings. Fold overhang under; make Ruffled or other Decorative Pie Edge (pages 152, 153, and 308).

6 With reserved dough trimmings, make "berries" (see Box, right). Score veins on reserved cutout leaves and arrange with berries on top crust. Brush top crust with milk and sprinkle with remaining 2 teaspoons sugar. Bake pie 15 minutes. Turn oven control to 350°F.; bake 25 minutes longer or until crust is golden brown.

7 Cool pie on wire rack before serving.

PASTRY LEAVES AND BERRIES

Pastry "leaves" can be made by cutting out shapes from top crust of pie with cookie cutter as in the recipe here for Sour-Cherry Pie, or by rolling out dough trimmings, then cutting dough into leaf shapes with sharp knife or cookie cutter. After making leaf shapes, score "veins" on surface of leaves with tip of sharp knife.

Between fingertips of both hands, roll dough trimmings into "berry" shapes. Arrange leaves and berries together, twisting leaves at base to give a more realistic look.

To garnish a large pie for a special occasion, group lots of berries together to make a cluster of grapes; for a Christmas pie, create a seasonal look by garnishing top or edge of pie with pastry holly leaves and berries.

CHOCOLATE-CREAM PIE

10 servings

Begin about 5 ½ hours before serving or early in day

35 vanilla wafers or 18 chocolate wafers

8 tablespoons margarine or butter (1 stick), softened

3 tablespoons cornstarch

¼ teaspoon salt

½ cup plus 1 teaspoon sugar

2 cups milk

3 1-ounce squares unsweetened chocolate, coarsely chopped

2 large egg yolks

1 teaspoon vanilla extract

¼ cup walnuts

½ cup heavy or whipping cream

1 Preheat oven to 375°F. Place vanilla or chocolate wafers, in batches, in heavy-duty, closed plastic bag and with rolling pin, roll wafers into fine crumbs. Or, in food processor with knife blade attached or in blender at medium speed, blend wafers, in batches, until fine crumbs form. (You should have about 1 ½ cups crumbs.)

2 In 9-inch pie plate, with hand, mix wafer crumbs and 6 tablespoons (³/₄ stick) softened margarine or butter; press mixture onto bottom and up side of pie plate, making small rim.

3 Bake crust 8 minutes; cool on wire rack.

4 While crust is cooling, prepare filling: In heavy 3-quart saucepan, mix cornstarch, salt, and ½ cup sugar. Stir in milk and chopped chocolate. Cook over medium heat, stirring constantly, until chocolate melts and mixture thickens and boils; boil 1 minute. Immediately remove saucepan from heat.

5 In cup, with fork, beat egg yolks; stir in small amount of hot chocolate mixture. Slowly pour egg mixture back into remaining chocolate mixture in pan, stirring rapidly to prevent lumping. Cook, stirring constantly, until mixture thickens and coats a spoon well (mixture should be about 170° to 175°F. but do not boil or it will curdle). Stir in vanilla extract and remaining 2 tablespoons margarine or butter until blended.

6 Into piecrust, pour chocolate filling; smooth top with rubber spatula.

Pouring chocolate filling into piecrust

7 To keep skin from forming as filling cools, press plastic wrap directly onto surface of hot filling. Refrigerate pie at least 3 hours or until well chilled.

8 Meanwhile, in small saucepan over medium heat, cook walnuts until toasted, stirring frequently; cool. Chop walnuts.

9 In small bowl, with mixer at medium speed, beat heavy or whipping cream with remaining 1 teaspoon sugar until soft peaks form.

10 Discard plastic wrap on filling. Spoon or pipe whipped cream onto filling and swirl to make attractive design.

TO SERVE
Sprinkle top of pie with toasted walnuts.

DOWN-HOME PEACH PIE

🍴 10 servings
🕐 Begin about 3 hours before serving or early in day

14 large peaches (5 pounds)

¼ cup quick-cooking tapioca

2 tablespoons lemon juice

1 teaspoon ground cinnamon

½ teaspoon ground ginger

1 cup plus 2 teaspoons sugar

2 ⅓ cups all-purpose flour

1 teaspoon salt

¾ cup margarine or butter (1 ½ sticks) plus 1 tablespoon

1 large egg yolk, beaten

1 Peel and thickly slice peaches.

2 In large bowl, gently toss peaches, tapioca, lemon juice, cinnamon, ginger, and 1 cup sugar. Let peach mixture stand 30 minutes to soften tapioca, stirring occasionally.

3 Meanwhile, prepare pastry: In medium bowl, with fork, stir flour, salt, and remaining 2 teaspoons sugar. With pastry blender or two knives used scissor-fashion, cut ¾ cup margarine or butter (1 ½ sticks) into flour mixture until mixture resembles coarse crumbs. Sprinkle 4 to 6 tablespoons cold water, a tablespoon at a time, into mixture, mixing lightly with fork after each addition until dough is just moist enough to hold together. With hands, shape dough into 2 balls, 1 slightly larger.

4 On lightly floured surface, with floured rolling pin, roll out larger ball of dough into round about 2 ½ inches larger all around than 9 ½" by 1 ½" deep pie plate. Ease dough into pie plate to line evenly; trim dough edge, leaving 1-inch overhang.

5 Spoon peach mixture into crust. Cut remaining 1 tablespoon margarine or butter into small pieces; sprinkle on top of peach mixture.

6 Preheat oven to 425°F. Roll out remaining dough into 13-inch round. Cut a few small slashes in center of round to allow steam to escape during baking.

7 Place dough round over peach filling; trim dough edge, leaving 1-inch overhang. Fold overhang under; make Fluted or other Decorative Pie Edge (pages 152, 153, and 308).

8 Reroll dough trimmings; cut out a few leaves. Arrange leaves on top of pie. Brush all over with beaten egg yolk.

9 Because peaches vary in juiciness, place sheet of foil underneath pie plate; crimp edges to form rim to catch any drips during baking. Bake pie 50 minutes or until crust is golden and peaches are tender. If piecrust begins to brown too much, cover loosely with foil.

10 Slightly cool pie on wire rack; serve warm. Or, cool pie completely to serve later.

Tarts

Open-faced tarts – crisp, rich, and sweet pastries filled with creamy custards, juicy fruits, fine chocolate, and crunchy nuts, make the most delectable of desserts. In this collection of recipes you will find old favorites next to new and exciting ideas, each one of them as good to look at as it is to eat, and you don't have to be a pastry chef to make them!

TART SHELL

1 1/4 cups all-purpose flour

1 tablespoon sugar

1/4 teaspoon salt

1/4 cup shortening or butter-flavor shortening

4 tablespoons cold margarine or butter (1/2 stick)

1 In medium bowl, with fork, stir flour with sugar and salt. With pastry blender or two knives used scissor-fashion, cut shortening and margarine or butter into flour mixture until mixture resembles coarse crumbs.

2 Sprinkle *2 to 3 tablespoons cold water*, a tablespoon at a time, into mixture, mixing lightly with fork after each addition until dough is just moist enough to hold together. With hands, shape dough into ball. Wrap with plastic wrap and refrigerate 1 hour.

3 Preheat oven to 425°F. On lightly floured surface, with floured rolling pin, roll out dough into round about 1 inch larger all around than 9- or 10-inch tart pan with removable bottom.

4 Ease dough into tart pan to line evenly; press onto bottom and up side of tart pan.

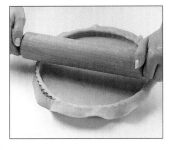

5 Roll rolling pin across top of pan to trim off excess dough; reserve trimmings for decoration.

6 With fork, prick dough in many places to prevent puffing and shrinkage during baking.

7 Line shell with foil, gently smoothing it onto bottom and up side of dough with fingertips. Bake shell 10 minutes. Remove foil; again prick dough. Bake shell 10 to 15 minutes longer until golden brown.

8 If pastry puffs up, gently press it to tart pan with spoon.

9 Cool Tart Shell in pan on wire rack.

TARTLET SHELLS

1 In medium bowl, with fork, stir *1/2 cup all-purpose flour, 1 teaspoon sugar*, and *1/4 teaspoon salt*. With pastry blender or two knives used scissor-fashion, cut *1/4 cup shortening* or butter-flavor shortening into flour mixture until mixture resembles coarse crumbs. Sprinkle *4 to 5 teaspoons cold water*, a tablespoon at a time, into mixture, mixing lightly with fork after each addition until dough is just moist enough to hold together. With hands, shape dough into ball. Wrap with plastic wrap and refrigerate 1 hour.

2 Preheat oven to 375°F. On lightly floured surface, with floured rolling pin, roll out half the dough 1/8 inch thick.

With floured 3-inch round cookie cutter, cut out as many rounds as possible. Repeat with remaining dough and reroll trimmings to make 18 rounds.

3 Gently press each round of dough onto bottom and up side of eighteen 2 1/2-inch round tartlet pans (about 3/4 inch deep).

4 With fork, prick tartlet shells in many places to prevent puffing and shrinkage during baking.

5 Place tartlet pans in jelly-roll pan for easy handling. Bake 12 to 15 minutes until lightly browned.

6 Cool Tartlet Shells in pans on wire racks 10 minutes. With knife, gently loosen tartlet shells from sides of pans; remove from pans and cool completely on wire racks. If not using right away, store in covered container.

TRUFFLE TARTLETS

🍴 18 servings
🕐 Begin about
3 ½ hours before
serving or early
in day

1   12-ounce package semisweet-chocolate pieces (2 cups)
1 cup heavy or whipping cream
6 tablespoons margarine or butter (³/₄ stick)
2 tablespoons orange-flavor liqueur (optional)
18 Tartlet Shells (see Box, page 175)
Shredded orange peel for garnish

*These individual
tartlets are easy
to serve and will
please a big crowd!*

1 In heavy 2-quart saucepan over low heat, heat chocolate, heavy or whipping cream, and margarine or butter, stirring frequently until melted and smooth. Remove saucepan from heat; if you like, stir in liqueur.

2 Refrigerate chocolate mixture about 2 ½ hours or until very thick and of easy piping consistency, stirring occasionally.

3 While chocolate mixture is chilling, prepare and bake Tartlet Shells as directed; cool on wire rack.

WHITE TRUFFLE TARTLETS

For a change, use white rather than semisweet chocolate to make the truffle filling for these elegant tartlets.

In step 1, substitute *12 ounces white chocolate* or, use four 3-ounce Swiss confectionery bars or two 6-ounce packages white baking bar for the semi-sweet-chocolate pieces, and *2 teaspoons vanilla extract* for the orange-flavor liqueur.
  For garnish, use *coffee-bean candies*, grated chocolate, or a cluster of raspberries.

4 Spoon chocolate mixture into large decorating bag with large star tube; pipe into shells.

5 Serve tartlets while truffle mixture is velvety soft, or refrigerate several hours so truffle is more firm and of candy-like consistency. Garnish with shredded orange peel just before serving.

BUTTERY PLUM TART

10 servings

Begin about 3 hours before serving or early in day

Cinnamon Pastry

1 ¹/₂ cups all-purpose flour
¹/₂ cup margarine or butter (1 stick), softened
¹/₃ cup sugar
¹/₄ teaspoon ground cinnamon

Filling

1 ¹/₂ pounds purple plums
¹/₂ cup sugar
2 tablespoons all-purpose flour
¹/₂ teaspoon ground cinnamon
¹/₄ teaspoon almond extract
¹/₄ cup slivered blanched almonds
1 cup heavy or whipping cream, whipped (optional)

1 Prepare Cinnamon Pastry dough: Into medium bowl, measure flour, margarine or butter, sugar, and cinnamon. With fingertips, mix just until blended.

2 Press pastry dough onto bottom and up side of 9-inch tart pan with removable bottom.

3 Preheat oven to 375°F. Prepare filling: Cut each plum in half and remove pit; slice plums.

4 In large bowl, toss plums, sugar, flour, cinnamon, and almond extract.

5 Arrange plum slices, closely overlapping, to form concentric circles in tart shell.

Sprinkling almonds over plums

6 Evenly sprinkle slivered almonds over plum slices.

7 Bake 45 minutes or until pastry is golden and plums are tender. Cool tart in pan on wire rack.

8 Carefully remove side from tart pan. Transfer tart to serving plate.

TO SERVE
Serve Buttery Plum Tart cut into wedges, with whipped cream, if you like.

PLUMS
These plump, fragrant fruits are in season from May through October, but are at their plentiful best in August.

• Plums come in a wide range of sizes, shapes, and colors, with skin color from bright yellow-green to reddish-purple to purplish-black, depending on variety. It doesn't matter which variety you choose – all plums can be used interchangeably in recipes.

• A perfect plum is richly colored and firm, with a slight softening at the stem end.

• Five or six plums weigh one pound, provide about 2 ¹/₂ cups sliced fruit, 3 cups quartered or halved fruit.

• Store ripe plums in refrigerator, for up to 3 to 5 days.

BERRIES AND CUSTARD IN COCONUT SHELL

🥄 10 servings
🕐 Begin about 3 ½ hours before serving or early in day

Coconut Pastry

1 cup all-purpose flour

³/4 cup shredded coconut

6 tablespoons margarine or butter (³/4 stick)

2 tablespoons sugar

1 large egg yolk

Lemon-Custard Filling

1 large lemon

6 tablespoons margarine or butter (³/4 stick)

¹/3 cup sugar

1 tablespoon cornstarch

4 large egg yolks

1 cup heavy or whipping cream

2 ¹/2-pints raspberries

1 pint blueberries

1 Prepare Coconut Pastry dough: Into medium bowl, measure flour, coconut, margarine or butter, sugar, and egg yolk. With fingertips, mix together just until blended.

2 Press dough onto bottom and up side of 10-inch tart pan with removable bottom. With fork, prick tart shell in many places to prevent puffing and shrinkage during baking.

3 Preheat oven to 350°F. Line tart shell with foil; bake 10 minutes. Remove foil; again prick dough. Bake tart shell 10 to 15 minutes longer until golden (if pastry puffs up, gently press it to pan with spoon). Cool tart shell in pan on wire rack.

4 While tart shell is baking, prepare Lemon-Custard Filling: From lemon, grate 1 teaspoon peel and squeeze 2 tablespoons juice; set aside. In heavy 2-quart saucepan over medium-low heat, heat margarine or butter, sugar, and cornstarch, stirring constantly, until mixture thickens and boils; boil 1 minute.

5 In small bowl, with fork, beat egg yolks; stir in small amount of hot sugar mixture. Slowly pour egg-yolk mixture back into sugar mixture in pan, stirring rapidly to prevent lumping.

6 Cook, stirring constantly, until mixture thickens and coats spoon well, about 1 minute (mixture should be about 170° to 175°F.). Remove saucepan from heat.

7 Stir lemon peel and lemon juice into custard; cover custard and refrigerate until very cold, about 1 hour.

8 In small bowl, with mixer at medium speed, beat heavy or whipping cream until stiff peaks form. With rubber spatula or wire whisk, fold whipped cream into custard.

RASPBERRIES

These small, juicy, thimble-shaped berries come in red, black, purple, and yellow varieties, and are best during June to July and September to October.

- Look for plump, fresh-looking berries.

- Do not buy berries that are crushed or bruised, or that have leaked moisture through carton.

- Keep refrigerated and use within 1 to 2 days.

- Eat raspberries out of hand, or use in fruit salads, pies, tarts, muffins, coffeecakes, jellies, and sauces.

9 Evenly spoon Lemon-Custard Filling into cooled tart shell.

Spooning Lemon-Custard Filling into tart shell

10 Around edge of tart, arrange raspberries in circular pattern.

11 Fill in center with blueberries and raspberries; refrigerate 1 hour or until custard sets.

With different fruits to match the seasons, this can be a year-round treat. Use bananas and oranges in winter; pineapple and papaya in spring; apricots and cherries in summer; grapes and pears in fall. Slice or dice fruit as needed for prettiest look, easy serving.

RASPBERRY TART ROYALE

10 servings
Begin about
3 ½ hours before
serving or early
in day

1 10-inch Tart Shell
(see Box, page 175)

¼ cup sugar

3 tablespoons all-purpose
flour

¼ teaspoon salt

1 envelope unflavored
gelatin

2 large eggs plus 1 large
egg yolk

1 ½ cups milk

½ cup heavy or whipping
cream

3 ½-pints raspberries

1 Prepare and bake Tart Shell as directed; cool on wire rack.

2 In 2-quart saucepan, combine sugar, flour, salt, and gelatin. In medium bowl, with wire whisk or fork, beat eggs and egg yolk with milk until well mixed; stir into gelatin mixture. Let stand 1 minute to soften gelatin slightly.

3 Cook over low heat, stirring constantly, until mixture thickens and coats spoon well, about 20 minutes (mixture should be about 170° to 175°F.). Remove saucepan from heat.

4 Pour custard into large bowl; cover and refrigerate until mixture mounds slightly when dropped from spoon, about 1 hour, stirring occasionally.

ALTERNATIVE RASPBERRY TOPPINGS

In our main picture, raspberries are piled high on top of custard filling. For a more formal effect, raspberries can be arranged in patterns, as here.

Windmill
Arrange raspberries in 4 triangular shapes, working from center of filling toward outside.

In the Round
Arrange raspberries in concentric circles, working from outside edge of filling to center.

5 In small bowl, with mixer at medium speed, beat heavy or whipping cream until stiff peaks form. With rubber spatula or wire whisk, fold whipped cream into custard.

6 Place Tart Shell on serving plate. Evenly spoon custard filling into Tart Shell. Pile raspberries on custard.

7 Refrigerate tart 1 hour or until custard is completely set.

Raspberry Tart Royale with fresh raspberries in center

NUTCRACKER TART

🍴 10 servings
🕐 Begin about 3 hours before serving or early in day

Ginger Pastry

1 1/4 cups all-purpose flour

2 tablespoons sugar

1/4 teaspoon ground ginger

1/2 cup margarine or butter (1 stick)

1 large egg

Filling

4 tablespoons margarine or butter (1/2 stick)

1 cup dark corn syrup

1/4 cup sugar

1 teaspoon vanilla extract

3 large eggs

1 4-ounce bag pecan halves

1 3 1/2-ounce jar macadamia nuts

Whipped cream and nontoxic flower (pages 134 to 135) for garnish

1 Prepare Ginger Pastry dough: In medium bowl, with fork, stir flour, sugar, and ginger. With pastry blender or two knives used scissor-fashion, cut margarine or butter into flour mixture until mixture resembles coarse crumbs. Add egg; mix lightly with fork until dough is just moist enough to hold together.

2 With hand, pat pastry on bottom and up side of 10-inch tart pan with removable bottom. Set aside.

3 Preheat oven to 350°F.

4 Prepare filling: In 2-quart saucepan over low heat, melt margarine or butter; remove from heat.

5 Into melted margarine or butter, with wire whisk, beat corn syrup, sugar, vanilla extract, and eggs just until blended.

6 Arrange pecans and macadamia nuts in concentric circles on bottom of tart shell.

7 Carefully pour egg mixture over nuts in tart shell.

8 Bake tart 35 minutes or until knife inserted in filling 1 inch from edge comes out clean. Cool tart in pan on wire rack.

9 To serve, remove side of pan; garnish center of tart with whipped cream and flower.

In Nutcracker Tart, concentric circles of pecans and macadamia nuts are crowned with cream and a flower

THIN-THIN APPLE TARTS

🍴 8 servings

⏱ Begin about 1 ½ hours before serving or up to 4 hours ahead

1 17 ¼-ounce package *frozen puff pastry*

4 medium-sized Golden Delicious apples

½ cup vanilla-wafer crumbs

3 tablespoons margarine or butter, melted

⅓ cup orange marmalade

Confectioners' sugar

Whipped cream (optional)

1 Thaw puff pastry as label directs.

2 Preheat oven to 425°F. Unfold 1 puff-pastry sheet on lightly floured surface; with floured rolling pin, roll out pastry to 14 ½-inch square.

3 Using 7-inch round plate as guide, cut out 4 rounds from pastry square.

4 Cut 2 apples lengthwise in half; remove cores and peel. Cut apple halves lengthwise into paper-thin slices.

5 Place pastry rounds on large cookie sheet. Top each with 1 table-spoon vanilla-wafer crumbs, then one-fourth of apple slices.

6 Brush apple slices with some melted margarine or butter.

7 Bake apple tarts 15 minutes or until pastry is lightly browned and crisp and apples are tender. With pancake turner, remove tarts to wire racks.

8 In small saucepan over low heat, heat orange marmalade until melted. Brush tarts while hot with some melted marmalade.

9 Repeat with remaining ingredients to make 4 more tarts.

TO SERVE
Sprinkle tarts with confectioners' sugar; serve warm or at room temperature, with whipped cream.

FRESH PEACH GALETTE

10 servings

Begin about 3 hours before serving or early in day

Pastry

1 1/4 cups all-purpose flour

2 tablespoons sugar

1/2 cup margarine or butter (1 stick)

1 large egg

Filling

8 medium-sized peaches (about 2 3/4 pounds)

1/2 teaspoon lemon juice

1/4 teaspoon ground ginger

3/4 cup apricot preserves

1 Prepare pastry dough: In medium bowl, with fork, stir flour and sugar. With pastry blender or two knives used scissor-fashion, cut margarine or butter into flour mixture until mixture resembles coarse crumbs. Add egg; mix lightly with fork until dough is just moist enough to hold together. (Or, in food processor with knife blade attached, blend flour, margarine or butter, cut into 8 pieces, and sugar about 10 seconds. Add egg through feed tube; blend 15 seconds longer or until dough holds together and leaves side of bowl.) Shape dough into ball. Wrap with plastic wrap and refrigerate 1 hour.

2 Meanwhile, prepare filling: Peel and slice 4 peaches. Place sliced peaches in saucepan. With potato masher, crush peaches; stir in lemon juice, ginger, and 1/4 cup apricot preserves. Heat to boiling; reduce heat to medium and cook 25 minutes or until mixture is thick and measures 1 1/4 cups, stirring often. Refrigerate.

3 Preheat oven to 350°F. On lightly floured surface, with floured rolling pin, roll out pastry dough into 14-inch round; transfer to large cookie sheet.

4 With fingertips, roll edge toward center until round measures 10 inches and edge is 3/4 inch high; push edge in toward center to make 7 large, evenly spaced scallops.

5 Bake 25 minutes or until pastry is golden. Cool on cookie sheet on wire rack.

6 With spoon, press remaining 1/2 cup apricot preserves through sieve into small saucepan; over medium heat, heat to boiling. Remove saucepan from heat.

7 Spoon filling over pastry. Peel remaining peaches; cut lengthwise into halves and remove pits. Cut halves into slices, maintaining peach shape; arrange on filling with broad-bladed knife.

8 Fan peach slices slightly; brush with apricot glaze. Transfer galette to serving plate.

Pushing edges of dough in toward center to make scallops

FRENCH APPLE TART

12 servings
Begin about
1 ½ hours before
serving or early
in day

---

1 10-ounce package frozen
ready-to-bake puff-pastry
shells

---

10 medium-sized Golden
Delicious apples (about
3 ½ pounds)

---

1 cup sugar

½ cup butter (1 stick)

¼ teaspoon almond extract

Heavy or whipping cream
(optional)

1 Let frozen puff-pastry
shells stand at room
temperature to thaw
slightly.

2 Meanwhile, peel and
core apples (Golden
Delicious apples with
greener skin retain shape
best; do not use other
apples). Cut each apple
lengthwise in half.

3 In heavy 10-inch
skillet with metal
handle (or with handle
covered with heavy-duty
foil), over medium heat,
heat sugar, butter, and
almond extract until
butter melts, stirring
occasionally (do not use
margarine because it
separates from sugar
during cooking). Sugar
will not be completely
dissolved. Remove skillet
from heat.

4 Arrange apple halves
on their sides around
side and in center of
skillet, fitting apples very
tightly together.

5 Over medium heat,
heat apple mixture to
boiling; boil 20 to
40 minutes, depending
on juiciness of apples,
until sugar mixture
becomes caramel-colored.
Remove from heat.

6 Preheat oven to
450°F. On lightly
floured surface, stack puff-
pastry shells, one on top of
the other, pressing firmly
together. With floured
rolling pin, roll out pastry
into 12-inch round.

7 Carefully place pastry
round over apple
halves in skillet.

8 With tines of fork,
press pastry to edge of
skillet.

9 Cut slits in pastry.
Bake 20 to 25 minutes
until pastry is golden.
Remove skillet from oven;
let cool on wire rack
10 minutes.

10 Place dessert
platter upside
down over skillet; grasping
them firmly together,
carefully invert tart onto
dessert platter (do this
over sink since tart may be
extremely juicy).

*Serve French Apple Tart
warm or cold, with cream,
if you like*

ELEGANT MINCEMEAT-PEAR TART

🍴 10 servings

⏱ Begin about 2 hours before serving or early in day

Pastry

1 1/4 cups all-purpose flour

2 tablespoons sugar

1/2 cup margarine or butter (1 stick)

1 large egg

Streusel Topping

1/4 cup all-purpose flour

2 tablespoons light brown sugar

2 tablespoons margarine or butter (1/4 stick)

Filling

1 20 1/2- to 28-ounce jar ready-to-use mincemeat

1 16-ounce can pear halves

Elegant Mincemeat-Pear Tart tastes especially delicious with tender pear slices and crisp Streusel Topping

1 Prepare pastry dough: In medium bowl, with fork, stir flour and sugar. With pastry blender or two knives used scissor-fashion, cut margarine or butter into flour mixture until mixture resembles coarse crumbs. Add egg; mix lightly with fork until dough is just moist enough to hold together. (Or, in food processor with knife blade attached, blend flour, margarine or butter, cut into 8 pieces, and sugar until mixture resembles coarse crumbs, about 10 seconds. Add egg through feed tube; blend 15 seconds more or until dough holds together and leaves side of bowl.) With hands, shape dough into ball. Wrap with plastic wrap and refrigerate 1 hour.

2 Prepare Streusel Topping: In small bowl, combine flour and light brown sugar. With pastry blender or two knives used scissor-fashion, cut margarine or butter into flour mixture until mixture resembles coarse crumbs. Refrigerate.

3 Preheat oven to 350°F. On lightly floured surface, with floured rolling pin, roll out dough into round about 1 inch larger all around than 10-inch tart pan with removable bottom.

4 Ease dough into tart pan to line evenly; trim edge. With fork, prick tart shell in many places to prevent puffing and shrinkage during baking.

5 Line tart shell with foil; bake 10 minutes. Remove foil; again prick dough. Bake 10 minutes longer. Remove tart shell from oven; turn oven control to 425°F.

6 Spoon mincemeat into partially baked tart shell and spread evenly.

7 Drain pears; pat dry with paper towels. Cut each pear half lengthwise into 1/4-inch-thick slices, being careful to keep slices from each half together. Arrange pears on mincemeat, fanning slices slightly.

8 With spoon, evenly sprinkle Streusel Topping over sliced pears in tart shell.

9 Bake tart 15 to 20 minutes until filling is heated through and crust and topping are lightly browned. Cool tart slightly in pan on wire rack.

10 Remove side of pan. Serve tart warm or cool completely to serve later.

Arranging pear slices on mincemeat

FRUIT TARTLETS

Petite and prettily shaped, tartlets filled with a variety of colorful fruits and topped with a sparkling glaze make an irresistible display on the table. Here we suggest a few ideas for presentation, and you'll find it easy to create your own filling and topping combinations. Use tartlet pans of as many different shapes as you can, and choose small whole fruits that lend themselves to the shapes of the shells, or cut up larger fruits to fit. Make the pastry shells from the recipe for Tartlet Shells (see Box, page 175); cool them, fill with Lemon-Custard Filling (page 178) or sweetened whipped cream, then top with fruits and brush with a little melted jelly – use red currant jelly for dark fruits, or apple jelly or strained apricot preserves for light-colored fruits. The thin glaze will provide an instant gloss and keep fruit looking its best for a few hours if necessary.

*Raspberry
and Blackberry*

Blueberry

Strawberry

*Orange and
Grapefruit*

*Red and
Green Seedless Grapes*

FRUIT TOPPINGS

Choose fruits that suit the size and shape of the tartlet shell. Dainty small, whole fruits such as berries and grapes can be used singly, or heaped, or clustered on filling. Dice larger fruits, or cut them into slices for dramatic effect.

Grapes can be left whole or sliced, according to their size

Carambola slices are star-shaped

Passion-fruit pulp can be sprinkled over other fruits as a garnish

PEARS AND CREAM TART

10 servings
Begin about 3 hours
before serving or
early in day

1 teaspoon ground cinnamon
1/4 teaspoon ground nutmeg
3/4 cup plus 3 tablespoons sugar
1 cup heavy or whipping cream
2 large egg yolks
1 1/2 cups all-purpose flour
1/4 teaspoon salt
6 tablespoons margarine or butter (3/4 stick)
1 29-ounce can sliced pears

1 In small bowl, with fork, mix cinnamon, nutmeg, and 3/4 cup sugar; set aside.

2 In another small bowl, with wire whisk or fork, beat heavy or whipping cream with egg yolks until blended; refrigerate.

3 Preheat oven to 400°F. Prepare pastry: In medium bowl, with fork, stir flour, salt, and 3 tablespoons sugar. With pastry blender or two knives used scissor-fashion, cut margarine or butter into flour mixture until mixture resembles coarse crumbs. (Mixture will be very dry and crumbly.)

4 With hand, firmly press mixture onto bottom and up side of 10-inch pie plate.

5 Drain pears; pat dry with paper towels. Arrange pear slices, fanning slightly, on bottom of tart shell.

6 Over pear slices in tart shell, evenly sprinkle cinnamon-sugar mixture.

7 Bake tart 5 minutes until cinnamon-sugar mixture is melted.

8 With pie plate still on oven rack, carefully pour cream mixture over pears.

9 Bake tart 20 to 30 minutes longer until top is browned and knife inserted in center of filling comes out clean.

10 Cool tart in pan on wire rack. Cover and refrigerate if not serving right away.

APRICOT LINZER TORTE

🍴 10 servings

⏰ Begin about 3 hours before serving or early in day

Filling

2 6-ounce packages dried apricot halves (2 1/4 cups)

1 cup orange juice

1/2 cup sugar

Almond Pastry

1 4-ounce can slivered blanched almonds (1 cup), ground

1 3/4 cups all-purpose flour

1 cup sugar

3/4 cup margarine or butter (1 1/2 sticks), softened

1/4 cup unsweetened cocoa

1 teaspoon ground cinnamon

1 teaspoon grated lemon peel

1 large egg

Confectioners' sugar for sprinkling

1 Prepare filling: In 3-quart saucepan over high heat, heat dried apricot halves, orange juice, sugar, and *1 cup water* to boiling. Reduce heat to medium; cook, uncovered, 30 minutes or until apricots are very tender and liquid is absorbed, stirring frequently.

2 Press apricot mixture through food mill or coarse sieve into bowl; cover and refrigerate.

3 Generously grease 11-inch tart pan with removable bottom.

4 Prepare Almond Pastry dough: In large bowl, with mixer at low speed, beat ground almonds, flour, sugar, margarine or butter, cocoa, cinnamon, lemon peel, and egg until well mixed, occasionally scraping bowl with rubber spatula.

5 Divide dough in half; press half the dough onto bottom and up side of tart pan. Spoon apricot mixture into pastry shell.

6 Preheat oven to 400°F. On lightly floured surface, with floured rolling pin, roll out remaining dough into 10-inch round. With knife, cut dough round into 1/2-inch-wide strips.

7 Carefully place half the dough strips, about 1/2 inch apart, over apricot filling.

8 Place remaining dough strips diagonally across first row of dough strips.

9 Press down with finger on either side of each crossing to create rippled lattice effect.

10 Press ends of strips to inside edge of pastry shell.

11 Bake torte 10 minutes. Turn oven control to 350°F.; bake 20 minutes longer. Cool torte in pan on wire rack.

12 To serve, remove side of pan. Sprinkle lattice with confectioners' sugar.

FRESH CHERRY TART

🥄 10 servings
⏱ Begin about 2 hours before serving or early in day

1 10-inch Tart Shell (see Box, page 175)

1 pound sweet cherries

3 large eggs

³/4 cup heavy or whipping cream

¹/3 cup sugar

2 tablespoons almond-flavor liqueur

1 ¹/2 teaspoons grated lemon peel

¹/4 teaspoon salt

Fresh Cherry Tart – a luscious, creamy dessert filled with juicy, sweet cherries

1 Prepare and bake Tart Shell as directed; cool. Turn oven control to 350°F.

2 While Tart Shell is cooling, with cherry or olive pitter, remove pits from cherries.

3 In large bowl, with mixer at low speed, beat eggs, heavy or whipping cream, sugar, almond-flavor liqueur, lemon peel, and salt until blended.

CUSTARDS AND CUSTARD PIES

Because custards are so delicate in texture, and can easily be overcooked, they should be removed from the oven when they are done at the sides – and still slightly undercooked at the center.

Testing for Doneness
To test custards and custard pies and tarts for doneness, insert knife 1 inch from edge – custard is ready if knife comes out clean. The custard will continue cooking after it is removed from the oven, so that after standing 10 to 15 minutes it will be done throughout.

4 Place cherries in Tart Shell.

5 Set pan on oven rack and carefully pour egg mixture over cherries.

6 Bake tart 30 minutes or until knife inserted in filling 1 inch from edge comes out clean.

7 Cool tart slightly in pan on wire rack.

8 Remove side of pan. Serve tart warm or cover and refrigerate to serve cold later.

BLUEBERRY CLAFOUTIS TART

🥄 12 servings
🕐 Begin about 4 hours before serving or early in day

Pastry

1 1/2 cups all-purpose flour

3/4 teaspoon salt

1 teaspoon sugar

1/2 cup margarine or butter (1 stick), softened

1 large egg

1 tablespoon milk

Filling

6 large eggs

1 cup sugar

1 1/2 cups milk

1/2 cup sour cream

1 1/2 teaspoons vanilla extract

1 pint blueberries

Confectioners' sugar

1 Prepare pastry dough: In medium bowl, with fork, stir flour, salt, and sugar. With pastry blender or two knives used scissor-fashion, cut margarine or butter into flour mixture until mixture resembles coarse crumbs. In cup, with fork, beat egg and milk until well blended; add to flour mixture and mix lightly with fork until dough is just moist enough to hold together. With hands, shape dough into ball. Wrap with plastic wrap and refrigerate 1 hour.

2 On lightly floured surface, with floured rolling pin, roll out dough into round about 1 inch larger all around than 12-inch quiche dish. Ease dough into dish to line evenly; trim edge. With fork, prick tart shell in many places to prevent puffing during baking. To prevent shrinkage, place tart shell in freezer 15 minutes.

3 Preheat oven to 425°F. Line tart shell with foil and evenly spread dry beans, pie weights, or uncooked rice over bottom.

4 Bake tart shell 20 minutes. Remove beans, weights, or rice and foil and again prick tart shell. Bake 3 to 4 minutes longer until pastry is lightly browned and no longer soft and raw (if pastry puffs up, gently press it to dish with spoon).

5 Prepare filling: In large bowl, with mixer at high speed, beat eggs and sugar until very thick and lemon-colored, about 3 minutes. Gradually beat in milk, sour cream, and vanilla extract, beating until well blended.

6 Sprinkle 1/2 pint blueberries into warm tart shell. Pour egg mixture over blueberries.

Pouring egg mixture over blueberries

7 Bake 30 to 35 minutes until filling is set and edge of crust is golden brown; cover with foil after 20 minutes to prevent overbrowning.

8 Cool tart in quiche dish on wire rack.

> ### TO SERVE
> *Top tart with remaining 1/2 pint blueberries and lightly dust with confectioners' sugar.*

EASY FRUIT TART

6 servings

Begin about 1 ½ hours before serving or early in day

½ 17 ¼-ounce package frozen puff pastry (1 sheet)

1 large egg

1 teaspoon sugar

2 tablespoons apple jelly

1 large nectarine

1 large kiwifruit

1 8-ounce container soft cream cheese with pineapple or strawberries

½ cup raspberries

½ cup blueberries

1 Thaw puff-pastry sheet as label directs.

2 Preheat oven to 350°F.

3 In cup, with fork, beat egg with *1 tablespoon water*. Unfold pastry sheet and place on lightly floured surface. With rolling pin, roll pastry to 14" by 11" rectangle.

4 With sharp knife, cut two 1-inch-wide strips from each edge of rectangle, leaving 10" by 7" rectangle. Place rectangle on ungreased cookie sheet; prick pastry with fork. With pastry brush, brush rectangle with some egg mixture.

5 To form sides of tart shell, arrange 4 pastry strips along edges of rectangle, so that strips overlap at corners.

6 With kitchen shears, trim pastry overhang.

7 Brush pastry strips with egg mixture. Repeat with remaining 4 pastry strips. Sprinkle tart shell with sugar.

8 Bake tart shell 15 to 20 minutes or until pastry is golden brown and crisp, pricking again with fork after 5 minutes if bottom of tart shell is puffed. With pancake turners, carefully remove to wire rack; cool completely.

9 In small saucepan over low heat, heat apple jelly until melted; remove pan from heat.

10 Thinly slice nectarine; peel and thinly slice kiwifruit.

11 Place tart shell on serving plate; spread cream cheese in tart shell. Arrange nectarine and kiwifruit slices, raspberries, and blueberries over cream cheese. Brush nectarines with apple jelly. If not serving right away, cover and refrigerate.

WALNUT TORTE

16 servings

Begin about 3 hours before serving or early in day

Sweet Cornmeal Pastry

1 1/2 cups all-purpose flour
1/3 cup yellow cornmeal
1/4 cup sugar
3/4 cup margarine or butter (1 1/2 sticks)
1 large egg

Filling

3/4 cup sugar
1 cup heavy or whipping cream
1/4 cup honey
1 teaspoon vanilla extract
1/4 teaspoon salt
1 16-ounce can walnuts (4 cups), coarsely chopped
1 tablespoon milk

Sweet Cornmeal Pastry gives lattice-topped Walnut Torte a golden color and accentuates the nutty flavor of the filling

1 Prepare Sweet Cornmeal Pastry dough: In large bowl, with fork, stir flour, cornmeal, and sugar. With pastry blender or two knives used scissor-fashion, cut margarine or butter into flour mixture until mixture resembles coarse crumbs. Add egg; mix lightly with fork until dough is just moist enough to hold together.

2 Press two-thirds of dough onto bottom and 1 1/4 inches up side of 10" by 2 1/2" springform pan.

3 Refrigerate torte shell and remaining pastry dough.

Stirring walnuts into filling

4 Prepare filling: In 10-inch skillet over medium heat, heat sugar, without stirring, just until it begins to melt. Cook, stirring constantly, 6 to 8 minutes until golden brown. Remove skillet from heat; slowly and carefully stir in heavy or whipping cream (mixture will spatter). Return skillet to medium heat; cook 5 minutes or until mixture is smooth, stirring frequently.

5 Remove skillet from heat; stir in honey, vanilla extract, and salt until well blended. Stir in walnuts.

6 Leave walnut filling in skillet to cool slightly.

7 Preheat oven to 350°F. Evenly spread walnut filling in torte shell. On lightly floured surface, with floured rolling pin, roll out remaining dough into 10" by 5" rectangle; cut lengthwise into ten 1/2-inch-wide strips.

8 Twist strips; arrange in lattice design on top of torte.

9 Brush strips lightly with milk. Bake torte 45 minutes or until golden brown. Cool torte in pan on wire rack.

10 To serve, carefully remove side from springform pan.

DELUXE APPLE TART

🍴 10 servings
🕐 Begin about 4 hours before serving or early in day

Pastry

1 cup all-purpose flour

5 tablespoons margarine or butter, softened

2 tablespoons sugar

1/8 teaspoon salt

Filling

6 medium-sized Golden Delicious apples (about 2 pounds)

1 10- to 12-ounce jar apricot preserves

1/4 cup sugar

1 teaspoon lemon juice

1 Prepare pastry dough: Into medium bowl, measure flour, margarine or butter, sugar, salt, and *2 tablespoons cold water*. With fingertips, mix together just until blended, adding more water, 1 teaspoon at a time, if needed.

2 Press dough onto bottom and up side of 9-inch tart pan with removable bottom; refrigerate.

3 Prepare filling: Peel and core 3 apples; cut into chunks. In blender, combine *1/4 cup water* with about one-third of apple chunks; cover and blend at high speed until apples are pureed. Add remaining apple chunks, a third at a time; blend until smooth.

4 Pour pureed apples into 3-quart saucepan; stir in 1/2 cup apricot preserves and 2 tablespoons sugar. Over high heat, heat to boiling. Reduce heat to medium-high; cook, uncovered, about 20 minutes until applesauce is very thick, stirring frequently.

5 Peel remaining 3 apples. Cut each apple lengthwise into quarters; remove cores.

Removing cores from apples

FILLING AND GLAZING TART

Spreading applesauce in tart shell: *Spoon applesauce into tart shell, then, with back of spoon, spread evenly.*

Arranging apples in center of tart: *Place apple slices, closely overlapping, in small circle in center of applesauce filling.*

Arranging remaining apple slices: *Place remaining apple slices, closely overlapping, in large circle around first small circle, to completely cover applesauce and fill tart shell.*

Glazing apples: *With pastry brush, gently spread hot apricot preserves over apple slices until evenly coated.*

6 Cut each apple quarter lengthwise into ⅛-inch-thick slices.

7 In large bowl, gently toss apple slices with lemon juice and remaining 2 tablespoons sugar.

8 Preheat oven to 400°F. Fill tart shell with applesauce and cover with apple slices (see Box, page 194).

9 Bake tart 45 minutes or until apple slices are tender and browned. Remove pan to wire rack.

10 With spoon, press remaining apricot preserves through sieve into small saucepan; over medium heat, heat to boiling. Cook 2 minutes longer or until preserves are thick enough to coat a spoon. Brush preserves evenly over apple slices (see Box, page 194). Cool tart in pan on wire rack.

11 To serve, carefully remove side of pan.

CARAMEL-PECAN TORTE

🍴 10 servings

🕐 Begin about 3 hours before serving or early in day

Filling

2 4-ounce packages pecan halves (2 1/4 cups)

2/3 cup sugar

1 cup heavy or whipping cream

1 tablespoon margarine or butter

Pastry

2 cups all-purpose flour

2 tablespoons sugar

1/2 teaspoon salt

1/3 cup shortening or butter-flavor shortening

6 tablespoons margarine or butter (3/4 stick)

Chocolate Coating

1 6-ounce package semisweet-chocolate pieces (1 cup)

4 tablespoons margarine or butter (1/2 stick)

1 Prepare filling: Reserve 10 pecan halves for garnish; finely chop remaining pecans. Set aside.

2 In 2-quart saucepan over high heat, heat sugar and 1/4 cup water to boiling, stirring frequently until sugar completely dissolves. Reduce heat to medium; cook sugar syrup 10 minutes, without stirring, until syrup turns a medium amber color. Remove saucepan from heat; slowly and carefully pour in heavy or whipping cream (mixture will spatter). Return saucepan to heat; cook until caramel dissolves, stirring occasionally. Increase heat to high; cook, stirring frequently, until mixture boils and thickens slightly.

3 Remove saucepan from heat; stir in chopped pecans and margarine or butter. Set aside to cool.

4 Prepare pastry dough: In medium bowl, with fork, stir flour, sugar, and salt. With pastry blender or two knives used scissor-fashion, cut shortening and margarine or butter into flour mixture until mixture resembles coarse crumbs. Sprinkle *4 to 6 tablespoons cold water*, a tablespoon at a time, into mixture, mixing lightly with fork after each addition until dough is just moist enough to hold together. With hands, shape dough into ball.

5 Preheat oven to 400°F. On lightly floured surface, with floured rolling pin, roll out two-thirds of pastry dough into round about 2 inches larger all around than 9 1/2-inch tart pan with removable bottom. Ease dough into tart pan to line evenly (you will have a 1-inch overhang).

6 Spoon pecan mixture into pastry shell. Roll out remaining dough into 9-inch round; place on top of pecan filling. Fold overhang over round; press gently to seal.

7 Bake torte 40 minutes or until lightly browned. Cool torte in pan on wire rack.

8 When torte is cool, prepare Chocolate Coating: In heavy 1-quart saucepan over low heat, heat chocolate pieces and margarine or butter, stirring frequently, until melted and smooth. Remove saucepan from heat; cool chocolate mixture slightly.

9 Carefully invert torte onto cake plate; remove tart pan. Spoon 1/4 cup chocolate mixture into decorating bag with small writing tube; spread remaining chocolate mixture over top and sides of torte. Arrange reserved pecan halves on top. Drizzle chocolate mixture in decorating bag over top of torte to make pretty design. Let torte stand 15 minutes until chocolate sets before serving.

LEMON CUSTARD TART

🍴 10 servings
🕐 Begin day before serving

Pastry

½ teaspoon grated lemon peel

6 tablespoons margarine or butter (¾ stick), softened

3 tablespoons sugar

1 large egg yolk

1 cup cake flour

Filling

4 large eggs

4 large egg yolks

¾ cup lemon juice

¾ cup plus 3 tablespoons sugar

4 tablespoons margarine or butter (½ stick)

2 tablespoons apricot preserves

Lemon slices for garnish

1 Prepare pastry dough: In small bowl, with mixer at medium speed, beat lemon peel, margarine or butter, and sugar until well blended; beat in egg yolk. Stir in cake flour until just blended. Shape dough into ball; wrap with plastic wrap and refrigerate 1 hour.

2 Preheat oven to 425°F. On lightly floured surface, with floured rolling pin, roll out dough into round about 1 inch larger all around than 9-inch tart pan with removable bottom. Ease dough into tart pan to line evenly; trim edge even with rim. With fork, prick tart shell in many places to prevent puffing and shrinkage during baking. Line tart shell with foil.

3 Bake tart shell 10 minutes; remove foil and again prick tart shell. Bake 5 minutes longer or until pastry is golden (if pastry puffs up, gently press it to pan with spoon). Cool tart shell in pan on wire rack.

4 Prepare filling: In heavy 2-quart saucepan, with wire whisk or fork, beat eggs and egg yolks until blended; stir in lemon juice and ¾ cup sugar. Cook over medium-low heat, stirring constantly, until mixture thickens and coats a spoon well, about 15 minutes (mixture should be about 170° to 175°F. but do not boil or it will curdle). Stir in margarine or butter until melted.

5 Into baked tart shell, pour lemon custard filling.

6 Refrigerate tart overnight so that filling is well chilled and firm.

> **TO SERVE**
> Garnish center of Lemon Custard Tart with lemon slices.

7 About 1 to 2 hours before serving, preheat broiler if manufacturer directs. Cover edge of crust with foil to prevent overbrowning. Evenly sprinkle remaining 3 tablespoons sugar over lemon custard filling.

8 Place tart in broiler at closest position to source of heat; broil 6 to 8 minutes until sugar melts and begins to brown, making a shiny crust. Chill.

9 Carefully remove side of tart pan; slide tart onto cake plate. In small saucepan over low heat, melt apricot preserves. Brush top of tart with melted preserves.

GRAPE-AND-KIWIFRUIT TART

🥄 10 servings

⏱ Begin about 3 ½ hours before serving or early in day

1 10-inch Tart Shell (see Box, page 175)

¼ cup sugar

3 tablespoons all-purpose flour

1 envelope unflavored gelatin

¼ teaspoon salt

2 large eggs plus 1 large egg yolk

1 ½ cups milk

2 tablespoons almond-flavor liqueur or ½ teaspoon almond extract

About ½ pound seedless green or red grapes

3 medium-sized kiwifruit

½ cup heavy or whipping cream

2 tablespoons apple jelly

1 Prepare and bake Tart Shell as directed; cool on wire rack.

2 While Tart Shell is baking, prepare filling: In heavy 2-quart saucepan, combine sugar, flour, gelatin, and salt. In small bowl, with wire whisk or fork, beat eggs and egg yolk with milk until well mixed; stir into gelatin mixture. Let stand 1 minute to soften gelatin slightly.

3 Cook over low heat, stirring constantly, until mixture thickens and coats a spoon well, about 15 minutes (mixture should be about 170° to 175°F. but do not boil or it will curdle).

The contrasting shades of two green fruits look stunning in Grape-and-Kiwifruit Tart

4 Remove saucepan from heat; stir in almond-flavor liqueur or almond extract. Cover and refrigerate until mixture mounds slightly when dropped from a spoon, about 1 hour, stirring occasionally.

5 Meanwhile, cut each grape lengthwise in half. Peel and thinly slice kiwifruit. Set grapes and kiwifruit aside.

6 In small bowl, with mixer at medium speed, beat heavy or whipping cream until stiff peaks form. With rubber spatula or wire whisk, fold whipped cream into almond custard.

7 Carefully remove side from tart pan; slide Tart Shell onto serving plate. Evenly spoon custard into cooled Tart Shell. Arrange grapes, cut side down, and kiwifruit on custard to make attractive design.

8 In small saucepan over medium heat, melt apple jelly, stirring occasionally. With pastry brush, carefully brush fruit with melted jelly. Refrigerate tart until filling is completely set, about 1 hour.

Pastries

All pastries are made with some kind of dough; and the different doughs, coupled with the wide variety of fillings that can be used, add up to an almost limitless choice of eye-catching, taste-tempting desserts. Tender pie dough can be used for fruit-filled rolls and dumplings. Flaky puff pastry makes handsome pies, tarts, and turnovers. Light and airy shells made from cream puff dough take to fillings from whipped cream to ice cream; and delicious desserts made with paper-thin phyllo range from fancy dessert cups to the incomparable Baklava.

PEAR DUMPLINGS À LA CRÈME

6 servings
Begin about 1 ½ hours before serving or early in day

¼ cup sugar

¼ teaspoon ground cinnamon

3 medium-sized Bartlett pears

1 ½ cups all-purpose flour

½ cup margarine or butter (1 stick), softened

1 3-ounce package cream cheese, softened

1 large egg, separated

2 cups half-and-half or light cream

4 teaspoons cornstarch

¼ teaspoon almond extract

6 whole cloves

1 In cup, with fork, stir 1 tablespoon sugar with cinnamon; set aside. Peel pears. Cut each pear lengthwise in half; remove cores.

2 Prepare pastry dough: Into medium bowl, measure flour, margarine or butter, and cream cheese; with fingertips, mix together just until blended.

3 On lightly floured surface, with floured rolling pin, roll out half the dough ⅛ inch thick. Using 7-inch round plate as guide, cut 3 rounds from dough; reserve trimmings.

4 Sprinkle rounds of dough with half the cinnamon-sugar mixture; place a pear half, cut-side up, on each round. Carefully fold round of dough over each pear half.

5 Pinch dough edges to seal. Place dumplings, seam-side down, on ungreased large cookie sheet. Repeat with remaining dough to make 6 dumplings in all.

6 Preheat oven to 375°F. Reroll dough trimmings; cut to make leaves. Brush dumplings with egg white; decorate with dough leaves and brush them with egg white.

7 Bake dumplings 35 minutes or until pastry is golden. Remove dumplings to wire rack; cool slightly.

8 Meanwhile, in 2-quart saucepan, combine egg yolk, half-and-half or light cream, cornstarch, and remaining 3 tablespoons sugar.

9 Cook over medium-low heat, stirring constantly, until mixture thickens and coats a spoon well, about 15 minutes (mixture should be about 170° to 175°F.). Remove saucepan from heat; stir in almond extract. Cool custard slightly.

> *TO SERVE*
> *Onto each of 6 dessert plates, spoon some custard. Place pear dumplings in custard; insert whole clove in tip of each to resemble stem. Or, refrigerate dumplings and custard separately to serve chilled later.*

PUFF-PASTRY PEAR PIE

🍴 8 servings

🕐 Begin about 1½ hours before serving or early in day

---

1 17 ¼-ounce package frozen puff pastry

---

6 medium-sized pears (2 pounds)

⅓ cup dried currants

¼ teaspoon anise seeds, crushed (optional)

½ cup sugar plus extra for sprinkling

---

2 tablespoons all-purpose flour plus extra for sprinkling

---

1 large egg

Spiced Cream (see Box, below)

---

1 Thaw puff pastry as label directs.

2 Meanwhile, prepare pear filling: Core and thinly slice pears (do not peel). In large bowl, toss pear slices with currants, crushed anise seeds, ½ cup sugar, and 2 tablespoons flour until mixed.

3 Preheat oven to 375°F. Unfold 1 puff-pastry sheet on ungreased large cookie sheet; with floured rolling pin, roll out into 13" by 10" rectangle.

SPICED CREAM

In 3-quart saucepan over high heat, heat 1 ½ cups heavy or whipping cream, 2 tablespoons sugar, and 1 teaspoon anise seeds to boiling, stirring occasionally. Boil until cream is reduced to about 1 ¼ cups. Strain cream into serving bowl; discard anise seeds. Allow cream to cool slightly to serve warm, or cover and refrigerate to serve cold later.

4 On lightly floured surface, with floured rolling pin, roll out second pastry sheet into 14" by 11" rectangle; sprinkle lightly with flour. Fold pastry sheet lengthwise in half.

5 With floured knife, cut pastry crosswise through folded edge to within 1 inch of unfolded edge at ½-inch intervals.

6 In cup, with fork, beat egg and 1 teaspoon water. Spoon pear filling onto pastry rectangle on cookie sheet to about 1 inch from edges. Brush edges of pastry with some egg mixture.

TO SERVE
Cut pear pie into slices; serve warm, or cool on wire rack to serve later. Pass Spiced Cream separately.

---

7 Place second pastry sheet over filling with fold at center; unfold pastry. Press edges of pastry together to seal. Brush pastry with remaining egg mixture; sprinkle lightly with sugar. Bake pie 30 minutes or until pastry is golden and puffed.

8 While pie is baking, prepare Spiced Cream.

FRUIT-FILLED PASTRY ROLL

- 🍴 16 servings
- ⏱ Begin 4 hours before serving or early in day

1 8-ounce package dried Mission figs, coarsely chopped (1 cup)

½ 10-ounce container pitted dates, coarsely chopped (1 cup)

½ 8-ounce package dried apricots, coarsely chopped (1 cup)

¼ cup golden raisins

2 tablespoons lemon juice

1 teaspoon ground cinnamon

½ cup sugar plus 2 tablespoons

1 4-ounce can walnuts (1 cup), chopped

2 cups all-purpose flour

1 teaspoon salt

¾ cup shortening or butter-flavor shortening

1 large egg

1 tablespoon milk

Whipped cream (optional)

1 In 4-quart saucepan over high heat, heat figs, dates, apricots, raisins, lemon juice, cinnamon, ½ cup sugar, and 2 ½ cups water to boiling. Reduce heat to low; simmer, uncovered, stirring occasionally, 30 minutes or until mixture is thick. Remove saucepan from heat; stir in chopped walnuts. Let stand until cool, at least 1 hour.

2 Meanwhile, prepare pastry dough: In medium bowl, with fork, stir flour, salt, and remaining 2 tablespoons sugar. With pastry blender or two knives used scissor-fashion, cut shortening into flour mixture until mixture resembles coarse crumbs. Sprinkle 5 to 6 tablespoons cold water, a tablespoon at a time, into flour mixture, mixing lightly with fork after each addition until dough is just moist enough to hold together. With hands, shape dough into ball. Wrap with plastic wrap and refrigerate until dried-fruit filling is cool.

3 Preheat oven to 425°F. Reserve about ½ cup dough. On lightly floured surface, with floured rolling pin, roll out remaining dough into 16" by 12" rectangle. Transfer to ungreased large cookie sheet.

TO SERVE
Serve pastry roll sliced, with whipped cream, if you like.

---

4 Spoon dried-fruit filling in about 4-inch-wide strip lengthwise over center of rectangle to about 2 ½ inches from each end. Fold one long side of dough rectangle over filling, then roll over to enclose filling, seam-side down. Fold dough under on each end of roll.

5 In cup, with fork, beat egg and milk. Brush roll with some egg mixture. With tip of knife, cut few shallow lines in top of roll. On floured surface, with floured rolling pin, roll out reserved dough. With knife, cut out small leaves and roll small pieces of dough into berries. Arrange leaves and berries on top of roll; brush with some egg mixture.

6 Bake roll 25 to 30 minutes until pastry is golden. With pancake turner, transfer pastry roll to wire rack to cool completely.

APPLE TURNOVERS

🥄 8 servings
🕐 Begin 5 hours before serving or early in day

2 cups all-purpose flour
1 teaspoon salt
1 cup margarine or butter (2 sticks)
2 large cooking apples
1/2 cup sugar
1 tablespoon cornstarch
1 teaspoon lemon juice
1/4 teaspoon ground cinnamon
1 large egg
Sugar Drizzle (see Box, below)

1 Prepare pastry dough: In medium bowl, with fork, stir flour and salt. With pastry blender or two knives used scissor-fashion, cut 1/2 cup margarine or butter (1 stick) into flour mixture until mixture resembles coarse crumbs. Sprinkle 1/2 cup cold water, a tablespoon at a time, into mixture, mixing lightly with fork after each addition until dough is just moist enough to hold together. With hands, shape dough into ball.

2 On lightly floured surface, with floured rolling pin, roll out dough into 18" by 8" rectangle. Cut 4 tablespoons margarine or butter (1/2 stick) into thin slices.

3 Starting at one of the 8-inch sides, place margarine or butter slices over two-thirds of rectangle to about 1/2 inch from edge of dough.

4 Fold unbuttered third of dough over middle third.

5 Fold opposite end of dough over to make 8" by 6" rectangle.

6 Roll out dough again into 18" by 8" rectangle. Slice remaining margarine or butter; place slices on dough and fold as before. Wrap with plastic wrap and refrigerate 15 minutes.

7 Roll out folded dough into 18" by 8" rectangle. Fold rectangle lengthwise then crosswise; wrap and refrigerate 1 hour.

8 Meanwhile, prepare filling: Peel, core, and slice apples. In 1-quart saucepan over low heat, cook apples with sugar, cornstarch, lemon juice, and cinnamon, stirring frequently, until apples are tender. Refrigerate until cool.

9 Preheat oven to 450°F. Cut dough crosswise in half. On lightly floured surface, with floured rolling pin, roll out half into 12-inch square (keep remaining dough refrigerated); cut into four 6-inch squares. In cup, with fork, beat egg and 1 tablespoon water; brush some egg mixture over dough squares.

10 Spoon one-eighth of apple mixture in center of each square; fold diagonally in half and press edges to seal. Place on ungreased cookie sheet; refrigerate. Repeat with remaining dough and apple mixture.

11 Brush turnovers with egg mixture. Bake 20 minutes or until pastry is golden. Cool on wire rack.

12 Prepare Sugar Drizzle; with spoon, drizzle on turnovers; allow to set before serving.

SUGAR DRIZZLE
In small bowl, mix together 1/2 cup confectioners' sugar and 1 tablespoon water.

RASPBERRY PUFF PASTRIES

🍴 6 servings

⏱ Begin about 2 hours before serving or early in day

½ 17 ¼-ounce package frozen puff pastry

---

1 ½ cups plus 2 tablespoons sugar

¾ cup half-and-half or light cream

---

1 cup heavy or whipping cream

½ teaspoon vanilla extract

---

2 ½-pints raspberries

---

1 Thaw puff pastry as label directs.

2 Preheat oven to 375°F. Unfold puff-pastry sheet on lightly floured surface. With sharp knife, cut thin strip of pastry, about ⅛ inch wide, from each side of pastry sheet (fresh-cut edges are needed for maximum puffing). Then, cut pastry along folds into 3 rectangles; cut each rectangle crosswise in half, making 6 rectangles in all.

3 Place pastry rectangles on ungreased large cookie sheet. Bake 15 minutes or until pastry is puffed and golden. Cool on wire rack.

4 About 30 minutes before serving, prepare caramel sauce: In 3-quart saucepan over medium heat, heat 1 ½ cups sugar and ⅓ cup *water* to boiling, stirring frequently. Cook, without stirring, until mixture becomes caramel-colored. Remove saucepan from heat; gradually stir in half-and-half or light cream (sugar mixture will harden). Cook over medium heat, stirring constantly, until sauce is smooth; keep warm.

5 In small bowl, with mixer at medium speed, beat heavy or whipping cream, vanilla extract, and remaining 2 tablespoons sugar until soft peaks form.

6 With serrated knife, carefully split each puff-pastry rectangle horizontally in half.

Splitting puff-pastry rectangles into halves

7 Spoon whipped-cream mixture onto bottom half of each puff-pastry rectangle.

8 With fingers, carefully place some raspberries on top of whipped-cream mixture.

9 Gently replace pastry tops over cream and raspberries.

TO SERVE
Pour warm caramel sauce onto 6 dessert plates. Arrange pastries on plates; garnish with remaining raspberries.

ELEGANT PUFF-PASTRY TARTS

The melt-in-the-mouth layers of puff pastry in these glorious French tarts are filled with juicy, colorful fruits. Here we've used a mixture of fresh and canned fruits – fresh strawberries, apples, grapes, and kiwifruit with canned mandarin oranges and peaches, but you can make the changes according to the season.

16 servings
Begin day before serving or up to 1 week ahead

3 cups all-purpose flour

1 cup cake flour

1 teaspoon salt

2 cups cold margarine or butter (4 sticks)

1 large egg, beaten

1 cup heavy or whipping cream

2 tablespoons sugar

1/4 teaspoon almond extract

Fresh or canned fruits

Mint leaves for garnish

MAKING PASTRY TARTS

1 Fold 1 square of dough diagonally in half to form triangle.

2 Starting at folded side, cut 1/2-inch border strip on both sides of triangle, leaving 1/2 inch uncut dough at triangle point so strips remain attached.

3 Unfold triangle. Lift up both loose border strips and slip one under the other, gently pulling to matching corners on base. Attach points of dough with drop of water.

1 In medium bowl, with fork, stir flours and salt. With pastry blender or two knives used scissor-fashion, cut 1/2 cup margarine or butter (1 stick) into flour until mixture resembles coarse crumbs. Add *1 cup cold water*, a few tablespoons at a time, mixing lightly with fork after each addition until soft dough is formed (add more water if needed, a tablespoon at a time). With hands, shape dough into ball. Wrap with plastic wrap and refrigerate 30 minutes.

2 Meanwhile, between 2 sheets of waxed paper, roll remaining 1 1/2 cups margarine or butter (3 sticks) into 6-inch square; wrap and refrigerate.

3 On lightly floured surface, with floured rolling pin, roll out dough into 12-inch square.

4 Place square of margarine or butter diagonally in center of dough; fold corners of dough over margarine or butter so they meet in center, overlapping slightly.

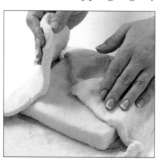

5 Press dough with rolling pin to seal seams.

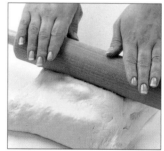

6 Roll out dough into 18" by 12" rectangle. Fold one-third of dough over center, then fold opposite one-third over first to form 6" by 12" rectangle of three layers.

7 Press rectangle of dough with rolling pin to seal seam.

8 Give dough quarter turn. Roll out dough into 15" by 8" rectangle; fold into thirds to form 5" by 8" rectangle. Wrap with plastic wrap and refrigerate at least 1 hour.

9 Repeat, rolling out dough into 15" by 8" rectangle and folding into thirds, 2 more times. Wrap and refrigerate 2 hours.

10 Repeat rolling, folding, and refrigerating 2 more times, or 6 times in all. After sixth time, wrap well and refrigerate at least 4 hours (or up to 1 week) before using.

11 Cut dough crosswise in half. On lightly floured surface, with floured rolling pin, roll out half the dough into rectangle about 20 1/2" by 10 1/2", gently lifting dough occasionally.

12 With sharp knife or pastry wheel, trim edges to make 20" by 10" rectangle.

13 Cut rectangle into eight 5-inch squares; place on large cookie sheet. Refrigerate 30 minutes.

14 Repeat with remaining dough half. (Or freezer-wrap and freeze remaining dough up to 6 months; thaw dough in refrigerator overnight before using.)

15 Make pastry tarts (see Box, page 204). Refrigerate 30 minutes.

16 Preheat oven to 400°F. Bake tarts 20 minutes. Reduce oven temperature to 375°F.; brush top of borders with beaten egg. Bake 20 minutes longer or until centers of tarts are lightly browned. Cool tarts on wire rack.

17 In small bowl, with mixer at medium speed, beat heavy or whipping cream, sugar, and almond extract until soft peaks form. Fill tarts with whipped-cream mixture; top with fruit and garnish with mint leaves.

BAKLAVA

24 servings
Begin about 3 ½ hours before serving or early in day

| 1 16-ounce can walnuts (4 cups), finely chopped |
| ½ cup sugar |
| 1 teaspoon ground cinnamon |
| 1 16-ounce package fresh or frozen (thawed) phyllo |
| 1 cup margarine or butter (2 sticks), melted |
| 1 12-ounce jar honey |

1 In large bowl, with fork, mix finely chopped walnuts, sugar, and cinnamon; set aside.

2 Cut phyllo into 13" by 9" rectangles. In greased 13" by 9" baking dish, place 1 phyllo sheet; brush with some melted margarine or butter. Repeat with phyllo and margarine or butter to make 5 more layers, overlapping any small strips of phyllo to make rectangles, if necessary.

3 Over phyllo in baking dish, sprinkle 1 cup walnut mixture.

4 Repeat steps 2 and 3 to make 3 more layers (4 layers total). Place remaining phyllo on top of last walnut layer; brush with margarine or butter.

5 With sharp knife, cut just halfway through layers in triangle pattern to make 24 servings (cut lengthwise into 3 strips; cut each strip crosswise into 4 rectangles; then cut each rectangle diagonally into 2 triangles).

6 Bake in 300°F. oven 1 hour and 25 minutes or until top is golden brown.

7 In small saucepan over medium-low heat, heat honey until hot but not boiling. Evenly spoon hot honey over hot Baklava.

ALTERNATIVE SHAPES

For a change from triangles, you can cut Baklava into diamond shapes, which are more traditional.

Diamond Baklava
In step 5, with sharp knife, cut just halfway through layers in diamond pattern (cut lengthwise into 4 strips, then cut diagonally across strips in parallel lines); finish cutting through layers in step 9.

8 Cool Baklava in dish on wire rack at least 1 hour; cover with foil and let stand at room temperature until serving.

9 To serve, with sharp knife, finish cutting through layers to make 24 Baklava triangles.

Spooning honey over Baklava

APPLE STRUDEL

16 servings

Begin about 2 hours before serving or early in day

3 large green cooking apples

$^1/_2$ cup sugar

$^1/_2$ cup dark seedless raisins

$^1/_2$ cup walnuts, chopped

$^1/_2$ teaspoon ground cinnamon

$^1/_4$ teaspoon ground nutmeg

$^1/_4$ teaspoon salt

About $^3/_4$ cup dried bread crumbs

$^1/_2$ 16-ounce package fresh or frozen (thawed) phyllo

$^1/_2$ cup margarine or butter (1 stick), melted

Confectioners' sugar

> **TO SERVE**
> *Sprinkle strudel lightly with confectioners' sugar; cut into slices.*

1 Grease large cookie sheet. Peel, core, and thinly slice apples. In large bowl, toss apples with sugar, raisins, walnuts, cinnamon, nutmeg, salt, and $^1/_4$ cup bread crumbs.

2 Cut two 24-inch lengths of waxed paper. Overlap 2 long sides about 2 inches; fasten with cellophane tape.

3 On waxed paper, arrange 1 sheet of phyllo. (It should be a 17" by 12" rectangle; if necessary, trim or overlap small pieces of phyllo to make it this size.) Brush with some melted margarine or butter.

4 Sprinkle phyllo with scant tablespoon bread crumbs. Continue layering phyllo, brushing each sheet with melted margarine or butter and sprinkling every other sheet with crumbs.

Spooning apple mixture onto phyllo

5 Preheat oven to 375°F. Starting along 1 long side of phyllo rectangle, spoon apple mixture to about $^1/_2$ inch from edges to cover about half the phyllo rectangle.

6 From apple-mixture side, roll phyllo, jelly-roll fashion, using waxed paper to help lift roll.

7 Place roll on cookie sheet, seam-side down. Brush with remaining melted margarine or butter. Bake 40 minutes or until golden. Cool on cookie sheet 30 minutes.

SWAN CREAM PUFFS

🥄 8 servings

🕐 Begin about 3 hours before serving or early in day

Cream-Puff Dough (see Box, below right)

---

1 cup heavy or whipping cream

---

1 package vanilla-flavor instant pudding and pie filling for 4 servings

---

1 ¼ cups milk

½ teaspoon almond extract

Pretty as a picture, Swan Cream Puffs are filled with the most luscious cream and vanilla-pudding mixture

1 Preheat oven to 375°F. Prepare Cream-Puff Dough. Spoon ½ cup batter into decorating bag with large writing tube (tip about ½ inch in diameter). Onto greased large cookie sheet, pipe eight 3-inch-long "question marks" for swans' necks, making small dollop at beginning of each for head.

2 Drop remaining batter by large spoonfuls, pushing off with rubber spatula, into 8 large mounds onto cookie sheet, about 3 inches apart.

3 With moistened finger, gently smooth batter to round slightly.

4 Bake 20 minutes or until necks are golden. Remove necks to wire rack to cool. Continue baking cream puffs 45 to 50 minutes longer until golden; remove to racks to cool.

5 When cream puffs are cool, prepare filling: In small bowl, with mixer at medium speed, beat heavy or whipping cream until stiff peaks form; set aside. In large bowl, with wire whisk, prepare instant pudding as label directs, but use only 1 ¼ cups milk. With rubber spatula or wire whisk, gently fold whipped cream and almond extract into prepared vanilla pudding.

6 Working quickly, before filling begins to set, cut off top third from each cream puff; set aside.

CREAM-PUFF DOUGH

In 2-quart saucepan over medium heat, heat *1 cup water* and *½ cup margarine* or butter (1 stick) until margarine or butter melts and mixture boils. Remove saucepan from heat. Add *1 cup all-purpose flour* all at once; with wooden spoon, vigorously stir until mixture leaves side of pan and forms a ball. Add *4 large eggs*, 1 at a time, beating well with wooden spoon after each addition until batter is smooth and satiny.

7 Spoon some filling into each of the cream-puff bottoms (swans' bodies). Cut each reserved top piece in half; set into filling for wings. Place swans' necks into filling. Refrigerate if not serving right away.

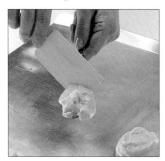

ALMOND CREAM-PUFF RING

🍴 10 servings
🕐 Begin about 3 hours before serving or early in day

Cream-Puff Dough (see Box, page 208)

1 cup heavy or whipping cream

1 package vanilla-flavor instant pudding and pie filling for 4 servings

1 ¼ cups milk

1 teaspoon almond extract

Chocolate Glaze (see Box, below)

1 Preheat oven to 400°F. Grease and flour large cookie sheet.

2 Prepare Cream-Puff Dough. Using 7-inch plate as guide, trace circle in flour on cookie sheet. Drop batter by heaping tablespoons, pushing off with rubber spatula, into 10 mounds, inside circle, to form ring.

3 Bake ring 40 minutes or until golden. Turn off oven; let ring remain in oven 15 minutes. Cool ring on wire rack.

4 With long serrated knife, slice ring horizontally in half.

5 Prepare filling: In small bowl, with mixer at medium speed, beat heavy or whipping cream until stiff peaks form; set aside. In large bowl, with wire whisk, prepare instant pudding as label directs, but use only 1 ¼ cups milk. With rubber spatula or wire whisk, gently fold whipped cream and almond extract into vanilla pudding.

6 Spoon whipped-cream mixture onto bottom of ring.

7 Replace top of ring.

8 Prepare Chocolate Glaze; spoon over top of ring.

9 Refrigerate cream-puff ring if not serving right away.

CHOCOLATE GLAZE
In heavy small saucepan over low heat, heat *½ cup semisweet-chocolate pieces, 1 tablespoon margarine* or butter, *1½ teaspoons light corn syrup,* and *1½ teaspoons milk,* stirring frequently, until melted and smooth.

FANCY PHYLLO CUPS

4 servings
Begin about
1 hour before
serving

*4 sheets fresh or frozen
(thawed) phyllo*

*2 tablespoons margarine or
butter (¹/₄ stick), melted*

¹/₂ pound fresh rhubarb

1 ¹/₂ teaspoons cornstarch

¹/₃ cup sugar

*³/₄ pint vanilla ice cream
or frozen yogurt*

1 Preheat oven to
375°F. On work
surface, stack sheets of
phyllo (about 17" by 12"
each), one on top of the
other; with knife, cut stack
lengthwise, then crosswise
into quarters to obtain
16 pieces.

2 Place 2 pieces phyllo,
one on top of the
other; brush top sheet with
some melted margarine or
butter. Arrange phyllo in
10-ounce custard cup or
heat-safe bowl.

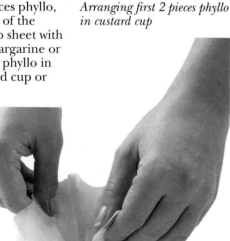

*Arranging first 2 pieces phyllo
in custard cup*

3 Place 2 more pieces
phyllo, one on top of
the other, and brush top
with some melted marga-
rine or butter; place
crosswise over phyllo in
cup, crimping to form
pretty edge. Repeat with
remaining phyllo, to make
4 phyllo cups in all.

4 Place custard cups in
jelly-roll pan for easier
handling.

5 Bake 10 to 12 minutes
until phyllo is crisp
and golden. Cool in cups
on wire rack.

6 Meanwhile,
wash rhubarb
and trim and
discard leaves and
discolored ends;
cut into ¹/₂-inch
pieces. In 2-quart
saucepan, stir
cornstarch and
*2 tablespoons
water* until
blended; add
rhubarb.

7 Over medium heat,
cook, stirring fre-
quently, until rhubarb is
very tender and mixture
thickens, about 10 min-
utes. Stir in sugar.
Remove saucepan from
heat; cool slightly.

8 Carefully remove
phyllo from custard
cups (pastry is very fragile);
place on dessert plates.
Spoon ice cream or frozen
yogurt into phyllo cups;
top with rhubarb mixture.

PHYLLO

Phyllo, also spelled fillo, is the tissue-paper-thin
pastry sheets of Greece - similar to the strudel leaves
of Austria and Hungary. It is used for making
layered, rolled, and otherwise-shaped appetizers
and pastries, the most famous of which
is Baklava (page 206).

• Phyllo is sold in 8- or
16-ounce packages in the
frozen-food section of
most supermarkets. It may
also be found fresh in
many Middle Eastern food
stores.

• Thaw wrapped phyllo
in the refrigerator for
8 hours or overnight.
Then, to prevent crumb-
ling, allow unopened
package to stand at room
temperature for an
additional 2 hours before
using.

• Once unwrapped, the
sheets should be kept
stacked and covered with
a damp towel, no matter
how rapid the assembly,
otherwise they will dry out
and become brittle.

• Unused thawed phyllo
may be refrigerated for up
to 5 weeks if tightly sealed
in plastic wrap or foil. It
may also be refrozen for
up to 2 months.

APPLE DUMPLINGS WITH CHEDDAR PASTRY

6 servings

Begin about 2 hours before serving

2 ½ cups all-purpose flour

1 teaspoon salt

³/₄ cup shortening or butter-flavor shortening

1 4-ounce package shredded sharp Cheddar cheese (1 cup)

¹/₃ cup packed light brown sugar

¹/₄ cup dark seedless raisins

¹/₄ cup walnuts, chopped

4 tablespoons margarine or butter (¹/₂ stick), softened

1 teaspoon ground cinnamon

6 small Golden Delicious apples (about 2 pounds)

1 large egg

6 whole cloves

1 ¹/₄ cups apple cider or apple juice

¹/₂ cup maple or maple-flavor syrup

1 Prepare pastry dough: In large bowl, with fork, stir flour and salt. With pastry blender or two knives used scissor-fashion, cut shortening into flour mixture until mixture resembles coarse crumbs; stir in cheese. Sprinkle *8 to 9 tablespoons cold water*, a tablespoon at a time, into mixture, mixing lightly with fork after each addition until dough is just moist enough to hold together. With hands, shape dough into ball.

2 In small bowl, with fork, mix brown sugar, raisins, walnuts, margarine or butter, and cinnamon.

> **TO SERVE**
> *Serve apple dumplings hot on individual plates, with cider mixture spooned around.*

3 Peel apples; remove cores but do not go all the way through apples.

4 Preheat oven to 400°F. Reserve ¹/₃ cup pastry dough. On well floured surface, with floured rolling pin, roll out remaining dough into 21" by 14" rectangle. With pastry wheel or knife, cut dough into six 7-inch squares.

5 In cup, with fork, beat egg and *1 teaspoon water*. Center an apple on square of dough.

6 Spoon one-sixth of sugar mixture into cavity in apple. Brush edges of square with some egg mixture.

7 Bring points of square up over apple, pinching edges together to seal well.

8 Repeat with remaining dough squares, apples, and sugar mixture. With pancake turner, place dumplings in greased 13" by 9" baking dish.

9 On floured surface, with floured rolling pin, roll out reserved dough ¹/₄ inch thick. Cut 12 leaves from dough; score with tip of knife to make "veins." Brush dumplings with some egg mixture; press 2 leaves on top of each dumpling and brush them with egg mixture. Press cloves, rounded-side down, into dumplings to resemble stems. Bake dumplings 35 minutes.

10 In bowl, with spoon, stir apple cider and maple syrup; pour cider mixture over dumplings. Bake dumplings 15 minutes longer (cover with foil after 5 minutes if dumplings are overbrowning), basting occasionally with cider mixture in baking dish, until pastry is golden brown and apples are tender when pierced with skewer.

PROFITEROLE GLACÉE

🍴 6 servings
⏱ Begin 1 1/2 hours before serving or early in day

5 tablespoons margarine or butter

1/2 cup all-purpose flour

2 large eggs

1 10-ounce package frozen raspberries in syrup, thawed

1 1/2 pints vanilla ice cream

2 tablespoons raspberry liqueur (optional)

2 1-ounce squares semisweet chocolate

2 tablespoons milk

1/4 cup shelled pistachio nuts, chopped

1 Preheat oven to 400°F. Grease and flour large cookie sheet.

2 Prepare cream-puff dough: In 2-quart saucepan over medium heat, heat 4 tablespoons margarine or butter (1/2 stick) and 1/2 cup water until margarine or butter melts and mixture boils. Remove saucepan from heat. Add flour all at once; with wooden spoon, vigorously stir until mixture leaves side of pan and forms ball. Add eggs, 1 at a time, beating well with wooden spoon after each addition until batter is smooth and satiny.

3 Drop batter by teaspoons into 18 mounds onto cookie sheet, 2 inches apart.

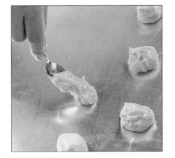

4 Bake 30 minutes or until golden. Turn off oven; let puffs remain in oven 10 minutes. Cool on wire rack.

5 While puffs are baking, over large bowl, with back of spoon, press and scrape thawed raspberries with their syrup firmly against medium-mesh sieve to separate seeds from pulp; discard seeds. Add 1/4 cup ice cream with liqueur to raspberry puree; stir to mix. Cover raspberry sauce and refrigerate.

ALTERNATIVE SERVING IDEA

As an alternative to raspberry sauce, you can serve Profiterole Glacée with other fruit sauces such as strawberry, apricot, or mango. This Peach Sauce goes especially well, both in color and flavor.

Peach Sauce
In blender at low speed, blend together *one 10-ounce package frozen peaches*, thawed, *1/4 teaspoon almond extract*, and *1/8 teaspoon ground nutmeg* until all ingredients are smooth.

6 When puffs are cool, in small heavy saucepan over low heat, heat chocolate, milk, and remaining 1 tablespoon margarine or butter, stirring frequently, until melted and smooth.

Profiteroles nestled together on a pool of raspberry sauce are drizzled with chocolate sauce and sprinkled with nuts

7 Cut each puff horizontally in half; fill bottom halves with remaining ice cream; replace tops. Drizzle cream puffs with chocolate mixture and sprinkle with nuts. Freeze.

TO SERVE
Spoon raspberry sauce onto 6 dessert plates; arrange 3 profiteroles on each plate.

Hot Fruit Desserts

Here you'll find homespun desserts: hot sweet fruit blanketed with crunchy topping in a "crisp" or "crumble," or covered with a tender biscuit crust in a "pandowdy" or "cobbler," or layered with buttered bread crumbs, sugar, and spices in a "brown Betty." Reheating at the same temperature at which they were baked will give desserts made ahead, or leftovers, fresh-baked goodness.

BANANA BROWN BETTY

4 servings
Begin about 40 minutes before serving

2 large oranges

6 medium-sized bananas

3 tablespoons sugar

6 tablespoons margarine or butter ($^3/_4$ stick)

$^1/_2$ cup fresh bread crumbs

3 tablespoons wheat germ

$^1/_3$ cup quick-cooking or old-fashioned oats

3 tablespoons brown sugar

$^1/_2$ teaspoon ground cinnamon

$^1/_4$ teaspoon salt

Whipped cream (optional)

1 From oranges, grate 1 teaspoon peel and squeeze $^3/_4$ cup juice. Cut bananas into chunks.

2 In 10-inch skillet over medium-high heat, cook sugar, 3 tablespoons orange juice, and 2 tablespoons margarine or butter ($^1/_4$ stick), stirring frequently, until light caramel color, about 3 to 4 minutes. Add bananas; toss to coat.

3 Remove skillet from heat. Preheat oven to 400°F.

4 In medium bowl, with fork, mix bread crumbs and wheat germ. Spoon half the banana mixture into four 8-ounce custard cups or ramekins.

5 Sprinkle each with 1 tablespoon bread-crumb mixture. Top with remaining banana mixture. Spoon about 2 tablespoons orange juice over banana mixture in each custard cup.

6 Into remaining bread-crumb mixture, with fingertips, mix oats, brown sugar, cinnamon, salt, orange peel, and remaining 4 tablespoons margarine or butter ($^1/_2$ stick) until mixture resembles coarse crumbs; sprinkle over bananas.

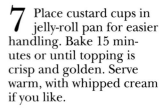

7 Place custard cups in jelly-roll pan for easier handling. Bake 15 minutes or until topping is crisp and golden. Serve warm, with whipped cream if you like.

APPLE PANDOWDY

RHUBARB CRUMBLE

🍴 6 servings

⏰ Begin 50 minutes before serving

1 ¹/2 pounds fresh rhubarb

1 teaspoon lemon juice

³/4 cup sugar

1 ¹/4 cups all-purpose flour

¹/2 cup margarine or butter (1 stick)

Half-and-half or vanilla ice cream (optional)

1 Wash rhubarb and trim and discard leaves and discolored ends. Cut rhubarb into 1-inch pieces (you should have about 4 cups). In 4-quart saucepan over medium heat, heat rhubarb, lemon juice, ¹/2 cup sugar, and ¹/4 *cup water* to boiling. Reduce heat to low; cover and simmer 10 minutes or until rhubarb is tender.

2 Preheat oven to 425°F. While rhubarb is cooking, in medium bowl, with fork, stir flour and remaining ¹/4 cup sugar. With pastry blender or two knives used scissor-fashion, cut margarine or butter into flour mixture until mixture resembles coarse crumbs.

3 Pour rhubarb mixture into 8" by 8" baking dish. Sprinkle flour mixture over rhubarb.

4 Bake 25 minutes or until crumble topping is golden.

TO SERVE
Serve Rhubarb Crumble and Apple Pandowdy warm, with half-and-half or ice cream.

🍴 6 servings

⏰ Begin 1 hour before serving

1 cup packed light brown sugar

1 ¹/4 cups all-purpose flour

1 teaspoon salt

2 tablespoons margarine or butter (¹/4 stick)

1 teaspoon lemon juice

1 teaspoon vanilla extract

¹/4 teaspoon ground cinnamon

Dash ground nutmeg

5 large cooking apples (about 2 pounds)

2 teaspoons baking powder

3 tablespoons shortening

³/4 cup milk

Half-and-half or vanilla ice cream (optional)

1 In 1-quart saucepan, mix brown sugar, ¹/4 cup flour, and ¹/4 teaspoon salt; stir in 1 cup water.

2 Heat over medium heat, stirring constantly, to boiling; cook until sauce is thick. Remove from heat. Stir in margarine or butter, lemon juice, vanilla extract, cinnamon, and nutmeg.

3 Peel, core, and thinly slice apples. Arrange apple slices in 12" by 8" baking dish; pour butter mixture over apples.

4 Preheat oven to 375°F. Into medium bowl, measure baking powder, remaining 1 cup flour, and ³/4 teaspoon salt. With pastry blender or two knives used scissor-fashion, cut shortening into flour mixture until size of peas. Add milk; stir until moistened but still lumpy.

5 Evenly drop dough by large spoonfuls on top of apples, not covering completely. Bake 40 minutes or until apples are tender and topping is golden brown.

STREUSEL-TOPPED APPLE COBBLER

16 servings

Begin about 2 ½ hours before serving or early in day

2 6-ounce packages dried apples

3 cups apple juice

6 medium-sized Golden Delicious apples (about 2 pounds)

1 teaspoon ground cinnamon

¼ teaspoon ground nutmeg

1 cup packed light brown sugar

3 cups plus 3 tablespoons all-purpose flour

2 teaspoons salt

1 ½ cups margarine or butter (2 ½ sticks)

1 In 3-quart saucepan over high heat, heat dried apples with apple juice to boiling. Reduce heat to low; simmer, uncovered, 15 to 20 minutes, stirring often, until liquid is absorbed. Remove from heat.

2 Meanwhile, peel, core, and thinly slice Golden Delicious apples to make 6 to 7 cups slices. In large bowl, toss apple slices with cinnamon, nutmeg, ½ cup packed brown sugar, 3 tablespoons flour, and ½ teaspoon salt. Set aside.

3 Prepare pastry: In another large bowl, with fork, stir remaining 3 cups flour with remaining 1 ½ teaspoons salt. With pastry blender or two knives used scissor-fashion, cut 1 cup margarine or butter (2 sticks) into flour until mixture resembles coarse crumbs. Reserve 1 ½ cups flour mixture in medium bowl.

4 To remaining flour mixture, add 5 to 6 tablespoons cold water, a tablespoon at a time, mixing lightly with fork after each addition until pastry is just moist enough to hold together. With hands, shape pastry into ball.

5 On lightly floured surface, with floured rolling pin, roll pastry into rectangle about 3 inches larger all around than 13" by 9" baking dish. Line baking dish with pastry. Trim edges, leaving 1-inch overhang. Fold overhang under; with back of floured 4-tined fork, press pastry to rim of baking dish.

6 Preheat oven to 425°F. Toss dried-apple mixture with Golden Delicious-apple mixture; spoon into pastry-lined baking dish.

APPLE JUICE

Made from the sweet juice of apples, apple juice is pasteurized and will keep well, unopened, in or out of the refrigerator; it is useful in fruit desserts for adding extra juiciness. Here it is used for this purpose, and to plump up the dried apples and intensify their apple flavor. Do not confuse apple juice with apple cider, which is also sold in supermarkets.

7 Into reserved flour mixture in medium bowl, stir remaining ½ cup brown sugar. With pastry blender or two knives used scissor-fashion, cut in remaining 4 tablespoons margarine or butter (½ stick) until mixture resembles coarse crumbs. Sprinkle over apple mixture.

8 Bake cobbler 60 to 70 minutes until apples are tender, covering loosely with foil after about 20 minutes if topping begins to brown too quickly. Cool cobbler slightly on wire rack. With spoon, scoop out portions to serve warm or cold.

BLUEBERRY COBBLER

8 servings
Begin about
40 minutes before
serving or early
in day

2 pints blueberries

3 tablespoons quick-cooking
tapioca

2 teaspoons lemon juice

1/2 cup plus 2 tablespoons
sugar

1/8 teaspoon plus
1/2 teaspoon salt

1 cup all-purpose flour

1 1/2 teaspoons baking
powder

2 tablespoons shortening

1/2 cup milk

Mint leaves for garnish

1 Reserve 1/4 cup
blueberries for
garnish. In 12-inch skillet,
stir together tapioca,
lemon juice, 1/2 cup sugar,
1/8 teaspoon salt, and
remaining blueberries.
Over medium heat, heat
mixture until hot and
bubbly and thickened
slightly, about 10 minutes,
stirring occasionally.

2 Meanwhile, prepare
cobbler topping: In
medium bowl, combine
flour, baking powder,
2 tablespoons sugar, and
1/2 teaspoon salt until
blended.

3 With pastry blender or
two knives used
scissor-fashion, cut in
shortening until mixture
resembles coarse crumbs.

4 Stir in milk until flour
is just moistened.
(Cobbler batter will be
lumpy.)

5 Preheat oven to
450°F. Spoon blue-
berry mixture into 3-quart
casserole or baking dish.
(Casserole should be at
least 2 inches deep so that
blueberry mixture does
not bubble over during
baking.)

ALTERNATIVE COBBLER TOPPING

There are many different types of cobbler topping.
This recipe for Whole-Wheat Cobbler Topping has a
nice nutty texture.

Whole-Wheat Cobbler Topping

In bowl, mix *1 cup whole-wheat flour, 1/2 cup all-purpose flour, 1/3 cup sugar, 1 tablespoon baking powder, and 1/2 teaspoon salt*. With pastry blender or 2 knives used scissor-fashion, cut in *1/2 cup margarine* or butter (1 stick) until mixture resembles coarse crumbs.

Add *1/2 cup heavy or whipping cream*; stir gently with fork until dough leaves side of bowl. Crumble dough over fruit in baking dish and bake in 400°F. oven for 25 to 30 minutes until topping is golden and fruit is hot and bubbly.

6 Spoon cobbler batter
on blueberry mixture,
leaving 1 1/2-inch border
on all sides.

7 Bake cobbler about
15 minutes or until
golden.

TO SERVE
*Garnish cobbler with
reserved blueberries and
mint leaves. Serve warm
or cold.*

INDIVIDUAL PEACH COBBLERS

🍴 4 servings
🕐 Begin about 1 hour before serving

4 large peaches (about 1 ³/₄ pounds)

¹/₄ cup plus 2 teaspoons sugar

³/₄ cup plus 3 tablespoons all-purpose flour

1 teaspoon baking powder

¹/₄ teaspoon salt

3 tablespoons margarine or butter

1 cup heavy or whipping cream

1 Peel and thinly slice peaches. In large bowl, toss peaches with ¹/₄ cup sugar (or to taste) and 3 tablespoons flour. Spoon peaches into four 1-cup ramekins or 10-ounce custard cups. Set aside.

2 In large bowl, with fork, mix baking powder, salt, remaining ³/₄ cup flour, and 2 teaspoons sugar. With pastry blender or two knives used scissor-fashion, cut in margarine or butter until mixture resembles coarse crumbs. Stir in ¹/₃ cup heavy or whipping cream; quickly mix just until mixture forms a stiff dough that leaves side of bowl.

3 Preheat oven to 400°F. Turn dough onto lightly floured surface. With floured rolling pin, roll out dough to about ³/₈-inch thickness.

4 Using floured biscuit cutter with diameter about ¹/₄ inch smaller than diameter of top of ramekin, cut out 4 biscuits.

5 Place biscuits over peaches; brush biscuits lightly with heavy or whipping cream.

6 If you like, press trimmings together; roll and cut into desired shapes to decorate top of cobblers.

7 Place cobblers in jelly-roll pan for easier handling. Bake 15 to 20 minutes until peach mixture begins to bubble and crust is golden.

> *TO SERVE*
> *Serve peach cobblers warm, with remaining heavy or whipping cream if you like.*

COOKIES

219-240

COOKIES

Cookies – perfect for after school, as a snack, for dessert, for anytime! Around the holidays, our festive Gingerbread Christmas Cookies and Sweet and Spicy Peppernuts are crowd-pleasers for children and adults alike. Elegantly accented Chocolate-Dipped Pecan Shortbread and Finnish Almond Cookies are ideal to accompany afternoon tea or after-dinner coffee, and delicate Brandy Snaps and dainty Pizzelles taste as good as they look – why not make a second batch to wrap as take-home gifts for guests? For all-around favorites, nothing can beat Apricot Rugelach and All-Oatmeal Crunchies – home-baked goodness your family and friends will love.

CONTENTS

Cookies

In our cookie collection you'll find dainty, elegant morsels for the tea tray, sturdy favorites for the school lunchbox, jolly sugary snowmen to delight the children at Christmastime, even oatmeal cookies that would be good for breakfast! There are different shapes, sizes, and decorations to catch the eye and match any occasion. Every palate is sure to be pleased with the choice of buttery, nutty, chocolatey, or sugar-and-spicy flavors and the variety of textures, which range from tender and chewy to crisp and crunchy.

BRANDY SNAPS

Makes about 3 dozen

Begin about 2 hours before serving or early in day

½ cup butter (1 stick)
3 tablespoons light molasses
½ cup all-purpose flour
½ cup sugar
1 teaspoon ground ginger
¼ teaspoon salt
2 tablespoons brandy

1 Preheat oven to 350°F. Grease large cookie sheet. In small saucepan over medium heat, heat butter and molasses, stirring occasionally, until butter melts (do not use margarine because it separates from molasses during heating). Remove saucepan from heat; with spoon, stir in flour, sugar, ginger, and salt until smooth. Stir in brandy until blended. Return saucepan to very low heat to keep mixture warm.

2 Drop 1 teaspoon mixture onto cookie sheet; with back of spoon, spread in circular motion to make 4-inch round (mixture spreads during baking to fill in any thin areas). Repeat to make 3 more rounds, spacing them about 2 inches apart.

3 Bake cookies about 5 minutes or until golden brown. Remove cookie sheet from oven; allow cookies to cool briefly, only until edges set. With pancake turner, flip cookies over quickly so lacy texture will be on outside after rolling.

4 Working as quickly as possible, roll each cookie into cylinder around handle of wooden spoon or dowel (about ½ inch in diameter). If cookies become too hard to roll, return to oven briefly to soften. As each cookie is shaped, remove from spoon handle; cool on wire racks.

5 Repeat until all mixture is used.

TWO-TONE HEARTS

Makes 2 ½ dozen

Begin about 4 hours before serving or early in day

2 1-ounce squares semisweet chocolate

2 ¼ cups all-purpose flour

¾ cup margarine or butter (1 ½ sticks), softened

1 tablespoon milk

1 ½ teaspoons baking powder

1 teaspoon vanilla extract

¼ teaspoon salt

1 large egg

¾ cup sugar plus extra for sprinkling

1 In heavy 1-quart saucepan over low heat, heat semisweet chocolate, stirring frequently, until melted and smooth. Remove saucepan from heat.

2 Into large bowl, measure flour, margarine or butter, milk, baking powder, vanilla extract, salt, egg, and ¾ cup sugar. With mixer at low speed, beat ingredients until well blended, occasionally scraping bowl with rubber spatula. With hands, shape half the dough into ball; wrap with plastic wrap and refrigerate 2 hours or until dough is firm enough to handle. (Or, place dough in freezer 40 minutes.)

3 With mixer at low speed, beat melted chocolate into dough remaining in bowl until blended. With hands, shape chocolate dough into ball; wrap and refrigerate 2 hours.

4 Grease and flour 2 large cookie sheets. On lightly floured surface, with floured rolling pin, roll out half the vanilla dough ⅛ inch thick; keep remaining dough refrigerated. With floured 3 ¼-inch heart-shaped cutter, cut dough into hearts. Place hearts, about ¼ inch apart, on 1 cookie sheet. Repeat with remaining vanilla dough and trimmings. Repeat with chocolate dough, placing hearts on second cookie sheet. Refrigerate until hearts are firm, about 20 minutes.

5 Preheat oven to 350°F. With 1-inch heart-shaped cookie cutter, cut small heart in center of each vanilla- and chocolate-heart cookie; set small hearts aside. With 2 ⅛-inch heart-shaped cookie cutter, cut another heart in center of each cookie. Remove medium-sized heart from each vanilla cookie and replace it with one from chocolate cookie. Fit 1-inch vanilla hearts into centers of medium-sized chocolate hearts; repeat with 1-inch chocolate hearts and medium-sized vanilla hearts to create two-tone cookies.

6 Sprinkle cookies lightly with sugar. Bake cookies 10 minutes or until golden. With pancake turner, remove cookies to wire racks to cool. Store cookies in tightly covered container.

CHRISTMAS SUGAR COOKIES

Makes about
4 dozen

Begin early in day
or day ahead

3 ¹/2 cups all-purpose flour

*1 cup margarine or butter
(2 sticks), softened*

³/4 cup sugar

¹/2 cup light corn syrup

1 tablespoon lemon juice

¹/4 teaspoon salt

2 large eggs

*Ornamental Frosting (see
Box, right)*

1 Into large bowl,
measure flour, marga-
rine or butter, sugar, corn
syrup, lemon juice, salt,
and eggs. With mixer at
low speed, beat ingre-
dients until well blended,
occasionally scraping bowl
with rubber spatula. Wrap
dough with plastic wrap;
refrigerate 2 hours or until
dough is firm enough to
handle. (Or, place dough
in freezer 40 minutes.)

2 Preheat oven to
350°F. On well
floured surface, with
floured rolling pin, roll
out one-fourth of dough
¹/8 inch thick, keeping
remaining dough refrige-
rated. With floured cookie
cutters, cut dough into
different shapes. (Or, use
3-inch round cookie
cutter.) With pancake
turner, place cookies,
about ¹/2 inch apart, on
ungreased cookie sheet.

3 Bake cookies 5 to
7 minutes until
golden. With pancake
turner, remove cookies to
wire racks to cool. Repeat
with remaining dough and
trimmings.

ORNAMENTAL FROSTING

In small bowl, with
mixer at low speed, beat
*one 16-ounce package
confectioners' sugar*
(4 cups), *¹/3 cup warm
water*, and *3 tablespoons
meringue powder* until just
mixed. Increase speed
to high; beat mixture
until so stiff that knife
drawn through mixture
leaves clean-cut path.
Divide frosting into
small bowls; tint each
bowl of frosting with
food coloring as desired.
Keep all bowls covered
to prevent frosting
drying out.

---

4 Prepare Ornamental
Frosting.

5 Place cookies on
waxed-paper-lined
cookie sheets. With small
metal spatula or small and
medium artist's paint
brushes and decorating
bags with writing tubes,
decorate cookies with
Ornamental Frosting as
desired. (If frosting is too
stiff for brushing on
cookies, dilute it with a
little water.) Set cookies
aside to allow frosting to
dry completely, about
2 hours. Store cookies in
tightly covered container.

Jingle Bells
*With skewer, make small hole
in dough at top of each bell
before baking. After cookies
have cooled, coat with yellow
frosting; allow to dry. With
decorating bag and small
writing tube, pipe decorative
designs in different colors on
top of yellow; allow to dry.
Thread string or ribbon
through holes.*

Holly Wreaths
*Coat each wreath shape with
green frosting; allow to dry.
With decorating bag and
small writing tube, pipe white
frosting in zig-zag design over
green. Then pipe red dots in
between white frosting to
resemble holly berries.*

Party Parcels
*With decorating bag and
small writing tube, pipe
decorative designs in
different-colored frostings on
plain rectangular-shaped
cookies. If you like, tie
parcels with ribbon.*

Jolly Snowmen
*Coat each cookie with white
frosting; allow to dry. With
decorating bag and small
writing tube and different-
colored frostings, pipe hats,
faces, scarves, buttons, and
other trimmings on snowmen.*

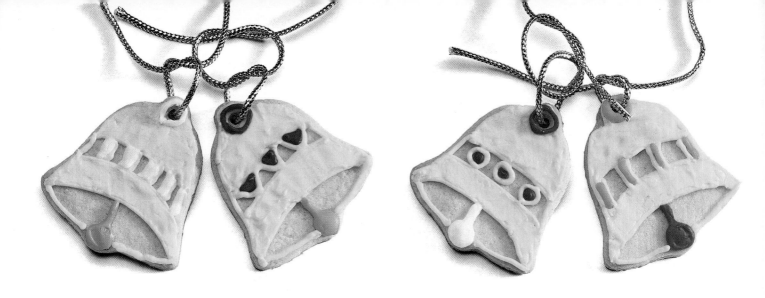

CHOCOLATE AMARETTI

Makes about 2 ½ dozen

Begin about 1 ½ hours before serving or early in day

1 4 ½-ounce can blanched whole almonds (1 cup)

½ cup sugar

2 large egg whites

⅛ teaspoon cream of tartar

½ teaspoon vanilla extract

½ teaspoon almond extract

2 tablespoons unsweetened cocoa

¼ cup confectioners' sugar plus extra for sprinkling

1 In 10-inch skillet over medium heat, cook almonds until lightly browned, shaking pan frequently. Remove skillet from heat; cool almonds completely.

2 In food processor with knife blade attached, blend almonds with ¼ cup sugar, pulsing on and off, until almonds are finely ground.

3 Preheat oven to 325°F. Line large cookie sheet with foil.

4 In small bowl, with mixer at high speed, beat egg whites and cream of tartar until soft peaks form; gradually sprinkle in remaining ¼ cup sugar, beating until sugar completely dissolves and whites stand in stiff, glossy peaks. Beat in vanilla and almond extracts. With rubber spatula or wire whisk, gently fold in ground-almond mixture, cocoa, and ¼ cup confectioners' sugar.

5 Spoon almond mixture into decorating bag with medium writing tube (tip about ½ inch in diameter). Onto cookie sheet, pipe mixture in 1 ½-inch mounds, about 1 inch apart.

6 Bake 15 minutes or until amaretti are crisp. Cool 10 minutes on cookie sheet on wire rack; with pancake turner, remove amaretti to wire rack to cool completely. Sprinkle amaretti with confectioners' sugar. Store cookies in tightly covered container.

CAPPUCCINO SQUARES

Makes 2 dozen

Begin about 2 hours before serving or early in day

1 cup margarine or butter (2 sticks)

1 8-ounce package unsweetened-chocolate squares (8 1-ounce squares)

3 ½ cups sugar

6 large eggs

1 8-ounce can walnuts (2 cups), coarsely chopped

1 ¾ cups all-purpose flour

¼ cup instant espresso-coffee powder

2 teaspoons vanilla extract

½ teaspoon ground cinnamon

½ teaspoon salt

Confectioners' sugar for garnish

1 Preheat oven to 350°F. Grease and flour 13" by 9" baking pan.

2 In heavy 4-quart saucepan over low heat, heat margarine or butter and chocolate, stirring frequently, until melted and smooth; remove saucepan from heat. With wire whisk or spoon, beat in sugar and eggs until well blended. Stir in walnuts, flour, espresso-coffee powder, vanilla extract, cinnamon, and salt.

3 Evenly spread mixture in baking pan. Bake 45 to 50 minutes until toothpick inserted in center comes out clean. Cool completely in pan on wire rack.

4 When cold, cut crosswise into 6 strips, then cut each strip into 4 pieces. With pancake turner, remove squares from pan; sprinkle half of each square with confectioners' sugar. Store cookies in single layer in tightly covered container.

APRICOT RUGELACH

Makes 3 dozen

Begin about 2 ½ hours before serving or early in day

2 cups all-purpose flour

1 cup plus 2 tablespoons margarine or butter (2 ¼ sticks)

¾ cup sour cream

6 tablespoons apricot preserves

6 tablespoons semisweet-chocolate mini pieces

⅓ cup sliced blanched almonds

2 tablespoons sugar

1 Into large bowl, measure flour. With pastry blender or two knives used scissor-fashion, cut 1 cup margarine or butter (2 sticks) into flour until mixture resembles small peas. Add sour cream and mix lightly with fork until dough is just moist enough to hold together. Divide dough into 3 pieces. Wrap with plastic wrap and refrigerate 1 hour or until firm enough to handle.

2 On lightly floured surface, with floured rolling pin, roll out 1 piece of dough into 11-inch round, keeping remaining dough refrigerated.

3 Spread dough round with 2 tablespoons apricot preserves; sprinkle with 2 tablespoons chocolate mini pieces. Cut dough round into 12 equal wedges; starting at curved edge, roll up each wedge, jelly-roll fashion. Place cookies, point-side up, about 1 ½ inches apart, on large ungreased cookie sheet. Repeat with remaining dough, preserves, and chocolate mini pieces.

4 Preheat oven to 375°F. In small saucepan over low heat, melt remaining 2 tablespoons margarine or butter (¼ stick); remove saucepan from heat. In small bowl, mix almonds and sugar.

5 Brush cookies with melted butter; sprinkle with almond mixture. Bake cookies 25 minutes or until golden brown. With pancake turner, immediately remove cookies to wire racks to cool. Store cookies in tightly covered container.

CHOCOLATE-DIPPED PECAN SHORTBREAD

Makes 3 dozen

Begin about 2 hours before serving or early in day

2 ½ cups all-purpose flour

¾ cup confectioners' sugar

½ cup cornstarch

1 3-ounce can pecans (1 cup), finely chopped

1 ½ cups margarine or butter (3 sticks)

6 1-ounce squares semisweet chocolate

1 Preheat oven to 325°F. In large bowl, with fork, stir flour, confectioners' sugar, cornstarch, and chopped pecans. With knife, cut margarine or butter into small pieces; add to flour mixture. With hand, knead ingredients until well blended and mixture holds together.

2 Pat dough evenly into 13" by 9" baking dish. Bake shortbread 35 to 40 minutes until golden. With sharp knife, immediately cut shortbread lengthwise into 3 strips, then cut each strip crosswise into 12 pieces. Cool shortbread in dish on wire rack. When cold, with pancake turner, carefully remove shortbread cookies from baking dish.

3 In heavy 1-quart saucepan over low heat, heat chocolate, stirring frequently, until melted and smooth; remove saucepan from heat. Dip one corner of each cookie diagonally into chocolate until half the cookie is coated with chocolate. Place cookies on tray or cookie sheet lined with waxed paper or foil. Refrigerate until chocolate is set, about 15 minutes.

FUNNEL CAKES

Makes 7
Begin about 30 minutes before serving

Salad oil for frying

1 cup plus 2 tablespoons all-purpose flour

3/4 cup milk

1 teaspoon baking powder

1 teaspoon almond extract

1/8 teaspoon salt

1 large egg

2 tablespoons confectioners' sugar for sprinkling

1 In 10-inch skillet over medium heat, heat about 3/4 inch salad oil to 325°F. on deep-fat thermometer. (Or, heat oil according to manufacturer's directions in deep-fat fryer set at 325°F.)

2 Meanwhile, in medium bowl, with wire whisk or fork, mix flour, milk, baking powder, almond extract, salt, and egg until well blended.

3 Holding narrow-spouted funnel (1/2-inch spout), close spout with finger; pour 1/4 cup batter into funnel. Over hot oil, carefully remove finger to let batter run out in a stream, while making a spiral about 6 inches in diameter.

4 Fry 3 to 5 minutes until golden brown, turning once with tongs. Drain well on paper towels; keep warm. Repeat with remaining batter, stirring well before pouring.

5 Sprinkle Funnel Cakes lightly with confectioners' sugar. Serve warm.

Pennsylvania Dutch country specialty

FRIED BOW TIES

Makes about 7 dozen
Begin about 4 hours before serving or early in day

3 large eggs

1/4 cup sugar

1/4 cup milk

1/2 teaspoon salt

2 3/4 cups all-purpose flour

Salad oil for frying

Confectioners' sugar for sprinkling (optional)

1 In medium bowl, combine eggs, sugar, milk, salt, and 1 cup flour. With wooden spoon, stir ingredients until well blended; stir in remaining flour until mixture holds together. With hands, shape dough into ball; wrap with plastic wrap and refrigerate 2 hours or until dough is easy to handle. (Or, place dough in freezer 40 minutes.)

2 On floured surface, with floured rolling pin, roll out half the dough until paper thin, keeping remaining dough refrigerated. With knife, cut dough into 4" by 1 1/2" rectangles. Twist each rectangular strip twice to form bow-tie shape, pinching center to flatten and seal. Repeat with remaining dough.

3 In 10-inch skillet over medium heat, heat 3/4 inch salad oil to 350°F. on deep-fat thermometer. (Or, heat oil according to manufacturer's directions in deep-fat fryer set at 350°F.)

4 Gently place several bow ties in hot oil; fry about 1 1/2 minutes or until golden. Drain bow ties on paper towels; cool. Fry remaining bow ties in batches; drain and cool. Store in tightly covered container.

5 If you like, sprinkle bow ties with confectioners' sugar just before serving.

CRISPY SNOWFLAKES

Makes 32
Begin about 4 hours before serving or early in day

3 large eggs

2 ³/₄ cups all-purpose flour

¹/₄ cup sugar

¹/₄ cup milk

¹/₂ teaspoon salt

Salad oil for frying

Confectioners' sugar for sprinkling (optional)

1 In medium bowl, combine eggs, flour, sugar, milk, and salt. With wooden spoon, stir ingredients until well blended and mixture holds together. With hands, shape dough into ball; wrap with plastic wrap and refrigerate 2 hours or until dough is easy to handle. (Or, place dough in freezer 40 minutes.)

2 Divide dough into 32 pieces. On lightly floured surface, with floured rolling pin, roll out 8 dough pieces into 5 ¹/₂-inch rounds; cover and refrigerate remaining 24 dough pieces. Let dough rounds stand, uncovered, until tops are fairly dry.

3 Fold each dough round in half, folding dry-top-side together; fold again into quarters, then into eighths. With sharp knife or canapé cutter, cut designs along edges of dough. Unfold snowflakes and let stand at room temperature. Meanwhile, repeat with remaining dough, working with 8 pieces at a time.

4 In 12-inch skillet over medium heat, heat about ¹/₂ inch salad oil to 350°F. on deep-fat thermometer. (Or, heat oil according to manufacturer's directions in deep-fat fryer set at 350°F.)

5 Gently place 2 or 3 snowflakes in hot oil; fry about 1 ¹/₂ minutes or until golden. Drain snowflakes on paper towels; cool. Fry remaining snowflakes in batches; drain and cool. Store in tightly covered container.

6 If you like, sprinkle snowflakes with confectioners' sugar just before serving.

PIZZELLES

- Makes about 2 dozen pizzelles or 8 dozen wedge- or heart-shaped cookies
- Begin about 2 hours before serving or early in day

3 1/2 cups all-purpose flour
1 1/2 cups sugar
1 cup margarine or butter (2 sticks), melted
2 tablespoons vanilla or anise extract
4 teaspoons baking powder
6 large eggs

PIZZELLE IRON
Pizzelle irons are available in electric and nonelectric models in various sizes. Be sure to follow manufacturer's directions for using the correct amount of batter in your iron.

1 Preheat 7-inch electric pizzelle iron as manufacturer directs (see Box, above right).

2 Into large bowl, measure all ingredients. With mixer at low speed, beat ingredients until well blended, occasionally scraping bowl with rubber spatula.

3 Pour 2 tablespoons batter onto center of pizzelle iron. Cover; bake as manufacturer directs (do not lift cover during baking).

4 When done, lift cover and loosen pizzelle with fork; remove to wire rack to cool. Repeat with remaining batter.

5 When cookies are cold, break each into 4 pieces to serve. (The 7-inch iron makes round cookies, each with 4 wedge- or heart-shaped sections.) Store in tightly covered container.

ALL-OATMEAL CRUNCHIES

- Makes about 2 1/2 dozen
- Begin about 2 hours before serving or early in day

3/4 cup margarine or butter (1 1/2 sticks), softened
3/4 cup packed light brown sugar
1 tablespoon grated lemon peel
1 teaspoon baking powder
1/8 teaspoon salt
1 large egg
3 1/4 cups quick-cooking oats, uncooked
1/3 cup blanched whole almonds, ground
2 large egg yolks, slightly beaten

1 Into large bowl, measure first 6 ingredients. With mixer at medium speed, beat ingredients 10 minutes or until light and fluffy, occasionally scraping bowl with rubber spatula. Add oats and almonds; with hand, knead until well blended and mixture holds together.

2 Preheat oven to 350°F. Grease well 2 large cookie sheets. Between two sheets of waxed paper, roll out half the dough 1/4 inch thick. With 2 1/2-inch round cookie cutter, cut dough into as many cookies as possible; place cookies, 1 inch apart, on cookie sheets. Brush tops of cookies with egg yolk.

3 Bake cookies 12 minutes or until golden. Immediately, with pancake turner, remove cookies to wire racks to cool. Repeat with remaining dough and trimmings. Store cookies in tightly covered container.

FINNISH ALMOND COOKIES

Makes 2 ½ dozen

Begin about 1 ½ hours before serving or early in day

2 cups all-purpose flour
³/₄ cup margarine or butter (1 ¹/₂ sticks), softened
1 teaspoon almond extract
¹/₄ cup plus 2 tablespoons sugar
1 large egg, separated
1 3 ¹/₂-ounce can sliced blanched almonds (1 cup)

1 Into large bowl, measure flour, margarine or butter, almond extract, ¹/₄ cup sugar, and egg yolk. With hand, knead ingredients until well blended and mixture holds together. (Mixture will appear dry at first – if too dry, add about *1 tablespoon water* while kneading.)

2 Preheat oven to 375°F. On lightly floured surface, with floured rolling pin, roll out half the dough into 10" by 9" rectangle. In cup, with fork, beat egg white slightly; with pastry brush, brush dough with some egg white. Sprinkle with half the almonds and 1 tablespoon sugar. Cut dough into fifteen 3" by 2" rectangles. With pancake turner, place cookies, ¹/₂ inch apart, on ungreased cookie sheet.

3 Bake cookies 10 to 12 minutes until lightly browned. With pancake turner, remove cookies to wire racks to cool completely. Repeat with remaining dough, almonds, and sugar. Store cookies in tightly covered container.

TOASTED SESAME COOKIES

Makes about 3 dozen

Begin about 2 hours before serving or early in day

2 2 ¹/₈-ounce jars sesame seeds (about 1 cup)
2 cups all-purpose flour
³/₄ cup sugar
¹/₂ cup margarine or butter (1 stick), softened
1 teaspoon baking powder
¹/₂ teaspoon vanilla extract
¹/₄ teaspoon salt
1 large egg

1 In 10-inch skillet over medium heat, cook sesame seeds until golden, shaking pan and stirring frequently. Remove skillet from heat; set aside.

2 Into large bowl, measure flour, sugar, margarine or butter, baking powder, vanilla extract, salt, egg, and *2 tablespoons water*. With mixer at low speed, beat ingredients until well blended, occasionally scraping bowl with rubber spatula. With wooden spoon, stir in ¹/₂ cup toasted sesame seeds.

3 Preheat oven to 350°F. Shape 2 teaspoons dough at a time into 2-inch-long oval; roll ovals in remaining sesame seeds. Place ovals, about 1 inch apart, on ungreased cookie sheets.

4 Bake cookies 20 minutes or until lightly browned. With pancake turner, remove cookies to wire rack to cool. Store cookies in tightly covered container.

SWEET AND SPICY PEPPERNUTS

 Makes about 6 cups

Begin about 2 ½ hours before serving or early in day

1 ³/₄ cups all-purpose flour
1 cup packed light brown sugar
4 tablespoons margarine or butter (¹/₂ stick), softened
¹/₄ teaspoon baking soda
¹/₄ teaspoon ground cinnamon
¹/₄ teaspoon ground cloves
¹/₄ teaspoon ground ginger
¹/₄ teaspoon white pepper
1 large egg

1 Preheat oven to 375°F. Into large bowl, measure all ingredients. With mixer at low speed, beat ingredients until well blended, occasionally scraping bowl with rubber spatula. (Mixture may be crumbly; if necessary, add 1 teaspoon water and, with hand, knead until mixture holds together.) Shape dough into ball.

2 For each cookie, pinch off ¹/₈ teaspoon dough; with hands, shape into ball. Place dough balls, about ¹/₂ inch apart, on ungreased cookie sheets.

3 Bake cookies 7 minutes or until lightly browned. Let cookies cool on cookie sheets. Store cookies in tightly covered container.

MAPLE LEAVES

 Makes about 4 dozen

Begin about 3 ½ hours before serving or early in day

4 cups all-purpose flour
1 cup margarine or butter (2 sticks), softened
³/₄ cup packed light brown sugar
¹/₂ cup maple or maple-flavor syrup
2 teaspoons cream of tartar
1 teaspoon baking soda
³/₄ teaspoon salt
2 large eggs

1 Into large bowl, measure all ingredients. With mixer at low speed, beat ingredients until well blended, occasionally scraping bowl with rubber spatula.

2 With hands, shape dough into ball; wrap with plastic wrap and refrigerate 1 hour or until dough is easy to handle. (Or, place dough in freezer 30 minutes.)

3 Preheat oven to 350°F. Grease large cookie sheet. On lightly floured surface, with floured rolling pin, roll out one-third of dough ¹/₈ inch thick; keep remaining dough refrigerated. With floured 3¹/₂-inch leaf-shaped cookie cutter, cut dough into leaves; score leaf "veins" in dough with tip of knife. Place cookies, 1 inch apart, on cookie sheet.

4 Bake cookies 10 minutes or until golden. With pancake turner, remove to wire racks to cool. Repeat with remaining dough and trimmings. Store in tightly covered container.

POPPY-SEED SWIRLS

Makes about 5 dozen

Begin about 4 hours before serving or early in day

1/2 cup sugar

3/4 cup margarine or butter (1 1/2 sticks), softened

1 3/4 cups all-purpose flour

1/2 teaspoon vanilla extract

1/4 teaspoon salt

1 large egg

1/2 cup walnuts

1/2 cup poppy seeds

1/4 cup honey

3/4 teaspoon grated orange peel

1/4 teaspoon ground cinnamon

1 In large bowl, with mixer at low speed, beat sugar and 1/2 cup margarine or butter (1 stick) just until blended. Increase speed to high; beat 10 minutes or until light and fluffy, scraping bowl often with rubber spatula. Reduce speed to low; add flour, vanilla extract, salt, and egg; beat just until blended, occasionally scraping bowl. With hands, shape dough into ball; wrap with plastic wrap and refrigerate 1 hour or until dough is firm enough to handle. (Or, place dough in freezer 30 minutes.)

2 Meanwhile, in blender at medium speed or in food processor with knife blade attached, finely grind walnuts. In small bowl, stir walnuts, poppy seeds, honey, orange peel, cinnamon, and remaining 1/4 cup margarine or butter (1/2 stick) until mixed; set aside.

3 On sheet of waxed paper, with floured rolling pin, roll out half the dough into 10" by 8" rectangle (keep remaining dough refrigerated); spread rectangle with half the poppy-seed mixture. Starting at 8-inch side, roll dough jelly-roll fashion. Wrap roll with plastic wrap and refrigerate 1 hour or until dough is firm enough to slice. (Or, place roll in freezer 30 minutes.) Repeat with remaining dough and filling.

4 Preheat oven to 375°F. With sharp knife, slice 1 roll crosswise into 1/4-inch-thick slices. Place slices, about 1/2 inch apart, on ungreased cookie sheets.

5 Bake cookies 10 to 12 minutes until lightly browned. With pancake turner, remove cookies to wire racks to cool. Repeat with remaining roll. Store cookies in tightly covered container.

PINWHEELS

Makes about 3 dozen

Begin about 3 1/2 hours before serving or early in day

2 cups all-purpose flour

1 cup packed light brown sugar

1/2 cup margarine or butter (1 stick), softened

1 tablespoon vanilla extract

1 teaspoon salt

1 teaspoon imitation maple flavor

1/2 teaspoon baking soda

1 large egg

1/2 3-ounce can pecans (1/2 cup), chopped

1 Into large bowl, measure all ingredients except pecans. With mixer at low speed, beat ingredients until well blended, occasionally scraping bowl with rubber spatula.

2 With hands, shape dough into ball; wrap with plastic wrap and refrigerate 1 hour or until dough is easy to handle. (Or, place dough in freezer 30 minutes.)

3 Preheat oven to 350°F. Grease large cookie sheet. On lightly floured surface, with floured rolling pin, roll out one-third of dough 1/8 inch thick; keep remaining dough refrigerated. With floured 3 1/2-inch round cookie cutter, cut dough into rounds. Place rounds, 1 inch apart, on cookie sheet. With knife, cut 4 lines from edge of each round almost to center, forming equal quarters; fold left corner of each quarter to center; press firmly to form pinwheel. Sprinkle chopped pecans on center of each.

4 Bake cookies 10 to 12 minutes until golden. Remove cookies to wire racks to cool. Repeat with remaining dough and pecans. Store cookies in tightly covered container.

PIGNOLI COOKIE CUPS

🥄 Makes 16
🕐 Begin about
2 ½ hours before
serving or early
in day

³/4 cup all-purpose flour

*5 tablespoons margarine or
butter, softened*

4 tablespoons sugar

¹/4 cup light corn syrup

¹/2 teaspoon vanilla extract

1 large egg

*1 3-ounce jar pine nuts
(pignoli)*

1 Preheat oven to
350°F. Into medium
bowl, measure flour,
4 tablespoons margarine
or butter (¹/2 stick), and
3 tablespoons sugar. With
hand, knead ingredients
until well blended and
mixture holds together.

2 Divide dough into
16 pieces. Press dough
pieces onto bottoms and
up sides of sixteen
1 ³/4-inch muffin-pan cups.

3 In 1-quart saucepan
over low heat, melt
remaining 1 tablespoon
margarine or butter.
Remove saucepan from
heat; stir in corn syrup,
vanilla extract, egg, and
remaining 1 tablespoon
sugar.

4 Into dough cups,
sprinkle pine nuts.

5 Spoon corn-syrup
mixture on top of
pine nuts. Bake cookies
about 25 minutes or until
crust is browned and toothpick inserted in center
of filling comes out clean.

6 Cool cookies in cups
on wire racks about
5 minutes or until firm.
With tip of knife or small
metal spatula, loosen
cookie cups from
muffin-pan cups;
place on wire racks
to cool completely.

FILBERT CRESCENTS

🥄 Makes about
3 dozen
🕐 Begin about 2 hours
before serving or
early in day

¹/4 cup filberts (hazelnuts)

1 ¹/4 cups all-purpose flour

*¹/2 cup margarine or butter
(1 stick), softened*

¹/2 cup confectioners' sugar

¹/2 teaspoon baking powder

¹/4 teaspoon salt

1 Preheat oven to
400°F. Place filberts
in 9" by 9" baking pan.
Bake 8 to 10 minutes until
lightly toasted. Remove
nuts from oven; turn oven
control to 350°F. Cool
nuts; finely chop.

2 Into large bowl,
measure flour, marga-
rine or butter, confectioners' sugar, baking powder,
and salt; add filberts. With
hand, knead ingredients
until well blended and
mixture holds together.
(Mixture may be crumbly;
if necessary, add *1 tablespoon water* while kneading
ingredients together.)

3 Shape dough into
1 ³/4" by ¹/2" crescents
(about 2 level teaspoons
each). Place cookies, about
1 inch apart, on ungreased
cookie sheets.

4 Bake cookies
10 minutes or until
lightly browned. With
pancake turner, remove
cookies to wire racks to
cool. Store cookies in
tightly covered container.

PISTACHIO BARS

🍴 Makes 20

🕐 Begin about 2 hours before serving or early in day

1 ³/₄ cups all-purpose flour

³/₄ cup margarine or butter (1 ¹/₂ sticks), softened

1 teaspoon vanilla extract

¹/₄ teaspoon salt

1 ¹/₂ cups confectioners' sugar

1 cup shelled pistachios

2 teaspoons lemon juice

1 Into large bowl, measure flour, margarine or butter, vanilla extract, salt, and 1 cup confectioners' sugar. With hand, knead ingredients until well blended and mixture holds together. Flatten dough to 1-inch thickness; wrap with plastic wrap and refrigerate 45 minutes or until dough is easy to handle. (Or, place dough in freezer 30 minutes.)

2 Meanwhile, coarsely chop pistachios; set aside. Preheat oven to 350°F.

3 On lightly floured surface, with floured rolling pin, roll out dough into 12" by 10" rectangle. If dough breaks apart, press cracks together with fingers. Cut rectangle lengthwise into 5 strips; cut each strip crosswise into 4 pieces. Sprinkle with pistachios; with rolling pin, gently press pistachios into dough.

4 Place bars on large ungreased cookie sheet. Bake cookies 15 minutes or until edges are lightly browned. With pancake turner, remove cookies to wire racks to cool.

5 In small bowl, with spoon, mix remaining ¹/₂ cup confectioners' sugar with lemon juice until smooth. Drizzle lemon glaze over bars; let stand until set. Store bars in tightly covered container.

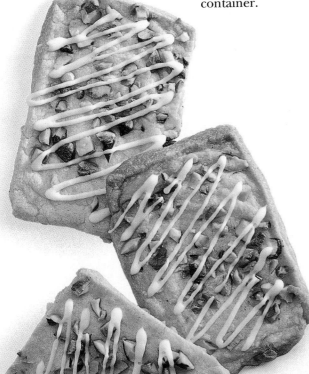

TOFFEE BARS

🍴 Makes 4 dozen

🕐 Begin about 2 hours before serving or early in day

1 ³/₄ cups all-purpose flour

1 cup sugar

1 cup margarine or butter (2 sticks), softened

1 teaspoon vanilla extract

1 large egg, separated

¹/₂ cup walnuts, finely chopped

1 Preheat oven to 275°F. Grease 15 ¹/₂" by 10 ¹/₂" jelly-roll pan. Into large bowl, measure flour, sugar, margarine or butter, vanilla extract, and egg yolk. With mixer at low speed, beat ingredients just until blended, occasionally scraping bowl with rubber spatula. Increase speed to medium; beat until well mixed, occasionally scraping bowl.

2 Pat dough evenly into jelly-roll pan. In cup, with fork, beat egg white slightly; with pastry brush, brush over top of dough. Sprinkle with walnuts.

3 Bake 1 hour and 10 minutes or until golden. With sharp knife, immediately cut crosswise into 12 strips, then cut each strip into 4 pieces to make 48 bars.

4 With pancake turner, remove bars from pan to wire racks to cool. Store bars in tightly covered container.

MOCHA FINGERS

Makes 27

Begin about 2 hours before serving or early in day

1 1/2 cups all-purpose flour

1/2 cup sugar

1/2 cup margarine or butter (1 stick), softened

1/4 cup unsweetened cocoa

1/2 teaspoon baking powder

1 large egg

Mocha Filling (see Box, above right)

MOCHA FILLING

In small bowl, with mixer at medium speed, beat 1 cup confectioners' sugar, 1/2 cup margarine or butter (1 stick), softened, 2 tablespoons unsweetened cocoa, and 2 teaspoons instant espresso-coffee powder until smooth.

1 Into large bowl, measure flour, sugar, margarine or butter, cocoa, baking powder, and egg. With mixer at low speed, beat ingredients until well blended, occasionally scraping bowl with rubber spatula.

2 Preheat oven to 350°F. Grease large cookie sheet. On lightly floured surface, with floured rolling pin, roll out half the dough into 9" by 9" square, about 1/8 inch thick. Cut dough square into thirds, then cut each third crosswise into nine 3" by 1" rectangles.

3 With pancake turner, place rectangles, about 1 inch apart, on cookie sheet.

4 With fork, prick each cookie in several places for decoration. Bake cookies 15 minutes or until firm. With pancake turner, remove cookies to wire rack to cool. Repeat with remaining dough.

5 While cookies are cooling, prepare Mocha Filling.

6 Assemble cookie sandwiches: Spread bottom of half the cookies with Mocha Filling; top with remaining cookies, top-side up. Store cookies in tightly covered container.

ALMOND DIAMOND COOKIES

Makes about 2 dozen

Begin about 4 1/2 hours before serving or early in day

1 1/3 cups all-purpose flour

3/4 cup sugar

1/2 cup margarine or butter (1 stick), softened

2 teaspoons baking powder

1/2 teaspoon vanilla extract

1/4 teaspoon salt

1/4 teaspoon almond extract

1 large egg

1 large egg yolk

1 Into large bowl, measure flour, sugar, margarine or butter, baking powder, vanilla extract, salt, almond extract, and egg. With mixer at low speed, beat ingredients until well blended, occasionally scraping bowl with rubber spatula.

2 On waxed paper, with hands, shape dough into 6 1/2" by 2" roll; wrap in waxed paper and refrigerate 2 hours or until dough is firm enough to slice. (Or, place dough in freezer 1 hour.)

3 Preheat oven to 350°F. With sharp knife, slice dough crosswise into 1/4-inch-thick slices. Place slices, about 1 inch apart, on ungreased large cookie sheets.

4 In cup, with fork, slightly beat egg yolk; with pastry brush, brush cookies with egg yolk. With dull edge of knife, score cookies to make criss-crossed diamond pattern.

5 Bake cookies 15 minutes or until lightly browned. With pancake turner, remove cookies to wire racks to cool. Store cookies in tightly covered container.

CHOCODAMIA COOKIES

🥄 Makes about
2 ½ dozen

🕐 Begin about 2 hours
before serving or
early in day

1 8-ounce package
semisweet-chocolate
squares (8 1-ounce
squares)

3 3 ½-ounce jars
macadamia nuts
(2 ¼ cups)

1 ¼ cups all-purpose flour

½ cup margarine or butter
(1 stick), softened

½ cup packed light brown
sugar

¼ cup sugar

1 teaspoon vanilla extract

½ teaspoon baking soda

½ teaspoon salt

1 large egg

1 Preheat oven to 375°F.
With sharp knife, cut
semisweet chocolate into
½-inch chunks. Coarsely
chop 2 jars of macadamia
nuts; reserve remaining
whole nuts for
topping
cookies.

2 Into large bowl,
measure flour, marga-
rine or butter, brown
sugar, sugar, vanilla
extract, baking soda, salt,
egg, and *1 tablespoon water*.
With mixer at low speed,
beat ingredients until well
blended, occasionally
scraping bowl with rubber
spatula. Stir in chopped
chocolate and chopped
macadamia nuts.

3 Drop mixture by
heaping tablespoons,
about 2 inches apart, onto
ungreased large cookie
sheets. With pancake
turner, flatten each cookie
to make 2-inch round;
press reserved whole
macadamia nuts onto
cookies.

4 Bake cookies 10 to
15 minutes until
lightly browned. With
pancake turner, carefully
remove cookies to wire
racks to cool. Store cookies
in tightly covered
container.

PEANUT-BUTTER SAND DOLLARS

🥄 Makes about
2 ½ dozen

🕐 Begin about 3 ½
hours before serving
or early in day

2 ½ cups all-purpose flour

½ cup margarine or butter
(1 stick), softened

½ cup light molasses

¼ cup sugar

1 tablespoon vanilla extract

1 teaspoon salt

½ teaspoon baking soda

2 large eggs

2 cups chunky peanut
butter

1 Into large bowl,
measure flour, marga-
rine or butter, molasses,
sugar, vanilla extract, salt,
baking soda, and 1 egg.
With mixer at low speed,
beat ingredients until well
blended, occasionally
scraping bowl with rubber
spatula. With hands,
shape dough into ball;
wrap with plastic wrap and
refrigerate 1 hour or until
dough is easy to handle.
(Or, place dough in
freezer 30 minutes.)

2 Preheat oven to
350°F. Grease large
cookie sheet. On lightly
floured surface, with
floured rolling pin, roll
out half the dough ⅛ inch
thick, keeping remaining
dough refrigerated. With
floured 3-inch round or
scalloped cookie cutter,
cut dough into 24 rounds,
rerolling trimmings.

3 Arrange 12 rounds,
1 inch apart, on
cookie sheet; place
1 tablespoon peanut
butter on center of each
round. With tip of knife,
cut 5 small slits, radiating
from center, on each of
remaining 12 rounds;
place them on rounds with
peanut butter. With fork,
seal edges.

4 In cup, with fork, beat
remaining egg
slightly; with pastry brush,
brush tops of cookies
lightly with some egg. Bake
cookies 10 to 12 minutes
until golden brown. With
pancake turner, remove
cookies to wire racks to
cool. Repeat with remain-
ing dough and peanut
butter. Store cookies in
tightly covered container.

GINGERBREAD CHRISTMAS COOKIES

Makes about
4 dozen

Begin early in day or
up to 1 month
ahead

²/₃ cup molasses

½ cup packed brown sugar

*½ cup margarine or butter
(1 stick), softened*

1 ½ teaspoons baking soda

½ teaspoon salt

½ teaspoon ground allspice

*½ teaspoon ground
cinnamon*

½ teaspoon ground cloves

½ teaspoon ground ginger

2 large eggs

*About 4 ½ cups
all-purpose flour*

*Ornamental Frosting (see
Box, above right)*

1 Into large bowl,
measure molasses,
brown sugar, margarine or
butter, baking soda, salt,
allspice, cinnamon, cloves,
ginger, eggs, and 1 ½ cups
flour. With mixer at low
speed, beat ingredients
until just mixed, constantly
scraping bowl with rubber
spatula. Increase speed to
medium; beat 2 minutes,
occasionally scraping bowl.
With wooden spoon, stir in
about 3 cups flour to make
stiff dough. Shape dough
into ball; wrap with plastic
wrap. Use dough imme-
diately or refrigerate to
use within 2 days.

2 Preheat oven to
350°F. On lightly
floured surface, with
floured rolling pin, roll
out half the dough ⅛ inch
thick.

**ORNAMENTAL
FROSTING**
In small bowl, with
mixer at low speed, beat
*one 16-ounce package
confectioners' sugar
(4 cups)*, *⅓ cup warm
water*, and *3 tablespoons
meringue powder* until just
mixed. Increase speed
to high; beat mixture
until so stiff that knife
drawn through mixture
leaves clean-cut path.

3 With desired shape
cookie cutter (about
3½ inches), cut out as
many cookies as possible.
With pancake turner,
place cookies, about
½ inch apart, on
ungreased large cookie
sheet.

4 Bake cookies
12 minutes or until
edges are firm. With pan-
cake turner, immediately
loosen cookies from
cookie sheet and remove
to wire racks to cool.
Repeat with remaining
dough and trimmings.

5 If not decorating
cookies right away,
wrap cookies with freezer
wrap; seal, label, and
freeze. Before decorating
frozen cookies, unwrap
and thaw 1 hour.

6 Prepare Ornamental
Frosting. Spoon
frosting into decorating
bag with small writing
tube, or use paper cone
with tip cut to make
⅛-inch-diameter hole;
pipe decorative outlines
and designs on each
cookie. Set cookies aside
to allow frosting to dry
completely, about 1 hour.

Big Tree

Twinkling Star

Rocking Horse Winner

Santa

Reindeer

LEMON-CHOCOLATE DRIZZLES

Makes about
8 ½ dozen

Begin about 5 hours
before serving or
early in day

2 ½ cups all-purpose flour

1 cup sugar

¾ cup margarine or butter
(1 ½ sticks), softened

2 teaspoons baking powder

¾ teaspoon grated lemon
peel

2 large eggs

Chocolate Drizzle (see Box,
above right)

1 Into large bowl, measure all ingredients except Chocolate Drizzle. With mixer at low speed, beat ingredients until well blended, occasionally scraping bowl with rubber spatula. With hands, shape dough into ball; wrap with plastic wrap and refrigerate 3 hours or until dough is easy to handle. (Or, place dough in freezer 1 hour.)

2 Preheat oven to 350°F. On lightly floured surface, with floured rolling pin, roll out half the dough ⅛ inch thick, keeping remaining dough refrigerated. With floured 2 ½-inch flower-shaped cookie cutter, cut dough into as many cookies as possible. Place cookies, ½ inch apart, on ungreased cookie sheet.

3 Bake cookies 6 to 8 minutes until lightly browned. With pancake turner, remove cookies to wire racks to cool. Repeat with remaining dough and trimmings.

CHOCOLATE DRIZZLE

In heavy 1-quart saucepan over low heat, heat *three 1-ounce squares semisweet chocolate* and *1 tablespoon margarine* or butter, stirring frequently, until melted and smooth.

4 Prepare Chocolate Drizzle; cool slightly for easier piping. Spoon chocolate mixture into paper cone with tip cut to make ⅛-inch-diameter hole, or use decorating bag with small writing tube.

5 On long sheet of waxed paper, arrange cookies in one layer as close together as possible. Hold chocolate-filled paper cone or decorating bag several inches above cookies; working quickly, drizzle chocolate mixture over cookies in zigzag pattern.

6 Let chocolate dry about 30 minutes or until firm. Store cookies in tightly covered container.

FROZEN
DESSERTS
241-272

Frozen Desserts

Summertime or winter, our cool, creamy frozen desserts will delight everyone. Many of our frozen tortes and iced drinks begin with basic vanilla ice cream (we've included our own delectable recipe) and we've suggested some pretty garnishes, such as mint leaves and fruit slices, and even coffee-bean candies. Individual Frozen Fruit Cupcakes and Ice-Cream Bonbons are ideal for casual entertaining and everyday eating. On the lighter side, Raspberry Sorbet and Two-Tone Granitas – elegant layers of icy coffee and citrus sorbet – are so refreshing in hot weather or to balance out a lavishly rich meal. When you're feeling especially creative, try our luscious Hazelnut Fantasy, smooth, frozen coffee and chocolate custards with hazelnut "crunch" topping. Or, for a special treat, Fudge-Sundae Pie, a deluxe concoction of vanilla and chocolate ice creams with a rich and chewy fudge center, all in a walnut crust. Scrumptious!

CONTENTS

Frozen Desserts

Nothing beats ice cream or frozen yogurt, sherbet, or sorbet for "instant" dessert: just dish it up, serve, and enjoy. You'll find the favorite flavors in this chapter, plus recipes to turn them (or their storebought counterparts) into chilly treats that money can't buy, such as dacquoises, frozen tortes, and more. For freezer storage, wrap them airtight to prevent freezer burn, and keep on hand to serve with easy elegance on very short notice or to end a feast superbly.

FROZEN PEANUT-BUTTER CUPS

6 servings
Begin about 3 1/2 hours before serving or day ahead

1 cup heavy or whipping cream

1 7- to 7 1/2-ounce jar marshmallow cream

1 3-ounce package cream cheese, softened

1/2 cup chunky peanut butter

Semisweet Chocolate Curls (page 158) and lemon leaves for garnish

1 In small bowl, with mixer at medium speed, beat heavy or whipping cream until stiff peaks form. In large bowl, using same beaters and with mixer at low speed, beat marshmallow cream, cream cheese, and peanut butter until smooth, occasionally scraping bowl with rubber spatula.

2 With rubber spatula or wire whisk, fold whipped cream into peanut-butter mixture.

3 Spoon peanut-butter mousse mixture into foil tart pans. Cover; freeze until firm, at least 3 hours.

4 Let stand at room temperature about 10 minutes to soften slightly for easier eating.

TO SERVE
Garnish with chocolate curls and lemon leaves.

RAINBOW ICE-CREAM TORTE

16 servings

Begin early in day or up to 1 week ahead

2 *pints chocolate ice cream*

2 *pints mint chocolate-chip ice cream*

2 *pints strawberry ice cream*

2 *pints vanilla ice cream*

About 20 gingersnap cookies

4 *tablespoons margarine or butter (¹/₂ stick), softened*

2 *16 ¹/₂- to 17-ounce cans pitted dark sweet cherries, well drained*

¹/₂ *cup walnuts, chopped*

1 Place ice creams in refrigerator to soften slightly.

2 Meanwhile, place cookies in heavy-duty, closed plastic bag; with rolling pin, roll cookies into fine crumbs. (You should have 1 ¹/₃ cups.)

3 Or, in food processor with knife blade attached or in blender at medium speed, blend gingersnap cookies until fine crumbs form.

4 In 10" by 3" spring-form pan, with hand, mix cookie crumbs with margarine or butter; press mixture firmly onto bottom of pan. Freeze until firm, about 10 minutes.

5 Evenly spread chocolate ice cream on top of crumb mixture. Place pan in freezer to harden ice cream slightly, about 15 minutes.

6 Spread mint choco-late-chip ice cream on chocolate ice-cream layer; top with cherries.

7 Return springform pan to freezer to harden ice creams and cherries slightly.

8 With metal spatula, evenly spread straw-berry ice cream over layer of cherries.

Spreading strawberry ice cream over cherries

9 Place pan in freezer to harden ice cream slightly, about 15 minutes. Evenly spread vanilla ice cream on strawberry ice-cream layer. Sprinkle top with walnuts. Cover and freeze until firm.

10 To serve, run knife or metal spatula, dipped in hot water, around edge of pan to loosen torte; remove side of pan. Let torte stand at room temperature about 10 minutes for easier slicing.

VANILLA ICE CREAM

About 3 ½ quarts or 28 servings

Begin early in day or up to 1 month ahead

2 cups sugar

⅓ cup all-purpose flour

1 ½ teaspoons salt

6 cups milk

6 large eggs

3 cups heavy or whipping cream

3 tablespoons vanilla extract

About 10 to 20 pounds cracked ice

About 3 cups rock salt for ice cream and cooling or 2 cups table salt

1 In heavy 4-quart saucepan, with spoon or wire whisk, mix sugar, flour, and salt; stir in milk. Cook over medium heat until mixture thickens slightly and boils, stirring frequently.

2 In medium bowl, with fork, beat eggs slightly; stir in small amount of hot milk mixture. Slowly pour egg mixture back into hot milk mixture in saucepan, stirring rapidly to prevent lumping; cook, stirring constantly, until mixture thickens and coats a spoon well, about 5 minutes (mixture should be about 170° to 175°F.).

3 Remove saucepan from heat. To keep skin from forming as custard mixture cools, press plastic wrap directly onto surface of hot custard. Refrigerate until completely chilled, about 3 hours, stirring occasionally.

4 Pour chilled custard mixture, heavy or whipping cream, and vanilla extract into 5- to 6-quart ice-cream freezer can. Place dasher in can and cover. Place can in freezer bucket; attach motor or hand crank. Add *2 cups water* to bucket.

5 Fill bucket half full with ice; sprinkle with ¼ cup rock salt or 3 tablespoons table salt. Add about 1 inch of ice and ¼ cup rock salt or 3 tablespoons table salt. Repeat layers of ice and salt until layers reach 1 inch below can lid. Freeze as manufacturer directs, adding more ice and salt as needed. Freezing takes about 35 minutes.

6 When freezing is finished, ice cream will be soft. Remove motor or crank; wipe lid clean; remove dasher. With spoon, pack down ice cream. Cover surface of ice cream closely with plastic wrap. Replace lid and put cork in hole in center; add more ice and salt to completely cover lid. Let ice cream stand to harden, about 2 to 3 hours, adding ice as needed. (Or, place container in home freezer 2 to 3 hours.)

ICE CREAM VARIATIONS

Once you've mastered the art of ice-cream making, you can make the changes by adding different fresh fruits, chocolate, nuts, or fudge to vanilla ice cream. Here are 3 delicious varieties for you to try:

Chocolate Ice Cream
Prepare custard mixture as in steps 1 through 3 for Vanilla Ice Cream, except add *one 8-ounce package semisweet-chocolate squares* (eight 1-ounce squares), chopped, with milk in step 1. Follow step 4 but use only 1 tablespoon vanilla extract in custard mixture. Then freeze and harden as in steps 5 and 6. Makes about 3 ¾ quarts ice cream or 30 servings.

Fudge-Swirl Ice Cream
Prepare Vanilla Ice Cream. While ice cream is freezing, prepare fudge sauce: In heavy 2-quart saucepan over medium-high heat, heat *1 cup sugar, 1 cup heavy or whipping cream, 2 tablespoons margarine* or butter (¼ stick), *1 tablespoon light corn syrup,* and *four 1-ounce squares unsweetened chocolate,* chopped, to boiling, stirring constantly. Reduce heat to medium; cook 5 minutes, stirring occasionally. Remove saucepan from heat; stir in *1 teaspoon vanilla extract.* Let sauce stand at room temperature to cool slightly, stirring occasionally. After freezing ice cream, spoon into 15 ½" by 1 ½" roasting pan or 6-quart bowl. With spoon or knife, quickly swirl fudge sauce into ice cream to create marbled design. Cover surface of ice cream with plastic wrap; cover pan with foil. Place pan in freezer 2 to 3 hours to harden. Makes about 4 quarts ice cream or 32 servings.

Strawberry Ice Cream
Prepare custard mixture as in steps 1 through 3 for Vanilla Ice Cream. While custard mixture is chilling, in medium bowl, with potato masher or slotted spoon, crush *1 ½ pints strawberries,* hulled, with *1 cup sugar* and *2 tablespoons lemon juice;* let stand at least 1 hour. Follow step 4, but add strawberry mixture and *¼ teaspoon red food coloring* (optional). Then freeze and harden as in steps 5 and 6. Makes about 4 quarts ice cream or 32 servings.

Chocolate Ice Cream
A piped chocolate design only hints at the rich taste of Chocolate Ice Cream. Make the designs as shown, using directions for Chocolate Squiggles (page 111); chill, and place on servings at the last minute.

Vanilla Ice Cream
Homemade Vanilla Ice Cream is America's favorite, so delicious that it can be served absolutely plain. Yet it's equally good topped off with sweet sauces, fruit, nuts, honey, liqueur, even crumbled cookies.

Strawberry Ice Cream
For incomparable flavor, use the reddest, ripest (but not overripe), juiciest berries you can find for Strawberry Ice Cream. Here, scoops of varied sizes make a pretty plateful.

Fudge-Swirl Ice Cream
The garnish is built right into Fudge-Swirl Ice Cream, with thick, fudgy sauce rippled through the frozen mixture. Elegant rolled cookies make a perfect go-along.

WALNUT ICE-CREAM ROLL

16 servings

Begin early in day or up to 1 week ahead

4 large eggs

³/4 cup sugar

1/2 cup cake flour

1 teaspoon baking powder

1/4 teaspoon salt

1/3 cup unsweetened cocoa plus extra for sprinkling

2 pints vanilla ice cream

1/2 6-ounce package semisweet-chocolate pieces (1/2 cup)

1/4 cup sweetened condensed milk

2 tablespoons orange-flavor liqueur

2 1/2 cups walnuts

1/2 12-ounce jar butterscotch-flavor topping (1/2 cup)

1 Preheat oven to 375°F. Grease 15 1/2" by 10 1/2" jelly-roll pan; line pan with waxed paper.

2 Separate eggs, placing egg whites in small mixing bowl and yolks in large mixing bowl. With mixer at high speed, beat egg whites until soft peaks form; gradually sprinkle in 1/4 cup sugar, beating until sugar completely dissolves and whites stand in stiff peaks.

3 In large bowl with egg yolks, using same beaters and with mixer at high speed, beat remaining 1/2 cup sugar until very thick and lemon-colored. Reduce speed to medium; add flour, baking powder, salt, and 1/3 cup cocoa; beat until well mixed, occasionally scraping bowl with rubber spatula.

4 With wire whisk or rubber spatula, gently fold beaten egg-white mixture into egg-yolk mixture.

5 Spoon batter into pan, spreading evenly. Bake 12 to 15 minutes until top of cake springs back when lightly touched with finger.

6 Sprinkle clean cloth towel with cocoa. When cake is done, immediately invert cake onto towel. Carefully peel waxed paper from cake. If you like, cut off crisp edges. Starting at 1 narrow end, roll cake with towel, jelly-roll fashion. Place cake roll, seam-side down, on wire rack; cool completely, about 30 minutes.

7 Place vanilla ice cream in refrigerator to soften slightly, about 30 minutes. Meanwhile, in heavy 1-quart saucepan over low heat, heat semi-sweet-chocolate pieces, stirring frequently, until melted and smooth. Remove saucepan from heat; stir in sweetened condensed milk and orange-flavor liqueur until blended. Refrigerate chocolate mixture until slightly cooled, about 15 minutes.

8 Unroll cooled cake; evenly spread top with softened ice cream.

9 Spoon chocolate mixture in crosswise strip along 1 narrow end, leaving 2-inch border.

10 Starting at same narrow end, roll cake without towel. Cover and freeze ice-cream roll until firm enough to handle, about 2 hours.

11 Meanwhile, in 10-inch skillet over medium heat, cook walnuts until toasted, stirring frequently; remove pan from heat. When walnuts are cool, chop coarsely.

12 With metal spatula, evenly spread butterscotch-flavor topping over ice-cream roll.

13 With fingertips, evenly pat walnuts into topping.

14 Cover and freeze until firm, at least 4 hours.

15 Place ice-cream roll on chilled platter; let stand at room temperature 10 minutes for easier slicing.

Spreading cake with ice cream

Cake and ice cream all rolled up in an easy-to-serve combination. Even the sauce is built in!

HAZELNUT FANTASY

16 servings
Begin early in day or
up to 1 week ahead

Hazelnut Crunch (see Box, below right)

12 large egg yolks

³/4 cup light corn syrup

2 tablespoons coffee-flavor liqueur

2 teaspoons instant espresso-coffee powder

1 6-ounce package semisweet-chocolate pieces (1 cup)

3 cups heavy or whipping cream

Toasted hazelnuts (sometimes called filberts) for garnish

1 Prepare Hazelnut Crunch.

2 In large bowl, with mixer at medium-high speed, beat egg yolks and corn syrup until slightly thickened and light-colored, about 4 minutes. Pour egg-yolk mixture into heavy 4-quart saucepan. Cook over low heat, stirring constantly, until mixture thickens and coats a spoon well, about 30 minutes (mixture should be about 170° to 175°F., but do not boil or it will curdle). Remove saucepan from heat.

3 Pour two-thirds of egg-yolk mixture into large bowl. In cup, stir coffee-flavor liqueur and espresso-coffee powder; stir into egg-yolk mixture in large bowl.

4 In small heavy saucepan over low heat, heat ¹/2 cup chocolate pieces, stirring frequently, until melted and smooth. Stir melted chocolate into remaining egg-yolk mixture in saucepan until blended.

5 In another large bowl, with mixer at medium speed, beat 2 ¹/2 cups heavy or whipping cream until stiff peaks form. With rubber spatula or wire whisk, fold two-thirds of whipped cream into coffee mixture until blended. Fold remaining whipped cream into chocolate mixture.

6 Spoon half the coffee mixture into 9" by 3" springform pan, spreading evenly; freeze until set, about 15 minutes. Evenly spread chocolate mixture over coffee layer in springform pan; freeze until set, about 15 minutes.

7 Sprinkle chocolate layer with Hazelnut Crunch; evenly spread with remaining coffee mixture. Cover and freeze until firm, at least 4 hours.

8 To serve, in small heavy saucepan over low heat, heat remaining ¹/2 cup chocolate pieces, stirring frequently, until melted and smooth; remove saucepan from heat. Cut waxed paper into two 4" by 4" squares. Moisten large cookie sheet with water; place waxed-paper squares on cookie sheet (water will prevent waxed paper from slipping). Use melted chocolate and waxed-paper squares to make Chocolate Triangles (see Box, page 251); refrigerate.

9 In small bowl, with mixer at medium speed, beat remaining ¹/2 cup heavy or whipping cream until stiff peaks form. Spoon whipped cream into decorating bag with rosette tube.

HAZELNUT CRUNCH
With sharp knife, coarsely chop *1 cup hazelnuts.*

In 10-inch skillet over medium heat, heat *¹/4 cup sugar* until sugar melts and turns golden brown. Stir in chopped hazelnuts; toss to coat well.

Pour into 8" by 8" baking pan; cool. Break into small pieces.

10 Run knife or metal spatula, dipped in hot water, around edge of springform pan to loosen cake; remove side of pan.

11 Pipe whipped cream into 8 "flowers" around edge on top of cake; place Chocolate Triangles between whipped-cream flowers. Garnish with toasted hazelnuts.

12 Let cake stand at room temperature about 10 minutes for easier slicing.

CHOCOLATE TRIANGLES

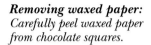

Removing waxed paper: *Carefully peel waxed paper from chocolate squares.*

Spreading melted chocolate: *With pastry brush or small metal spatula, evenly spread chocolate to cover waxed-paper squares. Refrigerate until chocolate is firm but not brittle, about 10 minutes. Remove chocolate from refrigerator; let stand about 5 minutes to soften slightly.*

Cutting triangles: *With sharp knife, quickly but gently cut each chocolate square into 8 triangles.*

Frozen chocolate and coffee mousses with a layer of crisp candy

DACQUOISE GLACÉE

🥄 16 servings

⏰ Begin early in day or up to 1 week ahead

5 large egg whites

¼ teaspoon cream of tartar

⅛ teaspoon salt

1 cup sugar

1 teaspoon vanilla extract

3 tablespoons unsweetened cocoa

1 tablespoon cornstarch

½ 3½-ounce can sliced blanched almonds (½ cup)

2 pints coffee ice cream

2 cups heavy or whipping cream

¼ cup confectioners' sugar

2 tablespoons coffee-flavor liqueur

1 Line 1 large and 1 small cookie sheet with foil. Using 8-inch round plate as guide, with toothpick, outline 2 circles on foil on large cookie sheet and 1 circle on small cookie sheet.

2 In large bowl, with mixer at high speed, beat egg whites, cream of tartar, and salt until soft peaks form. Beating at high speed, gradually sprinkle in sugar, 2 tablespoons at a time, beating well after each addition until sugar completely dissolves and whites stand in stiff, glossy peaks. Beat in vanilla extract.

3 In cup, with fork, mix cocoa and cornstarch. With rubber spatula or wire whisk, gently fold cocoa mixture into meringue until blended.

4 Preheat oven to 275°F. Spoon one-third of meringue inside each circle on cookie sheets; evenly spread meringue to cover circle.

5 Bake layers 1¼ hours or until meringue is crisp.

6 Cool meringue layers on cookie sheets on wire racks 10 minutes; carefully loosen and remove meringue layers from foil.

7 Place meringue layers on wire racks; leave to cool completely.

ASSEMBLING DACQUOISE GLACÉE

Spreading meringue with ice cream: With metal spatula, quickly and evenly spread first meringue layer with softened ice cream.

Topping with second meringue layer: Carefully lift chilled meringue round and place it over ice-cream layer.

Frosting frozen dessert: Evenly swirl whipped-cream mixture all over side and top of frozen dessert.

8 While meringue is cooling, turn oven control to 350°F. Spread almonds in 13" by 9" baking pan or cookie sheet. Bake almonds 10 to 15 minutes until browned, stirring occasionally. Cool; set aside.

9 Chill meringue layers in freezer about 30 minutes for easier handling. Place 1 pint coffee ice cream in refrigerator to soften slightly, about 30 minutes.

10 On freezersafe cake plate, place 1 meringue layer; spread with softened ice cream (see Box, page 252).

11 Place meringue with ice cream in freezer until firm, about 30 minutes. Meanwhile, place second pint of coffee ice cream in refrigerator to soften.

12 Remove meringue with ice cream from freezer. Top with second meringue layer (see Box, page 252).

13 Quickly and evenly spread with second pint of ice cream; place remaining meringue layer on top. Return to freezer until completely frozen, at least 4 hours.

14 In small bowl, with mixer at medium speed, beat heavy or whipping cream, confectioners' sugar, and coffee-flavor liqueur until stiff peaks form.

Sprinkling toasted almonds on top of frozen dessert

15 Frost frozen dessert with whipped-cream mixture (see Box, page 252). Evenly sprinkle toasted almonds on top of whipped cream.

16 Return dessert to freezer; when whipped cream has hardened, cover. Keep in freezer until ready to serve.

> *TO SERVE*
> *Let cake stand at room temperature about 10 minutes for easier slicing.*

VELVET HAMMER

 2 servings
Begin just before serving

1 pint vanilla ice cream, slightly softened

2 tablespoons orange-flavor liqueur

2 tablespoons brandy

Orange wedges and curls (see Citrus Curls, page 66) for garnish

1 In blender at medium speed, blend all ingredients just until smooth. Do not overblend, mixture should be thick.

2 Pour immediately into chilled wineglasses for sipping; garnish each serving with orange wedge and curls.

STRAWBERRY SODA

5 servings
Begin just before serving

1 ¹/₂ cups milk

1 10-ounce package frozen sliced strawberries, partially thawed

1 pint strawberry ice cream

1 16-ounce bottle club soda or strawberry soft drink, chilled

1 In blender at high speed, blend milk and strawberries 15 seconds until smooth. Pour into five 12-ounce glasses.

2 Add scoop of strawberry ice cream to each; slowly add soda or soft drink to fill almost to top. Serve immediately.

GARNISHES FOR ICED DRINKS

A pretty garnish atop an iced drink, or arranged decoratively on the rim of the glass, adds greatly to its appeal. Sprigs of fresh herbs and fruit slices go well with fruity drinks, while coffee-bean candies taste good with chocolate- and coffee-flavored drinks.

Mint sprig

Carambola (star fruit) slice

Coffee-bean candies

BLACK COW

🍴 1 serving
🕐 Begin just before serving

½ 12-ounce can root beer, chilled

Scoop of vanilla ice cream

1 Into chilled tall 10-ounce glass, pour chilled root beer.

2 Top with generous scoop slightly softened vanilla ice cream. Serve immediately with long straw and iced-tea spoon.

MOCHA FLOAT

🍴 1 serving
🕐 Begin just before serving

1 teaspoon cocoa mix

¾ teaspoon instant coffee powder

½ teaspoon sugar

Club soda, chilled

2 small scoops chocolate ice cream

1 Into 8-ounce glass, measure first 3 ingredients. Gradually add enough club soda to fill glass ¾ full; stir until sugar is dissolved.

2 Add chocolate ice cream; stir. Serve with spoon and straw.

FROZEN FRUIT CUPCAKES

12 servings

Begin about 3 ½ hours before serving or day ahead

1 small lemon

2 cups buttermilk

½ cup sugar

⅛ teaspoon salt

2 cups assorted fresh fruit (halved strawberries, chopped peaches, chopped nectarines, blueberries, or raspberries)

Garnish: Lemon leaves, halved strawberries, blueberries, raspberries, and nectarine wedges

1 Line twelve 2 ½" by 1 ¼" muffin-pan cups with fluted paper baking cups.

2 Into large bowl, grate peel from lemon. Add buttermilk, sugar, and salt; with wire whisk, mix until blended. Gently stir in 1 ¼ cups fruit.

3 Spoon mixture into paper baking cups; top with remaining ¾ cup fruit (some fruit will stay above mixture for pretty color).

4 Cover; freeze until firm, about 3 hours.

5 Peel off paper baking cups from dessert.

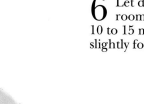

6 Let dessert stand at room temperature 10 to 15 minutes to soften slightly for easier eating.

> *TO SERVE*
> *Garnish each serving with lemon leaves, strawberry halves, blueberries, raspberries, and nectarine wedges.*

CHOLESTEROL-FREE CAKE ROLL

12 servings

Begin early in day or up to 1 week ahead

Nonstick cooking spray

1 cup cake flour

1 cup sugar

2 tablespoons unsweetened cocoa plus extra for sprinkling

10 large egg whites

1 teaspoon cream of tartar

1/2 teaspoon almond extract

1 pint orange-sorbet-and-vanilla light tofu-based frozen dessert

1 pint raspberry or strawberry light tofu-based frozen dessert

1 Preheat oven to 375°F. Line 15 1/2" by 10 1/2" jelly-roll pan with waxed paper; very lightly spray waxed paper with nonstick cooking spray.

2 In small bowl, with fork, stir cake flour, 1/2 cup sugar, and 2 tablespoons cocoa until evenly blended; set aside.

3 In large bowl, with mixer at high speed, beat egg whites, cream of tartar, and almond extract until soft peaks form.

4 Into egg-white mixture, gradually sprinkle remaining 1/2 cup sugar, beating until sugar completely dissolves and whites stand in stiff peaks.

5 With wire whisk or rubber spatula, gently fold flour mixture into egg-white mixture.

6 Spoon batter into pan, spreading evenly. Bake 15 to 20 minutes until top of cake springs back when lightly touched with finger.

7 Sprinkle clean cloth towel with cocoa. When cake is done, immediately invert cake onto towel. Carefully peel waxed paper from cake. If you like, cut off crisp edges. Starting at 1 narrow end, roll cake with towel, jelly-roll fashion. Place cake roll, seam-side down, on wire rack; cool completely, about 1 hour.

8 Remove tofu-based frozen desserts from freezer to soften slightly. Unroll cooled cake; with metal spatula, spread half the cake crosswise with one flavor tofu-based frozen dessert; evenly spread other half of cake with remaining flavor tofu-based frozen dessert.

9 Starting at same narrow end, roll cake without towel.

10 Place rolled cake, seam-side down, on long freezersafe platter. Cover and freeze cake until firm, at least 4 hours.

TOFU-BASED FROZEN DESSERT

Tofu-based nondairy frozen desserts have the richness of ice cream without its cholesterol and just a fraction of the calories. If you cannot find the light tofu-based frozen dessert in your supermarket, you might use your favorite flavors of low-fat frozen yogurt and fruit sorbet instead and still keep cholesterol and calories pleasantly low.

TO SERVE
Let cake stand at room temperature 15 minutes for easier slicing.

ICE-CREAM BONBONS

🥄 4 servings
🕐 Begin early in day or up to 1 week ahead

*These ice-cream balls covered with crisp chocolate coating are as sweet as the confection for which they are named. If you **must** save calories, eat only one – if you can!*

1 pint vanilla ice cream

1 ½ cups walnuts, finely chopped

1 6-ounce package semisweet-chocolate pieces (1 cup)

3 tablespoons margarine or butter

1 tablespoon light corn syrup

²/₃ cup confectioners' sugar

1 teaspoon lemon juice or water

1 Place ice cream in refrigerator to soften slightly, about 30 minutes. Chill small cookie sheet in freezer.

2 Place chopped walnuts on sheet of waxed paper.

3 Line chilled cookie sheet with waxed paper. Working quickly, with small ice-cream scoop, scoop a ball of ice cream; roll in walnuts; place on waxed-paper-lined cookie sheet. Repeat with remaining ice cream and walnuts to make 8 ice-cream balls. Freeze until firm, about 1 ½ hours.

4 In heavy 1-quart saucepan over low heat, heat chocolate pieces, margarine or butter, and corn syrup, stirring frequently, until melted and smooth. Remove saucepan from heat.

5 Remove cookie sheet with ice-cream balls from freezer; place 1 ice-cream ball at a time on spatula or fork over saucepan of melted chocolate. With large spoon or ⅛-cup measuring cup, quickly scoop up chocolate and pour over ice-cream ball to coat completely.

6 Place bonbons on same cookie sheet. Return to freezer; freeze until bonbons are firm, about 1 hour.

7 In small bowl, with spoon, mix confectioners' sugar and lemon juice or water until smooth and of easy spreading consistency. With spoon, drizzle sugar mixture over bonbons to make pretty design.

8 Return bonbons to freezer. If not serving on same day, when sugar glaze has hardened, wrap bonbons with foil or plastic wrap to use within 1 week.

9 Let bonbons stand at room temperature 10 minutes to soften slightly for easier eating.

Drizzling sugar mixture over bonbons

TARTUFO

🍴 6 servings

🕐 Begin early in day or up to 1 week ahead

---

2 pints vanilla ice cream

---

2 tablespoons almond-flavor liqueur or orange juice

---

6 amaretti cookies

---

1 6-ounce package semisweet-chocolate pieces (1 cup)

---

3 tablespoons margarine or butter

---

1 tablespoon light corn syrup

---

³/₄ cup walnuts, toasted and chopped

---

1 Place ice cream in refrigerator to soften slightly, about 30 minutes. Chill small cookie sheet in freezer.

2 Meanwhile, on plate, pour almond-flavor liqueur or orange juice over amaretti cookies; let stand until liqueur or juice is absorbed, turning cookies occasionally.

3 Line chilled cookie sheet with waxed paper. Working quickly, with large ice-cream scoop, scoop a ball of ice cream. Gently press an amaretti cookie into center of ball.

4 Reshape ice cream into ball around cookie; place on waxed-paper-lined cookie sheet. Repeat with remaining ice cream and cookies to make 6 ice-cream balls. Freeze until firm, about 1 ½ hours.

5 In heavy 1-quart saucepan over low heat, heat chocolate pieces, margarine or butter, and corn syrup, stirring frequently, until melted and smooth. Remove saucepan from heat.

6 Remove cookie sheet with ice-cream balls from freezer; place 1 ice-cream ball on spatula or fork over saucepan of melted chocolate. With large spoon or ⅛-cup measuring cup, quickly scoop up chocolate and pour over ice-cream ball to coat completely.

7 Place chocolate-coated ice-cream ball on same cookie sheet. Firmly pat some walnuts onto chocolate coating.

8 Repeat with remaining ice-cream balls, chocolate mixture, and nuts. Freeze until ice-cream balls are firm, about 1 hour.

9 If not serving on same day, wrap ice-cream balls with foil or plastic wrap; return to freezer to use within 1 week.

TO SERVE
Let ice-cream balls stand at room temperature 10 minutes to soften slightly for easier eating.

ICE-CREAM BOMBE

🍴 20 servings
🕐 Begin early in day or up to 1 week ahead

1 package devil's food or chocolate cake mix for 2-layer cake

1 pint strawberry ice cream

1 pint vanilla ice cream

3 tablespoons coffee-flavor liqueur (optional)

1 16 1/2- to 17-ounce can pitted dark sweet cherries, drained

1 pint chocolate ice cream

Chocolate Bow and Ribbon Streamers (see Box, right)

1 7-ounce bag flaked coconut (2 1/2 cups)

1 1/2 cups confectioners' sugar

1 cup margarine or butter (2 sticks), softened

1/2 teaspoon vanilla extract

1 Preheat oven to 350°F. Grease and flour two 9-inch round cake pans and one 9" by 9" baking pan.

2 Prepare cake mix as label directs. Spoon batter equally into pans, spreading evenly. Bake 25 minutes or until toothpick inserted in center of each cake comes out clean. Cool cakes in pans on wire racks 10 minutes. With metal spatula, loosen each cake from edge of pan; invert onto wire rack to cool completely.

3 Place strawberry and vanilla ice creams in refrigerator to soften slightly, about 30 minutes.

4 Line deep 3-quart bowl with plastic wrap. Cut 1 cake round into quarters; cut cake square into 3 equal strips. Line entire bowl using cake quarters to line bottom and cake strips to cover side; trim cake pieces to fit, if necessary. Press any cake trimmings into any open areas in cake in bowl. Brush cake in bowl with coffee-flavor liqueur.

5 Spoon half the strawberry ice cream into cake-lined bowl. Spoon one-fourth of vanilla ice cream in dollops onto strawberry ice cream. Scatter one-fourth of cherries between vanilla-ice-cream dollops.

6 Repeat with remaining strawberry ice cream, one-fourth of vanilla ice cream, and one-fourth of cherries; press down mixture to eliminate air pockets. Place bowl in freezer to harden ice cream slightly, about 20 minutes.

CHOCOLATE BOW AND RIBBON STREAMERS
In heavy 1-quart saucepan over low heat, heat *two 1-ounce squares semisweet chocolate*, stirring frequently, until melted and smooth. Remove saucepan from heat; quickly stir in *1 tablespoon light corn syrup*. Pour melted chocolate onto small cookie sheet; with metal spatula, evenly spread chocolate to cover sheet. Refrigerate until firm but not brittle, about 30 minutes.

Remove from cookie sheet and, with hands, knead until chocolate dough is soft. Wrap chocolate dough with plastic wrap or waxed paper; let stand at room temperature 1 hour for easier handling.

Place chocolate dough between sheets of waxed paper. With rolling pin, roll out dough into rectangle about 10 inches long and 6 inches wide.

Cut dough into six 10" by 1/2" strips for ribbon streamers. Cut three 8" by 3/4" strips for loops of bow. Tightly cover ribbon streamers with plastic wrap to prevent drying (ribbon streamers must be flexible to drape down on cake); keep at room temperature. Pinch ends of loop pieces to make bow; allow bow to sit at room temperature, uncovered, to set.

7 Meanwhile, place chocolate ice cream in refrigerator to soften slightly, and return remaining vanilla ice cream to freezer.

8 Remove bowl from freezer. Repeat layering as for strawberry ice cream, but use chocolate ice cream with remaining vanilla ice cream and cherries.

9 Place remaining chocolate-cake round on top of chocolate ice cream, pressing cake down firmly against ice cream. Cover bowl with plastic wrap; place bowl in freezer until ice cream is firm, at least 4 hours.

10 Prepare Chocolate Bow and Ribbon Streamers.

Spooning vanilla ice cream over chocolate ice cream in bowl

11 Preheat oven to 350°F. Evenly sprinkle coconut in 13" by 9" baking pan; bake 15 minutes or until lightly toasted, stirring occasionally. Set aside.

12 Prepare buttercream frosting: In large bowl, with mixer at medium speed, beat confectioners' sugar and margarine or butter until just mixed. Increase speed to high; beat until light and fluffy, scraping bowl often with rubber spatula. Reduce speed to medium; beat in vanilla extract until smooth.

13 Remove ice-cream cake from freezer. Invert cake onto chilled freezersafe cake stand or platter; remove plastic wrap. With metal spatula, thinly spread frosting over cake, covering a small area at a time and immediately pressing toasted coconut onto frosting.

14 Continue until cake is completely covered with frosting and toasted coconut. Garnish cake with Chocolate Bow and Ribbon Streamers. Keep cake in freezer until ready to serve.

TO SERVE
Let cake stand at room temperature 20 minutes for easier slicing.

CANTALOUPE SHERBET

About 2 quarts or
16 servings

Begin early in day or
up to 1 week ahead

1 small ripe cantaloupe
(1 ³/₄ pounds)

1 quart milk

2 envelopes unflavored
gelatin

³/₄ cup light corn syrup

¹/₂ cup sugar

³/₄ teaspoon salt

3 drops yellow food coloring
(optional)

1 drop red food coloring
(optional)

1 Remove and discard peel and seeds from cantaloupe; cut cantaloupe into chunks. In blender at medium speed or in food processor with knife blade attached, blend cantaloupe and 1 cup milk until smooth; set aside.

2 In 3-quart saucepan evenly sprinkle gelatin over 1 cup milk; let stand 1 minute to soften. Cook over medium heat until gelatin completely dissolves, stirring frequently.

3 Remove saucepan from heat; with wire whisk, stir in cantaloupe mixture, remaining milk, and remaining ingredients (mixture may look curdled).

4 Pour mixture into 13" by 9" baking pan; cover with foil or plastic wrap. Freeze until partially frozen, about 3 hours, stirring occasionally.

5 Spoon cantaloupe mixture into chilled large bowl; with mixer at medium speed, beat mixture until smooth but still frozen. Return mixture to baking pan. Cover; freeze until firm, about 3 hours.

6 Let sherbet stand at room temperature 10 minutes for easier scooping.

For this attractive presentation, different-sized scoops of Cantaloupe Sherbet are placed on waxed-paper-lined chilled cookie sheet and put in freezer to harden. They can then be lifted off easily and piled on top of each other without melting

TWO-MELON GRANITA

🥄 4 cups or 8 servings
🕐 Begin early in day or up to 1 week ahead

1 cup sugar
1/4 cup lemon juice
1 medium-sized ripe cantaloupe (about 2 pounds)
1 small ripe honeydew melon (about 2 pounds)

1 In small saucepan over high heat, heat sugar and *2 cups water* to boiling. Reduce heat to medium; cook 5 minutes. Remove saucepan from heat; stir in lemon juice.

2 Remove and discard peel and seeds from cantaloupe; cut cantaloupe into chunks. In blender at medium speed or in food processor with knife blade attached, blend cantaloupe until smooth; pour into 8" by 8" baking pan.

3 Repeat with honeydew melon; pour into another 8" by 8" pan.

4 Pour half the sugar mixture into each baking pan; stir until well mixed. Cover pans with foil or plastic wrap; freeze melon mixtures until firm, about 5 hours, stirring occasionally so mixtures freeze evenly.

5 Let granitas stand at room temperature 10 minutes to soften slightly.

6 With spoon or ice-cream scoop, scrape across surface of granitas in pans to create pebbly texture.

7 Spoon some cantaloupe granita and some honeydew granita into each of 8 chilled dessert bowls.

WATERMELON ICE

🥄 5 cups or 10 servings
🕐 Begin early in day or up to 1 week ahead

1 4-pound wedge watermelon
3 tablespoons confectioners' sugar
1 tablespoon lemon juice
1/4 teaspoon salt

1 Remove and discard peel and seeds from watermelon; cut enough watermelon into bite-sized chunks to make 6 cups. In blender at low speed or in food processor with knife blade attached, blend one-third of watermelon chunks with confectioners' sugar, lemon juice, and salt until smooth.

2 Pour watermelon mixture into 9" by 9" baking pan. Blend remaining watermelon chunks, half at a time, until smooth. Stir into mixture in pan. Cover with foil or plastic wrap; freeze until partially frozen, about 2 hours, stirring occasionally.

3 Spoon watermelon mixture into chilled large bowl. With mixer at medium speed, beat mixture until fluffy but still frozen. Return mixture to baking pan; cover and freeze until firm, about 2 hours.

4 Let ice stand at room temperature about 10 minutes to soften slightly. Then, with spoon, scrape across surface of ice to create fine "snowlike" texture; spoon into dessert dishes.

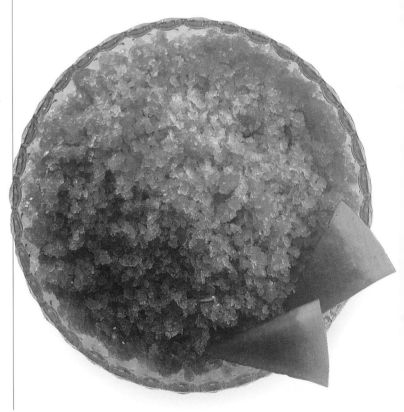

SPUMONI ELEGANTE

12 servings

Begin day ahead or up to 1 week ahead

2 cups milk
3 large eggs
¹/₄ teaspoon salt
1 cup sugar
¹/₂ teaspoon orange extract
1 large lime
1 cup heavy or whipping cream
¹/₃ cup diced mixed candied fruits
1 large strawberry for garnish

1 In heavy 2-quart saucepan, with wire whisk or fork, beat milk, eggs, salt, and ³/₄ cup sugar until blended. Cook over medium-low heat, stirring constantly, until mixture thickens and coats a spoon well, about 30 minutes (mixture should be about 170° to 175°F., but do not boil or it will curdle).

2 Remove saucepan from heat; stir in orange extract.

3 Pour custard mixture into bowl; cover with foil or plastic wrap and freeze until almost firm, about 3 hours.

4 With back of large spoon, evenly spread frozen custard mixture to line inside of 8 ¹/₂" by 4 ¹/₂" loaf pan.

FLOWER GARNISHES
With a little imagination, you can turn fruit into "flowers" for arranging on top of desserts. Here are a few ideas which look most effective yet are simple and quick to do.

5 Cover loaf pan; freeze about 1 hour.

6 Grate 1 teaspoon peel from half the lime; set aside. Wrap remaining lime with plastic wrap; refrigerate to use for garnish later.

7 In small bowl, with mixer at medium speed, beat heavy or whipping cream and remaining ¹/₄ cup sugar until stiff peaks form. With rubber spatula, fold in candied fruits and grated lime peel.

8 Into center of frozen custard in loaf pan, spoon whipped-cream mixture.

Spooning whipped-cream mixture into center of frozen custard

9 Smooth surface of whipped-cream mixture. Cover and return to freezer; freeze overnight or until firm.

10 Invert spumoni onto chilled platter; let stand at room temperature 10 minutes for easier slicing.

TO SERVE
Make flower garnish: Cut remaining peel from reserved lime for stem and leaves; slice strawberry for petals. Garnish dessert with lime peel and strawberry slices to resemble flowers.

Classic Italian Spumoni is made up of ice creams of different flavors and colors. Layered in a mold, it is easy to slice and the servings are extra pretty

BANANA-GINGERBREAD CAKE

16 servings
Begin early in day or day ahead

1 14- to 14 1/2-ounce package gingerbread mix

2 pints vanilla ice cream

3 ripe medium-sized bananas

3/4 cup walnuts, coarsely chopped

1/4 cup bottled caramel topping

1 Preheat oven to 350°F. Grease and flour two 8-inch round cake pans.

2 Prepare gingerbread mix as label directs. Spoon batter equally into cake pans, spreading evenly. Bake 20 minutes or until toothpick inserted in center of each cake comes out clean. Cool layers in pans on wire racks 10 minutes. With metal spatula, loosen layers from edges of pans; invert onto wire racks to cool completely. When cold, cover layers; set aside.

3 Meanwhile, place ice cream in refrigerator to soften slightly, about 30 minutes.

4 Line one 8-inch round cake pan with plastic wrap; set aside.

5 In blender at medium speed, blend 2 bananas until pureed. In large bowl, with rubber spatula, fold pureed bananas into ice cream. Spoon 1 1/2 cups banana mixture into freezer-safe small bowl; cover and freeze for garnish later. Pour remaining banana mixture into lined cake pan; cover and freeze until firm, about 6 hours.

6 On chilled cake plate, place one gingerbread layer; invert frozen banana mixture from cake pan onto gingerbread. Peel off plastic wrap; discard. Place remaining gingerbread layer on top. If necessary, with metal spatula, smooth banana mixture to fit cake layers. Spread remaining 1 1/2 cups banana mixture on top of cake. Freeze.

7 If not serving cake on same day, when banana mixture is hard, wrap cake with plastic wrap. Return to freezer.

8 To serve, let dessert stand at room temperature 15 minutes for easier cutting. Meanwhile, slice remaining banana. Garnish cake with banana slices and walnuts.

9 Pour caramel topping over cake.

BANANAS

Bananas, economical and available all year round, add flavor, texture, color, and nutrition to desserts. Not only are they low in sodium and calories (about 85 cals for one six-inch banana), but they are high in potassium, have virtually no fat, are cholesterol-free, and contain other minerals and important vitamins!

• Choose bananas that are firm, unblemished, and green-tipped. Avoid brown-skinned fruit, which is overripe and mushy.

• Ripen bananas at room temperature. When fully ripe, banana peel will be completely yellow and flecked with brown.

• Refrigerate fully ripe bananas. Peel will turn dark, but flavor and texture will stay fresh for 2 or 3 days.

• For even longer storage, mash bananas with a little lemon juice and freeze in airtight container. Thaw; use in baked goods.

CHOCOLATE PEANUT-BUTTER ICE-CREAM PIE

🍴 12 servings
🕐 Begin early in day or up to 1 week ahead

15 *chocolate sandwich cookies*

¹/₂ cup dry-roasted peanuts

Nonstick cooking spray

4 tablespoons margarine or butter (¹/₂ stick), melted

3 quarts chocolate ice cream

7 1.8-ounce packages milk-chocolate-covered peanut-butter cups

1 cup heavy or whipping cream

2 tablespoons sugar

Fudge Sauce (see Box, above right)

1 Preheat oven to 400°F.

2 In food processor with knife blade attached or in blender at medium speed, blend chocolate sandwich cookies and dry-roasted peanuts until finely chopped.

3 Spray 9-inch pie plate with nonstick cooking spray.

4 Reserve 1 tablespoon chopped cookie-and-peanut mixture for garnish later; in pie plate, with hand, mix remaining cookie-and-peanut mixture and margarine or butter. Press mixture onto bottom and up side of pie plate.

5 Bake crust 8 minutes. Cool crust in pie plate on wire rack.

6 Meanwhile, place chocolate ice cream in refrigerator to soften slightly, about 30 minutes. With knife, coarsely chop milk-chocolate-covered peanut-butter cups.

7 In large bowl, with spoon, mix softened ice cream with chopped peanut-butter cups. Evenly spoon ice-cream mixture into cooled cookie crust. Cover; freeze until firm, at least 6 hours or overnight.

8 In small bowl, with mixer at medium speed, beat heavy or whipping cream and sugar until stiff peaks form. Spoon whipped-cream mixture into decorating bag with large star tube; pipe rosettes on outside edge of pie and on top to make pretty design.

9 Sprinkle reserved cookie-and-peanut mixture on top of pie.

FUDGE SAUCE

In 1-quart saucepan over low heat, heat *one 8-ounce jar milk-chocolate fudge topping* until hot; stir in *¹/₄ cup strong brewed coffee* and *2 tablespoons coffee-flavor liqueur* (optional) until blended. Serve warm.

10 Return pie to freezer uncovered; when whipped-cream mixture has hardened, wrap pie with foil or plastic wrap. Return to freezer.

11 Let pie stand at room temperature 15 minutes to soften slightly for easier slicing.

12 Meanwhile, make Fudge Sauce.

TO SERVE
Cut pie into wedges and serve with warm Fudge Sauce.

FROZEN CAPPUCCINO SQUARES

20 servings
Begin about 5 hours before serving or up to 1 week ahead

1/2 gallon coffee ice cream

1 8 1/4-ounce package chocolate wafers, crushed

4 tablespoons margarine or butter (1/2 stick), melted

1 tablespoon coffee-flavor liqueur or to taste (optional)

4 1.4-ounce bars chocolate-covered toffee candy, chopped

Semisweet Chocolate Curls (page 158) for garnish

1 Remove coffee ice cream from container to large bowl; place in refrigerator 30 minutes to soften slightly, stirring occasionally.

2 Meanwhile, in 13" by 9" baking pan, mix crushed chocolate wafers and melted margarine or butter.

3 Reserve 1/2 cup chocolate-wafer mixture; press remaining mixture firmly to cover bottom of pan to make crust.

4 Place pan in refrigerator to chill chocolate-wafer crust.

5 Stir ice cream until smooth, adding coffee-flavor liqueur, if desired. Spread half the softened ice cream over chocolate-wafer crust.

Spreading ice cream over crust

6 Top with chopped candy and reserved chocolate-wafer mixture, pressing lightly.

7 Spread remaining ice cream over chocolate-wafer mixture; cover and freeze until firm, at least 4 hours.

> *TO SERVE*
> *Let ice-cream dessert stand at room temperature about 10 minutes for easier cutting. Cut into serving pieces. Garnish with chocolate curls.*

FUDGE-SUNDAE PIE

12 servings
Begin early in day or
up to 1 week ahead

1 8-ounce can walnuts
(2 cups), finely chopped

2 tablespoons brown sugar

7 tablespoons margarine or
butter, softened

1 pint vanilla ice cream

1/2 cup unsweetened cocoa

3/4 cup plus 2 tablespoons
sugar

2 cups heavy or whipping
cream

2 teaspoons vanilla extract

1 pint chocolate or coffee ice
cream

Grated Chocolate Curls
(page 116) for garnish

1 Preheat oven to
400°F. In 9-inch pie
plate, with hand, mix
walnuts, brown sugar, and
3 tablespoons margarine
or butter. Press mixture
onto bottom and up side
of pie plate. Bake
8 minutes. Cool crust on
wire rack. Meanwhile,
place vanilla ice cream in
refrigerator to soften
slightly, about 30 minutes.

2 With metal or rubber
spatula, evenly spread
softened vanilla ice cream
in crust; freeze until firm,
about 1 1/2 hours.

3 In 2-quart saucepan
over medium heat,
heat cocoa, 3/4 cup sugar,
1/2 cup heavy or whipping
cream, and remaining
4 tablespoons margarine
or butter (1/2 stick) to
boiling, stirring constantly
until smooth. Remove
saucepan from heat; stir in
1 teaspoon vanilla extract.
Cool fudge sauce to room
temperature.

4 Over vanilla-ice-cream
layer, pour fudge
sauce.

5 Return pie to freezer;
freeze until fudge
sauce hardens, about
30 minutes.

6 Remove chocolate or
coffee ice cream from
container to medium bowl;
let stand at room temperature, stirring occasionally,
until smooth spreading
consistency but not
melted. Spread chocolate
or coffee ice cream over
fudge layer; return pie to
freezer.

7 In small bowl, with
mixer at medium
speed, beat remaining
1 1/2 cups heavy or whip-
ping cream, 2 tablespoons
sugar, and 1 teaspoon
vanilla extract until stiff
peaks form. With metal
spatula, spread whipped-
cream mixture over pie.

TO SERVE
Let pie stand at room
temperature 15 minutes
for easier slicing.

8 Garnish pie with
chocolate curls.

9 Return pie to freezer,
uncovered; freeze
until firm, about 3 hours.
If not serving pie same
day, wrap frozen pie with
foil or plastic wrap and
freeze until ready to serve.

Spreading
whipped-cream
mixture over pie

LEMON ICE IN LEMON CUPS

6 servings

Begin early in day or up to 1 week ahead

6 large lemons

1 envelope unflavored gelatin

1 cup sugar

Mint leaves for garnish

These pretty little lemon "boats" filled with cool lemon ice are so good and refreshing that you would never dream they are fat-free!

1 Cut off one-third of each lemon from one lengthwise side.

2 Grate peel from cut-off pieces of lemons. Wrap half the grated peel in plastic wrap; refrigerate for garnish. Reserve remaining peel.

3 Squeeze ³/4 cup juice from bottom pieces of lemons. Remove all crushed pulp and membrane.

4 Cut thin slice off bottom of each lemon cup so it can stand level. Place lemon cups in plastic bag; refrigerate until ready to fill.

5 In 2-quart saucepan, with wire whisk, mix gelatin and sugar; stir in 2 ¹/4 cups water. Let stand 1 minute to soften gelatin slightly. Cook over medium heat, stirring constantly, until gelatin completely dissolves. Remove sauce-pan from heat; stir in lemon juice and reserved grated lemon peel.

6 Pour lemon mixture into 9" by 9" baking pan; cover with foil or plastic wrap. Freeze until partially frozen, about 2 hours, stirring occasionally.

7 Spoon lemon mixture into chilled large bowl; with mixer at medium speed, beat mixture until smooth but still frozen.

8 Return mixture to baking pan; cover and freeze until partially frozen, about 2 hours. Spoon mixture into chilled large bowl; beat again as before. Cover and freeze until firm.

9 With spoon, fill lemon cups with lemon ice.

10 Sprinkle lemon ice with grated lemon peel; arrange on dessert plates and garnish with mint. Serve immediately or freeze to serve later. If not serving on same day, when cups have hardened, wrap with plastic wrap and return to freezer.

RASPBERRY SORBET

🍴 About 4 cups or
8 servings

🕐 Begin early in day or
up to 1 week ahead

*1 envelope unflavored
gelatin*

*2 10-ounce packages frozen
quick-thaw raspberries
in light syrup, thawed*

¹/₂ cup light corn syrup

*¹/₃ cup raspberry-flavor
liqueur*

3 tablespoons lemon juice

¹/₄ teaspoon salt

*Kiwifruit, papaya, and
fresh raspberries*

1 In 1-quart saucepan, evenly sprinkle gelatin over *1 cup water*; let stand 1 minute to soften. Cook over medium heat until gelatin completely dissolves, stirring frequently. Remove saucepan from heat.

2 Over large bowl, with back of spoon, press and scrape raspberries with their syrup firmly against medium-mesh sieve to separate seeds from pulp; discard seeds.

*Stirring corn
syrup into sieved
raspberries*

3 With wire whisk, stir corn syrup, raspberry-flavor liqueur, lemon juice, salt, and gelatin mixture into sieved raspberries until well mixed.

4 Pour raspberry mixture into 9" by 9" baking pan; cover with foil or plastic wrap. Freeze until partially frozen, about 3 hours, stirring occasionally.

5 Spoon raspberry mixture into chilled large bowl; with mixer at medium speed, beat mixture until smooth but still frozen. Return mixture to baking pan; cover and freeze until firm, about 2 to 3 hours.

6 Arrange some kiwifruit, papaya, and fresh raspberries on individual plates. Place small scoops of sorbet next to fruit.

SERVING SORBET AND ICE CREAM

For an attractive presentation, sorbet and ice cream look best served in scoops: For easier serving, with ice-cream scoop, carefully scoop balls of sorbet or ice cream out of container and place on waxed-paper-lined chilled cookie sheet.

Immediately place cookie sheet in freezer; leave until sorbet or ice cream hardens. To serve, lift scoops off waxed paper and place on dessert plates or in dishes at last minute.

TWO-TONE GRANITAS

ESPRESSO

- About 3 cups or 6 servings
- Begin early in day or up to 1 week ahead

1/3 cup sugar

1/4 cup instant espresso-coffee powder

1 In 2-quart saucepan over high heat, heat sugar, espresso-coffee powder, and *3 cups water* to boiling, stirring occasionally. Reduce heat to medium; cook 5 minutes.

2 Pour mixture into 8" by 8" baking pan.

3 Cool mixture. Cover with foil or plastic wrap; freeze until firm, about 5 hours, stirring occasionally.

> **TO SERVE**
> *Let granitas stand at room temperature 10 minutes to soften slightly. Then, with spoon or ice-cream scoop, scrape across surface of granitas to create pebbly texture; spoon into tall glasses, alternating layers.*

LEMON

- About 3 cups or 6 servings
- Begin early in day or up to 1 week ahead

1 cup sugar

4 large lemons

1 In 2-quart saucepan over high heat, heat sugar and *2 cups water* to boiling, stirring occasionally. Reduce heat to medium; cook 5 minutes.

2 Meanwhile, from lemons, grate 2 teaspoons peel and squeeze 3/4 cup juice. Stir lemon peel and juice into cooled sugar syrup.

3 Pour mixture into 8" by 8" baking pan.

4 Cool; cover with foil or plastic wrap; freeze until firm, about 5 hours, stirring occasionally.

USEFUL INFORMATION AND BASIC RECIPES

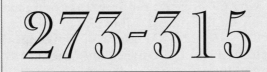

273-315

EQUIPMENT

Desserts require very little specialized equipment and a well-equipped kitchen will contain most of the things you need. Below and on page 275 is an illustrated guide to implements that you will find useful for making the desserts in this book. Measuring equipment and advice on measuring both dry and liquid ingredients are given on page 276.

For everyday use, rely on a good selection of different-sized mixing bowls, sharp knives, wooden and metal spoons. A blender or food processor will take the effort out of pureeing; fruit may need straining through a sieve afterward to remove seeds.

Wire whisks are excellent tools for stirring sauces to keep them smooth, and for incorporating beaten egg whites and whipped cream into mixtures. Should a sauce lump or curdle, a hand-held beater – electric or manual – will often restore its smooth consistency. For beating meringues, whipping cream, and mixing most batters, an electric mixer does the job with the greatest speed and efficiency.

It is a good idea, but not essential, to have a selection of sieves. Metal sieves are good for sifting dry ingredients; nylon sieves are better when rubbing fruits through to make a puree as a metal sieve can give the fruit a metallic taste. If you have to use a metal sieve, push the fruit through with a wooden spoon.

A double boiler is excellent for making delicate sauces and custards and for melting chocolate. It consists of two saucepans, one of which fits inside the other, and a lid. The handles of the pans are angled so that it is easy to pick up both as one unit. If you have not got a double boiler, use a heatproof bowl set over a saucepan of simmering, not boiling, water.

A candy thermometer is useful if you are making a sugar syrup or jelly where the correct temperature is vital, or for making sure egg-custard mixtures cook to at least 170°F. so that the eggs are cooked and the custard thickened properly.

A deep-fat thermometer is used for deep-frying in fat or oil.

Before you begin cooking, assemble all the utensils needed for the recipe and measure all the ingredients. Read through the recipe carefully to make sure that you have everything you need and that you have allowed enough preparation time. Do as much advance preparation as possible before you start mixing and cooking. Measure and mix ingredients carefully, using the correct equipment. Advance preparation of utensils is just as important as assembling ingredients: grease and flour a pan if directed and when a preheated oven is called for, turn it on when directed in the recipe, which will be at least 10 minutes before you need to put in the food to allow it to preheat to the required temperature.

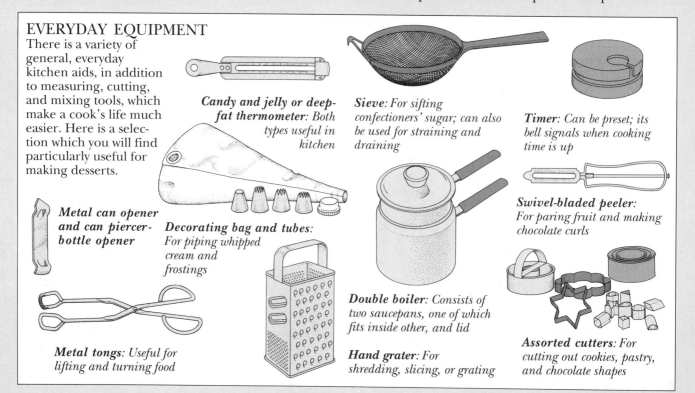

EVERYDAY EQUIPMENT

There is a variety of general, everyday kitchen aids, in addition to measuring, cutting, and mixing tools, which make a cook's life much easier. Here is a selection which you will find particularly useful for making desserts.

Candy and jelly or deep-fat thermometer: Both types useful in kitchen

Sieve: For sifting confectioners' sugar; can also be used for straining and draining

Timer: Can be preset; its bell signals when cooking time is up

Metal can opener and can piercer-bottle opener

Decorating bag and tubes: For piping whipped cream and frostings

Swivel-bladed peeler: For paring fruit and making chocolate curls

Metal tongs: Useful for lifting and turning food

Double boiler: Consists of two saucepans, one of which fits inside other, and lid

Hand grater: For shredding, slicing, or grating

Assorted cutters: For cutting out cookies, pastry, and chocolate shapes

BAKEWARE

While not essential, the bakeware shown here is useful for making desserts. Be sure pans are the size specified in the recipe.

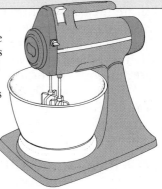

Cookie sheet: *Flat metal sheet with slightly raised edges on one or more sides*

Baking pan: *Useful for baking cakes, puddings, and other desserts*

Springform pan: *For easy removal of cakes, tortes, and cheesecakes*

Pie plate or pan: *Usually made of dull metal, glass, or glass-ceramic*

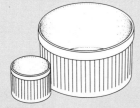

Soufflé dishes: *Straight-sided ovenproof dishes of different sizes, usually porcelain or glass*

Tart pan: *Fluted round pan with loose bottom to make it easy to remove pastry*

Custard cups: *Individual ovenproof porcelain, stoneware, or glass dishes*

MIXING TOOLS

Illustrated here are some of the basic types of tools available for stirring and beating all kinds of mixtures. Electric mixers come in two basic types: hand-held light duty beater, and heavier, stand-mounted multi-purpose one.

Electric mixer: *This multi-purpose machine has a range of attachments and bowls*

Hand rotary beater: *Useful for beating eggs and other light mixtures*

Blender: *Useful for pureeing, mixing, and finely chopping small quantities*

Wire whisk: *Ideal for beating egg whites, stirring sauces and folding in*

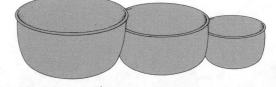

Set of mixing bowls: *Essential for all sorts of mixing jobs in the kitchen. A choice of three sizes is most useful*

SPOONS AND SPATULAS

A wide choice of long-handled spoons and spatulas is extremely useful in any cook's kitchen. This selection is particularly good for desserts.

Wooden spoon: *Ideal for stirring sauces or pushing purees through strainer*

Metal spatula: *Useful for glazing cakes or spreading cream or frosting on top and sides*

Slotted spoon: *Useful for lifting poached fruit out of poaching liquid*

Rubber spatula: *Use to fold in flour mixtures, whipped cream, or beaten egg whites, as well as for scraping bowls*

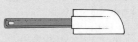

Metal spatula ...

Basting spoon: *Large metal spoon useful for spooning liquid over fruit while poaching*

Pancake turner: *Useful for transferring cake layers and cookies*

MEASURING

Accurate measurements are essential if you want consistently good results each time you follow a recipe. To measure very small amounts of liquids or dry ingredients, use measuring spoons. For larger amounts of liquids, use a 1-cup liquid measuring cup, which is also marked for smaller measurements. Larger cups are also available. For dry ingredients, use a set of graduated measuring cups.

MEASURING MARGARINE OR BUTTER
Each ¼-pound stick of margarine or butter measures ½ cup or 8 tablespoons. The wrapping is usually marked off in tablespoons for measuring smaller amounts.

Following guidelines on wrapper, cut off number of tablespoons needed

For margarine or butter not wrapped in this way, pack into measuring spoon or cup; level off

MEASURING SHORTENING
Liquid shortening such as salad oil and melted butter can be measured in the same way as liquids (see below right). Measure solid shortening such as vegetable shortening, lard, and even peanut butter as shown here.

Pack in shortening firmly, right to top of measuring spoon or cup

Level off shortening with straight edge of small kitchen knife, not flat side

MEASURING SUGAR
Lightly spoon sugar into graduated measuring cup; level off with straight edge of knife or spatula. If measuring brown sugar, pack sugar down lightly into cup with back of spoon, then level off.

Brown sugar will hold its shape when inverted from cup

MEASURING TOOLS
When measuring dry ingredients, level excess into small bowl, then add measured amount to mixing bowl.

Standard set of 4 graduated measuring cups consists of ¼-, ⅓-, ½-, and 1-cup measures

Liquid measuring cups are available in 1-, 2-, 4-, and 8-cup measures

Set of measuring spoons has ¼, ½, 1 teaspoon, and 1 tablespoon measures

MEASURING FLOUR
In recipes all flours are measured straight from flour package or canister. Never pack flour down into measure or shake or tap side of measure.

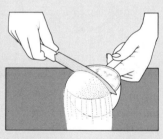

Lightly spoon flour from package into graduated measuring cup or spoon

Level off surplus flour with straight edge of small kitchen knife or metal spatula

MEASURING LIQUIDS
When measuring liquids, always place measuring cup on level surface and read line at eye level when checking volume of liquid.

Slowly pour liquid into level measuring cup until it reaches desired line

If using measuring spoons, carefully pour liquid just to top of spoon without letting it spill over

EQUIVALENT AMOUNTS

How many cups make a quart? Are three bananas enough to make one cup of mashed? For two tablespoons of grated orange peel and 1/3 cup orange juice, will you need more than one medium orange? How many cups are there in a pound of all-purpose flour? These questions, and many more like them, are answered in the charts on this page.

EQUIVALENT MEASURES	
Dash	2 to 3 drops or less than 1/8 teaspoon
1 tablespoon	3 teaspoons
1/4 cup	4 tablespoons
1/3 cup	5 tablespoons plus 1 teaspoon
1/2 cup	8 tablespoons
3/4 cup	12 tablespoons
1 cup	16 tablespoons
1 pint	2 cups
1 quart	4 cups
1 gallon	4 quarts
1 peck	8 quarts
1 bushel	4 pecks
1 pound	16 ounces

FOOD EQUIVALENTS		
Apples	1 pound	3 medium (3 cups sliced)
Bananas	1 pound	3 medium (1 1/3 cups mashed)
Breadcrumbs, fresh	1 slice bread with crust	1/2 cup
Butter or margarine	1/4-pound stick	1/2 cup or 8 tablespoons
Cheese, cottage	8 ounces	1 cup
Cheese, cream	3 ounces	6 tablespoons
Chocolate, semisweet pieces	1 6-ounce package	1 cup
Chocolate, unsweetened	1 ounce	1 square

Food equivalents continued		
Coconut, flaked	3 1/2-ounce can	1 1/3 cups
shredded	7-ounce bag	2 2/3 cups
Cream, heavy or whipping	1 cup	2 cups whipped cream
Cream, sour	8 ounces	1 cup
Egg whites, large	1 cup	8-10 whites
Egg yolks, large	1 cup	12 to 14 yolks
Flour, all-purpose	1 pound	about 3 1/2 cups
cake		about 4 cups
Gelatin, unflavored	1 envelope	1 tablespoon
Honey, liquid	16 ounces	1 1/3 cups
Lemon	1 medium	about 3 tablespoons juice 1 tablespoon grated peel
Lime	1 medium	2 tablespoons juice 1 teaspoon grated peel
Milk, evaporated	5-ounce can	2/3 cup
	12-ounce can	1 2/3 cups
Milk, sweetened condensed	14-ounce can	1 1/4 cups
Nuts	1 pound	
Almonds, in shell		1 to 1 1/4 cups nutmeats
shelled		3 cups
Brazil nuts, in shell		1 1/2 cups nutmeats
shelled		3 1/4 cups
Hazelnuts, in shell		1 1/2 cups nutmeats
shelled		3 1/2 cups
Pecans, in shell		2 1/4 cups nutmeats
shelled		4 cups
Walnuts, in shell		2 cups nutmeats
shelled		4 cups
Orange	1 medium	1/3 to 1/2 cup juice 2 tablespoons grated peel
Raisins	1 pound	3 cups, loosely packed
Sugar,	1 pound	
brown		2 1/4 cups packed
confectioners'		about 3 3/4 cups
granulated		2 1/4 to 2 1/2 cups
Syrup,		
corn	16 ounces	2 cups
maple	12 ounces	1 1/2 cups

DESSERTS

The recipes in this book fall into the following categories: mousses and soufflés, custards and creams, meringues, crepes and blintzes, fruit desserts, puddings, cakes and tortes, cheesecakes, fruitcakes, pies, tarts, pastries, hot fruit desserts, cookies, and frozen desserts. Within each category the recipes range from simple everyday desserts to internationally famous dishes, and popular recipes calling for slightly more advanced techniques. On this and the following two pages, you will find useful information on general dessert-making techniques.

USING GELATIN

Many desserts, such as fruit molds, mousses, and cold soufflés, depend on gelatin to make them set. Gelatin is available both flavored and unflavored. The two different types are not interchangeable, so always use the type specified in the individual recipe.

DISSOLVING GELATIN

For properly set, jelled mixtures, gelatin must be dissolved completely in hot liquid such as water, milk, or fruit juice in a bowl or saucepan; no visible granules of gelatin should remain in the mixture or they will spoil its clarity and/or smoothness. Constant stirring is essential to make sure gelatin is completely dissolved. Gelatin granules that splash up on side of bowl or saucepan are difficult to dissolve; so always stir mixture steadily but not too vigorously.

Flavored gelatins are dissolved in boiling water, according to package directions. Recipes using unflavored gelatin vary slightly in dissolving technique, depending on other ingredients used in the recipe. One rule must always be observed: never add unflavored gelatin directly to hot liquid. The granules will lump together and will not dissolve completely, and this will ruin the dessert.

To check gelatin has dissolved properly: Run rubber spatula through mixture, next to side of pan, to see if granules are all dissolved

---

UNMOLDING GELATIN DESSERTS

Individual desserts set with gelatin can be unmolded right onto dessert plates for serving. Unmold large desserts onto serving platter; moisten platter first so if dessert comes out off-center on platter, it can be moved easily to center of platter.

- Fill sink or large bowl with warm, not hot, water. Carefully loosen edges of gelatin from mold with metal spatula or knife.

- Dip mold into warm water just to rim for about 10 seconds. Be careful not to melt gelatin.

- Lift mold out of water and shake it gently to loosen it.

- Invert serving platter on top of mold, then quickly invert mold and platter together and gently lift off mold.

ADDING INGREDIENTS TO GELATIN

In most recipes, gelatin should be partially set before other ingredients are added, or solid ingredients such as cut-up fruit might sink to the bottom, and whipped cream could lose its volume by the time it is thoroughly blended in. When solids are to be added, gelatin mixture should be jelled to consistency of "unbeaten egg white." This partially thickened stage allows for even distribution of solids. When adding whipped cream, chill mixture slightly longer, until it "mounds when dropped from spoon."

If gelatin thickens too much before other ingredients are folded in or it is poured into a mold, place bowl of gelatin in hot water and stir occasionally for 1 minute or less to melt gelatin. Then chill gelatin again, stirring occasionally.

CHILLING GELATIN

In order to set, a gelatin mixture must be chilled. Stir mixture occasionally while it chills, so that it cools and thickens evenly. For faster thickening, place saucepan or bowl containing mixture in larger bowl of ice water. Stir mixture often until it reaches desired consistency. Or place saucepan or bowl in freezer and stir often until mixture is of desired consistency. Do not leave mixture in freezer until it sets; ice crystals will form and make gelatin watery, ruining the dessert.

To test consistency of gelatin mixture: Take up spoonful of mixture and drop it on top. It should "mound," not disappear

EGGS: HANDLE WITH CARE

Raw or undercooked eggs may pose a risk of salmonellosis, food poisoning caused by salmonella bacteria found in some eggs. While this risk is very small, it does exist; so the recipes in this book do not use raw eggs. When making a custard, be sure it reaches a temperature of 170° to 175°F. so that the eggs are cooked and custard thickened properly; but do not allow the custard to boil or it will curdle. Proper storage and cooking of eggs and handling of egg-rich foods is necessary to prevent growth of potentially harmful bacteria. For safety first, take these precautions:

• Buy only clean, uncracked grade AA or grade A eggs.

• Don't buy eggs that have not been kept stored in a refrigerator.

• When you bring eggs home, put them in the refrigerator as soon as possible - it is safer to leave eggs in the carton, not on the door. The temperature in the refrigerator should be 40°F. or colder.

• Don't keep eggs at room temperature longer than 1 hour.

• Use eggs within 5 weeks of purchase.

• Before and after working with eggs, wash hands, work surfaces, and equipment.

• If a speck of yolk gets into egg whites while separating eggs, use a spoon, not the egg shell, to remove it. The egg shell might not be clean.

• Serve eggs and egg-rich foods as soon as they are cooked; or, if you've made them ahead, refrigerate them at once and use within 3 days.

• The Center for Disease Control advises extra caution for the following:
  a) elderly whose immune systems are weakened with age
  b) infants whose immune systems are not yet fully developed
  c) pregnant women
  d) anyone with an immune system weakened by disease or anticancer treatments.

THICKENING WITH EGGS

Many different desserts use eggs as a thickening agent in the form of a custard. The key to successful custard is careful control of heat; too high a heat causes eggs to curdle, resulting in a lumpy, thin mixture. However, it is also important that the heat is high enough (see Eggs: Handle with Care, left).

For successful custards, use a heavy saucepan or double boiler, and stir mixture constantly until it thickens and coats a metal spoon well (temperature of mixture should be about 170° to 175°F.). Take care not to let mixture boil or it will curdle. Check thickness by lifting spoon from custard and holding it up for 15 to 20 seconds; if spoon does not show through it, custard has thickened to right consistency.

To test consistency of custard: *Lift spoon and hold it up for 15 to 20 seconds: Spoon should not show through mixture*

HOT SOUFFLÉS

Raised high with beaten egg whites, light, fluffy, hot dessert soufflés need to be carefully timed since they should be served as soon as they are taken from the oven: they tend to collapse if left to stand for more than a few minutes. Both the basic sauce and the soufflé dish itself can be prepared well in advance. Don't open oven door before end of specified baking time; a rush of cold air into the oven could cause soufflé to collapse.

With wire whisk, gradually folding soufflé mixture into egg whites

With back of spoon, making 1-inch indentation around top of soufflé for "top hat" effect

MOUSSES

The light, creamy texture of mousse comes from eggs or whipped cream, or a combination of both, blended into chocolate, fruit, or nuts. Mousses are often made with uncooked beaten egg whites but, because of the problem with raw eggs (see Eggs: Handle with Care, above), recipes in this book are made with cream or cooked eggs. Mousses using eggs must be cooked with care to raise their temperature to 170°F. without cooking them past the slightly thickened stage.

CUSTARDS

English Cream, classically called crème anglaise, is a stirred custard – a thick, sweet liquid that can be served alone as dessert or used as a sauce for other desserts. Constant stirring over low heat allows custard to thicken evenly without lumping.

• Serve English Cream as dessert, accompanied with crisp cookies.

• Use as sauce for toasted or plain pound-cake slices or angel-food-cake wedges; cut-up fresh or poached fruit; brownies; ice cream.

ENGLISH CREAM

8 servings
Begin early in day

2/3 cup all-purpose flour

1/2 cup sugar

8 large egg yolks

4 cups milk

1 teaspoon grated lemon peel

1/4 teaspoon vanilla extract

1 In large bowl, with wire whisk, beat flour, sugar, and egg yolks until well blended; then gradually beat in milk.

2 Strain mixture through fine strainer into heavy 3-quart saucepan. Over medium heat, cook, stirring constantly with wire whisk, until thickened and smooth (mixture should be about 170° to 175°F. but do not boil or it will curdle).

3 Remove saucepan from heat; stir in lemon peel and vanilla extract. Pour custard into bowl; cover; refrigerate until well chilled.

MERINGUES

Meringue is a mixture of stiffly beaten egg whites and sugar, which can be baked in varied shapes, small or large. Baked meringues are crisp and light. Shells can be filled with various sweet fillings such as ice cream; flat rounds can be layered with fillings, as in dacquoise.

MERINGUE KISSES

Preheat oven to 200°F. Line large cookie sheet with foil. Prepare meringue as for Meringue Pie Shell (right). Spoon meringue into large decorating bag with large rosette tube. Pipe meringue onto foil-lined cookie sheet in 48 rosettes, each about 1 inch in diameter, about 1/2 inch apart. Bake meringues 1 1/4 hours. Turn oven off; leave meringues in oven 45 minutes longer to dry completely. Cool on cookie sheet on wire rack. Store in tightly covered container. Serve as candy or use to garnish desserts.

SUCCESS TIPS FOR MERINGUES

• Make sure all sugar is dissolved; beat sugar in gradually, 2 tablespoons at a time, beating well after each addition.

• Egg whites and sugar should be beaten until meringue forms stiff, glossy peaks when beaters are lifted.

• For meringue recipes calling for 3/4 cup sugar to 3 egg whites, it may take about 15 minutes to beat in all sugar.

• Use low temperature (275° to 200°F.) for baking, so meringues dry out thoroughly without overbrowning.

• Use clean, dry beaters and metal or glass – not plastic – bowl.

• Make sure there is not slightest speck of egg yolk in egg whites.

• Beat egg whites until soft peaks form before adding sugar. If sugar is added too soon, whites will not reach maximum volume.

• Add sugar gradually and beat after each addition until sugar dissolves completely. Test by rubbing mixture between fingers: it should not feel grainy. A knife drawn through mixture should leave clean-cut path.

MERINGUE PIE SHELL

Preheat oven to 275°F. In small bowl with mixer at high speed, beat *3 egg whites* and *1/8 teaspoon cream of tartar* until soft peaks form. Gradually sprinkle in *3/4 cup sugar*, beating after each addition until sugar is dissolved. To test, rub meringue between fingers; if grainy, continue beating. Add *1/2 teaspoon vanilla extract*, beating at high speed until mixture stands in stiff glossy peaks. Spread meringue in well-greased 9-inch pie plate, using large spoon as shown below. Bake 1 hour. Turn off oven control, let meringue stand in oven 1 hour. Cool on wire rack.

Spooning meringue into pie plate, smoothing it at center

With back of spoon, pushing meringue high on sides to form pie "shell"

FRUIT

Fruit, with its many flavors and beautiful colors, offers scores of possibilities for superb desserts. Even when served alone, it can end a sophisticated dinner as perfectly as it ends a simple repast. One rule of thumb applies: whether fruit is used alone or in combination with other foods, it should always be at its best. Many fruits are ripe and ready to eat when you buy them: apples, berries, cherries, citrus fruits, grapes, pineapples, pomegranates, and rhubarb. Other fruits, particularly those that have been shipped long distances, usually need ripening at home. To ripen apricots, nectarines, peaches, pears, and plums, place them in a loosely closed paper bag or covered fruit-ripening bowl and leave them at room temperature (avoid direct sunlight) for a few days until ripe. Let bananas, kiwifruit, mangoes, melons, papayas, and persimmons stand, uncovered, at room temperature away from direct sunlight until ripe. Once it is completely ripe and ready to use, store fruit in refrigerator. The alphabetical guide on this and the following pages will show you when fruits are available, what to look out for, and how to store and prepare them for use.

APPLES

Season: All year round. Supplies are best from October through March.
Look for: Firm, crisp, well-shaped, and well-colored fruit, with color ranging from bright green to deep red, depending on variety of apple. Avoid any apples that are at all shriveled, feel soft and mealy, or have brown, bruised spots.
To store: Refrigerate apples; use within 2 weeks.

To prepare: Wash, then peel and core, depending on use. To prevent cut surfaces browning, if apples are peeled or sliced and are to stand for any length of time, sprinkle with a little lemon juice or ascorbic-acid mixture for fruit.

TO STEW DRIED FRUITS*

Fruit	Package size	Water	Sugar	Time
	ounces	*cups*	*cups*	*mins*
Apples	8	3 1/2 + 1/8 tsp salt	1/4	25
Apricots	8	2 1/2	1/4	15
	11 or 12	3	1/2	15
Figs	12	3 + 1 tblsp lemon juice	0	35
Mixed fruit	11 or 12	4	1/2	25
Peaches	11 or 12	4	1/4	25
Pears	11	3	1/4	25
Prunes	16	4	0	20

*Yield: 4 to 6 servings

BEST WAYS TO USE APPLE VARIETIES

All apples can be eaten fresh or cooked, but some lose their shape when baked, while others may be too tart for out-of-hand eating. Use this chart to guide your choice.

	Eating	Baking	Cooking	Sauce	Salad	Pie
Cortland	●	●	●	●	●	●
Golden Delicious	●	●	●	●	●	●
Granny Smith	●	●	●	●	●	●
Gravenstein	●		●	●	●	●
Jonathan	●	●	●	●	●	●
McIntosh	●		●	●	●	●
Newtown Pippin		●	●	●		●
Northern Spy	●	●	●	●	●	●
Red Delicious	●				●	
Rome Beauty		●	●	●		●
Winesap	●	●	●	●	●	●

Red Delicious

McIntosh

Newtown Pippin

Rome Beauty

Golden Delicious

Jonathan

APRICOTS

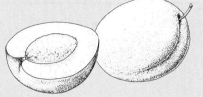

Season: June and July.
Look for: Plump, juicy looking orange-yellow fruit. Ripe apricots should yield to gentle pressure on skin. Avoid dull-looking, shriveled, or soft fruit.
To store: Refrigerate; use within 2 to 3 days.

To prepare: Wash apricots and cut in half to remove pit; peel if desired. To prevent browning if apricots are not to be eaten immediately, sprinkle them with lemon juice or ascorbic-acid mixture for fruit.

BANANAS

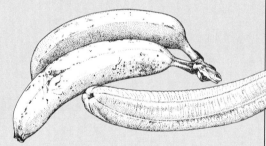

Season: All year.
Look for: Solid yellow bananas with some brown flecks for immediate use. Fruit with some green will ripen at home in a few days at room temperature. Brown skins usually indicate overripened fruit. Red bananas are a specialty in some areas.
To store: Refrigerate bananas after ripening and use within 2 to 3 days. Skin will darken but fruit inside will be ripe and fresh.

To prepare: Peel and slice or cut up bananas. To prevent browning, sprinkle with lemon juice or ascorbic-acid mixture for fruit.

BERRIES

Season: All year, depending on variety.
Look for: Plump, fresh-looking fruit. Avoid berries that are moldy, crushed, or bruised.
To store: Refrigerate; use blueberries within 10 days to 2 weeks, other berries within 1 or 2 days.

To prepare: Just before serving, wash berries; drain; remove hulls or stems; remove stem and "tail" from gooseberries.

Blackberries
Purplish-black, cone-shaped berries grown on climbing vines. Available mainly June and July.

Blueberries
Flat, round berries ranging in color from purplish-blue to almost black, with soft, silvery, powdery bloom. Blueberries vary from size of pea to more than 1 inch in diameter. Best from June through August.

Boysenberries
Large, dark, blackberry-like berries with rich, tart, raspberry flavor. Available during summer months.

Currants
Small, round berries red, black, or white in color. Red currants are most available; very tart but can be eaten fresh if sugared. Available mainly July and August.

Dewberries
Berries resembling blackberries in appearance and flavor. Available during summer months.

Gooseberries
Tart berries resembling small, striped grapes, ranging from pale green to amber and red. Generally cooked. Available June and July.

Loganberries
Large, long berries, reddish in color, with raspberry flavor. Available during summer months.

Raspberries
Thimble-shaped berries red, black, purple, or yellow in color. Best in June, July, September, and October.

Strawberries
Bright red, fragrant berries ranging from tiny wild ones to large cultivated ones. Stem caps should be attached. Available all year, best from April through June.

CHERIMOYAS (CUSTARD APPLES)

Season: November through May.
Look for: Large fruit, uniformly green, with rough, petal-like indentations.
To store: Ripen at room temperature until they yield to pressure. Refrigerate and use within 1 to 2 days.

To prepare: Wash fruit; cut lengthwise into halves or quarters.

CHERRIES

Season: Best in June and July.
Look for: Plump, bright-looking cherries with color ranging from amber to red to purplish-black. Sour cherries best for cooking; sweet cherries can be eaten fresh or used in cooking.
To store: Refrigerate; use within 1 week.

To prepare: Wash; remove stem and pit.

COCONUTS

Season: All year; best in November and December.
Look for: Heavy coconuts, full of liquid. Avoid nuts with wet or moldy eyes.
To store: Refrigerate and use within a week; shredded in 1 to 2 days.

To prepare: Pierce eyes with skewer and hammer; drain liquid. Hit shell hard with hammer around middle to break open. Pry out meat with small, sharp knife.

CRANBERRIES

Season: Best from October through December.
Look for: Plump, firm, glossy berries.
To store: Refrigerate; use within 1 to 2 weeks. Freeze for longer storage; leave in their original bag. Do not wash before freezing.

To prepare: Wash, remove stems, drain well. No need to thaw frozen ones, just rinse and drain.

DATES

Season: All year.
Look for: Lustrous, plump, golden-brown fruit.
To store: Keep tightly wrapped; when refrigerated will keep for several weeks.

To prepare: Cut out pits, if necessary.

FIGS

Season: Summer and fall.
Look for: Slightly firm fruit with no sour odor.
To store: Refrigerate; use within 1 to 2 days.

To prepare: Wash; remove any stems.

HOW TO PRESENT FRESH FRUIT

When cut in unusual ways, fresh fruits can be used on their own to create a spectacular effect or as a garnish. Here are a few ideas using apples, mangoes, and pomegranates; for more ideas, see Fruit Garnishes (pages 66 to 67).

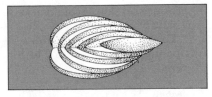

To make apple chevrons: Cut apple into 6 wedges, then cut each wedge into 4 layered V-shaped slices. Reassemble wedges, spreading them out slightly

To prepare mangoes: With sharp knife, cut lengthwise slice from each flat side, as close to seed as possible. Set aside inner section containing seed. Using sharp knife, score flesh of slices crosswise and then lengthwise, without cutting through skin. Gently push skin outward to eat cubes. Peel skin from inner section and either eat out of hand or slice flesh from seed lengthwise

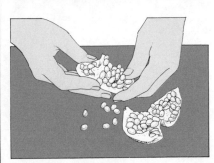

To prepare pomegranates: With sharp knife, 1 inch from blossom end, make shallow cut all around. With fingers, pull off top. Score fruit, through peel only, in about 6 wedges. Break pomegranate into separate sections and remove seeds

GRAPEFRUIT

Season: All year; best January through April.
Look for: Well-shaped, firm fruit, heavy for size.
To store: Refrigerate; use within 1 to 2 weeks.

To prepare: Cut in half parallel to stem end. With sharp, pointed knife cut sections from membrane. Cut out cores; remove seeds.

GRAPES

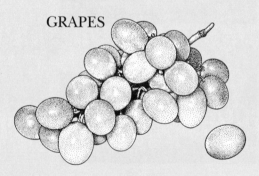

Season: All year, depending on variety (see below).
Look for: Plump, fresh-looking fruit with individual grapes firmly attached to stems. Avoid dry, brittle stems and shriveled grapes or ones leaking moisture. Varieties of table grapes include: Almeria, Black Beauty, Calmeria, Cardinal, Concord, Emperor, Exotic, Flame Seedless, Italia, Perlette, Queen, Ribier, Ruby Seedless, Tokay, and Thompson Seedless.
To store: Keep grapes in refrigerator; use within 1 week.

To prepare: Wash well just before serving and pat grapes dry with paper towels.

GUAVAS

Season: September through November.
Look for: Fruit with green to yellowish-red skin, depending on variety. Ripe guavas should yield to gentle pressure on skin. Avoid cracked skins.
To store: Refrigerate after ripening and use within 2 to 3 days.

To prepare: Wash fruit; cut off skin.

KIWIFRUIT (CHINESE GOOSEBERRY)

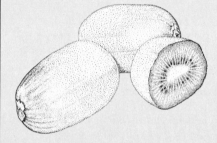

Season: All year.
Look for: Slightly firm fruit with fuzzy skin. When fully ripe, kiwifruit should yield to gentle pressure on skin. Some kiwifruit with smooth, not fuzzy, skin may be available soon.
To store: Firm, unwashed kiwifruit may be stored, away from other fruits, in refrigerator for several months. Ripen at room temperature; refrigerate when ripe and use within 1 to 2 days.

To prepare: With sharp knife, peel off skin; cut in wedges or slices. Or cut unpeeled fruit lengthwise in half to be eaten with spoon.

KUMQUATS

Season: November through April; best in early winter.
Look for: Firm, glossy, bright-orange kumquats. Avoid blemished or shriveled fruit.
To store: Refrigerate; use within 1 week.

To prepare: Wash fruit and remove stems; cut in half to remove seeds.

LEMONS AND LIMES

Season: All year.
Look for: Firm, bright fruits that are heavy for their size. Pale or greenish-yellow lemons usually indicate fruit of higher acidity. Limes should be glossy skinned; irregular purplish-brown marks on skins do not affect quality. Avoid soft, shriveled, or hard-skinned fruits.
To store: Keep for few days at room temperature, or refrigerate and use within 2 weeks.

To prepare: Cut fruit in half, parallel to stem end, for squeezing; slice or cut into wedges for garnishes; remove seeds. When grating or shredding lemon or lime peel, be sure to grate only zest – thin, colored part of peel – as white pith underneath will add bitter taste to food.

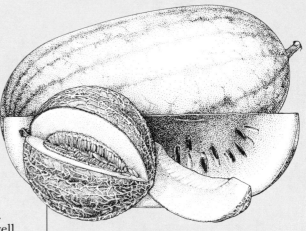

LYCHEES

Season: Late May through July.
Look for: Firm, rough, reddish-brown fruit with no indication of decay at stem end. Avoid blemished fruit.
To store: Refrigerate; use within 1 to 2 days.

To prepare: Beginning at stem, with thumb, pull off skin as you would orange skin; remove pit.

MANGOES

Season: Best May through August.
Look for: Plump, yellowish or orange, oval or round fruit, sometimes with speckled skin, and fresh aroma. Ripe mangoes should yield slightly to gentle pressure on skin. Avoid soft, bruised, or shriveled fruit.
To store: Ripen at room temperature, then refrigerate and use within 2 to 3 days. Keep refrigerated until ready to serve, as mangoes taste best when cold.

To prepare: With sharp knife, cut single lengthwise slice from each side of long flat seed, as close to seed as possible; set aside section containing seed. With spoon, carefully scoop out mango flesh in long, curved slices. Peel skin from reserved inner section and slice flesh from seed lengthwise. To eat out of hand, cut slices off each side, score crosswise and lengthwise without cutting through skin. Gently push outward to eat cubes.

MELONS

Season: April through December, depending on variety.
Look for: Fully ripened melons for best sweetness and flavor, heavy for size. Avoid bruised or cracked fruit.
To store: Ripen at room temperature, then refrigerate. Use within 2 to 3 days. Keep well wrapped after cutting.

To prepare: Cut small round melons in half, remove seeds with spoon. Cut large melons in half from stem to blossom end. Slice thickly lengthwise.

Cantaloupe
Golden- or greenish-beige skin with thick, coarse netting. Scar at stem should be smooth, without any stem remaining. When ripe, it has pleasant aroma and salmon-colored flesh, and feels tender but not mushy at blossom end. Available June through September.

Casaba
Round with pointed end, chartreuse-yellow with lengthwise furrows and no netting; flesh is cream-colored. When ripe, rind is rich yellow and blossom end yields to gentle pressure. Best July through October.

Crenshaw
Globe-shaped and pointed at stem end, with shallow furrows and gold-and-green rind that turns all-gold when ripe. Blossom end yields to gentle pressure when ripe. Pink flesh with rich aroma. Available July through October.

Gallia
Small and round with netting on rind. When ripe, rind turns from green to golden yellow and should yield to pressure.

Honeydew, Honeyball
Similar except that honeyball is smaller. Rind is cream-colored with patches of netting. When ripe, skin should feel velvety and rind should give slightly. Look for honeyballs from July through November, honeydews all year.

Persian
Resembling cantaloupe but larger, with finer netting, and dark-green background that turns lighter green when ripe. Skin gives under slight pressure. Flesh is orange-pink with distinctive aroma. Available June through November.

Watermelon
Can weigh up to 20 pounds, with red or yellow flesh. Should be firm and symmetrically shaped (either round or oval). Ripeness not easy to judge, so look for melons sold in halves or quarters. Flesh should be firm, of good red color. Avoid melons with hard white streak running through flesh. Available May through September.

NECTARINES

Season: May through September; best June through August.
Look for: Plump, smooth-skinned fruit; reddish to yellowish color. Avoid hard, soft, or shriveled fruit.
To store: Ripen at room temperature; then refrigerate and use within 3 to 5 days.

To prepare: Wash fruit; cut in half to remove pit. To prevent browning, sprinkle with lemon juice.

ORANGES

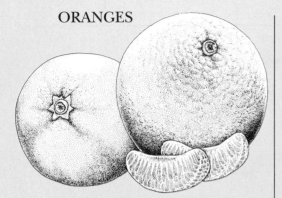

Season: All year; best winter and early spring.
Look for: Firm fruit, heavy for size. Strict regulations help assure tree-ripened fruit; slight greenish color or russeting on skin does not affect quality. Navel and Temple oranges easily peeled and sectioned; Valencias, Parson Browns, Pineapples, Hamlins have abundant juice.
To store: Keep at room temperature for few days or refrigerate and use within 2 weeks.

To prepare: Peel; separate into sections, slice or chop. Or cut in half, parallel to stem end, for squeezing. When grating peel, only grate zest—white pith underneath is bitter.

PAPAYAS

Season: All year.
Look for: Greenish-yellow to almost yellow fruit that yields to gentle thumb pressure. Avoid shriveled or bruised fruit.
To store: Refrigerate; use within 3 to 4 days.

To prepare: Cut in half lengthwise and scoop out seeds. Peel and slice or cut them up.

PASSION FRUIT

Season: February through July.
Look for: Fruit with leathery, mottled, purple skin. Flesh light orange in color, with numerous small dark edible seeds. Ripe and ready to eat when skin becomes wrinkled; flavor somewhat like sweet, delicately perfumed grapefruit.
To store: Refrigerate; use within 3 days.

To prepare: Cut in half crosswise; spoon out pulp and seeds.

PEACHES

Season: May to October.
Look for: Fairly firm to slightly soft fruit, yellow or cream-colored fruit with red blush, depending on variety. Avoid green, shriveled, or bruised fruit.
To store: Refrigerate; use within 3 to 5 days.

To prepare: Peel and halve to remove seed. To prevent browning, if cut peaches are not eaten immediately, sprinkle with lemon juice or ascorbic-acid mixture for fruit.

PEARS

Season: All year; best August to December.
Look for: Well-shaped, fairly firm fruit; color depends on variety. Ripe pears yield readily to soft pressure in palm of hand. Avoid shriveled, discolored, cut or bruised fruit. Select Bartlett, Anjou, and Bosc pears for eating fresh or cooking; Comice, Seckel, Nelis, and Kieffer for eating fresh.
To store: Let firm pears ripen at room temperature for few days, then refrigerate and eat within 3 to 5 days.

To prepare: Peel, cut lengthwise in half, and remove seeds, core, and stem.

PERSIMMONS

Season: October through December.
Look for: Slightly firm, plump fruit with smooth, unbroken skin and stem cap attached. Avoid bruised or too-soft fruit. Oriental varieties are most common; smaller native persimmons are usually homegrown.
To store: When ripe, refrigerate and use within 1 to 2 days.

To prepare: Remove caps. Press native persimmons through food mill or strainer to remove seeds and skin before using fruit in recipes. For dessert or snack, place Oriental persimmon, stem end down, on plate; cut gashes through top skin so that pulp can be eaten with spoon.

PHYSALIS
(CAPE GOOSEBERRY)

Also called: Chinese Lantern, Goldenberry, Ground Cherry, Peruvian Cherry, Husk Tomato.

Season: Late fall.
Look for: Unblemished bright orange berries with smooth, shiny skin, each encased in papery calyx. Skin contains numerous edible seeds.
To store: Refrigerate and use within 1 week.

To prepare: For garnish, leave in calyx, otherwise remove calyx and wash fruit.

PINEAPPLES

Season: All year.
Look for: Firm fruit, heavy for size, with distinct aroma and plump, glossy eyes. Color will depend on variety, but usually dark green indicates fruit is not fully ripe (once picked, it will not ripen further).
To store: If you like, refrigerate before serving.

To prepare: For chunks, cut off crown and stem ends; stand pineapple on one cut end. Cut off rind in large strips and remove eyes. Cut pineapple from core in large strips; discard core. Cut pineapple into chunks. For pineapple wedges, cut unpeeled fruit into halves, then quarters, through crown to stem end. Cut off core along tops of wedges; run knife between rind and flesh close to rind. Leaving flesh in shell, cut it into $1/4$- to $1/2$-inch slices. Or remove flesh; use pineapple shell for serving fruit salad.

PLUMS

Season: June through September.
Look for: Plump fruit that yields to gentle pressure on skin and is well colored. Color varies from yellow-green to reddish-purple to purplish-black, depending on variety. Avoid hard, shriveled, or cracked fruit.
To store: Refrigerate; use within 5 days.

To prepare: Wash plums; cut into each center to remove pit. Slice or cut up fruit for serving, with or without skin. Varieties vary in tartness, and some need more sugar than others when cooked.

POMEGRANATES

Season: September through December; best in October.
Look for: Fresh-looking fruit, heavy for size. Avoid shriveled fruit or broken rinds.
To store: Refrigerate; use within a week.

To prepare: With sharp knife, 1 inch from and parallel to blossom end, make shallow cut all around. With fingers, pull off top. Score fruit, through peel only, into about 6 wedges. Break wedges apart and gently remove kernels (which are very juicy). To extract juice, with spoon, press kernels through strainer; discard seeds.

QUINCES

Season: October and November.
Look for: Golden-yellow, round or pear-shaped fruit with rather fuzzy skin. Avoid small, knotty or bruised fruit.
To store: Refrigerate; use within 2 weeks.

To prepare: Peel fruit, cut in half, and remove all seeds and every bit of core. Slice fruit; in saucepan over medium heat, in 1 inch boiling water, place slices; when water begins to boil again, cover pan, reduce heat to low, and cook slices until tender. Add sugar to taste. Cooked fruit will remain firm though tender.

RHUBARB

Season: Best April and May.
Look for: Firm, crisp stalks that are either red or pink in color, depending on variety. Avoid flabby stalks.
To store: Refrigerate; use within 3 to 5 days.

To prepare: Wash and trim discolored ends; cut off and discard any leaves (they should not be eaten).

TANGERINES AND TANGELOS

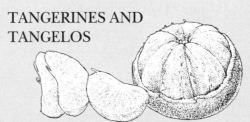

Season: Tangerines November through May; tangelos December through April.
Look for: Tangerines that are deep yellow to deep orange in color and heavy for size, often with loose skin that can be peeled away easily. Tangelos should have bright orange color and be firm and heavy for size; they peel and section easily, have few seeds, and are juicy.
To store: Keep at room temperature few days or refrigerate and use within 2 weeks.

To prepare: Starting from stem end, with fingers, pull off skin. Break fruit into natural sections; if you like, cut into center of each section to remove seeds.

UGLI FRUITS

Season: December through May.
Look for: Grapefruit-shaped citrus fruit, yellow with greenish splotches and wrinkled, bumpy skin.
To store: Refrigerate; use within 1 week.

To prepare: Remove peel with fingers as you would with tangerines; or cut fruit in half and section as grapefruit.

SAUCES

Sweet sauces enable the cook to give desserts a special finish. Here you'll find sauces to step up the flavor and appeal of fresh, canned, and frozen fruits; pies and cakes; frozen desserts; bread and rice puddings. Today's sauces aren't just poured over foods. They can be puddled on the plate or spooned around food to frame it.

More, sauces themselves can be decorated, with designs piped or stirred in; see Saucy Garnishes (pages 26 to 27) for ideas.

When choosing a sauce, think "contrast." A good sauce will differ – compatibly – in flavor, texture, color, and, on occasion, even in temperature, from the dessert it accompanies.

CHOCOLATE SAUCES

CHOCOLATE SAUCE

1 6-ounce package semisweet-chocolate pieces (1 cup)

1/2 cup light corn syrup

1/4 cup half-and-half

1 tablespoon margarine or butter

1 teaspoon vanilla extract

1 In 1-quart saucepan over low heat, melt chocolate with corn syrup, stirring. Remove from heat; stir in remaining ingredients.

2 Serve warm over baked custard, cream pies, cream puffs, or ice cream.

BITTERSWEET CHOCOLATE SAUCE

1/3 cup sugar

2 1-ounce squares unsweetened chocolate

2 1-ounce squares semisweet chocolate

2 tablespoons margarine or butter (1/4 stick)

3/4 teaspoon vanilla extract

1 In heavy 1-quart saucepan over medium heat, heat *1/3 cup water* with all ingredients except vanilla extract to boiling, stirring. Reduce heat to medium-low; simmer, stirring until mixture thickens and is smooth, about 3 minutes. Remove from heat; stir in vanilla extract.

2 Serve sauce warm over pound cake, ice cream, or poached pears.

CHOCOLATE-MARSHMALLOW SAUCE

2 cups miniature marshmallows

1/3 cup heavy or whipping cream

1/3 cup honey

2 1-ounce squares unsweetened chocolate

1/8 teaspoon salt

1 In 2-quart saucepan over low heat, cook marshmallows, cream, honey, chocolate squares, and salt, stirring, until chocolate and marshmallows are melted.

2 Serve hot over bananas or yellow or chocolate cake.

CREAM AND CUSTARD SAUCES

SWEETENED WHIPPED CREAM

1 cup heavy or whipping cream

1 to 2 tablespoons sugar

1/2 teaspoon vanilla or almond extract

1 In bowl, with hand beater or with mixer at medium speed, beat cream, sugar, and vanilla extract until soft peaks form (overbeating causes cream to curdle and turn to butter).

2 On hot days, chill bowl and beaters. Serve cream on fruit or nut pies, or ice-cream sundaes.

Berry Whipped Cream
Beat cream as above until soft peaks form; fold in *1/2 cup drained, crushed, and sweetened strawberries*, raspberries, blackberries, or blueberries.

Chocolate Whipped Cream
Place *2 tablespoons instant-cocoa mix* (or 2 tablespoons sugar and 2 tablespoons unsweetened cocoa) in bowl; add 1 cup heavy or whipping cream. Beat as above.

Coffee Whipped Cream
Place *2 teaspoons instant-coffee powder* and 2 tablespoons sugar in small bowl; add 1 cup heavy or whipping cream. Beat as above.

CUSTARD CREAM

3 tablespoons sugar

1 3/4 cups half-and-half

1 large egg yolk

1 tablespoon cornstarch

1/8 teaspoon salt

1/2 teaspoon vanilla extract

1 In heavy 2-quart saucepan, combine all ingredients except vanilla extract. Cook over medium heat, stirring, until mixture coats back of spoon, about 15 minutes (mixture should be about 170° to 175°F., but do not boil or it will curdle). Remove from heat; stir in vanilla extract. Chill. Serve over fruit pies, gingerbread, plain chocolate cake, fresh or poached fruit.

CUSTARD SAUCE

4 large egg yolks

⅓ cup sugar

⅛ teaspoon salt

2 cups milk

1 teaspoon vanilla extract

1 In heavy 2-quart saucepan over low heat, or in double boiler over hot, not boiling, water, with wire whisk, stir egg yolks, sugar, and salt.

2 Gradually add milk and cook, stirring, until mixture thickens and coats back of spoon, about 25 minutes (mixture should be about 170° to 175°F., but do not boil or it will curdle). Stir in vanilla extract. Serve warm or cold over apple pie, fruitcake, fresh or stewed fruit.

SUGAR SAUCES

BUTTERSCOTCH SAUCE

1 cup packed light brown sugar

½ cup half-and-half

2 tablespoons margarine or butter (¼ stick)

2 tablespoons light corn syrup

1 In 1-quart saucepan over medium heat, heat brown sugar, half-and-half, margarine or butter, and corn syrup to boiling, stirring occasionally.

2 Serve warm over vanilla or chocolate-ripple ice cream, pound-cake slices, peach or apple pie, or baked custard.

HOT FUDGE SAUCE

1 ½ cups sugar

½ cup milk

⅓ cup light corn syrup

2 1-ounce squares unsweetened chocolate

1 tablespoon margarine or butter

1 teaspoon vanilla extract

⅛ teaspoon salt

1 In 2-quart saucepan over medium heat, heat first 4 ingredients to boiling, stirring constantly. Set candy thermometer in place and continue cooking, stirring occasionally, until temperature reaches 228°F. or until small amount of mixture dropped from tip of spoon back into mixture spins ¼-inch thread.

2 Remove from heat; stir in margarine or butter, vanilla extract, and salt. Serve sauce hot over vanilla ice cream, poached pears, or toasted pound-cake slices.

CARAMEL SAUCE

2 tablespoons margarine or butter (¼ stick)

2 tablespoons all-purpose flour

1 ½ cups half-and-half

¾ cup packed light brown sugar

¾ cup sugar

¼ teaspoon salt

1 In 2-quart saucepan over medium heat, melt margarine or butter, then stir in flour.

2 Gradually stir in half-and-half; cook, stirring constantly, until mixture boils and thickens.

3 Add brown sugar, sugar, and salt; stir until well mixed. Serve warm or cover and refrigerate to serve cold; serve over baked bananas or apples, or vanilla or chocolate ice cream.

PRALINE SAUCE

1 cup packed brown sugar

½ cup light corn syrup

1 tablespoon margarine or butter

⅛ teaspoon salt

½ cup pecans, finely chopped

1 In 1-quart saucepan over medium heat, stir all ingredients, except nuts, with 2 tablespoons water until sugar dissolves. Stir in nuts.

2 Serve hot over bread or rice pudding, pancakes, or waffles.

HARD SAUCE

1 cup confectioners' sugar

6 tablespoons margarine or butter (¾ stick), softened

½ teaspoon vanilla extract

1 In small bowl, with mixer at medium speed, beat confectioners' sugar with margarine or butter until creamy; beat in vanilla extract.

2 Spoon sauce into small bowl and refrigerate if not serving right away. Serve on steamed pudding, fruitcake, or warm fruit pie.

Deluxe Hard Sauce
Prepare as above but fold in ¼ cup heavy or whipping cream, whipped.

Brandied Hard Sauce
Prepare as above but use 1 ½ cups confectioners' sugar, ½ cup margarine or butter (1 stick), 2 tablespoons brandy, and ½ teaspoon vanilla extract.

FRUIT SAUCES

BLACKBERRY SAUCE

1 20-ounce bag frozen, unsweetened blackberries	**1** In 2-quart saucepan over medium heat, heat berries, sugar, lemon juice, and ground cinnamon, stirring occasionally, until hot and bubbly. Cover; chill.
½ cup packed light brown sugar	
2 tablespoons lemon juice	**2** Serve sauce over ice cream, cake, and other fruits.
½ teaspoon ground cinnamon	

CHERRY SAUCE

1 pound sweet cherries, pitted	**1** In 2-quart saucepan over medium heat, in ⅔ cup boiling water, heat cherries to boiling.
¼ cup sugar	
	2 Reduce heat to low; cover pan and simmer cherries 5 minutes or until tender.

3 During last minute of cooking, add sugar. Serve hot, poured over crepes and waffles; or serve cold over tapioca cream.

PEACH SAUCE

1 10-ounce package frozen peaches in syrup, thawed	**1** In blender at low speed, blend together all ingredients until smooth.
¼ teaspoon almond extract	**2** Serve with ice cream or over angel-food-cake slices.
⅛ teaspoon ground nutmeg	

RASPBERRY SAUCE

2 ½-pints raspberries	**1** In blender at high speed, blend raspberries and sugar until smooth, adding *a little water* if needed to thin sauce.
1 tablespoon sugar	

2 If you like, press sauce through fine sieve with wooden spoon to remove seeds. Serve with peaches, ice cream, angel-food cake, or pound cake.

HOT FRUIT SAUCE

3 large nectarines	**1** Cut fruit into wedges.
3 large plums	**2** In 2-quart saucepan over low heat, cook fruit and juice 10 minutes or until tender, stirring occasionally. Remove from heat.
½ cup orange juice	
½ cup sugar	
2 tablespoons brandy (optional)	**3** Stir in sugar and brandy until sugar is dissolved. Serve over vanilla ice cream.

MAPLE AND ORANGE SAUCE

1 11-ounce can mandarin-orange sections, drained and chopped	**1** In 1-quart saucepan over low heat, heat all ingredients until hot and margarine or butter melts.
¾ cup maple or maple-flavor syrup	**2** Serve warm over crepes, waffles, French toast, or ice-cream sundaes.
2 tablespoons margarine or butter (¼ stick)	

MELBA SAUCE

1 10-ounce package frozen raspberries in syrup	**1** In 2-quart saucepan over low heat, heat raspberries and red currant jelly until raspberries thaw and mixture is hot. In cup, mix cornstarch with *1 tablespoon water* until smooth; stir into berries.
¼ cup red currant jelly	
4 teaspoons cornstarch	

2 Over medium heat, cook berries, stirring constantly, until mixture boils and thickens slightly; boil 1 minute. Press through strainer.

3 Serve warm over ice cream or poached peaches or pears.

ORANGE SAUCE

4 tablespoons margarine or butter (½ stick)	**1** In 1-quart saucepan over low heat, melt margarine or butter. Stir in confectioners' sugar, orange juice, and peel.
1 ½ cups confectioners' sugar	
⅓ cup orange juice	**2** Cook over low heat, stirring frequently, until heated through. Serve sauce over crepes, waffles, and blintzes.
2 tablespoons grated orange peel	

ORANGE-FLUFF SAUCE

¹/₂ cup sugar

¹/₂ cup frozen orange-juice concentrate, thawed

¹/₈ teaspoon salt

2 large egg yolks

1 cup heavy or whipping cream, whipped

1 In 1-quart saucepan over low heat, cook sugar, orange-juice concentrate, and salt; stir until sugar dissolves. Set aside.

2 In small bowl, with mixer at high speed, beat egg yolks until light and fluffy; at medium speed, gradually beat in orange-juice mixture.

3 Return mixture to saucepan; over low heat, cook, stirring until slightly thickened (mixture should be 170° to 175°F., but do not boil or it will curdle).

4 Cool, then fold in whipped cream. Refrigerate until well chilled. Serve over fresh fruit.

STRAWBERRY SAUCE

1 pint strawberries

1 tablespoon sugar

In blender at high speed, blend strawberries and sugar until smooth. Serve over ice cream, rice pudding, angel-food or chocolate cake.

BRANDIED STRAWBERRY SAUCE

3 10-ounce packages frozen sliced strawberries in syrup, thawed

¹/₂ cup red currant jelly

1 tablespoon cornstarch

Few drops red food coloring

¹/₄ cup brandy

1 Drain strawberries, reserving ¹/₂ cup juice. In 2-quart saucepan over low heat, melt red currant jelly, stirring constantly.

2 In small bowl, mix reserved strawberry juice and cornstarch until smooth. Stir cornstarch mixture into melted jelly in saucepan, stirring constantly; increase heat to medium and cook until thickened, stirring.

3 Add food coloring; then stir in berries and brandy. Serve sauce hot over rolled crepes and waffles, or refrigerate and serve chilled over ice cream, or vanilla or tapioca pudding.

PINEAPPLE-CASSIS SAUCE

1 8-ounce can crushed pineapple in juice

4 large egg yolks

2 tablespoons sugar

¹/₈ teaspoon salt

¹/₄ cup cassis (black-currant-flavor liqueur)

1 Drain pineapple, reserving ¹/₄ cup juice. Set aside.

2 In double-boiler top, with hand-held mixer at high speed, beat egg yolks, sugar, and salt until very thick, about 5 minutes. Stir cassis and reserved ¹/₄ cup pineapple juice into beaten egg yolks.

3 Place double-boiler top over hot, not boiling, water in double-boiler bottom. Cook, beating at medium speed, until mixture is fluffy and warm, and mounds slightly when beater is lifted, about 5 minutes (mixture should be 170° to 175°F., but do not boil or it will curdle).

4 Remove double-boiler top from bottom; fold in reserved crushed pineapple. Spoon warm sauce into dessert bowls and top with ice cream, sorbet, or fresh berries, or spoon over crepes.

RUM AND FRUIT SAUCE

2 ¹/₄ cups sugar

6 thin orange slices

6 thin lemon slices

¹/₄ cup light rum

1 In 2-quart saucepan over medium heat, heat sugar, *3 cups water*, and orange and lemon slices to boiling. Reduce heat to low; cover; simmer 5 minutes.

2 Cool sauce to lukewarm; discard orange and lemon slices. Stir rum into sauce. Serve over pound-cake slices or fresh fruit compote.

RHUBARB SAUCE

1 ¹/₂ pounds rhubarb, cut up

²/₃ cup sugar

1 In 2-quart saucepan over medium heat, heat rhubarb and *¹/₄ cup water* to boiling. Reduce heat to low; cover and simmer 5 minutes or until rhubarb is tender, but not broken up.

2 During last minutes of cooking time, stir sugar into sauce. Serve hot or cold over orange or lemon sorbet, or sponge-cake slices.

CAKES

The cakes in this book all follow one of two basic methods. Most contain margarine, butter, or solid shortening, and are mixed and beaten in one bowl. Others, such as tortes, roulades, and tube cakes, have beaten egg whites folded in at the end to give them a light and fluffy texture. Whichever type you bake, if you follow the directions given here you can be assured of success every time.

Before you start, read the recipe carefully and assemble all ingredients and equipment. Prepare pans, set oven racks in position, and preheat oven.

BEFORE YOU START

INGREDIENTS
In the recipes in this book large eggs are used and flour is measured – without sifting – right from the package or canister. Don't be tempted to substitute different ingredients for the ones given in the recipe; they will give different results.

MEASURING
Measure dry and liquid ingredients following directions on pages 276 to 277.

PANS
Use shiny metal pans or pans with nonstick finish. Avoid dull, dark, or enamel pans which can cause uneven and excessive browning. If using glass or porcelain-coated aluminum pans with a nonstick finish, reduce oven temperature by 25°F. Cake pans are available in round, square, or rectangular shapes. Be sure your pans are the size and shape called for in the recipe. Measure the top inside of bakeware for length, width, or diameter; measure perpendicular inside for depth. Prepare pans according to recipe directions (see How to Grease and Line Pans, page 293).

Springform pan: *Has side section which can be removed without disturbing contents*

Tube cake pan: *Has center tube; pan may or may not have removable bottom*

Jelly-roll pan: *Shallow rectangular pan, usually 1 inch deep*

Bundt pan: *Fluted pan with center tube; designed for elegant cakes and desserts*

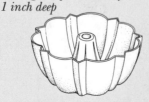

STORING AND FREEZING CAKES

Storing
Layer and tube cakes frosted with fudge- or butter-cream-type frostings or confectioners'-sugar glaze should be kept in a cake keeper or under an inverted bowl or pan to protect frosting.

In this book we have eliminated homemade frostings made with beaten egg whites, such as seven-minute frosting and fluffy white frosting (see Eggs: Handle with Care, page 279), as the egg whites might not reach the temperature at which salmonella bacteria are destroyed. Ornamental (or Decorator's) Frosting is made with meringue powder and is safe to use.

Cakes covered with whipped-cream or cream-cheese frosting, or those that have any sort of cream filling should be kept refrigerated and are best eaten within 1 or 2 days.

Wrap fruitcakes closely in plastic wrap and keep in cool place; they will improve with storage. For very rich cakes, before storing, sprinkle cake with wine or brandy, or wrap in wine- or brandy-dampened cloth, then overwrap with plastic wrap and store for up to 2 months. Redampen cloth weekly with more wine or brandy. Glaze or decorate cake just before serving.

Freezing
Cakes in the freezer make wonderful standby desserts. For storage for longer than 1 month, cake must be wrapped or packaged in materials specifically designed for freezer use. Wrapping materials for foods must be moistureproof; use heavy-duty foil, freezer paper, or freezer plastic wrap. Secure packages with freezer or masking tape. Use waterproof felt-tip pens or markers for writing on labels, freezer tape, or freezer paper.

Unfrosted cakes should be closely wrapped in freezer paper, plastic wrap, or foil, and securely sealed with tape. Most cakes keep from 4 to 6 months, fruitcakes for up to 12 months.

Freeze cakes frosted with butter-cream, whipped-cream, or fudge frostings, unwrapped, on sheet of cardboard covered with foil until frosting hardens. Then closely wrap in freezer wrap, plastic wrap, or foil, then seal with tape; return cake to freezer. Frosted cakes can be kept frozen for 2 to 3 months.

Don't freeze cakes which have fruit fillings; they can become soggy when thawed.

Never freeze uncooked batter or cakes with fillings made with cornstarch or flour.

Thaw unfrosted cakes and cakes with butter-cream or fudge frosting in their freezer wrapping at room temperature. Unfrosted cakes take about 1 hour; frosted tube and layer cakes, 2 to 3 hours.

Cakes with whipped-cream toppings or fillings should be carefully unwrapped before they are thawed. Thaw in refrigerator 3 to 4 hours and keep refrigerated until served. Be sure to cover and refrigerate leftovers.

MEASURING PANS

Be sure your pans are the kind and size specified in recipe. Measure top inside for length, width, or diameter; measure perpendicular inside for depth.

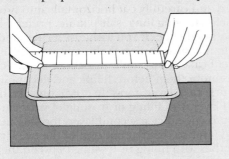

HOW TO GREASE AND LINE PANS

Make sure pans are size called for in recipe, and prepare them before you start mixing batter. Prepare pans according to individual recipe directions.

If pans are to be greased and floured, grease both bottom and sides with shortening, using crumpled waxed paper or paper towels. You can also grease pans with melted shortening using pastry brush to grease evenly. Sprinkle pan with a little flour or, for dark-colored batter, with cocoa so cake doesn't have white coating. Shake pan until coated, then invert it and tap to remove any excess flour or cocoa. For fruitcakes, grease pans generously, line with foil, then grease foil. Some recipes call for bottoms of pans to be lined with waxed paper. The pans are greased, lined with paper, then greased again.

Greasing pan: *Using brush, waxed paper, or paper towels, spread pans evenly with shortening*

Lining pan: *Where specified, line bottom of greased pan with waxed paper; grease paper*

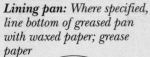

Flouring pan: *In some recipes, pans are floured after greasing. Sprinkle with flour and shake and turn pan until evenly coated; knock out surplus*

HOW TO BEAT MIXTURE

When mixing batter, beat it at recommended mixer speed for length of time specified in recipe. During beating, scrape bowl frequently with rubber spatula so that all cake ingredients are well mixed together. If you use a wooden spoon instead of mixer, you will need to give ingredients about 150 vigorous strokes for every minute of beating time in order to blend ingredients thoroughly. Before adding fruits and nuts to mixture, toss them in about ½ cup of the measured flour, so that they do not sink in batter.

To beat mixture: *Be sure to beat at recommended mixer speed for specified time, constantly scraping sides of bowl with rubber spatula to make sure ingredients are well mixed in*

HOW TO FOLD IN

For cakes made with egg whites, beat egg whites into stiff peaks in bowl. In separate bowl, beat remaining ingredients according to recipe directions. Using rubber spatula, gently fold egg whites into beaten mixture, cutting down through center, across bottom and up side of bowl. Give bowl a quarter turn and repeat until mixture is uniformly blended, but do not overfold or egg whites will break down.

To fold mixture: *Use rubber spatula to fold egg whites into beaten ingredients*

FILLING PANS

Pour batter into prepared pan and tap pan sharply on counter or cut through batter several times with rubber spatula or knife to break any large air bubbles. Spread evenly with spatula.

For mixtures containing beaten egg white, push batter into pan with rubber spatula. Smooth and level it very lightly, then cut through it with rubber spatula to break any large air bubbles.

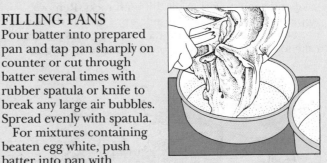

To fill pan: *With rubber spatula, push batter into pan, then smooth and level it very lightly*

OVEN SPACE

For cakes baked in tube pans, which are deep, set oven rack lower so that cake is in middle of oven. For loaves or layers that fit on one rack, set rack so that center of cake or layers is close to center of oven. For 3 or 4 cake layers, 2 oven racks are needed. Place them so they divide oven into thirds, and stagger pans so one is not directly underneath another. Place pans so that they do not touch each other or sides of oven. Preheat oven so that it is at temperature called for in recipe when cake is put into it.

TESTING FOR DONENESS

Do not open oven door to test cake until it has been baking for minimum baking time specified in recipe, or cake might sink. Test for doneness by inserting cake tester or toothpick into center of cake. If it comes out clean and dry, cake is done and should be removed at once to cool. Otherwise bake cake 5 to 10 minutes longer and test it again.

To test cake made with beaten egg white, press top lightly with finger. Cake is done if top springs back when lightly pressed and cracks in top look dry, not moist.

COOLING CHIFFON, ANGEL-FOOD, AND SPONGE CAKES

Invert tube pan on bottle neck or funnel so that its top does not touch counter; air can then circulate underneath, as well as over and around it, and cake can cool evenly. Cooling in this position also enables cake to hold its shape; if cooled top-side up, it will fall.

Allow cake to cool completely in pan, then remove it by cutting around side and tube of pan with metal spatula, using an up-and-down motion and pressing spatula firmly against pan. Invert pan and gently shake cake out onto plate.

COOLING LAYER CAKES

Most cakes should be cooled in their pans for 10 minutes or so on wire rack before removing them. Once cake has cooled slightly, run metal spatula around edge to loosen it from pan. Invert a second rack over top of cake. Turn over pan with both racks; cake should drop from pan. Remove upper rack and lift off pan. Replace rack over cake and again invert cake with both racks. Remove upper rack leaving cake top-side up. This way there will not be any marks from wire rack on top of cake. Allow cake to cool completely before frosting or storing it.

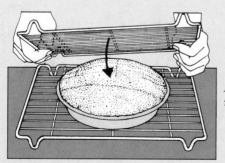

Inverting second rack over top of cake

SPLITTING, FROSTING, AND FILLING LAYERS

To split a tall cake into layers before frosting, put it on a board and carefully cut horizontally into two halves (see below), using long, sharp knife, preferably one with serrated edge. If you wish, use a ruler and toothpicks to measure and mark the midpoint all around cake; cut cake horizontally just above toothpicks and then remove them before filling and decorating cake. Place first cake layer, top-side down, on cake plate; spread layer with filling or frosting of your choice almost to edge. Place second layer, top-side up, on frosted layer so that flat bottoms of the two layers face each other with filling or frosting between them.

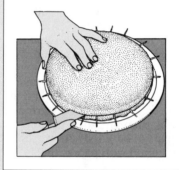

To split cake: *Using long, serrated knife, carefully halve cake horizontally*

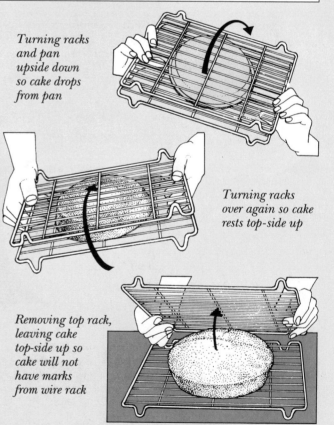

Turning racks and pan upside down so cake drops from pan

Turning racks over again so cake rests top-side up

Removing top rack, leaving cake top-side up so cake will not have marks from wire rack

CUTTING CAKES

Different cakes need to be cut in different ways, depending on their type. To get fluffy, high wedges from angel, chiffon, and sponge cakes, with cake breaker or 2 forks, gently pull pieces apart. Or "saw" cake lightly with serrated or very sharp knife. For layer cakes, use long thin, sharp, knife and cut with gentle sawing motion; don't press down. If cutting cake in kitchen, after each cut, wipe off crumbs clinging to knife; rinse knife in hot water.

CUTTING WAYS

To cut your cake to best advantage, try one of the ways diagrammed here. Dotted lines show first cuts to be made.

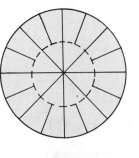

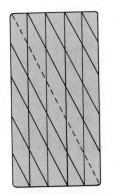

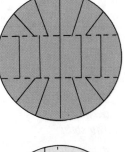

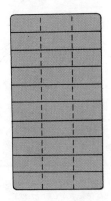

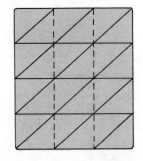

CUTTING THREE-TIER CAKE

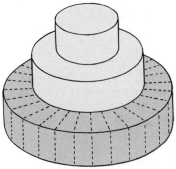

1 With cake knife held close to base of second tier, cut down to base of bottom tier and around to make a complete circle. Now cut bottom tier into serving slices, cutting just to circle. Remove slices.

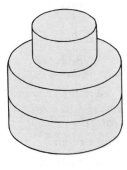

2 Cake now has two lower tiers of same size and small top tier.

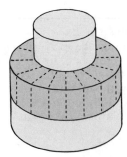

3 Repeating procedure in step 1, cut second tier by making circular cut around base of smaller top tier. Cut into serving slices from second tier, cutting just to circle. Remove slices. Now remove top tier on its foil-covered cardboard. Cut into slices; serve.

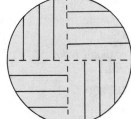

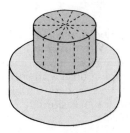

4 Cut remaining center of second tier into serving slices and remove.

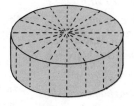

5 Remove foil-covered cardboard on which second tier had rested and cut remaining center of bottom tier into serving slices.

BASIC CAKE RECIPES

The cake recipes on this page provide a good basis for making a variety of different desserts. The recipes are carefully balanced, so be sure to follow directions exactly for successful results every time.

ANGEL-FOOD CAKE

Angel-food cakes should be high, light, and fluffy. For perfect results, it is important that egg whites are beaten stiff enough. Bowl and beaters must be absolutely free from grease or any specks of egg yolk, which contains fat, or egg whites cannot be beaten stiff.

1 1/4 cups confectioners' sugar

1 cup cake flour

1 2/3 cups large egg whites (12 to 14 egg whites)

1 1/2 teaspoons cream of tartar

1/2 teaspoon salt

2 teaspoons vanilla extract

1/2 teaspoon almond extract

1 1/4 cups sugar

1 Preheat oven to 375°F. In small bowl, stir confectioners' sugar and cake flour; set aside. In large bowl, with mixer at high speed, beat egg whites, cream of tartar, and salt until soft peaks form; beat in extracts. Beating at high speed, sprinkle in sugar, 2 tablespoons at a time, beating until sugar is completely dissolved and whites stand in stiff peaks. Fold in flour mixture just until flour disappears.

2 Pour batter into ungreased 10-inch tube pan. Bake 30 to 35 minutes, until cake springs back when lightly touched. Invert cake in pan on funnel or bottle; cool completely in pan. With metal spatula, carefully loosen cake from pan; place on cake plate.

YELLOW CAKE

2 1/4 cups cake flour

1 1/2 cups sugar

3/4 cup shortening

3/4 cup milk

2 1/2 teaspoons baking powder

1 teaspoon salt

1 teaspoon vanilla extract

1/2 teaspoon almond extract

3 large eggs

1 Preheat oven to 375°F. Grease and flour two 9-inch round cake pans.

2 Into large bowl, measure all ingredients. With mixer at low speed, beat ingredients until well mixed, scraping bowl with rubber spatula. Increase speed to high; beat 2 minutes, occasionally scraping bowl.

3 Pour batter into pans. Bake 25 minutes or until toothpick inserted in center of cake comes out clean. Cool. Fill and frost as desired.

POUND CAKE

2 cups sugar

1 cup margarine or butter (2 sticks), softened

3 1/2 cups cake flour

1 1/4 cups milk

1 1/2 teaspoons baking powder

2 teaspoons vanilla extract

1/8 teaspoon salt

6 large egg yolks

1 Preheat oven to 350°F. Grease and flour 10-inch Bundt pan or two 9" by 5" loaf pans.

2 In large bowl, with mixer at low speed, beat sugar and margarine or butter just until blended. Increase speed to high; beat until light and fluffy. Reduce speed to low; add flour and remaining ingredients; beat until well mixed, scraping bowl with rubber spatula. Increase speed to high; beat 2 minutes, occasionally scraping bowl.

3 Spoon batter into pan. Bake in Bundt pan 1 hour or in loaf pans 45 to 50 minutes, until toothpick inserted in center comes out clean. Cool on wire rack 10 minutes, then remove from pan.

CHOCOLATE CAKE

3/4 cup unsweetened cocoa, plus extra for dusting

2 cups cake flour

1 3/4 cups sugar

1 1/4 cups milk

3/4 cup shortening

1 1/4 teaspoons baking soda

1 teaspoon salt

1 teaspoon vanilla extract

1/2 teaspoon baking powder

3 large eggs

1 Preheat oven to 350°F. Grease two 9-inch round cake pans; dust with cocoa.

2 Into large bowl, measure all ingredients. With mixer at low speed, beat until mixed, scraping bowl with rubber spatula. Increase speed to high; beat 2 minutes, scraping bowl occasionally.

3 Pour batter into pans. Bake 30 to 35 minutes until toothpick inserted in center of cake comes out clean. Cool in pans on wire racks 10 minutes, then remove from pans.

Beating mixture at low speed, scraping bowl with rubber spatula

Inserting toothpick in center of cake, to test for doneness

FROSTINGS AND ICINGS

Most uncooked butter-cream-type frostings can be made in advance and stored until needed in tightly covered container to prevent crust forming on top. If they are refrigerated and as a result become too firm to spread easily, let them stand at room temperature or stir well to soften to spreading consistency.

Allow your cake to cool completely before frosting or filling. Trim off any crisp edges with knife or kitchen shears and brush away all loose crumbs. Keep cake plate clean by covering edges with strips of waxed paper. Lay cake on paper strips, centering it on plate. After frosting cake, carefully slide out paper strips. Cakes frosted with cream-cheese, sour-cream, or whipped-cream frostings should be refrigerated until served.

Each of the recipes on this and the following page makes enough to frost 13" by 9" cake or to fill and frost a 2-layer cake.

To frost cake: Cover plate edges with strips of waxed paper; lay cake on strips

After frosting, carefully slide out strips; if necessary, touch up base with frosting

WHIPPED-CREAM FROSTING

2 cups heavy or whipping cream

¼ cup confectioners' sugar

⅛ teaspoon salt

1 teaspoon vanilla extract

In small bowl, with mixer at medium speed, beat heavy or whipping cream, sugar, and salt until stiff peaks form; fold in vanilla extract. Keep frosted cake refrigerated until ready to serve.

TECHNIQUES

Layer cake
Place one layer of cake, top-side down, on serving plate. Cover this layer with either filling or frosting, spreading it almost to edge. If filling is soft, spread it only to within 1 inch of edge. Place second cake layer, top-side up, on filling, so that flat bottoms of two layers face each other, keeping top layer from cracking or sliding off. Frost sides of cake thinly to set any loose crumbs, then apply second, more generous layer of frosting, swirling it up to make ½-inch ridge above rim of cake. Finally, frost top of cake, swirling frosting or leaving it smooth, as you like. Decorate frosted cake if desired.

Oblong cake
Frost top and sides of cake as for layer cake, or leave cake in pan and frost just top.

Tube or ring cake
Frost sides, then top and inside center of cake as for layer cake.

Cupcakes
Dip top of each cupcake in frosting, turning it slightly to coat evenly.

Glazing
Brush crumbs from top of cake. Spoon or pour glaze onto top of cake, letting it drip down sides. Spread thicker glazes over top and sides of cake with metal spatula.

Drizzling
To make decorative pattern, pour thin icing or glaze from spoon, quickly waving spoon back and forth over cake.

Chocolate Whipped-Cream Frosting
Prepare as Whipped-Cream Frosting but fold in *one 6-ounce package semisweet-chocolate pieces* (1 cup), melted and cooled.

Coffee Whipped-Cream Frosting
Prepare as Whipped-Cream Frosting but add *1 teaspoon instant-coffee powder* with sugar.

Orange Whipped-Cream Frosting
Prepare as Whipped-Cream Frosting but add *1 teaspoon grated orange peel* and *⅛ teaspoon orange extract* with vanilla extract.

Peppermint Whipped-Cream Frosting
Beat cream and salt (no sugar) as Whipped-Cream Frosting and fold in *¼ cup crushed peppermint candy*; omit vanilla extract.

BUTTER-CREAM FROSTING

1 16-ounce package confectioners' sugar

6 tablespoons margarine or butter (³/₄ stick), softened

3 tablespoons milk or half-and-half

1 ¹/₂ teaspoons vanilla extract

In large bowl, with mixer at medium speed (or with spoon), beat all ingredients until smooth, adding more milk or half-and-half if necessary until frosting is smooth with an easy spreading consistency.

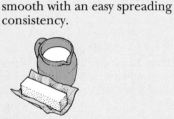

Lemon Butter-Cream Frosting
Prepare as Butter-Cream Frosting but substitute *lemon juice* for milk and omit vanilla.

Mocha Butter-Cream Frosting
Prepare as Butter-Cream Frosting but add *¹/₂ cup unsweetened cocoa*; substitute *¹/₃ cup cold coffee* for milk and reduce vanilla to ¹/₂ teaspoon.

CHOCOLATE SOUR-CREAM FROSTING

1 6-ounce package semisweet-chocolate pieces (1 cup)

1 tablespoon margarine or butter

²/₃ cup sour cream

¹/₄ cup confectioners' sugar

¹/₄ teaspoon salt

1 In heavy 1-quart saucepan over low heat, heat chocolate and margarine or butter until melted and smooth, stirring occasionally. Remove from heat.

2 In small bowl, with mixer at medium speed, beat melted chocolate mixture, sour cream, confectioners' sugar, and salt until smooth.

CREAM-CHEESE FROSTING

2 3-ounce packages cream cheese, softened

2 tablespoons milk

1 teaspoon vanilla extract

¹/₈ teaspoon salt

1 16-ounce package confectioners' sugar

1 In small bowl, with mixer at medium speed, beat cream cheese and milk just until smooth.

2 Blend in vanilla extract, salt, and confectioners' sugar.

Coffee-Cheese Frosting
Prepare as Cream-Cheese Frosting but add *4 teaspoons instant-coffee powder* with confectioners' sugar.

BUTTERMILK-PECAN ICING

3 cups sugar

1 cup margarine or butter (2 sticks)

1 cup buttermilk

2 tablespoons light corn syrup

1 teaspoon baking soda

1 3-ounce can pecans (1 cup), finely chopped

1 In 4-quart saucepan over medium heat, heat sugar, margarine or butter, buttermilk, light corn syrup, and baking soda to boiling, stirring constantly.

2 Set candy thermometer in place in saucepan; cook buttermilk mixture, stirring occasionally, until temperature reaches 238°F., or until a little of buttermilk mixture dropped in cup of cold water forms soft ball.

3 Pour icing into large bowl; with mixer at high speed, beat icing to spreading consistency, about 7 minutes, occasionally scraping bowl. Gently fold in finely chopped pecans.

SEMISWEET-CHOCOLATE ICING

1 6-ounce package semisweet-chocolate pieces (1 cup)

2 tablespoons shortening

2 tablespoons light corn syrup

3 tablespoons milk

1 In heavy 2-quart saucepan over low heat, or in double boiler over hot, not boiling, water, heat semisweet-chocolate pieces and shortening until melted and completely smooth, stirring occasionally. Remove from heat.

2 With wire whisk or fork, beat in corn syrup and milk until mixture is smooth. Spread while icing is still warm.

MOCHA-SUGAR ICING

3 cups confectioners' sugar

2 tablespoons unsweetened cocoa

1 teaspoon instant-coffee powder

1 teaspoon vanilla extract

In small bowl, mix together all ingredients with ¹/₃ cup water.

CHOCOLATE-SUGAR ICING

3 cups confectioners' sugar

¹/₄ cup unsweetened cocoa

1 teaspoon vanilla extract

In small bowl, mix together all ingredients with 7 *tablespoons water*.

GLAZES

Each of the following recipes makes enough to glaze 13" by 9" cake.

CITRUS GLAZE

1 cup confectioners' sugar	In small bowl, stir all ingredients until smooth.
5 teaspoons orange juice	
1 teaspoon each grated orange and lemon peel	
¹/₂ teaspoon vanilla extract	
¹/₈ teaspoon salt	

RICH CHOCOLATE GLAZE

³/₄ 12-ounce package semisweet-chocolate pieces (1 ¹/₂ cups)	**1** In 2-quart saucepan over low heat, heat all ingredients until chocolate melts and mixture is smooth, stirring constantly.
2 tablespoons confectioners' sugar	
3 tablespoons orange-flavor liqueur	**2** Remove saucepan from heat. Allow glaze to stand at room temperature to cool slightly until of spreading consistency, then spread while still warm.
3 tablespoons milk	
1 teaspoon instant-coffee powder	

Spreading Rich Chocolate Glaze over cake: *Stand cake on wire rack over sheet of waxed paper; spread glaze over top and sides with metal spatula, letting excess glaze drip onto paper*

DECORATIVE TOUCHES

It is easy to add decorative touches to cakes that are covered in frosting. To make spiral pattern below left, place cake on turntable or lazy Susan.

Press tip of spatula into center; turn cake, slowly moving spatula outward

Draw tines of fork across frosting in parallel rows; repeat rows at right angles

DRIZZLES

You only need a very small amount to make a cake or dessert look very glamorous.

ESPRESSO DRIZZLE

1 tablespoon margarine or butter	**1** In small saucepan over low heat, melt margarine or butter with coffee and *1 tablespoon water* until coffee dissolves; remove from heat.
2 teaspoons instant espresso-coffee powder	
¹/₃ cup confectioners' sugar	**2** Stir in sugar until smooth; add more water if needed for drizzle consistency.

CHOCOLATE DRIZZLE

2 1-ounce squares unsweetened chocolate	In heavy 1-quart saucepan, over low heat, melt unsweetened-chocolate squares.

WHITE DRIZZLE

¹/₂ cup confectioners' sugar	In small bowl, mix together confectioners' sugar and lemon juice.
2 teaspoons lemon juice	

TOPPINGS

Each of the following recipes makes enough to spread on top of 13" by 9" cake.

MACADAMIA-FUDGE TOPPING

1 cup heavy or whipping cream

½ cup sugar

2 tablespoons margarine or butter (¼ stick)

1 tablespoon corn syrup

4 1-ounce squares semisweet chocolate

1 teaspoon vanilla extract

1 7-ounce jar macadamia nuts

1 In 2-quart saucepan over medium-high heat, heat first 5 ingredients to boiling, stirring constantly.

2 Reduce heat to medium and then cook 5 minutes, stirring constantly. Remove pan from heat; stir in vanilla extract. Cool slightly, about 10 minutes, then stir in macadamia nuts.

3 Quickly pour topping evenly over cake, allowing some to run down sides. Refrigerate until topping is firm, about 1 hour.

BROILED PRALINE TOPPING

½ cup margarine or butter (1 stick)

1 3½-ounce can flaked coconut (1⅓ cups), chopped

¾ cup chopped nuts

¾ cup packed brown sugar

¾ teaspoon vanilla extract

1 Start to prepare topping about 10 minutes before end of cake's baking time. In 2-quart saucepan over low heat, melt margarine or butter.

2 Stir in flaked coconut, chopped nuts, sugar, and vanilla extract. Remove saucepan from heat.

3 When cake is done, turn oven control to broil. Spread coconut mixture over hot cake. Broil cake 2 minutes or until golden.

CRACKED CARAMEL

¼ cup sugar

1 In heavy small saucepan over medium heat, heat sugar until melted and a light brown color (about 6 minutes), stirring constantly.

2 Immediately pour onto greased cookie sheet. Cool.

3 With rolling pin, crack caramel. If not using right away, store in tightly covered container.

FILLINGS

Each of the following recipes makes enough filling for 2-layer cake.

ALMOND FILLING

1 4-ounce can slivered blanched almonds (1 cup)

½ cup confectioners' sugar

2 tablespoons margarine or butter (¼ stick), softened

2 tablespoons orange juice or orange-flavor liqueur

1 In blender at medium speed or in food processor with knife blade attached, finely grind slivered almonds.

2 In bowl, mix ground almonds with remaining ingredients.

CREAMY CUSTARD FILLING

2 cups milk

¼ cup sugar

3 tablespoons cornstarch

¼ teaspoon salt

2 large egg yolks

1 teaspoon vanilla extract

1 In heavy 2-quart saucepan, stir together all ingredients except vanilla extract.

2 Over medium-low heat, cook until mixture thickens and boils, about 20 minutes (mixture should be about 170° to 175°F.). Stir in vanilla extract. Cool in refrigerator 30 minutes.

FRESH LEMON FILLING

¼ cup lemon juice

1 tablespoon grated lemon peel

¼ cup sugar

4 teaspoons cornstarch

¼ teaspoon salt

1 tablespoon margarine or butter

1 In 1-quart saucepan over medium heat, stir all ingredients except margarine or butter with *½ cup water* until well blended. Cook until mixture thickens and boils, stirring.

2 Reduce heat; simmer 1 minute, stirring occasionally. Remove from heat; stir in margarine or butter. Cool mixture at room temperature.

Fresh Orange Filling
Prepare as Fresh Lemon Filling but substitute *orange juice and peel* for lemon juice and peel.

LEMON CURD FILLING

3 tablespoons lemon juice

1 tablespoon lemon peel

³/₄ cup margarine or butter (1 ¹/₂ sticks)

1 cup sugar

3 large eggs

1 In double boiler over hot, not boiling, water, or in heavy 2-quart saucepan over low heat, stir lemon juice, lemon peel, margarine or butter, and sugar until melted.

2 In small bowl, beat eggs slightly. Add to mixture and cook, stirring constantly, until mixture thickens and will coat the back of a spoon, about 15 minutes. (Mixture should be 170° to 175°F., but do not boil or it will curdle.)

3 Pour filling into bowl; cover surface with plastic wrap and refrigerate 3 hours or until filling is well chilled.

CREAMY CHOCOLATE-WALNUT FILLING

1 cup evaporated milk, undiluted

¹/₂ cup packed brown sugar

¹/₂ cup margarine or butter (1 stick)

2 1-ounce squares semisweet chocolate

3 large egg yolks, lightly beaten

1 8-ounce can walnuts (2 cups), chopped

1 teaspoon vanilla extract

1 In 3-quart saucepan over medium heat, heat milk, sugar, margarine, chocolate squares, and egg yolks, stirring frequently, about 10 minutes, until mixture thickens slightly. (Mixture should be 170° to 175°F., but do not boil or it will curdle.)

2 With wooden spoon, stir in chopped walnuts and vanilla extract until mixed.

3 Remove pan from heat and cool slightly until thick enough to spread, stirring occasionally.

PINEAPPLE FILLING

¹/₄ cup sugar

3 tablespoons cornstarch

¹/₈ teaspoon salt

³/₄ cup canned pineapple juice

2 tablespoons margarine or butter (¹/₄ stick)

1 tablespoon lemon juice

1 teaspoon grated lemon peel

1 In 1-quart saucepan, mix sugar, cornstarch, and salt. Stir in juice; add remaining ingredients.

2 Over low heat, heat to boiling, stirring constantly. Boil 1 minute or until smooth and thickened; cool.

MOCHA-CREAM FILLING

1 ¹/₂ cups heavy or whipping cream

¹/₂ cup unsweetened cocoa

¹/₄ cup confectioners' sugar

2 tablespoons coffee-flavor liqueur

In large bowl, with mixer at medium speed, beat all ingredients until stiff peaks form.

EASY CREAM FILLING
Makes enough to fill and spread on top of 3-layer cake or fill 4-layer cake.

1 package regular vanilla-flavor pudding and pie filling for 4 servings

1 ¹/₂ cups milk

¹/₂ cup heavy or whipping cream

Few drops of vanilla or almond extract

1 Prepare pudding mix as label directs but use only 1¹/₂ cups milk. Cover surface with plastic wrap and refrigerate until chilled.

2 When pudding is cold, beat heavy or whipping cream until stiff peaks form. Fold whipped cream and extract into pudding until blended.

Easy Orange-Cream Filling
Prepare as Easy Cream Filling but substitute *1 ¹/₂ cups orange juice* for milk. Fold in *1 tablespoon grated orange peel* with whipped cream.

Easy Pineapple-Cream Filling
Prepare as Easy Cream Filling but fold *¹/₂ cup drained canned crushed pineapple* into chilled pudding with whipped cream.

Easy Chocolate-Cream Filling
Prepare as Easy Cream Filling but substitute *1 package regular chocolate-flavor pudding and pie filling for 4 servings* for vanilla pudding; use only 1 ¹/₂ cups milk. Into hot pudding, stir *2 tablespoons brown sugar.*

Easy Butterscotch-Cream Filling
Prepare as Easy Cream Filling but substitute *1 package regular butterscotch pudding and pie filling for 4 servings* for vanilla pudding; use only 1 ¹/₂ cups milk.

Easy Lemon-Cream Filling
Prepare as Easy Cream Filling but substitute *1 package regular lemon-flavor pudding and pie filling for 4 servings* for vanilla pudding; use only 1 ¹/₂ cups milk.

PIPING

With decorating bag fitted with coupler, and a selection of tubes, you can make a wide range of shapes and designs in icing to decorate your cakes. Follow directions (below right) for fitting and filling decorating bag. Decorating bags come in various sizes – select the size that is appropriate for the amount of icing used.

Consistency of icing is very important. If necessary, thin icing slightly by adding a few drops of water or milk. Keep bowl covered with a damp cloth while working to prevent icing from drying out. Make flowers ahead by piping them onto waxed paper. Freeze butter-cream flowers ahead of time; they will keep a week. Air-dry flowers made from Ornamental Frosting; they will keep for months in tightly covered container.

BASIC EQUIPMENT

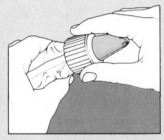

Decorating bag

Flower nail

Coupler

Tubes

Coupler ring

TUBES

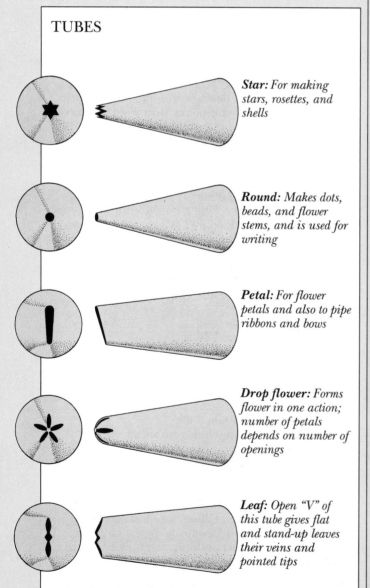

Star: *For making stars, rosettes, and shells*

Round: *Makes dots, beads, and flower stems, and is used for writing*

Petal: *For flower petals and also to pipe ribbons and bows*

Drop flower: *Forms flower in one action; number of petals depends on number of openings*

Leaf: *Open "V" of this tube gives flat and stand-up leaves their veins and pointed tips*

FITTING AND FILLING BAG

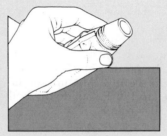

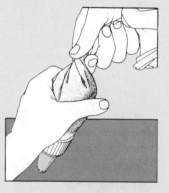

1 Unscrew coupler ring and drop coupler, narrow end first, into decorating bag so that some threads extend past bag opening; if necessary, trim bag opening slightly to fit.

2 Fit chosen decorating tube over coupler, then screw coupler ring in place. To change tube, simply unscrew coupler ring and replace tube with different one.

3 Holding bag in left hand, fold down open end of bag to make deep cuff. With rubber spatula, push icing deep into bag, filling it half full.

4 Keep half-filled decorating bag twisted shut while piping icing decorations; as you apply steady pressure to bag, icing will flow down tube in even stream.

HOLDING DECORATING BAG

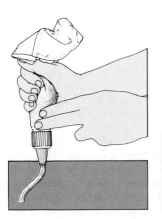

For a perfect shape, hold bag at 90° angle (left) or 45° angle (right) to surface being decorated. Use fingertips of other hand to steady bag

PIPING RIBBONS AND BOWS

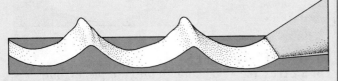

Ribbon: *With petal tube at 45° angle, place wide end of opening on surface of cake, narrow end slightly up. Then squeeze bag, while making series of curves*

Ribbon swag: *Follow technique for making ribbon, but as you complete each curve, move petal tube up and down in three short strokes*

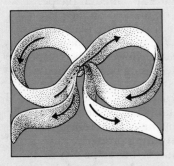

Bow: *With bag pointing toward you, hold petal tube at 45° angle, wide end on surface and narrow end straight up. Squeeze to make left loop; stop at cross starting point. Make right loop. From center, make two streamers*

PIPING STARS, ROSETTES, AND SHELLS

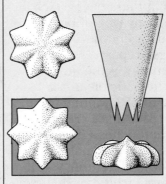

Stars: *With star tube at 90° angle and almost touching surface, squeeze decorating bag to form star, then lift tube slightly, keeping tip in icing. Stop applying pressure and lift tube away from icing*

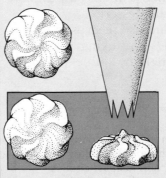

Rosettes: *Holding star tube at 90° angle and almost touching surface, squeeze to form star, but as you squeeze move tube up and to left in circular motion. Stop applying pressure and lift tube away from icing*

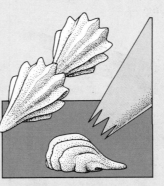

Shells: *Holding star tube at 45° angle and touching surface, squeeze decorating bag, lifting it slightly as icing fans out. Then relax pressure on bag and at same time bring tube down and toward you*

PIPING LEAVES

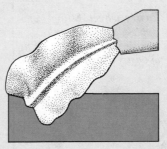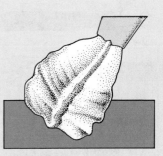

Plain leaf: *Hold leaf tube at 45° angle. Squeeze until icing fans out; relax pressure and draw leaf to point. Stop pressure and pull tube away*

Stand-up leaf: *Hold tube at 90° angle. Squeeze to fan icing; relax pressure as you raise tube, drawing leaf to point. Stop pressure and lift tube*

PASTRY-MAKING

You can make your own "designer" pies and tarts with the recipes and ideas in these pages. Pick a pastry to make the crust for any type of pie, whether served hot or cold; or choose a crumb crust to hold chilled fillings prepared separately. (Unbaked piecrust, incidentally, is the quickest piecrust you can make.) The basic piecrusts are here and on pages 150 to 153, waiting to be filled with fruit, pudding, custard, ice cream, or mousse, plus the decorative touches – edges, tops, garnishes, arrangements – that make a pie or tart your very own creation. Here, too, you'll find the recipes for the simple fruit pies that have been made in America since pioneer days and still rank as a family-favorite dessert.

If you take a short cut and use piecrust mix, follow the same techniques for mixing, handling, rolling, and using the dough in double- or single-crust pies and tarts.

EQUIPMENT
Using the right utensils can help make pastry-making easy and speedy. Chilling the rolling pin makes rolling dough easier and keeps it cool. A pastry cloth makes it easier to roll out dough and helps prevent it from sticking.

Rolling pin: Choose one with handles and ball bearings for rolling out dough

Pastry scraper: Use for scraping off any dough that sticks to work surface

Pastry wheel: Straight or ripple-edged wheel with handle, which speeds cutting of pastry dough

Pastry blender: For cutting fats evenly into dry ingredients

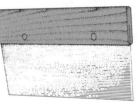

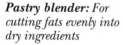

Pastry brush: For brushing on egg and milk glazes, or jelly glaze on fruit tarts

PASTRY-MAKING TECHNIQUES

ROLLING OUT DOUGH
Dough should be rolled with floured rolling pin on lightly floured surface. Slightly flatten ball of dough and roll it out, moving from center to edges, keeping it circular. Push sides in occasionally by hand, if necessary, and lift rolling pin slightly as you near edges to avoid making them too thin.

Lift dough from time to time to make sure that it is not sticking. If it does stick, loosen it with pastry scraper and sprinkle a little more flour on surface underneath. Mend any cracks or breaks as they appear, patching tears with strip of dough cut from edge. Moisten torn edges, lay patch over tear, and press it carefully into position.

Rolling out dough: Roll dough from center to edges, keeping it circular. Push sides in occasionally by hand, if necessary, and lift rolling pin slightly as you near edges to avoid making them too thin

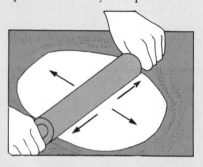

LINING PIE PLATES
For a 2-crust pie, divide dough into two pieces, one slightly larger than other. Use larger piece for bottom crust. For two bottom crusts, divide dough evenly in half.

Roll dough into round $1/8$ inch thick and $1 1/2$ inches larger all around than upside-down pie plate. Roll loosely around rolling pin and lift onto pie plate, centering it over plate. Unroll and ease it into pie plate, pressing it lightly onto bottom and side. Do not stretch dough at any point; it will just shrink back while baking. Make Decorative Pie Edge (pages 152, 153, and 308) and fill pie, or make top crust if it is 2-crust pie, then make edge.

PIE PLATES
Be sure your pie plates are size specified in recipe. To check, if size has not been marked on pie plate by manufacturer, use a ruler to measure plate from inside edge to inside edge. Pie plates of same diameter may differ in capacity, however; the recipes in this book have been tested using larger capacity pie plates.

For nicely browned piecrusts, use heatproof glass, porcelain, or nonshiny metal (such as anodized aluminum) pie plates. Shiny metal pans reflect heat and keep piecrusts from browning properly.

Don't grease pie plates unless the recipe says to do so. Most pastry contains enough shortening to keep from sticking to the pie plate.

BAKING BLIND

A pie or tart shell that is baked "blind" is baked first without a filling. If it is to be filled with a very juicy filling, it should not be pricked with a fork before baking. Instead, after lining the pie plate with dough and making a decorative edge, cut a sheet of foil and place it in the piecrust, pressing it gently to the bottom and side. If recipe directs, half fill foil liner with pie weights (available in department stores or specialty cookware stores) or dry beans or rice. Bake in preheated 425°F. oven 10 minutes; carefully remove liner with pie weights and continue baking pie shell until golden. Cool pie shell completely before filling. Dry beans and rice can be stored, after cooling, in covered container and used again and again for baking blind; do not use them in cooking.

Half filling foil liner with dry beans for baking blind

A BAKING PRECAUTION

Sometimes, despite the cook's best efforts, juices from very ripe fruit will bubble over the pie-plate rim onto the oven floor. If you are using very juicy fruit and suspect that this might happen, tear off a 12-inch square of foil and turn the edges up ½ inch on all sides; place on another oven shelf directly below the pie to catch any dripping juices, and bake the pie as recipe directs. Even if the pie does bubble over, the foil should catch all the drips and save an oven-cleaning job.

GLAZING AND BAKING

For a golden glaze, brush top crust (not edge) with milk, half-and-half, undiluted evaporated milk, or slightly beaten egg white; sprinkle crust with sugar, if you like. If piecrust edges begin to brown too much during baking, cover them with strips of foil to prevent burning. If top crust seems to be browning too much, cover pie loosely with foil for the last 15 minutes of the baking time.

Covering piecrust edges with strips of foil to prevent burning

FREEZING PIES, TARTS, AND PASTRY

Uncooked Pastry Dough
Roll pastry (made with solid shortening) into rounds 1 ½ inches larger all around than upside-down pie plates, stack with 2 sheets of waxed paper between each, wrap, and freeze. To use, place round of dough on pie plate; thaw 10 to 15 minutes before shaping. Use within 2 to 3 months.

Pie Crusts
Freeze baked or unbaked piecrusts in their pie plates, or in reusable foil pie plates. Store baked piecrusts 4 to 6 months; thaw, unwrapped, at room temperature 15 minutes. Store unbaked crusts 2 to 3 months. Prick unfilled piecrusts well with fork and bake, without thawing, for about 20 minutes in 425°F. oven; or fill and bake as directed in recipe.

Fruit Pies and Tarts
Freeze baked or unbaked fruit pies 2 to 3 months. To freeze unbaked fruit pies, if fruit is very juicy, add 1 to 2 tablespoons extra thickening per pie. Do not cut slits in top crust. Freezer-wrap and freeze. Or, if pie is fragile, first freeze until firm, then cover top with paper plate for protection, freezer-wrap and store.
   To cook unbaked, frozen fruit pie, unwrap, cut slits in top crust and bake still frozen, allowing 15 to 20 minutes additional baking time or until fruit is bubbling.
   Thaw baked pies at room temperature 30 minutes, then bake in 350°F. oven 30 minutes or until warm.

Pumpkin Pies
Bake pumpkin pies before freezing, or crust may become soggy. Use within 3 months. Thaw as for fruit pies. Or, freeze filling and unbaked crust separately; thaw and complete pie as recipe directs.

Frozen Fillings
Pies with ice cream or frozen filling will not only be easier to cut, but also have more flavor, if allowed to stand at room temperature for 15 minutes after removal from freezer.

STORING PIES, TARTS, AND PASTRY

Most fruit pies and tarts can be kept at room temperature overnight, even in warm weather, covered with foil or plastic wrap. For longer storage (2 or 3 days), refrigerate; then freshen by warming them in conventional or microwave oven.
   Pies with cream, custard, whipped-cream, cream-cheese, or gelatin-based fillings should be refrigerated and used within a day or so. Balls of unbaked pastry, made with shortening, margarine, or butter (not salad oil), may be wrapped in either plastic wrap or foil, and stored in refrigerator for a day or two.

BASIC PASTRY RECIPES

On pages 150 to 151, you'll find the basic recipes for tender, flaky pastry made with solid shortening. The recipe right, made with salad oil, is equally delicious and easy to mix, but it should be rolled out and used immediately after mixing. On a lazy day – or an extra-busy one – make the no-roll pastry crust and topping for your favorite fruit pie.

NO-ROLL PASTRY FOR 1-CRUST PIE

2 cups all-purpose flour

1 teaspoon salt

³/₄ cup shortening

1 In medium bowl, with fork, stir flour and salt. With pastry blender or two knives used scissor-fashion, cut shortening into flour until mixture resembles coarse crumbs. Reserve 1 cup of mixture.

2 Sprinkle *2 to 3 table-spoons cold water* into flour mixture, a tablespoon at a time, mixing lightly with fork after each addition, until dough is just moist enough to hold together.

3 Press dough to bottom and side of 8- or 9-inch pie plate; flute edges. Fill crust; sprinkle reserved flour mixture over pie and bake as recipe directs.

BAKED OIL-PASTRY PIE SHELL
Preheat oven to 425°F. Prepare dough and line pie plate as for Oil Pastry for 1-Crust Pie (right); with fork, prick dough in many places to prevent puffing during baking. Bake 15 minutes or until golden. Cool before filling.

OIL PASTRY FOR 2-CRUST PIE

2 ¹/₃ cups all-purpose flour

1 teaspoon salt

¹/₂ cup plus 1 tablespoon salad oil

1 In bowl, stir flour and salt. Stir in oil until mixture resembles coarse crumbs.

2 Sprinkle *3 to 4 table-spoons cold water*, a tablespoon at a time, into mixture, mixing lightly with fork after each addition until dough is moist and cleans side of bowl. Shape dough into 2 balls, one slightly larger.

3 Dampen countertop slightly; place 12-inch waxed-paper square on dampened surface. Center larger ball on paper; cover with second waxed-paper square. Roll dough into round about 1 ¹/₂ inches larger all around than upside-down pie plate.

4 If top waxed-paper sheet wrinkles, lift it off carefully, smooth it out, and replace; continue rolling.

5 Gently peel off top paper. Lift dough round on bottom sheet and place in 8- or 9-inch pie plate, pastry-side down; peel off paper and ease round onto bottom and up side of pie plate. Fill pie as recipe directs.

6 For top crust, roll smaller ball same way; peel off top sheet of paper and cut few slashes or design in center of dough. Center round, pastry-side down, over filling in bottom crust; peel off waxed paper. Trim edges, leaving 1-inch overhang.

7 Fold overhang under, bring up over pie-plate rim, then make Decorative Pie Edge (pages 152, 153, and 308) of your choice; bake filled pie as recipe directs.

OIL PASTRY FOR 1-CRUST PIE
Prepare dough as above, but use *1 ¹/₃ cups all-purpose flour, ¹/₂ teaspoon salt, ¹/₃ cup salad oil,* and *2 tablespoons cold water.* Line pie plate as above; trim edge, leaving 1-inch overhang. Fold overhang under, then make Decorative Pie Edge (pages 152, 153, and 308) of your choice. Fill and bake pie as recipe directs.

PIE TOPS

The simplest top for a 2-crust pie is one with steam vents cut into the pastry before it is placed over the filling. For attractive – and impressive – variety, try the different tops shown on these pages. They can be made with surprisingly little effort. Pastry trimmings can be used for decorating both covered and open-face pies. For the finishing touch – a beautiful edge – see the intriguing choices on pages 152, 153, and 308.

SIMPLE LATTICE

Prepare dough as in Pastry for 2-Crust Pie (page 150). Prepare bottom crust and fill as recipe directs. Trim edge to 1½-inch overhang.

1 Roll top crust into 11-inch round; cut into ½-inch strips. Moisten edge of bottom crust with water.

2 Place strips of dough about ¾ inch apart across filling; press each strip at both ends to seal.

3 Repeat with equal number of strips placed at right angles to first strips to make lattice design. Turn overhang up over ends of strips; pinch to seal and make high stand-up edge that will hold juices in; flute edge.

CARTWHEEL

Pastry strips placed over a filling like the spokes of a wheel; quick and easy to do.

1 For 9-inch pie plate, roll out dough for top crust and cut twelve ½-inch strips. Arrange 6 strips over filling in "V" shapes.

2 Use more strips to make smaller "V" shapes inside larger ones.

3 Moisten edge of bottom crust and press strips to edge. Make decorative edge. Bake as recipe directs.

Six pastry strips arranged over filling in "V" shapes

Making smaller "V" shapes inside larger ones to complete cartwheel

WOVEN LATTICE

A woven lattice top using strips of dough as for Simple Lattice (below left) gives a really professional-looking finish to a pie.

1 Place strips over filling; do not moisten edge of crust and do not seal ends. Fold every other strip back halfway from center. Place center cross-strip on pie; replace folded strips.

2 Fold back alternate strips; position second cross-strip.

3 Repeat to weave lattice. Pinch to seal ends, then make fluted edge.

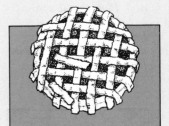

TWISTED LATTICE

This is an attractive variation on Simple Lattice (above left).

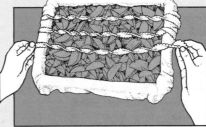

1 Twist long strips of dough lengthwise before attaching to bottom crust.

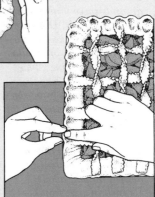

2 Trim edges. Fold overhang over strip ends. Pinch to make high edge, then make decorative edge.

DECORATIVE PIE EDGES

Making a pretty edge on a pie, even if it is as simple as pressing with a fork, helps keep the piecrust from shrinking, by fastening it to the pie-plate rim. In some pies, a high edge keeps liquid mixtures such as custards in and prevents juices from boiling out onto the oven floor.

Fork-Scalloped Edge: *Pinch to form stand-up edge. Place thumb against outside edge and press it toward pie while pressing down next to it with 4-tined fork*

Rope Edge: *Pinch to form stand-up edge. Then pinch edge between thumb and index finger to make a slanted deep indentation. Repeat all around pie edge*

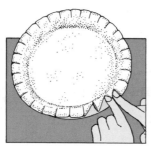

Polka-dot Edge: *Trim pastry, leaving 1/2-inch overhang; fold overhang under and press gently all around rim with fingertips to flatten evenly. Dip blunt end of wooden skewer into flour and gently press into pastry around rim, almost but not quite all way through, 1/4 inch from edge and at 1/2-inch intervals to make even row*

Cutouts Edge: *Trim edge even with pie plate. Cut desired shapes (about 3/4 inch in size) from remaining pastry using tiny cookie cutter, thimble, or bottle cap. Moisten rim; place cutouts on rim, slightly overlapping. Press into place*

Pinwheel Edge: *Fold edge under; press flat. Cut slits around edge of pastry the width of rim, leaving about 1 inch between slits. Fold under on diagonal to form pinwheel points*

Turret Edge: *Pinch to form stand-up edge. Cut edge at 1/2-inch intervals, then press alternate strips flat*

PASTRY DECORATIONS

It is very easy work to make a pie look extra special simply by cutting rolled-out trimmings of dough into various shapes, using knife, cookie or canapé cutter, or pastry wheel, and placing them on top of pie or around edge in a decorative pattern. Use our easy directions to create a "special occasion" look, and lightly brush shapes with milk or beaten egg before baking, to give them a shiny glaze.

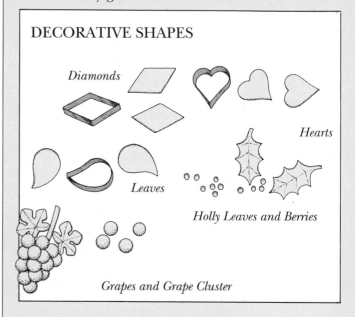

DECORATIVE SHAPES

Diamonds

Hearts

Leaves

Holly Leaves and Berries

Grapes and Grape Cluster

HOLLY LEAVES AND BERRIES

Roll out dough trimmings 1/8 inch thick. With floured 2 1/2-inch leaf-shaped cookie cutter, cut out leaves; with toothpick or small knife, mark veins on leaves. Shape scraps of dough into 1/4-inch balls. Brush some egg white on back of leaves and balls to make them stick to piecrust. Make design on top of pie, placing several leaves together and top with few balls. Lightly brush top of pie with milk or beaten egg before baking.

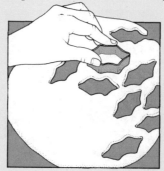

Cutting out leaves with floured cookie cutter

Brushing egg white on back of leaves to make them stick to piecrust

FAVORITE FRUIT PIES

When fresh fruits are in season, showcase them in a delectable homemade pie, or beautiful open-face tart. Out of season you can use frozen blueberries, cranberries, peaches, and rhubarb (if frozen without sugar or syrup); canned cherries rate a special recipe of their own.

FRUIT PIE

- 10 servings
- Begin about 3 hours before serving or early in day

Pastry for 2-Crust Pie (page 150) or 1 10- to 11-ounce package piecrust mix

Fruit filling (see below and right)

1 tablespoon margarine or butter, cut into bits

Dotting filling with margarine or butter

1 Prepare pastry and line 9-inch pie plate as directed for 2-crust pie. Preheat oven to 425°F.

2 Spoon filling into piecrust; dot filling with margarine or butter.

3 Place top crust on filling; make Decorative Pie Edge (pages 152, 153, and 308).

4 Bake pie 40 to 50 minutes until golden. Cool slightly on wire rack to serve warm; or cool pie completely to serve later.

Apple-Pie Filling
Peel, core, and thinly slice *6 medium-sized cooking apples* (about 2 pounds) to make 6 to 7 cups slices. In large bowl, toss apple slices with *²/₃ cup sugar* (half brown sugar, if you like), *2 tablespoons all-purpose flour, 1 to 2 teaspoons lemon juice, ¹/₂ teaspoon ground cinnamon, ¹/₂ teaspoon grated lemon peel,* and *¹/₄ teaspoon ground nutmeg* until well mixed.

Blueberry-Pie Filling
In large bowl, with rubber spatula, toss *2 pints blueberries* (about 5 cups) with *³/₄ cup sugar, ¹/₃ cup all-purpose flour, ¹/₂ teaspoon ground cinnamon, ¹/₂ teaspoon grated lemon peel,* and *¹/₈ teaspoon salt* until well mixed.

Cherry-Pie Filling
Remove pits from *2 pounds fresh tart cherries.* In large bowl, toss cherries with *1 cup sugar, ¹/₄ cup cornstarch,* and *¹/₂ teaspoon salt* until well mixed.

Canned-Cherry-Pie Filling
Drain *two 16-ounce cans pitted tart cherries,* reserving ¹/₂ cup juice. In medium bowl, stir *1 cup sugar, 3 tablespoons quick-cooking tapioca, ¹/₄ teaspoon salt,* and *¹/₄ teaspoon ground cinnamon;* stir in reserved cherry juice, cherries, *¹/₂ teaspoon vanilla extract,* and *¹/₈ teaspoon red food coloring* (optional). Let mixture stand 15 minutes to soften tapioca.

Cranberry-Walnut-Pie Filling
Prepare filling and let cool while making pastry. For filling, in 3-quart saucepan, stir *³/₄ cup sugar* with *1 tablespoon cornstarch;* stir in *¹/₄ cup water* until blended, then stir in *³/₄ cup light corn syrup,* and *1 teaspoon grated lemon peel.* Over medium heat, heat to boiling. Stir in *one 12-ounce package cranberries* (3 cups), *¹/₂ cup dark seedless raisins,* and *¹/₂ cup walnuts,* chopped; cover and cook until cranberry skins pop, about 4 minutes. Remove saucepan from heat; stir in *2 tablespoons margarine* or butter (¹/₄ stick).

Gooseberry- or Fresh-Currant-Pie Filling
In medium bowl, combine *2 pints gooseberries* or currants (about 4 cups), *1 ¹/₂ cups sugar, ¹/₄ cup cornstarch, ¹/₂ teaspoon ground cinnamon,* and *¹/₄ teaspoon salt.* With slotted spoon or potato masher, coarsely mash berries so that all sugar is moistened; mix well.

Green-Tomato-Pie Filling
Prepare filling before making pastry: Remove stem ends from *9 medium-sized green tomatoes* (about 3 pounds); dice tomatoes. In 4-quart saucepan over medium-high heat, heat diced tomatoes, *1 cup dark seedless raisins, 1 cup packed light-brown sugar, ¹/₄ cup red wine vinegar, 4 tablespoons margarine* or butter (¹/₂ stick), *¹/₂ teaspoon ground cinnamon,* and *¹/₂ teaspoon ground allspice* to boiling. Reduce heat to medium-low; cook, uncovered, stirring occasionally, until very thick, about 1 hour and 15 minutes.

Peach-Pie Filling
Peel, pit, and slice *8 medium-sized peaches* (about 2 pounds) to make 6 cups slices. In large bowl, toss peach slices with *³/₄ cup sugar, ¹/₃ cup all-purpose flour, 1 tablespoon lemon juice, ¹/₂ teaspoon ground cinnamon,* and *¹/₂ teaspoon grated lemon peel* until well mixed.

Pear-Pie Filling
Prepare as for Apple-Pie Filling (left) but substitute *6 pears* (about 2 pounds), peeled, cored, and thinly sliced, for apples.

Rhubarb-Pie Filling
Prepare filling before making pastry: In large bowl, stir *1 ¹/₂ cups sugar* with *¹/₄ to ¹/₃ cup all-purpose flour, 1 tablespoon grated orange peel* (optional), and *¹/₄ teaspoon salt.* Add *1 pound rhubarb* (without tops), cut into 1-inch pieces (about 4 cups); toss lightly to mix well.

CRUMB, COCONUT, AND NUT CRUSTS

Piecrusts made with different kinds of cookies, wafers, coconut, and nuts, are used mostly with fillings that are not baked, such as those made with gelatin, custard, or ice cream. They add flavor and are favorites for frozen desserts, because when frozen they are easier to cut than frozen pastry.

Each of the following recipes makes enough for one 8- or 9-inch piecrust.

BAKED GRAHAM-CRACKER CRUMB CRUST

1 ½ cups graham-cracker crumbs

6 tablespoons margarine or butter (³/4 stick), softened

¹/4 cup sugar

1 Preheat oven to 375°F. In pie plate, with hand, mix all ingredients well. Press mixture onto bottom and up side of pie plate, making small rim.

2 Bake 8 minutes; cool on wire rack. Fill as recipe directs or with chilled filling.

Unbaked Crumb Crust
Prepare as Baked Graham-Cracker Crumb Crust, but do not make rim and do not bake. Chill well; fill as recipe directs or with any chilled filling. Refrigerate.

Vanilla- or Chocolate-Wafer Crust
Prepare as Baked Graham-Cracker Crumb Crust, using *1 ½ cups vanilla- or chocolate-wafer crumbs* and *6 tablespoons margarine* or butter (³/4 stick), melted.

Nut-Crumb Crust
Prepare as Baked Graham-Cracker Crumb Crust, substituting *½ cup finely chopped nuts* (such as walnuts, almonds, pecans, or filberts) for *½ cup crumbs*.

Corn- or Wheat-Flake Crumb Crust
Prepare as Baked Graham-Cracker Crumb Crust, using *1 ½ cups corn- or wheat-flake crumbs, 6 tablespoons margarine* or butter (³/4 stick), melted, and *3 tablespoons sugar*.

NO-ROLL NUT CRUST

1 cup all-purpose flour

¹/2 cup margarine or butter (1 stick), softened

¹/4 cup confectioners' sugar

¹/4 cup walnuts, finely chopped

1 Preheat oven to 400°F. In pie plate, mix flour, margarine or butter, sugar, and walnuts until soft and pliable.

2 Press mixture evenly onto bottom and up side of pie plate. With fork, prick bottom of crust well. Bake 12 minutes or until golden. Cool on wire rack. Fill as recipe directs or with chilled pie filling.

BAKED COCONUT CRUST

2 tablespoons margarine or butter (¹/4 stick), softened

1 3 ¹/2-ounce can flaked coconut (1 ¹/3 cups)

1 Preheat oven to 300°F. Onto bottom and up side of pie plate, evenly spread margarine or butter. Pat coconut into margarine or butter.

2 Bake 15 minutes or until golden. Cool on wire rack. Fill as recipe directs or with chilled pie filling.

UNBAKED COCONUT CRUST

1 3 ¹/2-ounce can flaked coconut (1 ¹/3 cups)

¹/4 cup confectioners' sugar

3 tablespoons margarine or butter, softened

1 In pie plate, mix coconut, confectioners' sugar, and margarine or butter.

2 Press mixture onto bottom and up side of pie plate, making small rim. Refrigerate 1 hour or until firm. Fill as recipe directs or with chilled pie filling.

Unbaked Chocolate Coconut Crust
Grease pie plate. In small saucepan over low heat, heat margarine or butter, *2 squares unsweetened chocolate, ½ cup confectioners' sugar,* and *2 tablespoons water* until chocolate melts; stir to blend well. Stir in coconut. With back of spoon, press mixture onto bottom and up side of pie plate. Refrigerate 1 hour or until firm. Fill as recipe directs or with chilled pie filling.

BAKED NUT CRUST

1 ¹/2 cups blanched almonds, Brazil nuts, peanuts, pecans, or walnuts, finely ground

3 tablespoons sugar

2 tablespoons margarine or butter (¹/4 stick), softened

1 Preheat oven to 400°F. In pie plate, with hand, mix all ingredients well. Press mixture onto bottom and up side of pie plate.

2 Bake 8 minutes or just until golden. Cool on wire rack. Fill as recipe directs or with chilled pie filling.

HINTS AND TIPS

Here you'll find some do's and don'ts of good cooking and baking, selected to help you make the recipes in this book with the least time and effort, and the greatest of ease.

One very important rule should be observed with every single recipe: Before you start to cook, read the recipe through from beginning to end, to make sure you understand the directions; then assemble ingredients and equipment to make sure you have everything you need.

Finally, protect your cookbook while you cook! Slide the opened book into an extra-large, clear plastic bag so pages are covered yet visible; then drips and splashes won't stain them.

GENERAL HINTS

• When recipe calls for margarine or butter, it refers to solid, stick form. Don't substitute whipped varieties (they have air beaten in); also avoid "light" margarines and vegetable-oil spreads, which contain more water and less fat; and may give different results.

• Solid shortening can be stored at room temperature. Keep margarine and butter refrigerated.

• When softened margarine or butter is needed in a hurry, cut the amount needed into small pieces; it will soften more quickly at room temperature than if left in a large piece.

• If brown sugar is stored in freezer it will be soft and usable when thawed.

• Dry ingredients – flour, sugar, baking powder, baking soda – should be kept in airtight containers in a cool, dry place.

• To cut sticky foods like candied fruit, dates, or marshmallows, frequently dip knife or scissors in flour.

• When measuring ingredients to add to those already in mixing bowl, never hold the measuring spoon or cup over the bowl. One slip of the hand and the recipe could be ruined by too much vanilla extract, salt, baking powder, or whatever.

• Place a folded damp kitchen towel under the bowl when mixing by hand or folding ingredients into a mixture; then bowl won't slide or slip while mixing.

• To determine volume of mold, simply count number of cups of water it takes to fill it to the brim.

• Use the right knife and cutting techniques and slices will be perfect when you cut cakes and desserts.
For layer cakes, use a well-sharpened French or chef's knife.
For angel-food cakes, use a serrated knife or cake breaker.
For meringue desserts and cake rolls, use a knife with a thin, sharp blade and wipe it with a damp cloth or paper towel after every cut.
Before cutting cheesecake, mousse cakes, and other "sticky" desserts, dip knife blade in very hot water and dry quickly with a paper towel. The heated blade will cut through without sticking.
In all cases, use a sawing motion and a light touch to avoid mashing the cake or dessert out of shape.

• If you have leftover whipped cream, drop it by heaping spoonfuls onto a baking sheet and freeze. When it's firm, loosen with a metal spatula and store in plastic bag in freezer. To use, place frozen dollops on top of desserts; they'll thaw in just minutes.

CUSTARDS AND PUDDINGS

• Stirring a little hot liquid into eggs heats eggs so they won't curdle when added to more hot liquid.

• Always remove a custard mixture from the heat when checking to see if it is thick enough. Even a few seconds extra cooking could be too much!

• If you use an instant-read thermometer to check the temperature of a custard, be sure at least 2 inches of the thermometer are covered with custard.

• If cooked custard needs to be cooled before adding other ingredients, cover the custard directly with a sheet of plastic wrap. Otherwise, the surface of the custard may form a tough skin and cause the dessert to have a lumpy texture.

• To avoid spilling hot water, place filled custard cups in large pan and center pan on a partially pulled-out oven shelf. Fill pan with hot water to come halfway up custard cups, then gently push shelf back into oven and bake custards as directed.

• A water bath helps custards bake evenly because it keeps the temperature constant and moderate, not too hot.

• Wear a heavy rubber glove for a sure grip to remove custard cups from a water bath.

FRUIT AND NUTS

• An easy way to core apples and pears is with a melon baller. Just slice fruit in half and scoop out core in one smooth stroke.

• Fragile fruit such as raspberries or strawberries must be handled with care. Refrigerate berries and wash just before using. Quickly rinse in a large bowl of cold water – never a colander under running water, which might bruise berries. Drain on paper towels.

• To get maximum amount of juice when squeezing citrus fruit such as oranges, lemons, or limes, gently roll fruit on counter, pressing lightly, before cutting in half and squeezing.

• When recipe calls for lemon peel, that means thin yellow outer layer of skin – called zest – not spongy white part, which is bitter. Grate only fresh, colored layer, using sharp grater. Grate just before needed, because peel dries out quickly. ▶

• To thicken fruit juices of pie fillings, substitute 1 tablespoon quick-cooking tapioca for each tablespoon of all-purpose flour called for. Juices will be clear and glossy as well as thick.

• Do not use fresh figs, kiwifruit, papaya, pineapple, or prickly pears in mixtures containing gelatin; they contain an enzyme with softening effects on gelatin that prevents setting properly. These fruits can be used if canned or fully cooked.

• When buying nuts in shell, check that they are clean and free of scars and holes. Shake a few – if kernels rattle, nuts are old and dried out.

• Delicate torte or cake recipes often call for "finely ground nuts" to replace some of the flour. For successful results, nuts must be ground very fine, yet dry and light. Be careful not to over process nuts in blender or food processor; if they're thick and pasty, they will be too oily and heavy. If you are grinding the nuts by hand, grind 2 or 3 times to achieve correct texture. Packaged "ground" nuts are not fine enough.

CHOCOLATE

• *Unsweetened* chocolate is also known as bitter or baking chocolate. It is chocolate liquor which has been cooled and molded, usually into blocks; it contains 50 to 58 percent cocoa butter. Do not substitute semisweet chocolate for unsweetened.

• *Bittersweet* chocolate is at least 35 percent chocolate liquor. It has varying amounts of sugar added, together with butterfat, lecithin, and flavorings.

• *Semisweet* chocolate can be used interchangeably with bittersweet, but has more sugar added, so chocolate flavor is less intense.

• *Sweet, dark* chocolate (such as German sweet cooking chocolate) is a blend of at least 15 percent chocolate liquor and varying amounts of sugar, cocoa butter, milk solids, butterfat, lecithin, and flavorings.

• *Milk* chocolate must contain at least 3.6 percent butterfat, 12 percent milk solids, and at least 10 percent chocolate liquor. Because of low amount of chocolate liquor it cannot be used as a substitute in recipes calling for sweet, semisweet, or bittersweet chocolate.

• *White* chocolate is really not chocolate at all, but a cooked-down mixture of milk and sugar, with flavorings added. Some white chocolate contains some cocoa butter to give it a slight chocolate taste. It should only be used in recipes specifying white chocolate.

• *Unsweetened cocoa* is a powder made from chocolate liquor that has had nearly all cocoa butter removed. Instant cocoa mixes for drinks contain dry milk powder, sugar, and flavorings; do not substitute them for unsweetened cocoa in recipes.

• If you run out of unsweetened chocolate: For each square (1 ounce) of unsweetened chocolate, melted, substitute 3 tablespoons unsweetened cocoa plus 1 tablespoon shortening, salad oil, butter or margarine. Or use 1 envelope (1 ounce) unsweetened baking chocolate flavor.

For each 6-ounce package (1 cup) semisweet-chocolate pieces or six 1-ounce squares of semisweet chocolate, use 6 tablespoons unsweetened cocoa, plus 7 tablespoons sugar and ¼ cup shortening.

For 4-ounce bar sweet cooking chocolate, use 3 tablespoons unsweetened cocoa plus ¼ cup plus 1½ teaspoons sugar, and 2 tablespoons plus 2 teaspoons shortening.

• Store chocolate in cool, dry place. It keeps best if temperature is about 68°F., but not over 75°F.

• Chocolate stored in too cold conditions will "sweat" when brought to room temperature.

• If chocolate is stored in too warm conditions cocoa butter will start to melt and appear on surface of chocolate as a gray coating. This does not affect flavor and chocolate will return to its original color when melted.

• Melt chocolate any of these ways: (1) Place in top of double boiler and melt over hot, not boiling, water. (2) Or, place in custard cup or heat-safe measuring cup and set in pan of hot water. (3) Or, place in heavy, small saucepan; melt over low heat – if pan is too thin, it will transfer heat too fast and burn chocolate. (4) Or, for small amounts, leave blocks in original wrapper; place on piece of foil and set in warm spot on range.

• If chocolate does stiffen during melting, for each 3 ounces of unsweetened or semisweet chocolate, start with 1 teaspoon and add up to 1 tablespoon solid vegetable shortening (not salad oil, butter or margarine, which contain moisture), stirring until chocolate liquefies again and becomes smooth.

• Stir chocolate after it has begun to liquefy. If melting more than 16 ounces chocolate, start with 8 ounces and add remaining chocolate in 2-ounce amounts.

• To speed melting, break chocolate into small pieces and stir frequently.

• When adding liquid to melted chocolate, always add at least 2 tablespoons at a time, to avoid chocolate stiffening.

• When making chocolate garnishes, work with chocolate as soon as it is melted and smooth. When heated too long it can become grainy.

• To avoid breaking chocolate curls when transferring them, pick them up with toothpick.

BAKING

• If recipe says to preheat oven, allow at least 10 minutes for it to reach correct baking temperature.

• Make sure pans are size called for in recipe and prepare them before you start.

• If you don't have a springform pan, use a cake pan of the same size with a removable bottom – and vice versa.

• If pans are to be greased with margarine, butter, or shortening, use crumpled waxed paper or paper towels, to grease evenly.

• Grease fluted and Bundt pans very generously, especially the ridges up the side and tube, so cake can be unmolded easily. The best way to do this is to brush pan with melted shortening or salad oil.

• Place pans on oven shelf so they don't touch one another, or sides of oven.

• Wait until minimum baking time given in recipe has elapsed before opening oven door; opening it too soon can "jar" batter with inrush of cold air and make batters and doughs fall.

LAYER CAKES

• When baking 3 or 4 cake layers in oven at same time, 2 oven shelves are needed: place oven shelves so that oven is divided into thirds and stagger cake pans so that one is not directly beneath another.

• To line bottom of cake pan with waxed paper, place pan on paper and trace around bottom with tip of small knife. Then cut out tracing and place in greased cake pan; grease paper. It will fit bottom of pan exactly.

• For chocolate cakes, dust pans with unsweetened cocoa powder rather than flour – cocoa powder will not leave white film on surface of cake.

• Be sure to follow timing guide for mixing cake batter given in individual recipes. If you under-mix cake batter, ingredients will not be evenly distributed throughout and cake will fall; if you over-mix batter, cake may be tough and dry and will not rise properly.

• Beat cake batter for time recommended in individual recipes, scraping bowl often with rubber spatula for even mixing of ingredients.

• Stir in ingredients like nuts and raisins after mixing, as they could clog beaters.

• For even texture without any large holes, cut through batter in pans with rubber spatula to remove any air bubbles.

• Cake layers are done when they shrink away from side of pan and top springs back when lightly pressed with finger.

• After removing cake from oven, allow to cool in pan on wire rack about 10 minutes before removing from pan. If cake is cooled completely in pan, cake may stick and be difficult to remove; if cake is removed from pan while too hot, it may break.

• When transporting a filled layer cake, as to a picnic, insert a few pieces of dry spaghetti straight down through layers to hold them in place When spaghetti is removed, the small holes it made in frosting won't be noticed.

FROSTING AND FILLING

• For layer cakes, place first layer, top down, on plate; spread with filling, then place second layer, top up, on first, so flat bottoms of layers face each other.

• Spread frosting or firm filling to ½ inch of edge of cake, very soft filling to 1 inch of edge - weight of top layer will push it to edge.

• Spread cake with thin layer of frosting first, to "set" crumbs, then frost again.

• When filling decorating bag, stand narrow end in measuring cup or drinking glass, for easier handling.

• To keep decorating bag fresh-smelling, after each use, boil it in water with a little baking soda.

• A sturdy plastic bag makes a good substitute for decorating bag. Fill with frosting, close with twist tie, and snip small hole in corner.

FRUITCAKES

• Line cake pan with foil to make cake easy to remove. Smooth out all creases, so side of cake will be smooth.

• Move oven shelf to lower position to ensure whole cake is in middle of oven while baking.

• Mix candied fruit and nuts with a little flour before adding to batter; this keeps them evenly suspended in batter and prevents them sinking to bottom while cake is baking.

• Spoon cake batter evenly into pan and pack firmly to eliminate any air pockets that will leave holes in baked cake.

• Test fruitcakes with a cake tester or toothpick inserted in center; it should come out clean.

• Turn leftover fruitcake into an elegant dessert: slice cake into wine goblets or small custard cups, moisten with fruit juice or sherry, and top with whipped cream.

PASTRY

• When making cream-puff dough, flour must be added as soon as liquid boils or water could evaporate and dough would not puff.

• Add flour for cream-puff dough all at once. Beat until smooth and formed into ball that cleans side of saucepan.

• Pastries made with cream-puff dough should be eaten on day they are made, as pastry softens quickly.

• Thaw frozen phyllo pastry in its package; otherwise pastry might dry out and crack.

• Once thawed, keep phyllo covered with damp cloth or plastic wrap.

• Brush sheets of phyllo with melted margarine or butter – it adds flavor and keeps them pliable so they can be rolled or folded. ▶

PIES

• What's the key to making tender piecrust? It's accurate measurement of ingredients, to ensure the correct balance of fat and flour, and not too much liquid. Too much flour gives a tough crust; too much fat results in a greasy, crumbly crust. Too much liquid will require the excess flour that results in a tough crust.

• When rolling out pastry on a cutting board, place a damp dish cloth under board; this will keep board from slipping.

• Roll out pastry dough as evenly thick as possible so edges are not too thin.

• When rolling out pastry dough, slide a pastry scraper or pancake turner under it occasionally to make sure it isn't sticking to the work surface. If it sticks, sprinkle work surface with more flour before continuing rolling.

• Never stretch pastry dough to fit into pie plate; it will just shrink back when baking.

• After making a rope or fluted edge on a piecrust, hook points of pastry dough under pie-plate rim so edge will stay in place as it bakes.

• For a shiny top to pies, brush pastry dough with slightly beaten egg white. For a golden-brown glazed top, brush with beaten whole egg or egg yolk.

• To help keep oven clean when baking fruit pie, place second oven shelf below the one pie is on. Tear off sheet of foil, turn all edges up $1/2$ inch, and place it on second shelf to catch drips.

• To prevent soggy crusts on cream pies, try this: as soon as baked pie shell comes out of oven, brush it with lightly beaten egg white, making sure to cover areas pricked with fork. The heat from the hot pie shell will cook the egg white and form a protective seal to help eliminate sogginess after filling.

• Before refrigerating a cream-topped pie, insert 4 or more toothpicks around the pie, then cover with plastic wrap. Toothpicks prevent cover from touching topping, and won't leave marks when removed.

• If crumb crusts stick to the pie plate, set the pie plate on a kitchen towel that has been wrung out in hot water and let it stand briefly. It should be easy to remove slices perfectly.

• After preparing your favorite pie, use leftover pastry to make a special treat for children: roll out dough and cut pretty shapes using a cookie or canapé cutter. While pie bakes, brown "cookies", then spread with jam or peanut butter or sprinkle with cinnamon-sugar.

COOKIES

• For your cookies to have a light, tender texture, mix cookie dough gently. Take care not to overwork dough or cookies will be tough.

• No space to roll out cookies? Shape dough into small balls, place balls 2 or 3 inches apart on cookie sheet then press dough flat with bottom of a glass that has been dipped in sugar.

• Always start cutting at edge of dough and work toward center, cutting cookies as close together as possible to minimize scraps.

• Rehandling dough toughens cookies, so press dough trimmings together – do not knead – before rolling again.

• Transfer fragile cookies from board to cookie sheet with pancake turner to preserve shape.

• Short on cookie sheets? If you have only one cookie sheet, you'll save time by placing your cookie dough on sheets of aluminum foil. Then slide cookie sheet under one sheet of foil and bake as usual. Lift off the foil, baked cookies and all, and place another foil sheet with dough onto the cookie sheet.

• Cookie sheets should be at least 2 inches smaller all around than your oven, so heat can circulate and cookies can bake evenly.

• Always place dough on a cool cookie sheet. It will spread too much on a hot one.

• Grease cookie sheet only if recipe says so; very rich cookies will spread too much if baked on greased sheets.

• After baking, remove small cookies at once from cookie sheet to wire rack (they continue to bake on hot sheet).

• Don't overlap cookies on wire rack or place on top of each other – they will become soggy and out of shape.

• Cool bar cookies completely in pan before removing from pan.

• Always cool cookies completely before storing in airtight containers.

• Cookies that are too hard can be softened by placing a slice of bread in the cookie jar; change the slice every other day. A bread slice will also keep soft cookies soft, just as it softens hardened brown sugar.

ICE CREAM AND FROZEN DESSERTS

• Ice cream, whether bought or homemade, keeps best in freezer at 0°F. or lower.

• Ice cream will keep for up to 1 month in freezer compartment of refrigerator, or up to 2 months in home freezer.

• Do not refreeze partially melted ice cream – a coarse, icy texture will result.

• To store open containers of ice cream, press plastic wrap right onto exposed surface to protect ice cream from refrigerator odors and prevent development of "skin" or ice crystals.
• Partially frozen mixtures are ready for beating when frozen firm 1 inch around edge, though center is mushy.

GLOSSARY OF FOOD AND COOKING TERMS

Ascorbic-acid mixture for fruit: Crystalline or powdered mixture used to prevent darkening and loss of flavor in fruit low in ascorbic acid.

Batter: Mixture of fairly thin consistency, made of flour, liquid, and other ingredients.

Blintz: Thin pancake filled and rolled, usually with cottage cheese.

Bombe: Dessert of frozen mixtures, arranged and frozen in mold.

Brush with: Use pastry brush to spread food lightly with liquid such as melted fat, heavy cream, or beaten egg.

Cappuccino: Espresso coffee mixed with foamy hot milk or cream and often flavored with cinnamon.

Caramelize: To stir sugar in skillet over low heat until it melts and develops characteristic flavor and golden-brown color.

Chantilly: Prepared or served with whipped cream.

Charlotte: Dessert made in mold lined with ladyfingers, sponge cake, or bread, and filled with custard, whipped cream, or fruit.

Coat: To sprinkle food with, or dip it into, flour, chocolate, sauce, etc.

Compote: Dessert of fresh or dried fruit cooked in syrup.

Crème Brûlée: Literally, "burnt cream." A rich, creamy custard topped with sugar and broiled until the sugar melts and caramelizes.

Crème Caramel: Custard baked in a mold that has been lined with caramelized sugar. The caramel melts as the custard stands and forms a sauce for the dessert.

Crepe: Thin, delicate pancake.

Dacquoise: Nut meringue layers, filled and frosted like cake.

Flambé: Food that has had brandy or liqueur poured over, which is then set alight.

Flute: To make small, decorative indentations in food, such as piecrust, using fingers, or a knife.

Fold in: To combine delicate ingredients such as whipped cream or beaten egg whites with heavier ingredients by using gentle up-and-down circular motion with rubber spatula or wire whisk.

Fool: A cold dessert of pureed or cooked fruit mixed with whipped cream or custard.

Ganache: Rich mixture of whipped cream and chocolate, used to fill or cover cakes.

Grenadine: Pomegranate-flavored syrup used as flavoring or sauce.

Julienne: To cut into long, thin strips.

Marsala: Sweet Sicilian dessert wine.

Marzipan: Sweetened almond paste, used for confections and cake covering.

Meringue: A mixture of stiffly beaten egg whites and sugar. In this book, meringue is baked until crisp, dry, and fully cooked, for such desserts as meringue shells and dacquoise.

Mocha: Flavored with coffee, or coffee and chocolate combined.

Mousse: A rich, airy, cold dessert made with whipped cream or beaten egg whites, often with gelatin, and combined with fruit puree, chocolate, or custard.

Parfait: Dessert made by layering fruit, syrup, whipped cream, and ice cream in tall, thin glass.

Phyllo: Tissue-thin sheets of dough, usually layered to make very flaky pastries such as baklava and strudel.

Praline: Mixture of caramelized sugar and nuts, crushed and used as garnish or ingredient.

Profiterole: Tiny cream puff, made of cream-puff dough, filled with cream or chocolate and served as dessert.

Puff pastry: A rich dough made with a large quantity of margarine or butter. It is rolled and folded many times to make tissue-thin layers that, when baked, rise to many times their height, resulting in exceptionally flaky pastry.

Roulade: Thinly layered food, such as jelly roll, rolled around filling.

Sorbet: Sherbet

Soufflé: A light, fluffy dessert consisting of a sauce made with egg yolks, flavoring, and beaten egg whites (if the soufflé is baked) or whipped cream (if the soufflé is served cold or frozen). Whether baked or molded, the top of the soufflé rises well above the rim of the special dish in which it is made, making this one of the most dramatic of desserts.

Streusel: A crumbly topping used on cakes, coffee cakes, and pies, made of margarine or butter, sugar, flour, and sometimes spices.

Strudel: Dessert made of paper-thin sheets of pastry rolled around filling, usually fruit.

Torte: Cake or meringue-type dessert, usually rich in eggs and nuts.

Trifle: A dessert usually containing sponge cake or plain cake, custard, jelly or jam, sherry, and whipped cream.

Truffle: A candy made of chocolate, butter, and sugar, shaped into balls and coated with cocoa, made to resemble the edible fungus of the same name.

Whip: To beat rapidly with mixer, wire whisk, or hand beater, to incorporate air and increase volume, as of egg whites.

Zest: Colored part of peel of citrus fruit which contains flavorful fruit oils.

INDEX

ACKNOWLEDGMENTS

Photography	All original photography by David Murray
Photographer's Assistant	Jules Selmes
Photographs of finished desserts from Good Housekeeping	Arthur Beck: pages 23, 25, 33, 77, 101, 106, 107, 131, 140, 192; Charles Gold: 54, 64; Victor Scocozza: 142, 166, 189, 267, 271
Copy Editor	Norma MacMillan
Assisted by	Felicity Jackson, Sally Poole, Alexa Stace, Elizabeth Thompson, Stella Vayne
Page make-up	Rowena Feeny
Production Consultant	Lorraine Baird
Reproduced by	Colourscan, Singapore
Home Economists	
Step-by-steps and finished desserts	Elizabeth Wolf-Cohen
Finished desserts	Maxine Clark, Hilary Foster, Carole Handslip, Kathy Man, Janice Murfitt, Berit Vinegrad, Mandy Wagstaff
Stylist	Angi Lincoln

The companies listed here very graciously lent tableware

Arthur Price of England p. 147 (pie slice); p. 154 (serving spoon); p. 159 (pie slice); p. 160 (napkin rings); p. 170 (forks); p. 179 (napkin rings); p. 184 (pie slice); p. 191 (sugar spoon); p. 197 (silver platter); p. 198 (pie slice); p. 203 (fork); p. 261 (forks)

Classical Creamware Limited p. 81 (plate); p. 93 (plates, sugar bowl and shaker); p. 97 (plate); p. 117 (tea service and plate); p. 128 (plate); p. 149 (plate); p. 159 (plate); p. 164 (plate)

Dartington Crystal p. 195 (glass bowl)

George Butler of Sheffield Limited p. 148 (pie slice); p. 149 (forks); p. 155 (pie slice); p. 157 (pie slice); p. 165 (forks); p. 177 (forks); p. 179 (pie slice and forks); p. 182 (forks); p. 195 (forks); p. 197 (pie slice); p. 207 (pie slice); p. 211 (forks)

Guy Degrenne p. 136 (pie slice); p. 173 (pie slice)

Josiah Wedgwood & Sons Limited p. 177 (plates); p. 196 (plates); p. 203 (plate); p. 205 (coffee service and plates); p. 207 (tray and plate)

Villeroy & Boch Tableware Limited p. 113 (glass platter); p. 138 (glass platter); p. 155 (glass platter); p. 170 (glass plates); p. 180 (glass platter); p. 202 (plate); p. 212 (plate); p. 213 (plate); p. 268 (plates)

Carroll & Brown Limited would also like to thank these companies for their assistance

Corning Limited
Neff U.K. Limited
Siemens Domestic Appliances Limited